Asghar Seyed-Gohrab

Martyrdom, Mysticism and Dissent

Studies on Modern Orient

Volume 34

Asghar Seyed-Gohrab

Martyrdom, Mysticism and Dissent

The Poetry of the 1979 Iranian Revolution and the Iran-Iraq War (1980-1988)

DE GRUYTER

ISBN 978-3-11-127714-1
e-ISBN (PDF) 978-3-11-074873-4
e-ISBN (EPUB) 978-3-11-074885-7

Library of Congress Control Number: 2021938132

Bibliographic information published by the Deutsche Nationalbibliothek
The Deutsche Nationalbibliothek lists this publication in the Deutsche Nationalbibliografie; detailed bibliographic data are available on the Internet at http://dnb.dnb.de.

This volume is text- and page-identical with the hardback published in 2021.
Cover image: Gettyimages / Mansoreh Motamedi
Printing and binding: CPI books GmbH, Leck

www.degruyter.com

Contents

Acknowledgements — IX

Notes on Translations, Transliterations and Footnotes — XI

Preface — XIII

Outline of the Book — XVII

1 Towards Justifying Violence — 1
1.1 Introduction — **1**
1.2 Poetry as a Persuative Force — **2**
1.3 Poetry in Modern Politics — **8**
1.4 Poetry in the Service of Politics — **9**
1.5 Conclusion — **23**

2 'The Scent of Martyrdom' — 26
2.1 Introduction — **26**
2.2 Poems Celebrating Martyrdom — **34**
2.3 Conclusion — **69**

3 Qeyṣar Amīnpūr on War — 71
3.1 Introduction — **71**
3.2 A Poem about War (1) — **77**
3.3 A Poem about War (2) — **85**
3.4 Chemical Weapons in War Poetry — **90**
3.5 Poems on Peace — **94**
3.6 Conclusion — **98**

4 Love in Persian War Poetry — 99
4.1 Introduction — **99**
4.2 School of Love (*madrasa-yi ʿishq*) — **102**
4.3 Love and Reason — **105**
4.4 The Heart as an Intimate Companion — **108**
4.5 Love Poems as a Homage to Martyrs — **113**
4.6 Love as a Ubiquitous Being — **124**
4.7 Conclusion — **129**

5 “In the Trenches of my Small Room…” Ideologically Committed Children’s Poetry — 131
5.1 Introduction — 131
5.2 Dream of Paradise — 134
5.3 Angels of the Town — 136
5.4 Painting of War — 137
5.5 Rain of Kisses (Martyr Daddy) — 138
5.6 “When do you come back?” — 140
5.7 Āmina — 142
5.8 My good father — 143
5.9 The Street of Angels — 144
5.10 Memories of Spring — 146
5.11 You Are with us Again … — 149
5.12 A Sparrow’s Chatter — 150
5.13 You Became a Butterfly! — 152
5.14 Jasmine Petals Like Snow — 154
5.15 Conclusion — 155

6 Sīmīn Bihbahānī on the 1979 Revolution and Iran-Iraq War — 157
6.1 Introduction — 157
6.2 Bihbahānī as a War Poet — 170
6.3 A Poem on the Oil City of Khurramshahr — 182
6.4 Conclusion — 185

7 Nādir Nādirpūr on the 1979 Revolution — 187
7.1 Introduction — 187
7.2 Nādir Nādirpūr’s Life and Work — 188
7.3 Nādirpūr’s Poetic Genius — 189
7.4 The Sermon of Perdition — 191
7.5 The Satanic Verse — 197
7.6 From Żahhāk to Fireydūn — 205
7.7 Conclusion — 217

8 Iran and Saudi Arabia — 220
8.1 Introduction — 220
8.2 Demonstrations in the Holy Cities of Mecca and Medina — 222
8.3 Shiite versus Wahhabi — 235
8.4 Khomeini vs Arabism — 237
8.5 Mystical Dimensions of the Ḥajj — 238
8.6 The Persian and Arab Rivalries — 246

Acknowledgements

A generous grant from the Netherlands Organisation for Scientific Research (NWO) in 2009 offered me a unique opportunity to initiate a new research line to study the role of classical Persian poetry and Islamic mysticism in Iranian politics. I am exceptionally grateful to the NWO for funding the project, entitled *Of Poetry and Politics: Classical Poetic Concepts in the New Politics of Twentieth Century Iran*, and to the anonymous reviewers who saw potential in this project. The grant enabled two PhD students, Mahnia Nematollahi Mahani and Diede Farhosh-Van Loon, and myself to study the Persian poetic forms, themes and concepts utilised in modern times and in political contexts. Later Mohammed Alsulami and Saeedeh Shahnahpur joined us, with their topics to conduct a PhD research. Part of Saeedeh's dissertation has been published under the title *Writing War in Contemporary Iran: The Case of Esma'il Fasih's Zemestan-e 62* (New York: Peter Lang, 2019). The *Of Poetry and Politics* project has also attracted several enthusiastic MA students to conducting research into the related topics. I am also very grateful to all of my students who, with their enthusiasm, engagements and critical attitude, contributed to this project during our classes.

I am also grateful to several individuals with whom I have been discussing the topic. I am especially grateful to Rokus de Groot, whose friendship and intellectual vigour are always inspiring and motivating; to Koushyar Parsi, Maaike Warnaar, Mohammad Forough, Siavash Rafiee Rad and Noa Schonmann (in the order in which I came to know them). Special thanks go to Amin Ghodratzadeh who devotedly served as my student assistant for several years during which we talked about the subject of this book. Also I would like to thank my colleagues at Utrecht University, especially Christian Lange, for creating an inspiring and vibrant sholarly context. Last but by no means least, I would like to extend my gratitude to my friend Sen McGlinn who did an excellent job in polishing my English. I am of course responsible for any inconsistency to be found.

The publication of this book has been delayed for several years due to other research projects and personal circumstances. The book is by no means a comprehensive history of the events of the 1979 Revolution and the Iran-Iraq war (1980 – 1988); rather it offers a perspective which has been almost entirely neglected. I have tried to analyse the voices of the committed revolutionary poets and the counter-voices of the established poets, several of whom, such as Nādirpūr, lived in exile.

Chapter Three on Qayṣar Amīnpūr was previously published in *Zeitschrift der Deutschen Morgenländischen Gesellschaft* (2016, Band 166 – Heft 2, pp. 347 – 363). Part of Chapter Two entitled "The Scent of Martyrdom" was orig-

https://doi.org/10.1515/9783110748734-001

inally published in *The International Journal of Persian Literature*, Vol. 1, 2016, pp. 89 – 119. This article is used by permission of The Pennsylvania State University Press, the copyright holder. But I have added new materials to these chapters. For instance, the second part of "A Poem for War" by Amīnpūr is generally unknown. This is the first time the poem has been translated, analysed and published in a scholarly work in the West.

Writing a book is a passionate enterprise but it also means spending hours in isolation, unable to reciprocate the love and affection one receives from the family as one would wish. I would like wholeheartedly to thank my mother, who has always selflessly offered everything to smooth the road for all of us. I convey my intense love and gratitude to Miriam for her proverbial patience, and her encouragement through the years, motivating me to finish this book and always encouraging me to launch new projects. To the lights of my life, Nora and Sam, who have never seen Iran and hopefully will never experience tumultuous events such as those depicted in this book, I wish them a life full of inspiration, intellectual challenges, affection and, above all, love.

Notes on Translations, Transliterations and Footnotes

My translation of Persian poems is meant to reveal the meaning without any pretence of presenting these translations in a literary form. Persian poets apply many rhetorical embellishments, adorning their speech with metaphors, similes, anagrams, anaphora and a host of other rhetorical figures. I have tried to remain as close to the original text as possible, keeping these figures, especially the metaphors, intact. My analyses are based on the Persian texts.

Except for quoted titles and citations, which keep their own original orthography, Angelicised words and names such as Khan, Shah, and Khomeini keep their English forms. I refer to the 1979 Revolution and the Constitutional Revolution (1906–1911) using capital letters while all other revolutions are written in lower case. Many words are transliterated in their Persian pronunciation and not the Arabic, such as Siyyid and not Sayyid. It is always a challenge to use a transliteration system close to the original language, expressing the pronunciation exactly. My system is mainly based on reading the Persian words correctly and not for a proper pronounciation. For the transliteration of the Persian words I have employed the IJMES transliteration system. The Common Era dates are used throughout the book.

Consonants

ا	a	ط	ṭ
ب	b	ظ	ẓ
پ	p	ع	ʿ
ت	t	غ	gh
ث	th	ف	f
ج	j	ق	q
چ	ch	ک	k
ح	ḥ	گ	g
خ	kh	ل	l
د	d	م	m
ذ	dh	ن	n
ر	r	ه	h
ز	z	و	v
ژ	zh	ی	y
س	s		
ش	sh		
ص	ṣ		
ض	ż		

Vowels

Short	َ	a
	ِ	i
	ُ	u
Long	آ / ا	ā
	و	ī
	ی	ī
Diphtongs	ی	ey
	و	ow

https://doi.org/10.1515/9783110748734-002

Preface

The idea of writing this book is as much personal as professional. When I was a young teenager, the experience of the 1979 Revolution and the Iran-Iraq War (1980 – 1988) made such a deep impression on my soul that after years of living in exile, I am still haunted by the images of the war and ponder about the events of the Revolution. I will never forget the first references to the Revolution. My teachers at a school in the southern part of Tehran were involved with the Revolution. Our school was among the few Islamic schools in the Pahlavi period in which we were trained to memorise the Quran and had extra theological lessons and extracurricular activities such as calligraphy. During our theology lessons, our devout teacher furtively told us that he could bring us Ayatollah Khomeini's rare book *Kashf al-asrār* ("Unveiling of the Secrets," 1943). Fascinated by Khomeini's personality, I immediately ordered it. I can remember how enthusiastic I was when my teacher gave me the light green covered book a few weeks later. I took the book home and did not dare to share it with my pious grandfather, a learned man who remained distanced from politics. He was critical of Khomeini and the Revolution. My father being in Europe, we lived with my grandparents in one of those nostalgic old Southern Tehran houses with *bīrūnī* ("outside") and *andarūnī* ("inner parts") architecture. In the *bīrūnī* area, with a nice little garden and a small pool, and several rooms, my grandfather received visitors who came for advice, while the inner area was for us, with its large garden, old plane trees, a large pool, many rooms and a beautiful cool cellar where we used to spend the hot afternoons. I cannot remember that I ever understood the book in those days, especially because I was so immersed in all the events taking place around me.

The Revolution was developing very swiftly. The bazaaris went on strike, followed by the workers at oil refineries. Every day we witnessed larger groups demonstrating on the streets, chanting slogans such as "Death to the Shah," "Death to Tyranny," or "Independence, Freedom and Islamic Republic." Soon the presence of the army changed the peaceful streets I had known. As the demonstrations and destruction of public buildings such as banks and cinemas intensified, a curfew followed. We also heard that the government forces readily opened fire on demonstrations. Every morning, when I went to school or to play football in the street, I would see new slogans, and the image of a red hand with a stencil of Khomeini's face on the walls. The walls had become signboards, participating in the protests. The first time I saw the impression of a red hand on the wall a friend told me that it was a symbol of demonstrators who had been killed or wounded, some of whom put their blood-stained hands on a wall.

https://doi.org/10.1515/9783110748734-003

The Revolution was everywhere. The shootings were heard not only at night, but more and more during the day. The climax was the Black Friday massacre, just a few kilometres from my grandparents' house, when the Shah's police opened fire on hundreds of people.

From this moment, the Revolution was inevitable. People around me were repeating that the Shah's attempts to change the course of events were futile. I remember heated discussions in family circles. Some were hypnotised by the idea of freedom; others were enchanted by Ayatollah Khomeini, whom they considered to be mystically minded, or an Iranian Mahatma Gandhi. Others, such as my grandfather, were completely against the involvement of religion in politics. One day, our teacher brought a picture of Khomeini, sitting under an apple tree in Neauphle-le-Château in France, wearing a brown woollen mantle over a blue shirt. One could see his self-confident smile and picture his slow speech and gentle movements which had become a symbol for the fight against western imperialism. Soon we heard that the Shah had decided to leave the country and that preparations were being made to bring Khomeini back to Iran after 15 years of exile. It was a tense and emotional period. His arrival marked a short interval of openness and a period in which ministers, generals and advocates of the Pahlavi regime were executed by the Revolutionary Courts. I can still remember the front pages of the newspapers with disturbing pictures of the blood-soaked bodies of those who had been pitilessly executed. My grandfather removed all such papers from my sight. My safe Tehran had changed: Iran was transformed into a theocracy in less than two years.

In the first months after the Revolution I thought a period of normalisation would soon appear, but this was not the case as, a few months later, Saddam Hussein's army invaded Iran, occupying the oil-rich city of Khorramshahr. I remember how newspapers, radio and TV were reporting Saddam's killing of hundreds of innocent people and the destruction of the city. With the outbreak of the war all the political activities of diverse parties and movements were banned. Many politically engaged Iranians, who had been among the core participants in the Revolution, had to flee the country. My father, who had returned to Iran just a few months earlier, fled the country as well. People were still hoping that the war would end and a more democratic system would come to power. While people kept hoping, the situation worsened when the students of "the line of Imam" occupied the American embassy and held the personnel hostage for 444 days.

The war was devastating. When we heard that Iraqi fighter jets could fly over Tehran, we felt especially unsafe. Shortly afterwards, several of my friends, who were just a few years older than I but had certainly not reached the age of conscription, went to the front. The news of their deaths, wrapped in the term martyrdom, soon reached us. Already, the names of most streets and alleys had been changed to the names of those killed during the Revolution and the war. Tehran's identity was changing.

A few years later, the war of the cities started. Missiles and bombing of the cities meant that we could be attacked every night. Having no shelters, we all came together on the streets, waiting to hear the sound of the bombs, which meant the destruction of a large area and death for many innocents. I witnessed how many of my generation went to the front and were killed, or came back disabled or shell-shocked, while a few of them fled the country. It was my destiny to join my parents in the Netherlands, but memories of my friends who were killed during the war, of the frightening moments we experienced during the Revolution and the war, are still with me.

This book is just a droplet of those memories, moulded into an academic form. During the whole of my career I have been engaged mainly with the notion of love, Persian romances, Persian mystical poetry and Islamic piety. Several friends have asked why I have been engaged in writing this book, which analyses the poetry of the Revolution and the Iran-Iraq War, a poetry stained with blood, violence and death. For me, writing this book has been a way to understand how these two epoch-making events during my teenage years have been commented on, how they have changed many aspects of Persian culture, and how my generation is still stunned by the swift pace of so many developments. Moreover, I have been curious about the role of poetry, a lasting icon of Persian culture, in all these events.

Outline of the Book

This book focusses on depictions of the 1979 Revolution and Iran-Iraq War in Persian poetry, and how the Persian poetic tradition was used to feed politics, to spur people to action, to express the ideology of the Islamic Republic, and also in opposition, to assert the human and individual nature of experience. It does not claim to be comprehensive regarding either the state-sponsored poets or the responses from oppositional and diasporic poets. It aims to reveal enough about the ways poets and both classical and contemporary poetry functioned in the first decades of the Revolution to encourage other scholars to launch investigations on this fascinating topic.

There are several leitmotifs in this book, the most important being martyrdom, which is part and parcel of Persian culture. While there are ample martyrological paradigms in Shiite Islam, Persian secular culture also has its narrative of martyrdom. One example is Prince Siyāvash, a pre-Islamic hero, whose death is interpreted as martyrdom. Siyāvash is admired for his faithfulness, innocence and altruism. His problems start when his stepmother, Sūdāba, is attracted to him, but Siyāvash rejects her sexual advances. She accuses him of sexual transgression, which forces Siyāvash to prove his innocence by riding through fire, a Zoroastrian tradition. Siyāvash leaves Persia and chooses exile in Turan, the arch-enemy of Persia. He is first hospitably received by Persia's arch-enemy, Afrāsiyāb, but after a series of events Siyāvash is killed.[1]

The notion of martyrdom is also used in metaphors. One recurrent metaphor is the moth and the candle flame. In several interpretations, the moth stands for the lover who is ready to offer his soul to be united with the fire. The fire is the light, a window on the world of non-existence, where the lover lives with the beloved forever. Such a death is the ultimate way of showing one's devotion and dedication. As we will see in this book, many Iranian soldiers compared themselves to moths running towards the enemy's fire. Some poets even state that the candle itself is a lover as it is gradually burning up while giving light to others. It gives up its substance, made of beeswax, because that has been separated from its essence, the honey.

As poetry has been a national icon of Iran and is still a marker of identity for Iranians, the first chapter investigates how poetry is related to politics, and why it is so essential for Iranians in voicing their ideas. The introductory chapter is devoted to the role of poetry, specifically the relationship between it and politics.

1 See the insightful introduction by Dick Davis in his translation, *Ferdowsi: The Legend of Seyavash*, New York: Penguin Classics, 1992, especially pp. xxii-xxiv.

https://doi.org/10.1515/9783110748734-004

The aesthetic aspect of poetry relating to politics is also considered, as much of Persian poetry has been written in the service of politics and could be characterised as aesthetised politics. After this theoretical framework, the role of poetry in forming a new revolutionary culture is addressed by delving into a wide range of sources upholding the ideals of the 1979 Revolution, severely condemning the "Western cultural invasion" and secular Iranian movements, and introducing new Islamist conventions of literature. Committed revolutionaries chiefly treated topics such as martyrdom, militant engagement against the West and foregrounding a politically laden Shiism and a poetic mysticism with much common ground with Sufism. The new revolutionary literati fiercely reacted against the pre-revolutionary poets and intellectuals, depicting them as pawns of the Western powers who aimed to weaken traditional Persian Islamic culture by stimulating people to drink alcohol and to adopt Western manners, and reducing women to sex objects. The chapter concludes with an analysis of what is widely regarded as an ideal revolutionary poem, in which resistance, martyrdom, the justification of violence and classical themes such as love and wine are integrated in a vehemently political context.

Chapter Two offers an analysis of the dynamics of martyrdom and how the Islamic government utilised poetry to make death meaningful, so justifying violence and a loss of life. The cultivation of martyrdom is a pillar of Shiism, but during the 1979 Revolution and especially during the war against Iraq (1980–1988), martyrdom became an ideological pillar of the Islamic Republic. This chapter addresses its roots in classical Persian culture by focusing on the lover's spiritual death in medieval Persian love poetry and why an ideal lover was expected to sacrifice everything to attain union with the beloved. Why is union with the spiritual beloved depicted in terms of annihilation, or literally "offering one's head"? These themes are interwoven with the paradigmatic story of the third Shiite Imam, Ḥuseyn, who was killed in the city of Karbala in present-day Iraq and is known as the "prince of martyrs." Shiites were politically quietist for much of their long history. Enduring suffering was regarded as a mark of piety. The situation changed in the 1960s as Shiites in the Persian cultural sphere increasingly engaged with politics, interpreting Ḥuseyn's death as a paradigm for fighting contemporary political injustice. ʿAlī Sharīʿatī (1933–1977) and Ruḥullāh Khomeini (1902–1989) were among the most influential Iranian intellectuals in popularising political Shiism. Their concept of activist martyrdom was central to the 1979 Revolution and during the Iran-Iraq war. Following this discussion, the chapter examines several poems that praise martyrdom, inviting people to offer their lives. The analysis highlights the integration of mystical themes, such as the spiritual stages on the mystic path and the prophet's ascension, in order to contextualise death as a step – indeed, a leap – forward on the mystic path, leading to union with the immaterial beloved. What is fascinating in these poems is the polyphonic use of themes and motifs and how pre-Islamic Persian history is combined with the Shiite tradition and Sufism to produce a new poem that is both familiar to the audience and effective in mobilising people for the front. While many of these poems have a high literary value, they were composed as propaganda. Their message is that dying in a just cause is essential for personal growth. Such a death also had a social impact, as the families of the fallen were congratulated rather than receiving condolences. The Islamic government offered a wide range of privileges for family members.

Chapter Three focuses on Qeyṣar Amīnpūr (1959–2007), an influential poet of the Iran-Iraq War who started his career as a committed revolutionary poet, writing many poems on war and martyrdom, but later adopted a more apolitical stance. Amīnpūr receives a chapter to himself because he has written on virtually every aspect of the Iran-Iraq War, using both classical and modern poetic forms, and his poetry is very well received in Iran. His poetry is a balanced example of the development of Persian poetry in a period in which bullets, missiles and aircraft became part of the poetic universe. It gives tangible depictions of the horrors of war and the suffering of innocent people. Several of his poems, notably "A Poem about War," are still used to commemorate the war. Concentrating on one poet offers us insights into the poet's intellectual and political development. In Amīnpūr's case, we see that after the war he composed poems on peace, showing the war's irreparable impact and traumas. This chapter also discusses the choices the poet made in selecting the poems in his collected volume of poetry. It is fascinating to see why he removed some published poems from the collection. Are his choices personal or politically motivated? In a country such as Iran, where ideology and political developments are central, it is essential to see what is excluded when analysing a poet's political stance. Amīnpūr is an excellent example of how committed revolutionary poets altered their political stance.

Chapter Four delineates the notion of love in Iran-Iraq War poetry. This notion is ubiquitous in the war setting, referring to a wide range of realities, all intended to motivate soldiers to fight and achieve their final goal, i.e., to die as lover martyrs. Poets rely heavily on classical Persian poetry and Islamic mysticism to define love, its working and impact. Soldiers are depicted as lovers or mystics, and the front line as a mystic itinerary leading to the divine. The front line is also depicted as an academy of love, Khomeini as the teacher, and the soldiers as students. The chapter addresses whether the definitions of love as an active agent that kills the lover and the beloved in classical Persian love poetry have contributed to the inclusion of love in a militant and violent modern war context. In medieval depictions of love, the lover is advised to abandon the rational faculty and to focus on the heart in order fully to engage with spiritual illumination. Beheading is used as a metaphor for bidding farewell to reason to concentrate on the heart, while in modern war contexts the metaphor becomes the reality. The discussion contributes to our understanding of the application of these medieval mystical concepts in a militant modern setting and how peaceful metaphors of love are transformed into a violent reality.

The 1979 Revolution began a new chapter in Iranian history. The revolutionary intellectuals wanted to create a new human being, cleansing universities and other public teaching organisations of pre-revolutionary "elements" during what they called "the cultural revolution." Textbooks at all levels were changed to instil the new ideology into students. Chapter Five is devoted to part of this ideological engagement, communicated to children through committed revolutionary poetry. It analyses one collection of poetry for children. All the poems are composed from the perspective of a child, dealing with the themes of martyrdom, heroism, experiences of war and the *basīj*-soldiers. The themes and perspectives in this collection make it a good example of the type of poems written for children. Such collections are intended to inculcate in children how to cope with the war's traumatic experiences and how they themselves can become revolutionaries, ready to sacrifice life itself for the Revolution. The chapter examines how such poems make a connection between martyrs and angels, for example by showing how angels take the martyrs to an eternal world, as promised in the Quran. This use and abuse of the aesthetic power of poetry has not been studied before.

Chapter Six is devoted to the poetry of Sīmīn Bihbahānī (1927–2014), a leading established poet who also courageously voiced her concerns about a wide range of vital human rights issues violated by the Islamic Republic after the 1979 Revolution. Never allied herself with the revolutionary camp, Bihbahānī is perhaps the most productive established female poet who wrote on the Revolution and the war. Her poetry lifts events to a higher plane, depicting them from a humanistic perspective, aloof from Islamic ideological colouring. The chapter outlines crucial events such as "Black Friday," which became the turning point of the 1979 Revolution, the anti-war mood in Iran, her interpretation of martyrdom, her poems on the liberation of the oil city Khurramshahr from the Iraqis, and her war poem "Once more, I will build you, my homeland," which has become a national poem in post-war Iran, sung by several pop singers from Los Angeles to Tehran. The chapter offers a different perception of the Revolution and the war, appraising from a secular viewpoint the same subjects that were addressed by revolutionary poets.

Chapter Seven analyses the poetry of a central diasporic Persian poet, Nādir Nādirpūr (1929–2000), who fled Iran after the Revolution and lived first in Europe and then in Los Angeles until his passing. After 1979 many Iranian intellectuals chose exile, where they continued to write on political events in Iran. Nādirpūr is a pre-eminent example of the intellectuals in exile. The chapter examines several key poems in which the poet, as an exile, assesses the events in his home country, using a catalogue of pre-Islamic myths and legends to depict current political developments. The chapter offers a new perspective on the Revolution and the war from a frustrated and infuriated poet whose hopes of returning home have been shattered. He is stunned at the way his fellow Iranians could discover Khomeini's image miraculously visible in the moon, or how they were responding to their discovery of Khomeini as a poet of mystic love and wine. It is in such a state of bewilderment that the poet compares Khomeini to mythical characters in the Persian national epic *Shāh-nāma* by Firdowsī (circa 935–1020). The chapter offers insights into the ways a secular poet of the diaspora voiced his view on the Revolution and war. He is exceptionally critical of the Islamic regime, its founder and the recent course of Iranian history.

Chapter Eight examines Iran's international relations during the Iran-Iraq War, demonstrating how the majority of the Arab countries, especially Saudi Arabia, wholeheartedly supported Saddam Hussein (1937–2006) in his fight against Iran. It investigates the relationship between Iran and Saudi Arabia on several grounds, such as the rivalry between the Persians and the Arabs, Iranian resentment of the Saudis' support for Saddam, and the divergence of religious affiliations and practices: while Iran relies on her Shiite and Sufi tradition, the Saudis base their politics on Salafism and Wahhabism, which are diametrically opposed to Iranian religiosity. The chapter gives medieval examples showing how the Persians and Arabs have challenged each other in verse, each claiming the more praiseworthy qualities. The rivalry is not based on ethnicity alone, but also on piety. The chapter offers examples from Khomeini's poetry in which he emphasises that piety is not achieved simply by a pilgrimage (*ḥajj*) to the House of God, because the believer's heart is God's actual residence. The heart is more important than the Kaʿba in Mecca. Such views contradict the Wahhabi ideology, highlighting a completely different appreciation of the pilgrimage. The chapter examines why revolutionary Iranians demonstrated in the holy cities of Mecca and Medina, provoking the Saudis' anger in the 1980s. The chapter analyses several poems composed in reaction to the violent responses of the Saudi police to Iranian demonstrators, who were injured and even killed. In sum, the chapter offers new insights into the dynamics of the opposing ideologies, displaying how much Iranian Shiism and Persian Sufism differ from the Wahhabi ideology, and how these ideological incongruities impact deeply on the international relations between the two countries.

The Conclusion, Chapter Nine, is devoted to an analysis of the use of poetry in modern politics, examining how the revolutionary intellectuals created a new version of Sufism in which love-death, martyrdom and a new type of piety were central. The chapter examines the role of poetry as a mobilising force, but also as a therapeutic medium, used to heal traumas. The chapter also asks whether the revolutionaries' new poetic norms and conventions were successful. How do Iranians appreciate the committed war poetry? Why have several of the revolutionary intellectuals become dissidents?

1 Towards Justifying Violence

دلیر آمدی سعدیا در سخن
چو تیغت به دست است فتحی بکن
بگو آنچه دانی که حق گفته به
نه رشوت ستانیّ و نه عشوه ده
طمع بند و دفتر ز حکمت بشوی
طمع بگسل و هرچه دانی بگوی[2]

O Saʿdī! You are brave in speech;
As you have the blade in hand, make a victory.
Say what you know, for saying the truth is best;
You neither ask for a bribe, nor give tithe.
Bind in your hopes, wash prudence from the book;
Break your hopes, say all you know.

1.1 Introduction

Persian literature is the jewel in the crown of Persian culture, as Ehsan Yarshater says.[3] It is universally acknowledged that Persians are predisposed to poetry as they use poetry in everyday speech, in rites and rituals and especially in emotional personal moments, and at times of socio-political crisis. As Hossein Ziai states, "Poetry is to Iranian civilisation what philosophy is to the Greek and prophecy to the Judaic."[4] The role of poetry for Persian-speaking peoples comes very close to the definition of Gaston Bachelard (1884 – 1962) who characterises poetry as "the soul and the mind, thus giving us back our dreams and opening up possibilities for creating 'images which have not been experienced, and which life does not prepare.'"[5] Poetry is an extremely powerful means to reflect on developments in society and in oneself. It has a reflexive function, allowing the reader to compare reality described in a literary work with his or her own reality. Given that poetry is omnipresent in Iranian life, the developments in twentieth-century Iran cannot be properly understood without one considering

---

2 Muṣliḥ al-Dīn Saʿdī, *Būstān*, ed. G.H. Yūsufī, Tehran: Khᵛārazmī, 1375/1996, p. 53, lines 503 – 505.
3 Yarshater emphasises this on the blurb of each of the books published in the History of Persian Literature series at I.B. Tauris.
4 Hossein Ziai, "Ḥāfeẓ, Lisān al-Ghayb of Persian Poetic Wisdom," in *Gott ist schön und Er liebt die Schönheit* (*God Is Beautiful and He Loves Beauty*), A. Giese, and C.J. Bürgel, Bern: Peter Lang, 1994, p. 449.
5 As cited by Roland Bleiker, *Aesthetics and World Politics*, Basingstoke: Palgrave Macmillan, 2009, p. 85.

https://doi.org/10.1515/9783110748734-005

the poetic documents produced by core political figures, the literary elite and ordinary people. Due to its centrality, socio-political events have been depicted in poetry for various purposes, ranging from military mobilisation, developing individuals' spiritual potential, showing respect to Shiite saints, and as private therapy to process an emotional event. Many of the poems cited in this book have an unmistakable layer of processing pain, for the poet and the collective.

The sheer beauty and musicality of many of these poems invite repeated readings and "viral" sharing. The poems' aesthetic value is an essential aspect of their use in a political setting. From the beginnings of the New Persian poetry in the ninth century, it has been deeply connected to politics and social developments. What Frits van Oostrom says about medieval Dutch literature is seamlessly applicable to Persia and Persian literature: poetry is aestheticised politics and politics of aesthetics.[6] In his book *Aesthetics and World Politics*, Bleiker characterises poetry as a "perfect illustration of an aesthetic engagement with politics: a kind of micro-biotope in which we can observe, in an experimental way, why and how the aesthetic matters to politics."[7] The Persian poetry of the 1979 Revolution and the Iran-Iraq War (1980 – 1988) is not only an aesthetic engagement with specific socio-political events: one could argue that emotion is the engine igniting and running this poetry, perhaps more so than in other periods of modern Iranian history. Many of the decisions and actions of politicians, intellectuals and individuals are driven by emotions, but these are often omitted in examining the events of the 1979 Revolution and the Iran-Iraq War (1980 – 1988). The poetry is an aesthetic engagement, but it is deeply political and deeply emotional.

1.2 Poetry as a Persuative Force

For over a millennium poetry has been applied in various ways to comment on and interpret politics and political developments. In medieval times poetry was mainly a repository of Persian myths, legends, history and wisdom, as in the case of Firdowsī's monumental epic *Shāh-nāma*, but it was also a courtly practice, publicising the exploits of the rulers and courtiers and recording for posterity an essential aspect of politics in Persian cultural areas. Rulers retained dozens of poets to preserve their names for future generations and to publicise their exploits and power to far-off regions. During each period, Persian poetry was in

6 Frits van Oostrom, *Het woord van eer: literatuur aan het Hollandse hof omstreeks 1400*, Amsterdam: Ooievaar, 1996, pp. 22 – 25.
7 Roland Bleiker, *Aesthetics*, p. 86.

one way or another connected with politics. For centuries the connection was the place of poetry in court life. During and after the Constitutional Revolution (1906–1911), major poets shunned court service and increasingly directed their attention to the people, conveying messages on democracy, human rights, the position of women and many other topical subjects, which they published in newly-founded journals and newspapers. Often these materials were recited in public places such as coffee-houses where they reached a wide public.

While Persian poetry informs readers about events taking place in the world, it is also used to convince, to rouse the listener to action. The comparison between the Greeks and philosophy and the Persians and poetry is intriguing, as Persian poetry is not meant to convey a reality through discursive reasoning, syllogism or other philosophical devices. Persian poetry includes a space of ambiguity in which each reader can define and interpret for her/himself what the poetry means – although a reader familiar with the poetic conventions may discern the meanings that are juxtaposed.[8] The poet uses this space to demonstrate his superior poetic skills by employing a wide range of literary figures and novel metaphors within the strictly limited frame of poetic conventions. While embellishing his poetry to outshine all other poets, one of the poet's main tasks is to convince his reader or audience. The poet often uses original arguments wrapped in mesmerising poetic attire to capture the audience's attention. It is often not about logical reasoning but mere persuasion to stimulate an action, a decision, or to confirm an attitude, such as admiration for the ruler. The poet is successful when he has convinced his audience. Medieval literary manuals emphasise persuasion as a yardstick of the superiority of poetry. ʿAbd al-Qāhir al-Jurjānī (d. 1078 or 1081) refers positively to *takhyīl*, "make-believe," when it is applied in argumentative discourse to persuade.[9] Heinrichs calls this "poetic argumentation," which is based on analogy and simile, with the aim of convincing the audience through apt metaphors and similes. Both in classical and in modern po-

---

8 For a comprehensive study of ambiguity in Islam see Thomas Bauer, *Die Kultur der Ambiguität: Eine andere Geschichte des Islam*, Berlin: Verlag der Weltreligionen, 2011; also see M.R. Ghanoonparvar, *Prophets of Doom: Literature as a Socio-Political Phenomenon in Modern Iran*, Lanham / New York: University Press of America, 1984, chapter 6, pp. 149–177, in which the author discusses various adventages and disadventages of ambihuity in modern Persian fiction, while also dealing with censorship as a cause of ambiguity.

9 W.P. Heinrichs, in the *Encyclopaedia of Islam, Second Edition*, s.v. Takhyīl; also compare *idem*, "Observations on an Arabic Literary Debate," in *Dispute Poems and Dialogues in the Ancient and Mediaeval Near East: Forms and Types of Literary Debates in Semitic and Related Literatures*, ed., G.J. Reinink and Herman L.J. Vanstiphout, Leuven: Peeters, 1991, pp. 180–182. Heinrichs discusses this in the context of Arabic prose, but such argumentative discourse is equally applicable to poetry.

etry such literary tools are deployed to rouse the audience's imagination, to evoke emotions and to stir them into action. There are many examples showing how the audience is emotionally moved without logical thinking. In such cases, the emotive values of poetry overwhelm the audience's reasoning. A proverbial example of stirring the audience to action is Rūdakī's (860 – 940) poem, cited by Niẓāmī ʿArūżī in his *Chahār-maqāla* ("Four Discourses," 1155 – 1157) to highlight the power of poetic argument. Rūdakī's *qaṣīda* moved Amīr Naṣr II ibn Aḥmad (re. 914 – 43) to go back to Bukhara after many months of living in Herat.[10] The courtiers – from Bukhara – saw that the Amīr had no intention of returning. Many notables failed to convince the Amīr to return, but then Rūdakī composed a poem, accompanied by music, evoking nostalgic memories of Bukhara and stimulating the Amīr's senses to such a degree that when the poet reached the sixth couplet, the Amīr descended from his throne and, without boots, mounted his steed and galloped in the direction of Bukhara.

Discussions on the superiority of the power of conviction over the naked truth appear in the works of literary theoreticians such as the philosopher Naṣīr al-Dīn Ṭūsī (1201 – 1274).[11] He starts his *Miʿyār al-ashʿār* ("the Standard of Poetry") with a discussion on the nature of poetry, stating "*takhyīl* is the effect of speech on the soul in one way or another, affecting contraction (*qabż*) and expansion (*basṭ*), and there is no doubt that the intention of a poem is *takhyīl* so that its setting (*ḥuṣūl*) in the soul (*nafs*) will be a reason for taking an action, for instance, initiating a deed or refraining from doing something, or that *takhyīl* causes the creation of a figure (*hayʾat*) [in the soul], such as contentment or annoyance, or any type of joy desired."[12] In this definition of the impact of poetry, the evident premise is that poetry should persuade the individual to adopt a stance and take action.

Shams al-Dīn Muḥammad ibn Qeys al-Rāzī also refers to the power of poetry in his poetic manual, *al-Muʿjam fī maʿāyir ashʿār al-ʿajam* (1232 – 33). Here he gives the story of a governor who is sentenced to death but is saved by poetry.

---

10 See Niẓāmī ʿArūżī, *Chahār-maqāla*, pp. 31 – 34.

11 For an excellent analysis of Rūdakī's poem see J. Landau, "Naṣīr al-Dīn Ṭūsī and Poetic Imagination in the Arabic and Persian Philosophical Tradition," in *Metaphor and Imagery in Persian Poetry*, ed. A.A. Seyed-Gohrab, Leiden / Boston, MA: Brill, 2012, p. 16.

12 *Shiʿr va shāʿirī dar āthār-i khᵛāja Naṣīr al-Dīn Ṭūsī*, ed. Muʿaẓẓama Iqbālī (Aʿẓam), Tehran: Sāzmān-i Chāp va Intishārāt-i Vizārat-i Farhang va Irshād-i Islāmī, 1992, p. 159. Also see Landau's translation of this passage (ibid, p. 59): "The cause of an action has an origin similar [in the soul] to the impulse to set about doing one thing or to refrain from doing [one thing], or to the advent of a figure [in the soul], such as satisfaction or displeasure, or whatever kind of pleasure is sought after."

While in one case eloquence and poetry can save a life, in other cases Shams-i Qeys emphasises that "one verse has been the stimulus," stirring up "great sedition and becoming the occasion for the momentous shedding of blood." He then cites the following lines:

به بیتی شود مرد با کینه نرم
بجوشد به بیتی دگر خون ز تن
بسا دل کی گشت از پی شعر رام
بسا سر کی ببرید نظم سخن[13]

A line of poetry may soften one man's wrath
Another line may set blood rushing from the body.
Many a heart has been calmed by poetry
Many a neck has been severed by verse.[14]

The author tells this particular story to emphasise how poetry stays with the attentive reader as a resource for life. One of his arguments is that in such grave moments, truth and logical reasoning are of no avail. The power of poetry appeals to other human faculties to elicit mercy and sympathy:

> ... where with one *bait* [verse] the most important matters are resolved, where the necks of reason are subjugated to a halter, and an inherited vengeance is transformed into love and affection. The opposite has as often occurred, where one verse has been the stimulus that stirred up great seditions and became the occasion for the momentous shedding of blood.[15]

"The momentous shedding of blood" is not empty hyperbole and does not belong to medieval times, as Persian poetry is a living tradition and both poetry and theories on the power of poetry exist in contemporary Iran. During the 1979 Revolution and the Iran-Iraq War, poetry was consciously used by the revolutionary faction to convince people to offer their lives, even if this went against logical reasoning.

The Persian "mirror for princes" manual, *Chahār maqāla* ("Four Discourses"), containing four chapters on indispensable court offices, namely the secretary, poet, astronomer and physician, opens with the following paragraph emphasising the role of ambiguity and the power of poetry:

---

13 Shams al-Dīn Muḥammad ibn Qeys al-Rāzī, *al-Muʿjam fī maʿāyir ashʿār al-ʿajam*, ed. S. Shamīsā (this edition is based on the original critical edition by Muḥammad ibn ʿAbd al-Vahhāb Qazvīnī, and a re-edited version by Muḥammad-Taqī Mudarris Rażavī), Tehran: Rāmīn, 1388/ 2009, p. 451.
14 Clinton, "Shams-i Qays on the Nature of Poetry," in *Edebiyāt*, No. 2, Issue I, 1989, p. 110.
15 Ibid.

> Poetry is an art through which the poet creates imaginary propositions and blends fruitful analogies in such a way that he can alter the idea/meaning of a little thing to appear great or a great thing to appear small. Or he dresses good in the garb of evil and evil in the form of good. Through ambiguity (*īhām*) he arouses the faculties of anger and concupiscence in such a way that by his ambiguity men's temperaments (*ṭabāʿ*) become affected with tightening (*qabż*) or expansion (*basṭ*); whereby he conduces to the accomplishment of great things in the order of the world.[16]

In addition to the power of poetry to move people to save lives or to sacrifice their lives, Persian poetry incorporates ambiguity, which has allowed generations of readers from different walks of life to produce their own interpretations within an expansible space. This poetry is rich in metaphors and paradoxes which allow the reader to adopt a purely secular reading or read through that to find metaphysical signification. In this ambiguous space, antithetical concepts become each other's complement in such a coherent way that they make contradictions meaningful.[17] Metaphors retain ambiguity, creating ever newer meanings to make poetic arguments expressive. This ambiguity is so much at the heart of Persian poetry that it has become part and parcel of Persian culture. Poetry, as part of religion, supports faith in the possible coherence between the views one holds, the inherent structure of reality, and how one ought to live. Concepts such as *kufr* ("unbelief") and *ʿishq* ("passionate love") are commonly preferred over Islamic tenets and *ʿaql* ("intellect") to emphasise a paradoxical piety in which other types of religiosity, solely based on the literal reading of Islamic law and corroborated by discursive reasoning, are labelled as outward show. Such dualities are needed to create a paradox, which in turn allows an epistemological space to take the reader beyond the mundane terminology and antithesis. The goal of such paradoxes is to merge all things in selfless Love.[18]

---

16 *Chahār maqāla*, ed. Muḥammad ibn ʿAbd al-Vahhāb Qazvīnī, Berlin: Iranschahr, 1927, p. 30; translated by Edward G. Browne as *The Four Discourses of Niẓámí-i-ʿArúḍí of Samarqand*, followed by an abridged translation of Mírzá Muḥammad's notes to the Persian text, London: Luzac, 1921, p. 27. I have changed Browne's translation at several points.

17 See Shahab Ahmed's discussion on the notions of contradictions and ambiguity and how such concepts, together with paradox, have formed the intellectual and religious thoughts of Islam, *What Is Islam? The Importance of Being Islamic*, Princeton, NJ: Princeton University Press, 2016, pp. 405–541. Also see Thomas Bauer, *Die Kultur der Ambiguität*.

18 In this tradition, this pure piety, in which paradoxes play an essential role, reveals the limitations of ratiocinative intellectual faculty, emphasising why attaining gnosis and direct knowledge from God requires an experience of unbelief. Outstanding mystical poets such as Sanāʾī (d. about 1130), Niẓāmī (c. 1141–1209), ʿAṭṭār (c. 1145–1221), Saʿdī (c. 1210–1292), Rūmī (1207–1273) and Ḥāfiẓ (1315–1390) have produced a theory of this paradoxical piety and recount stories

While the ambiguity of the spiritual and profane is the essence of Persian poetry, it has been used in new ways in the Persian war poetry analysed in this book. Connoisseurs of classical Persian poetry will be amazed to see how a wide range of classical motifs, themes and imagery are interlocked in the violent reality of war, in which life and death are at stake. This war poetry derives from the millennium-old tradition which is universally known to speakers of the Persian language.

---

to illustrate the necessity of oppositional and seemingly blasphemous concepts. The story of Sheykh Ṣan'ān, the key-holder of the Ka'ba and the religious figure of his age, is often cited to explain this piety. Ṣan'ān dreams of a girl in Rome and goes to the Christian city where he falls in love with her. The girl asks four things before she can reciprocate his love: "There are four things you must / Perform to show that you deserve my trust: // Burn the Quran, drink wine, seal up Faith's eye, / bow down to images." Ṣan'ān agrees. There follows a long period during which his followers come to convince him to return, as he has become a disgrace to the Islamic community. He hurls stones at them and stays with the girl, but she keeps postponing union with him. When he has fulfilled all her wishes, she completely humiliates him by asking him to take care of her pigs for a year, before she will requite his love. The story is designed to show that Ṣan'ān, the great religious scholar of his age, lacks the love that so transforms the lover that he assumes the identity of the beloved. Persian mystics have depicted losing one's own identity in union with the beloved through colour symbolism, emphasising that all colours must be removed so that the lover achieves the colour of colourlessness (*bīrangī*). It is at this moment that Ṣan'ān dreams of the Prophet who tells him that the goal of his journey has been achieved and he can return to Mecca. Ṣan'ān's radical submission to *kufr* is a necessary transgression of exoteric religious conventions to achieve loving illumination. While these mystics push the centre occupied by religious scholars to the periphery, they also show that there is a plane beyond temporal dualities such as *kufr* and Islam. This antinomian philosophy introduced by poets such as Sanā'ī, 'Aṭṭār, and Ḥāfiẓ has been an inspiration for poets in subsequent centuries, including modern Persian war poets, creating a ubiquitous poetic idiom in which outward religiosity and the piety of religious jurists are severely criticised, whereas sinful behaviour is promoted to protect the individual against the dangers of hypocrisy. These mystic poets believed that the slightest show of religiosity would garner people's respect and this would lead to hypocrisy. A truly pious life could be covered by outwardly sinful behaviour. This antinomian approach to piety generated a rich space for paradox. In the space between "belief" and "unbelief" or "sober" and "drunkenness," the poet could create mesmerising metaphors, playing with the audience about the profane and spiritual contents of his poem, elevating sheer blasphemy to becoming the highest ideal of piety. See Farīd al-Dīn 'Aṭṭār, *Manṭiq al-ṭayr*, ed. Siyyid Ṣādiq Gowharīn, Tehran: Shirkat Intishārāt-i 'Ilmī va Farhangī, 1368/1989, p. 75, lines 1342–1343, transl. by D. Davis & A. Darbandi, *The Conference of the Birds*, New York: Penguin Classics, 1984 (reprinted 2011), p. 64. On antinomian piety see A.A. Seyed-Gohrab, "Rūmī's Antinomian Poetic Philosophy," in *Mawlana Rumi Review*, Issue IX, No. 1–2, 2018, pp. 159–99.

1.3 Poetry in Modern Politics

Poetry was used to convey a wide range of sometimes antithetical ideas: pan-Islamism, secularism, traditionalism, anti-imperialism and nationalism in the nineteenth century. This literature served both as a "recorded chronicle" and "as a decisive factor in Iran's social reformation."[19] Many Persians wished to follow the Western political philosophy in introducing a parliament, a code of law, educational and social reforms, but at the same time several of these ideas clashed with traditional Persian culture and were resisted. A good example of such a tension and paradox is the issue of unveiling, which was connected to concepts such as chastity. Some poets regarded unveiling as a Western intervention, an assault on Persia's traditional culture, while others wholeheartedly encouraged women to remove the veil and participate in society.[20]

The relationship between Persia and Europe (including Russia) intensified during the nineteenth century, as Persians journeyed through Europe and brought back new ideas, including the introduction of codified law and the idea of a constitution, and new concepts of education. The European presence and strategic interests in Iran also intensified. More European texts were being translated into Persian, and Persian thinkers acquired wider audiences within Persia through the introduction of printing and greater literacy.

At the same time, there were concerns about the loss of independence as Britain and Russia developed economic and political interests in Iran. With the granting of the Constitution in August 1906, Persian poets began to address social and political events for a mass audience. As the Qajar court declined, the institution of courtly poets began to crumble, but the social and political developments gave poets a new task. Poetry became topical, treating political issues published in newspapers or "recited by orators at emotion-packed demonstra-

---

19 M. Shaki, "An Introduction to Modern Persian Literature," in *Critical Perspectives on Modern Persian Literature*, ed. T.M. Ricks, Washington, DC: Three Continents Press, 1984, pp. 26–41; S. Soroudi, in *Encyclopaedia Iranica*, s.v. Constitutional revolution, vii. the Constitutional Movement in Literature.

20 A.A. Seyed-Gohrab, "Poetry as Awakening: Singing Modernity," in *Literature of the Early Twentieth Century: From the Constitutional Period to Reza Shah*, ed. A.A. Seyed-Gohrab, London/New York: I.B. Tauris, 2015, pp. 30–132; also see Paul Sprachman, "The Poetics of *Hijāb* in the Satire of Iraj Mirzā," in *Iran and Iranian Studies: Essays in Honor of Iraj Afshar*, ed. K. Eslami, Princeton, NJ: Zagros, 1998, pp. 341–357; M.R. Shafīʿī-Kadkanī, *Chirāgh-u āyina: dar justijū-yi taḥavvul-i shiʿr-i muʿāṣir-i Iran*, Tehran: Sukhan, 4th print 1392/2013, pp. 81–87; J. Afary, *Sexual Politics in Modern Iran*, Cambridge: Cambridge University Press, 2009, pp. 44–47, 187–188, 206–211.

tions and rallies."[21] The European imperialists in Persia, women's rights, education and participation in a changing society provided new poetic themes. Poets used accounts of pre-Islamic Persian history in classical Persian literature to rouse nationalistic sentiments against foreign interventions. Yet there was an intense sense of being "backward" in comparison to Europe, and a search for explanations. The canon of Persian poetry was re-appraised in terms of poets' contribution to the nation, or to its backwardness. In their new politically engaged roles, poets used poetry to stir their audience to political action, instructing them about the virtues of patriotism, fuelling their emotions against European imperialistic plans, while proposing that democracy, a novel western concept, could remedy the country's "backward" position. The position of women in Iran was contrasted not just to European examples, but also to the women of newly-founded states in central Asia in which Persian is spoken, such as Tajikistan.[22]

1.4 Poetry in the Service of Politics

The literature of the Constitutional Revolution had such an effect on the concepts of literature, poetry and poets that from this period onwards literature was increasingly in the service of and was a force in politics. Poets and writers were champions of new political ideas, defended the country with their pens, and became heroes of the nation. Throughout the first half of the twentieth century literature remained heavily politicised, especially due to the nationalist ideals of the Pahlavi dynasty (1925–1979) on the one side and Marxist ideology on the other. The millennium celebration of Firdowsī's *Shāh-nāma* in 1934 and the change of the name of Persia to Iran were accompanied by state initiatives to usher Iran into a new era in which its pre-Islamic glory and the Aryan heritage were central.[23] The Islamic heritage and the role of the *ʿulamāʾ* had been circum-

21 M.A. Jazayeri, "Recent Persian Literature: Observations on Themes and Tendencies," in *Critical perspectives on Modern Persian Literature*, ed. T.M. Ricks, Washington, DC: Three Continents Press, 1984, p. 73.

22 See, for instance, several poems by Lāhūtī. Also see A. Karimi-Hakkak, *Recasting Persian Poetry: Scenarios of Poetic Modernity in Iran*, Salt Lake City, UT: University of Utah Press, 1995, pp. 188–202.

23 See Afshin Marashi, "The Nation's Poet: Ferdowsi and the Iranian National Imagination," in *Iran in the 20th Century Historiography and Political Culture*, ed. T. Atabaki, London: I.B. Tauris, 2009, pp. 93–111.

scribed from the start of Riżā Shah's reforms in 1925.[24] During Riżā Shah's reign, from 1925, there was little freedom of expression, but in 1941 the allied forces removed him from power due to his sympathies for the Germans, and his son and successor, Muḥammad Riżā, allowed more latitude for writers and poets. The literature of this period, until the 1953 *coup d'état* that, with the aid of the CIA, overthrew Muḥammad Muṣaddiq's (1882–1967) government, was thriving, at least by the measure of freedom of expression.[25] Between the coup and the 1979 Revolution, Iranian poets and writers experienced a repressive atmosphere in which literature was censored and authors faced detention. In such a situation there were two types of literature, one treating social and political issues and the other engaging with non-political subjects. During these three decades, politically engaged literature gained the ascendency as topics such as justice, freedom and equality captured the common people's attention. Both religious and secular writers and poets treated these subjects alike, often speaking in the same language about topics such as the negative western cultural impact –usually termed Westoxification (*gharbzadagī*)– martyrdom and censorship.

The 1979 Revolution brought fundamental changes in Iran, which affected Persian literature.[26] While several established poets were criticised and their works censored, a new wave of poets came on the scene to compose poetry with the aim of safeguarding the principles of the newly-founded Islamic government. The 1979 Revolution created a shift in literary values, launching a new type of censorship on poets, writers and artists. The first response to pre-Revolutionary literature was entirely negative, associating this poetry with the West, which encouraged free sexual morals, the excessive use of alcohol, secularism and preferring Western assumptions to Persian cultural values. According to the new Islamic revolutionaries, literature had to be pious, ideological and instrumental in fighting despotic regimes. Many established poets were considered leftists, or other labels were put on them. Although the poets had their own diverse political

24 K. Talattof, *The Politics of Writing in Iran: A History of Modern Persian Literature*, Syracuse, NY: Syracuse University Press, 2000, pp. 66–72; also see the excellent study by M.R. Ghanoonparvar, *Prophets of Doom*, especially the first chapter, pp. 1–33.

25 See Abbas Amanat, *Iran: A Modern History*, New Haven, CT, & London: Yale University Press, 2017, see index under Mosaddeq, pp. 965–966; also see H. Katouzian, "The Campaign against the Anglo-Iranian Agreement of 1919," in *British Journal of Middle Eastern Studies*, 25, No. 1, 1998, pp. 5–46; idem, *Musaddiq and the Struggle for Power in Iran*, London: I.B. Tauris, 1990; M.J. Gasiorowski, in *Encyclopaedia Iranica*, s.v. Coup d'Etat of 1332 sh./1953.

26 For an excellent analytical overview of the literature from 1977 to 1997 see Ahmad Karimi-Hakkak, "Introduction: Iran's Literature 1977–1997," in *Iranian Studies*, Vol. 30, No. 3/4, 1997, pp. 193–213.

preferences, by being labelled as disloyal to the ideals of the Revolution, they were rendered inactive, or in some cases were arrested, executed or driven into exile.

The first generation of revolutionary literati sternly condemned most of the literature written before 1979. A new type of literature with its own specific literary conventions appeared after the revolution and was called the "Literature of the Islamic Revolution" (*adabiyyāt-i inqilāb-i islāmī*).[27] Most of the established Persian literary critics ignored this new revolutionary literature, believing that the movement was intended to circumscribe their power in society, while those who did respond took the side of the revolutionaries. The proponents of the revolutionary literature were deeply committed to Islamic revolutionary ideals, dismissing any literary texts that would harm revolutionary principles such as a sanctification of Khomeini's position, the cult of martyrdom and political Islam. This movement consisted mainly of young dilettante poets who praised the ethics of the Revolution. They wrote poetry in praise of Khomeini, and with the advent of the war against Iraq they started to write war poetry. They were generously financially supported to create a new literature that would contrast with pre-revolutionary poetry. For these committed revolutionary poets poetry had to have visible effects in promoting Islamic ideals, often involving a justification of violence and presenting death as the apogee of spiritual attainment. This poetry contrasted itself to the pre-Revolution literature, which was composed by Iranian intellectuals mainly for elites, whereas the young revolutionary poets and writers wrote for the common people to instil in them the values of the Revolution.

The essays of these committed literati rigorously censure the poetry of the previous generation and define new literary conventions and a new role for literature in general, and poetry in particular.[28] Manūchihr Akbarī, a member of the Academic Board of the University of Tehran, identifies essential aspects of this literature and contrasts it to pre-Revolution literature in his article "A Look at the Poetry of Revolution of the Light." This is one of the introductory articles in a volume of essays reflecting critically on the literature of the 1979 Revolution. Akbarī starts apologetically to defend the early poetry of the committed revolutionary poets. He says that even where this poetry is weak and superficial, it is still "poetry" because the poets were young and inexperienced, having no

---

27 In this book I avoid problematising the diverse names used for the literature of the 1979 Revolution and the Iran-Iraq War, to focus rather on its contents.

28 Khorrami rightly speaks of a "permanent revolution" carried out by the Islamic republic to remove the Other. This other comprises anything other than what the state promotes as "good literature" or "committed literature." See *Literary Subterfuge*, pp. 1–14.

time to embellish their poetry. In the following excerpt he defines Islamic committed poetry:

> The poetry of the Revolution is serious, modest and at the same time rebellious and stormy. The poetry of revolution is young but fruitful and robust, chaste, dynamic and alive. This is the poetry of anger, commotion, resistance and struggle. It is the poetry of protest and vociferation. It is the poetry of life and manliness. It is an admixture of love and wrath, kindness and rage, a murmur of monotheistic faith and righteous living, a running stream of supplication and prayer, and at the same time an ocean of heroism and fire. It is not the poetry of "sweet Aida unclothed," who is stripped naked from top to toe in the mirror of the poet and has completely possessed the poet's existence. The poetry of Revolution is a mixture of love, gnosis, and heroism. The gnosis in this poetry is not making a shop, acquiring disciples and desperate Sufi-mongering or endless waiting without any action or hope. Gnosticism in this poetry fights the idol (*ṭāghūt*) in the arena of fire and flowers,[29] bullets and blood, in the trenches and the front lines of light against darkness [i. e. probably Saddam Hussein's army]. The mystics and the travellers of the path, having consciously chosen this Gnosticism, have registered their names in a battalion waiting for martyrdom, or in groups striving for martyrdom running on the minefields. These are loved ones who are waiting for the moment to start the soul's flight to the spiritual garden. The mystics of the poetry of Revolution are youths such as Fahmīda who invented the new [arithmetic] formula of body against tank, which forms another manifestation of the victory of blood over sword, and body over tank. This poetry is not the poetry of beastly love and satanic descriptions of an irrational poet who is always drunk. The poetry of Revolution is not the belch of an irresponsible poet or a corrupt drunkard. This is not the poetry of the illegitimate spawn of selfish intellectuals. [...]. This poetry is not the intellectual belch of some stranger towards the people. This poetry is not the idle talk of some prostitute-poet who in the shelter of hashish, opium and addiction violates the bounds of discretion. This is not the poetry of "Without you I passed once more from that alley on a moonlit night." The poetry of Revolution is not the poetry of those who have not suffered, the frequenters of wine-houses,[30] strangers to gnosis, to acts of worship, and the spiritual journey; those who have not tried, even once in their lives, to place their foreheads on the prayer tablet (*muhr*) ..."[31]

---

29 The compound *gul u gulūla* refers to bullets and flowers, especially carnations (*mīkhak*) that people placed on the soldiers' gun barrels, inviting them to join the demonstrations.

30 The term used here is *kharābāt* which literally means "ruins." The term is a common reference to wine-houses, brothels and other localities of ill-fame at the periphery of Islamic towns in classical Persian poetry, but due to the popularity of antinomian mysticism the term became central to the Persian mystical poetry. During the Pahlavi period, *kharābāt* was used to refer to cafes, wine-houses and cabarets. The word cabaret derives from the Persian word *kharābāt*.

31 M. Akbari, "Nigāhī ba shiʿr-i inqlāb-i nūr," in *Majmūʿa-yi maqālāt-i simīnār-i barrasī-yi adabiyyāt-i inqilāb-i islāmī*, Tehran: Samt, 1373/1994, pp. 18 – 19. Also see Mahani, *'Do not say they are Dead,'* pp. 44 – 45.

This violent tirade is intended to condemn the literature written before the revolution and to define a new committed poetry.[32] The author alludes to eminent poets and writers who are stigmatised as whoremongers and drunkards, people who have damaged the Islamic Persian culture. It is certainly painful to read such a prejudiced evaluation of the undoubted masterpieces produced by poets and writers such as Aḥmad Shāmlū (1925–2000), the author of *Aida in the Mirror*, Furūgh Farrukhzād (1934–1967) and Fireydūn Mushīrī (1926–2000).[33] The allusion to Shāmlū is certainly unjustified, as he used his poetry to fight the despotic politics of the Pahlavi regime. This volume of essays on the literature of the 1979 Revolution makes no mention of the essential contribution of the pre-revolutionary poets and other writers to toppling the Shah's regime.[34] Several of the poets alluded to in Akbarī's piece, and in other articles in that volume, were imprisoned and tortured at the hands of the Pahlavi regime due to their writing and their resistance to censorship and oppression. The resistance to censorship started with the foundation of the Writers' Association of Iran (1968), whose members were suppressed by the Pahlavi government.[35] Despite the suppression, the Association undertook activities addressing essential topics such as freedom of expression. One of the Association's activities was the organisation of a series of poetry readings and speeches, held by prominent poets and writers at the Goethe Institute in Tehran from 10 to 19 October 1977, which was later called the Ten Nights (*dah shab*). These nights had a tremendous social impact. In Karimi-Hakkak's words, "*The Ten Nights* is beyond question the most significant group event in Iranian intellectual history and must be considered an early milestone in the 1979 Revolution. It not only provided an occasion for young literate Iranians to see and hear in person and for the first time those

---

32 This tirade is not an isolated case as we see such violent condemnations in other sources. See, for instance, Yūsuf-ʿAlī Mīrshakkāk, *Sitīz bā khīshtan: Majmūʿa-yi maqālāt*, Tehran: Barg, 1369/1990, pp. 9–22.

33 The first line of Firaydūn Mushīrī's poem entitled "The Alley." Despite the enormous popularity of these poets in contemporary Iran, the government censurs these poets. See A. Abiz, *Censorship of Literature in Post-Revolutionary Iran: Politics and Culture Since 1979*, New York/London: I.B. Tauris, 2021, pp. 38, 94–95. Abiz cites Khamenei, "I'm not naming some other female poets. I've mentioned Forough because, firstly, Forough is dead and, secondly, I believe that she achieved redemption toward the end of her life. But some others did not achieve and will never achieve redemption." According to Abiz, this is an allusion to Bihbahānī.

34 On Shāmlū's literary impact on modern Persian poetry see M.R. Shafīʿī-Kadkanī, *Chirāgh-u āyina*, pp. 216–218, 511–532

35 For an excellent history of the Writers' Association of Iran see Ahmad Karimi-Hakkak, *A Fire of Lilies: Perspectives on Literature and Politics in Modern Iran*, Leiden: Leiden University Press, 2019, pp. 53–84; idem, "Introduction: Iran's Literature 1977–1997," pp. 200–203.

writers and poets who had for years remained wrapped in a reverential halo of intellectual opposition to a repressive regime, but, what is more, it dispelled much of the popular fear of assembly and peaceful demonstration of that opposition."[36] After the 1979 Revolution, the Writers' Association did not last long. It was disbanded in 1982 and its members, mostly secular Iranian intellectuals, had to succumb to the Revolution or live underground, or secretly leave the country, or be killed. Saʿīd Sulṭānpūr (1940–1981), a poet and playwright, is an example: he was arrested at his wedding and later executed.[37]

In Akbarī's new definition of poetry, the poet is a mystic who participates in society and fights for Revolutionary ideals. Poetry is a mixture of themes about love, gnosis, struggle and martyrdom. A poet is both a mystic and a soldier. In the war poetry and war songs soldiers are commonly referred to as mystics or lovers of God. Akbarī also dismisses organised Sufism. He criticises the master-disciple relationship as "making a shop, acquiring disciples" and "Sufi-mongery," with the connotation of a ruse. It is not at all clear what Akbarī prefers to the master-disciple relationship, because in the Islamist committed literature Khomeini functions as a spiritual leader for his followers, who avidly read his poetry and mystical texts and comment upon them. Khomeini himself never claimed to be a mystical master, but his followers treated him as such. A large corpus of Persian war poetry is imbued with mystical themes and *topoi*, but these elements are selective. To begin with, several articles on this subject foreground Khomeini as a mystic who is a source of inspiration for committed poets. References are made to Khomeini's mystical exegesis of the Quran and to his poetry, emphasising that the committed poetry stems from one source, the desire for union with the Beloved. Ismāʿīl Ḥakīmī compares Khomeini to great medieval mystics and poets, citing and analysing one of his *ghazals*. In his appreciation of the *ghazal*, he comments on individual words in a mystical context, also citing passages from *Nahj al-balāgha* ("The Road of Eloquence").[38] This trend of commenting on Khomeini's vocabulary started quite early and led to the publication

---

36 See Ahmad Karimi-Hakkak, *A Fire of Lilies*, p. 71.

37 See ibid., p. 83; for the collected speeches and poetry presented on these nights see *Dah shab: shabhā-yi shāʿirān va nivisandigān dar anjuman-i farhangī-yi Iran va ālmān*, compiled by N. Mu'adhin, Tehran: Amīr Kabīr, 1357/1978; also see K. Talattof, *The Politics of Writing in Iran*, pp. 91–93; on these nights and the deeply rooted notion of commitment see M.R. Ghanoonparvar, *Prophets of Doom*, pp. 73–101; see also the comprehensive analysis of Olmo Gölz, "Dah Šab: Zehn Literaturabende in Teheran 1977: Der Kampf um das Monopol literarischer Legitimität," in *Die Welt des Islams*, 55, Nr. 1, 2015, pp. 83–111; H. Naficy, *A Social History of Iranian Cinema, The Islamicate Period 1978–1984*, Durham, NC/London: Duke University Press, 2012, vol. 3, p. 84.

38 Ismāʿīl Ḥakimī, "Barrisī-yi adabiyyāt-i inqilāb az buʿd-i ʿirfānī," in *Majmūʿa-yi maqālāt-i simīnār-i barrasī-yi adabiyyāt-i inqilāb-i islāmī*, Tehran: Samt, 1373/1994, pp. 149–166.

of voluminous dictionaries of mystical explications of his terminology.[39] Other prominent themes for the committed poets, which I will elaborate upon in the different chapters of this book, are those of love, ascension and union with the beloved.

Akbarī's criticism is directed at the secular character of Persian poetry prior to 1979. He refers to Shāmlū's collection of poetry entitled *Aida in the Mirror* (1965), in which the poet depicts his beloved wife Aida in an aesthetically superb way. Akbarī represents a generation of revolutionary intellectuals who were against open expressions of love, especially when they were connected to the female body. Moreover, for him, love has a specific type of mystic dimension whereas earthly love generates lustful passion. His other allusion to profane love "without you I passed through the alley once again," is a sarcastic appraisal of the popular poem, *Kūcha* ("Alley"), by Fireydūn Mushīrī, known by almost all Persians, starting with the splendid lines, "Without you I passed once more from that alley on a moonlit night, / My whole body became an eye, gazing in search of you / longing to see you overflowing from the cup of my existence / I become again the mad lover I was."[40] In the new revolutionary ethics, love and erotic emotions for a woman would lead to immorality: emotions should be channelled towards a religious, spiritual and political purpose. But a thousand years of Persian poetry is evidence that love, sex and eroticism, and also the praise of wine, are constitutive of Persian culture and of Islam.[41] The ideas of revolutionaries such as Akbarī are an ideological mask by means of which they present themselves as pious Muslims committed to the Revolution and dismiss other intellectuals as un-revolutionary and un-Islamic. Scholars such as Akbarī are part of the movement that turned the 1979 Revolution into an Islamic Revolution, erasing the contributions of secular intellectuals. Mushīrī's opus includes poems such

---

39 See, for instance, *Farhang-i dīvān-i ash'ār-i imām Khomeini*, Tehran: Institute for the Compilation and Publication of Imam Khomeini's Works, 1372/1993. On Khomeini's poetry see L. Ridgeon, "Hidden Khomeini: Mysticism and Poetry," in *A Critical Introduction to Khomeini*, ed. A. Adib-Moghaddam, Cambridge: Cambridge University Press, 2014, pp. 193–210; also see Alexander Knysh, "*'Irfān* Revisited: Khomeini and the Legacy of Islamic Mystical Philosophy," in *Middle East Journal*, 46, 4, 1992, pp. 631–653. A.A. Seyed-Gohrab, "Khomeini the Poet Mystic," in *Die Welt des Islams: International Journal for the Study of Modern Islam*, 51, 2011, pp. 438–458, and the unpublished PhD dissertation by D. Farhosh-van Loon, *Of Love and Longing: A Study of Ayatollah Khomeini's Mystical Poetry and its Reception in Iran and Abroad*, Leiden: 2016.

40 See Firaydūn Mushīrī, *Guzīna-yi ash'ār*, Tehran: Murvārīd, 1371/1992, pp. 88–91. The poem was composed in 1339/1960 and was published in the *abr-u kūcha* ('Cloud and Alley') collection in 1340/1961.

41 For an excellent examination of why wine is constitutive of Islam see Shahab Ahmed, *What Is Islam?*, especially chapters one and six.

as *Yāghī* or "Rebel" which openly call on people to rise and protest against the Shah's political system, even if it may cost them their lives.[42]

Akbarī is by no means alone in his crusade against pre-revolutionary poetry.[43] Muḥammad Taqavī dismisses modernism, condemning intellectuals such as Zeyn al-ʿĀbidīn Marāgha'ī (1840 – 1910), Muḥammad-ʿAlī Jamālzāda (1892 – 1997), Ṣādiq Hidāyat (1903 – 1951), and Nīmā Yūshīj (1897 – 1960) as writers who did not know their own culture. They were spellbound by Western culture, desiring to introduce it to Iran at the expense of their own national and religious values. In his view, writers such as Ṣādiq Hidāyat and Buzurg ʿAlavī (1904 – 1997) depict the apprehensive Freudian love leading the youth astray.[44] Another revolutionary critic, Muḥammad Kāẓim Kahdūʾī, takes Hidāyat as an example of a pro-Western intellectual who expresses the futility of this life, the pointlessness of religion, and other dubious ideas. It was due to the impact of western culture, Kahdūʾī adds, that Hidāyat committed suicide.[45]

Another critic, Aḥmad Aḥmadī, devotes his attention to the secularism which, in his view, was introduced to Iran before the Constitutional Revolution (1906 – 1911). Aḥmadī equates secularism with nationalism (*millī-garā'ī*), citing Khomeini's view that "nationalism is opposed to Islam," bringing corruption and immorality.[46] Without giving a clear definition of secularism, he concludes

---

42 See Talattof, *The Politics of Writing in Iran*, p. 91, in which he gives a translation of the poem: "I am not afraid of death since life / has poured nothing but the poison of sorrow into my glass/ if I have rested a moment of this long, boring life / let it be taken from me." Mushīrī also participated in the Ten Nights event, voicing his protest against the Shah's repressive regime. See *Dah shab*, pp. 371 – 378. On the process of islamising the Revolution see M.M. Khorrami, *Literary Subterfuge and Contemporary Persian Fiction: Who write Iran?*, London/New York: Routledge, 2015, pp. 18 – 20.

43 Also see the chapter by Abū ʾl-Qāsim Rādfar, "Digargūnīhā va vīzhigīhā-yi adabiyyāt-i inqilāb-i islāmī dar yik nigāh," in *Majmūʻa-yi maqālāt-i simīnār*, pp. 183 – 192, especially p. 186, in which the author refers to "the state of losing oneself in the face of the deceptions of the West (*farīb-hā-yi gharb*), the dissemination of the vulgar beauties of its culture, the distribution of ethical and sexual corruptions, belittling Islam (*islām-zudā'ī*) in various ways such as exaggerating the manifestations of pre-Islamic history and culture..."

44 Muḥammad Taqavī, "Jahat-gīrī-yi adabiyyāt-i muʿāṣir va taḥavvul-i ān pas az inqilāb," in *Majmūʿa-yi maqālāt-i simīnār-i barrasī-yi adabiyyāt-i inqilāb-i islāmī*, Tehran: Samt, 1373/1994, pp. 103 – 113; also see the chapter by Muḥammad Kāẓim Kahdūʾī, "Barrisī-yi adabiyyāt-i takhdīrī, bī-hadaf va mutiʿahhid dar dowrān-i muʿāsir va taḥavvul-i ānhā dar dowra-yi inqilāb-i islāmī," in *Majmūʿa-yi maqālāt*, pp. 479 – 493.

45 M.K. Kahdūʾī, "Barrasī-yi adabiyyāt-i takhdīrī ...," in *Majmūʿa-yi maqālāt-i simīnār-i barrasī-yi adabiyyāt-i inqilāb-i islāmī*, Tehran: Samt, 1373/1994, pp. 480 – 481.

46 Aḥmad Aḥmadī, "Khāstgāh-i adabiyyāt-i qabl va baʿd az inqilāb," in *Majmūʿa-yi maqālāt-i simīnār-i barrasī-yi adabiyyāt-i inqilāb-i islāmī*, Tehran: Samt, 1373/1994, p. 4.

that the "foundation of secularism, heresy and its culture and literature is an unbridled freedom, especially sexual freedom, the examples of which are in the poetry and prose of those days [the Shah's period] and especially in the poetry of many poets and a few poetesses."[47] Furūgh Farrukhzād may be the target of his criticism here, for her taboo-breaking poems in which she gracefully comments on gender and female sexuality. When Aḥmadī was writing his piece, the Islamic Republic was facing a huge problem with sexuality on the streets. The deaths of young men in eight years of war with Iraq and deplorable economic conditions in the first two decades of the Republic had created such a situation that the President at the time, ʿAlī-Akbar Hāshimī Rafsanjānī (1934–2017), delivered a Friday sermon in Tehran in November 1990, pointing to societal needs for the gratification of sexual desires. He pointed to the institution, accepted in Shiite Islam, of "temporary marriage" for a specified period, from ten minutes to 90 years. His speech could be regarded as a milestone admission that the Islamic Republic had problems with regard to prostitution, low marriage rates and sexuality. It astonished many by its candour and advocacy of temporary marriages. He defined sexual desire as *fiṭrat,* an inborn nature, bestowed by God: suppressing such needs was "wrong and un-Islamic."[48] In this speech Rafsanjānī suggests to control sexuality within a marriage contract, ignoring the significant number of problems that such temporary marital bonds create in society. Aḥmadī's criticism of sexual freedom and Rafsanjānī's call for temporary marriages show how the Islamic Republic was struggling to oust the pre-revolutionary ethos on sexuality and at the same time cope with sexuality within the ideological framework of the Revolution. Sexuality could be recognised if framed by a religious construction. Despite Rafsanjānī's open call, I have not seen any erotic poetry of the calibre of Farrukhzād's work by the committed female poets, and Farrukhzād and her poetry are still very popular in Iran.

While Iranian society struggles with issues around gender and sexuality, the subject is taboo in revolutionary literature and remains behind closed doors, as any expression of sexuality is associated with the West and pre-revolution times. Medieval Persian literature in which there is a rich *topos* of love-making scenes is

---

47 Ibid., p. 4.

48 Shahla Haeri, "Temporary Marriage and the State in Iran: An Islamic Discourse on Female Sexuality," *Social Research* 59, no. 1, Spring 1992, p. 201. The theologians Seyed Muḥammad Ḥuseyn Tabātabā'ī (1904–1981) and Murtiżā Muṭahharī (1919–1979) had made similar points before Rafsanjānī. On temporary marriages in Iran see Haeri, *Law of Desire: Temporary Marrigaes in Shi'i Iran*, Syracuse, NY: Syracuse University Press, 1989; also see J. Afary, *Sexual Politics in Modern Iran*, pp. 60–66.

entirely ignored.[49] Moreover, the Islamic ethos on sexuality is, unlike the Christian, very open. Both of these incongruities show that the ideas of the revolutionaries were partly cultural and partly ideological. Islamist literary critics supposed that eroticism was sex-driven, turning women into objects of lust. It is true that during the Shah's period nakedness had become to a certain degree a *leitmotiv*, especially on TV and in commercialised Iranian films. In a society in which women had, in living memory, been fully veiled, walking on the beach wearing a bikini was an affront to religious people. In Film-Farsi, as Talattof has shown, several women were erotic dancers in cafes and cabarets, and subject to the male gaze.[50] It is in such contexts that committed intellectuals considered love and sexuality as means to devalue female dignity. Many of these films had titles such as *Bed for Three* (1972), sometimes with a didactic message, but one that was too weak for the common audience to grasp. It is interesting that the authors of the essays in the volume on *Revolutionary Islamic Literature* do not refer to such Iranian films but direct their arrows at pre-revolutionary poets and writers with whom they had fought side by side against the repressive Pahlavi dynasty. A quick look at the subjects treated during the Ten Nights at the Goethe Institute in Tehran, such as freedom of expression, censorship, westernisation, Gnosticism, imprisonment, martyrdom, sympathy with Palestinians, etc., shows how close the original goals of all the intellectuals were. In fact, several of the revolutionary poets and writers, such as Ṭāhira Ṣaffārzāda and ʿAlī Musavī Garmārūdī, were speakers at these Ten Nights, but after the 1979 Revolution a clear split appeared between the intellectuals, poets and writers.[51] As Talattof observes, secular opposition to the Shah was strong, and when the Muslim

---

49 For examples of such scenes see Niẓāmī's *Khusrow and Shīrīn* and *Haft Paykar.* Many of his imitators followed his example. See for instance, Vaḥshī Bāfqī, *Nāẓir and Manẓūr*, in *Dīvān*, ed. P. Bābā'ī, Tehran: Nigāh, 1373/1994, p. 200. In 1381/2002, Sīrūs Shamīsā published *Shāhid-bāzī dar adabiyyāt-i Fārsī* (Tehran: Firdows, 1381/2002), but it was immediately banned. His book mostly cites and analyses the erotic and homo-erotic gaze in classical Persian texts. They are often intentionally open to being read as metaphors of mystic desire. Homo-erotic passages are so prevalent in the Persian literary tradition that, without an understanding of this aspect of literature, one cannot understand Persian court life and Islamic mysticism.

50 Kamran Talattof, "Sexuality and Cultural Change: The Presentation of Sex and Gender in Pre- and Post-revolutionary Iranian Cinema," in *Conflict and Development in Iranian Film*, Leiden: Leiden University Press, 2010, pp. 31–48, especially pp. 34–35; for a broader discussion of sexuality see idem, *Modernity, Sexuality, and Ideology in Iran the Life and Legacy of a Popular Female Artist*, Syracuse, NY: Syracuse University Press, 2011, and J. Afary, *Sexual Politics in Modern Iran*, pp. 221–228.

51 See Ahmad Karimi-Hakkak, "Introduction: Iran's Literature 1977–1997," pp. 203–204; Talattof, *The Politics of Writing*, pp. 112–113; also see F. Shams, *A Revolution in Rhyme: Poetic Co-option under the Islamic Republic*, Oxford: Oxford University Press, 2021, pp. 168–172.

activists joined that opposition they "eventually overwhelmed the secular revolutionary movement."[52] Talattof rightly adds, "Even though their literary activism was minimal, they began to mobilise their supporters, using religious institutions such as mosques, and during the last eighteen months of the Shah's rule Islamic forces gained hegemony over the movement. They gained it almost too easily, because the secular literary activists and culture producers and their readers were not averse to Islam."[53]

In Aḥmadī's view, "if literature starts from God, it reaches people and like a Paradisical river it streams through the entire existence of people, leading to fruits which are all purity, chastity, truth-speaking, freedom of heart, defence of religion and country, of one's family, possessions, and people's lives. Is this literature not the highest of all literature in the world?"[54] As an example of such literature Aḥmadī cites the following *ghazal* by the poetess Sipīda Kāshānī (1936–1992), one of the prominent poets of war whose poem became a hit in Iran as it was set to music and broadcast several times a day in the 1980s:

به خون گر کشی خاک من، دشمن من
بجوشد گل اندر گل از گلشن من
تنم گر بسوزی، به تیرم بدوزی
جدا سازی ای خصم، سر از تن من
کجا می‌توانی، ز قلبم ربایی
تو عشق میان من و میهن من
مسلمانم و آرمانم شهادت
تجلّیِ هستی‌ست، جان کندن من
مپندار این شعله افسرده گردد
که بعد از من افروزد از مدفن من
نه تسلیم و سازش، نه تکریم و خواهش
بتازد به نیرنگ تو، توسن من
کنون رود خلق است دریای جوشان
همه خوشه خشم شد خرمن من
من آزاده از خاک آزادگانم
گل صبر می‌پرورد دامن من
جز از جام توحید هرگز ننوشم
زنی گر به تیغ ستم گردن من
بلند اخترم، رهبرم، از در آمد
بهار است و هنگام گل چیدن من[55]

52 Ibid., p. 92.
53 Ibid.
54 Aḥmad Aḥmadī, "Khāstgāh...," p. 6.
55 Aḥmadī's citation is not complete as he leaves out two couplets. See "Khāstgāh...," pp. 6–7.

My enemy! If you soak my soil in blood,
Red roses will blossom in my bed of roses.
If you burn my body, if you stitch my body with bullets
O enemy, if you cut the head from my body,
How can you steal from my heart
The love between me and my homeland?
I am a Muslim,[56] my ideal is martyrdom;
My life-sacrifice is the manifestation of Being.
Do not fancy that this flame will be quenched
For after my death it will glow from my grave.
Neither submission nor sufferance, giving honour, or sympathy:
My wild horse will attack your deception.
Now the river of the people has become a raging ocean;
All my harvest has become a sheaf of rage.
I am free-born from the soil of the free;
My lap is the seedbed for roses of patience.
I will not drink except from the cup of God's oneness
Even if you sever my neck with the blade of oppression.
My star, my leader, has risen, has come;
It is Spring, my time to pick roses.

It is stimulating to analyse which elements make Kāshānī's revolutionary poem an example for critics such as Aḥmadī. The poem is couched in the traditional *ghazal* form. It is a political poem, directed at the enemies of Iran. In each couplet the poet introduces a new topic related to one of the ideals of the Revolution. While the first three couplets refer to the individual's readiness to offer her soul to defend the country, in the fourth couplet the individual's religion is emphasised. Here the poet says that the ideal of martyrdom is a corollary of Islam, or at least of her concept of being Muslim. Then the poet relates this Islamic martyrdom to Sufism, as the term *tajallī*, translated as "manifestation," is a mystical term connoting the revelation of God's beauty in His creation. The poet is justifying martyrdom because as soon as the person submits the soul, she becomes a manifestation of Being itself. The martyr does not die but becomes one with the source of Being, the object of Love. The poet emphasises that such a union is not the end, but rather the flourishing, of the martyr. This is a reference to the idea that martyrs achieve eternal life. In the sixth couplet these subjects are linked to patriotic resistance and especially rising against tyranny, whether in Iran or from foreign powers. This uprising is accompanied by fury and vehemence as depicted in the seventh couplet. The people are a raging

56 In another version, which is cited by Sipīda Kāshānī herself, it is *man īrānī-am* or "I am an Iranian." The *musalmānam-u* is metrically incorrect.

ocean destroying anything in their way. The harvest of the martyr's death in this world is a bundle of rage: the blood of the martyrs waters the tree of resistance, in effect. Another topic introduced in the eighth couplet is the notion of freedom, which in the 1980s was interpreted as independence from western powers and reliance on traditional Persian culture. The poet does not define what type of freedom is meant, and the word used could easily allude to pre-Islamic Persian history, which was frowned upon in the early years of the Revolution. By introducing the notion of *towḥīd* or "unicity of God" in the ninth couplet the poet contextualises the subjects she has treated. The term *towḥīd* is here linked with Sufism, since it is depicted as the contents of a cup that the poet drinks. The poet is combining the *khamriyya* or "wine poetry" motif with God's oneness, the holiest tenet of Islam. In the concluding couplet Kāshānī praises Khomeini's arrival in Iran and the victory of the Revolution on 22 Bahman (11 February), a month before the arrival of Spring with the New Year festival of Nowrūz on 21 of March.

This short poem contains several subjects which, for Aḥmadī, are the core of revolutionary poetry. These are warnings against the enemy who wants to violate Iran; emphasis on the faith as a Muslim of the individual who is ready to die; interpreting martyrdom in a mystical sense; God as a beloved; an emphasis on eternal life; resistance and protest against tyranny; freedom and independence; antinomian motifs, which combine wine imagery with sacred elements of Islam; and, finally, greeting Khomeini, showing devotion to his ideology, praising the victory of the Revolution, and celebrating the Persian New Year.

The poet, Sipīda Kāshānī, has contributed an article to the same collection on revolutionary literature with the title "Revolutionary Literature and the Battle Against Arrogance" (*Adabiyyāt-i inqilābī va mubāriza bā istikbār*), in which she uses the first four couplets of the above ghazal to criticise Iranian secular intellectuals.[57] She addresses the meaning of commitment, and why people criticise the 1979 Revolution and its ideology. She condemns these intellectuals as the enemies of Iran and of Islam:

> Isn't the most beautiful and comprehensive form of commitment the defence of rights and equality on the way to humanity's salvation from oppression and inequality? Isn't commitment the protection of bloodshed on the earth [meant] for the elevation and protection of Islam's freedom and the sanctified realm of the Quran? Today, a group of lookalike humans imitating modern fashions (*insān-namā-yi mutijaddid-ma'āb*) are ridiculing the divine goals

57 Sipīda Kāshānī, "Adabiyyāt-i inqilābī va mubāriza bā istikbār," in *Majmū'a-yi maqālāt*, pp. 401–410. By the time the volume was published the author had died and the article has appeared posthumously. The word *istikbār* literally means "pride" or "arrogance" and since the 1979 Revolution it has been used by Islamic revolutionaries to refer to the Western imperialist powers. It is sometimes translated as "global arrogance," referring to the United States.

(*ahdāf-i ilāhī*) and the pure ideology of a community and nation (*ummatī va millatī*) with the sting of their pens. Where have these people been in the last ten years when our suffering people, children, young and old, were fighting against the worst and most menacing enemy of humanity, and were offering their lives in farm fields, factories, ministries, schools and universities under the enemy's ruthless bombardments, without lowering their heads to submit, but rather shouting."[58]

Afterwards, she quotes her own poem. This is a unique example of how a poet uses her own poetry to comment on socio-political events. In her article the poet is probably attacking Iranian intellectuals who did not fully follow the revolutionary ideals but vented their opinions about the deplorable situation of post-war Iran. Her critique shows that the revolutionary ideas were not embraced by all Iranians, especially those who, despite the war, censorship and oppression, stayed in Iran and stealthily and sometimes not so stealthily criticised the polity of the Islamic Republic. The poem is forcefully used to dismiss any criticisms against the government's policy. After citing the four couplets of the poem, Kāshānī goes on to say that the poetry of the Islamic poets does not recognise any boundaries, as it is addressed to all those oppressed by world-devouring tyrants. She states that "those who do not believe in the revolutionary literature are certainly strangers to Islam and the Quran. Who is going to build a dam against the footsteps and pens of those who are creating ruins with a pleasing appearance?"[59] Kāshānī's views reflect the opinions of committed literati some thirteen years after the revolution, illustrating how a redefinition of revolutionary literature was still going on. Many revolutionary poets and intellectuals embraced the ideologies of the Revolution, while others such as Qeyṣar Amīnpūr tried gradually to reconcile with the pre-revolutionary poets such as Shāmlū. Reading through much of this revolutionary poetry, we see traces of the poetry that the Islamic hardliners originally criticised. The impact of pre-revolutionary poetry was too ubiquitous to be ignored, as both groups were fighting for essentially the same goals. For instance, the imagery and metaphors of poets such as Shāmlū are sometimes easily recognisable in Amīnpūr's poetry.[60] As an

---

58 Ibid., p. 408.

59 Ibid., p. 409.

60 For an analysis of Amīnpūr's development from a fully committed revolutionary poet to a distanced poet see F. Shams, "From Revolution to Silence: The Political and Literary Life of Qaysar Amīnpūr," in *The Layered Heart: Essays on Persian Poetry, A Celebration in Honor of Dick Davis*, ed. Asghar Seyed-Gohrab, Washington, DC: Mage Publishers, 2019, pp. 551–588. There are several examples of committed intellectuals who left the revolutionary camp and even became dissidents. A well-known case is Muḥsin Makhmalbāf who became a film director, living

example I give the first stanza of Amīnpūr's poem *Dardvārahā (1)* followed by Shāmlū's poem *ʿishq-i ʿumūmī*, without deeper analysis, since Shāmlū's impact is evident in the choice of words, negation and in the rhythm of the original which is lost here in translation. Both poems are talking about pain, comparing pain to different realities and then negating them in order to emphasise how intense the poet's pain is:

My pains	دردهای من
are not a garment	جامه نیستند
to be removed from my body	تا ز تن در آورم
they are not a poem or a song	چامه و چکامه نیستند
to be threaded into my speech,	تا به رشته ی سخن درآورم
they are not screams	نعره نیستند
to be brought out of the depth of my soul.	تا ز نای جان بر آورم
My pains are unspeakable	دردهای من نگفتنی
My pains are to be hidden.[61]	دردهای من نهفتنی است

And Shāmlū's poem runs as follows:

The tear is a secret	اشک رازی ست
The smile is a secret	لبخند رازی ست
Love is a secret	عشق رازی ست
The tears of that night were my love's smile.	اشک آن شب لبخند عشقم بود
I am not a tale to tell,	قصه نیستم که بگویی
I am not a strain to sing,	نغمه نیستم که بخوانی
I am not a sound to hear,	صدا نیستم که بشنوی
Or something that you may see	یا چیزی چنان که ببینی
Or something that you may know	یا چیزی چنان که بدانی
I am a shared pain	من درد مشترکم
Cry me out.	مرا فریاد کن[62]

1.5 Conclusion

The revolutionary Islamic scholars and poets wanted to distance themselves from pre-revolutionary literature in order to create a literature based entirely

---

outside Iran. The number of examples increases as we move from the end of 1990s to the present.

61 Amīnpūr, *Majmūʿa-yi kāmil-i ashʿār*, Tehran: Gulshan, 9th edition 1391/2012, p. 241. The poem comes from the āyina-hā-yi nāgahān or 'The Sudden Verses' collection.

62 Shāmlū, *Majmūʿa-yi āthār*, Tehran: Nigāh, 1382/2003, p. 213.

on the ideals of the Revolution. One tactic was categorically to reject and eject the secular poets, scholars and writers, who were systematically purged from their positions by the broad cultural revolution, on the charge of being un-revolutionary. By employing a very charged terminology, characterising events simply in terms of right and wrong, the revolutionaries identified themselves as the protectors of Islam and the Quran and any even slightly disparate opinions as un-Islamic. This happened for a long time after the advent of the 1979 Revolution. Another tactic was to emphasise Islam rather than Iranian national identity. While Muḥammad Riżā Shah propagated an image of Iran based on the pre-Islamic glories of the great Persian Empire, and relying partly on the Aryan race theory, Ayatollah Khomeini dismissed this altogether, emphasising Islam "as the sole basis for legitimate rule in Iran."[63] Writing on pre-Islamic Iran was seen as an opposition activity. For example, Akhavān Thālith's (1929–1990) popular poem "I Love You, Ancient Homeland," was regarded as such.[64] The tragic result was that these intellectuals could be persecuted and even executed on charges of heresy or of being a marionette of the West. The passage by Kāshānī I have cited above is a random and typical example of how these revolutionaries sanctified the revolution, with its divine goals (*ahdāf-i ilāhī*), presenting themselves as guardians of Islam and their opponents as combatants ready to attack Islam.[65] In such a black and white paradigm of revolutionary literature there is no place for nuances, no space to reflect on social themes such as censorship, inequality and sexuality, and no room at all for counter-arguments. The censorship that writers and poets had experienced before the 1979 Revolution was repeated in a more intense and violent form.

This strict revolutionary approach to literature could not be sustained on all fronts. Talented key figures such as Amīnpūr increasingly distanced themselves from the hard-line policy, increasingly appreciating the poetry of some pre-revolutionary poets. Others, such as Makhmalbāf, became dissidents, leaving the country. The committed Islamic revolutionary literature developed into a broad panoply of categories. There are still hardliners who write on the same subjects, keeping the ideals of the 1979 Revolution alive. Their chief representatives are the poets who gather at Ayatollah Khamenei's residence and recite their poetry on a

63 Ahmad Karimi-Hakkak, "Introduction: Iran's Literature 1977–1997," p. 204.

64 See ibid.

65 The divinisation of the revolution started with calling Khomeini Imam, which in Shiism is a title reserved for the twelve infallible Imams. A later example was the use of *labayk yā Khomeini* ("Here I am for you, O Khomeini"), the first part of which is used only during the *ḥajj* rituals in Mecca, by pilgrims addressing God. There are many examples of this sanctification process which warrants a separate study.

wide range of subjects, from socio-political satire to the grave themes of martyrdom, condemnation of the US and other Western allies, and war.[66] Another group, which is sometimes hard to distinguish from the hardliners, are those who write poetry reflecting on the horrors and traumas of the Iran-Iraq war in different literary forms, including the haiku.

66 For an extensive analysis of these literary sessions see F. Shams, *A Revolution in Rhyme*, especially chapter seven, pp. 286–331.

2 'The Scent of Martyrdom'

کی داعیه حور و بهشت است مرا
زین داعیه ها مگو که زشت است مرا
چون ملک ازآن تست گو دوزخ باش
هرجا که تو با منی بهشت است مرا[67]

How could I have desires for houris and Paradise?
Do not talk of such desires, they are ugly to me.
You may say, "go to hell," but you are the Lord of Hell.
Wherever you are with me, that is Paradise for me.

2.1 Introduction

One of the awful results of the culture of martyrdom after the 1979 Revolution was a widespread willingness to give one's life in a way that would qualify as martyrdom. In the years prior to the Revolution, but even more during the Iran-Iraq War (1980–1988), martyrdom was idealised and even glamorised. The newly established Islamic government accorded an elevated position to martyrs, and their families, friends and even acquaintances. Such a death brought public respect and financial security for the family, who would receive money. The brothers or sisters of the martyr could secure one of the limited university places, their children could go to better schools, and alleys and streets would be immediately renamed after the martyr, so that it was very much discernible which streets, alleys and neighbourhoods had offered their youth. This has changed the public sphere into a museum of martyrdom, even today.

Martyrdom is a central pillar of the Islamic Republic. In the Iran-Iraq war poetry, martyrdom is exploited with a heavy reliance on classical Persian poetry in terms of imagery, historical allusions to prominent martyrs of Islam such as the third Shiite Imam Ḥuseyn, and Ḥuseyn Manṣūr Ḥallāj (executed 922), and the layer of mystical reading to which many classical Persian poems are open. The main difference between the treatment of martyrdom in the war poetry and that in classical poetry is that the latter is pacifist and metaphoric, using martyrdom as a metaphor for the supplicant lover's sacrifice of "self," whereas in the war poetry metaphor becomes reality. Soldiers wish to become metaphors,

67 The quatrain belongs to khᵛāja ʿAlī Naʿīm cited in Ḥ. Āzād Tabrīzī, *Gulzār-i maʿrifat*, Leiden: Brill, 1906, p. 194. Line three may also be translated as follows: "As the kingdom belongs to You, [even if You] say, 'Be in hell.'"

https://doi.org/10.1515/9783110748734-006

which is to say that they wish to become meaningful, by literally sacrificing their lives.[68] While the lovers in classical poetry radically renounce his/her ego, the soldiers radically renounce their lives. Both desire to fulfil their longings for the union with the immaterial Beloved.

In the earliest periods of Persian poetry we often find references to martyrdom in the context of love. In such cases, the predicate of martyr is a trait of the selfless lover who would die for the beloved. This voluntary death could be interpreted as violent, yet these references are metaphoric exaggerations to show how far the lover would go to show his steadfastness in love. In addition to the historical examples mentioned above, there are literary narratives in which the lover chooses to die for the beloved without even having consummated his love. Perhaps the most popular of these is the romance of *Laylī and Majnūn*, originating in early Arabic literature. Versions of various anecdotes in this story were popular among Islamic mystics, who took Laylī as a figuration of God and the selfless Majnūn as a supplicant lover. In the twelfth century, the Persian poet Niẓāmī Ganjavī (c. 1141–1209) welded these into a massive epic romance which is a landmark in both literary and popular culture. Subsequent authors from the Balkans to Bengal have produced over 100 creative emulations of his *Laylī and Majnūn*. In Niẓāmī's version, the lover and the beloved die in separation, not having consummated their love. First Laylī dies and in her emotional message to her mother emphasises that she is a martyr. She asks her mother to adorn her body like a bride and then bury her:

خون کن کفنم که من شهیدم
تا باشد رنگ روز عیدم
آراسته کن عروس‌وارم
بسپار به خاک پرده دارم

68 There are a large number of studies on martyrdom related to the 1979 Revolution, the Iran-Iraq War and beyond. While I refer to many of these sources in this book, the following are indispensable sources: *Martyrdom: Canonization, Contestation and Afterlives*, ed. I. Saloul & J.W. van Henten, Amsterdam: Amsterdam University Press, 2020; *Martyrdom in Literature: Visions of Death and Meaningful Suffering in Europe and the Middle East from Antiquity to Modernity*, ed. D. Pannewick, Wiesbaden: Reichert Verlag, 2004; M. Dorraj, "Symbolic and Utilitarian Political Value of a Tradition: Martyrdom in the Iranian Political Culture," in *The Review of Politics*, 59, 3, 1997, pp. 489–521; the special issue of *Visual Anthropology*, No. 25, 2012, ed. Pedram Khosronejad; *The "Other" Martyrs: Women and the Poetics of Sexuality, Sacrifice and Death in World Literatures*, ed. Alireza Korangy & Leyla Rouhi, Wiesbaden: Harrassowitz Verlag, 2019, pp. 87–102; A. Korangy, "A Literary and Historical Background of Martyrdom in Iran," in *Comparative Studies of South Asia, Africa and the Middle East*, 29, No. 3, 2009, pp. 528–543; and the special issue of the journal *Persica: Annual of the Dutch-Iranian Society*, No. 22, 2008, ed. H.E. Chehabi, and F. Christia.

Put blood on my shroud for I am a martyr,
So that should be the colour of my festive day.
Adorn me like a bride,
Entrust me to the earth of my chamberlain.

Laylī is presented as a martyr because of her pure love, not contaminated by lust, and her patient and quietist endurance. She lives a life full of pain and agony for the sake of love. Niẓāmī depicts Laylī's complex position by creating tensions between tribal, religious and ethical laws. To respect the tribal laws, she accepts her father's suggestion and is married off to a man whom she does not love, but defends her virginity against her husband, flouting religious laws. She meets with Majnūn, but always remains at a distance so as not to touch him. Her complex life is full of agony, suffering and loneliness. On hearing of her death, Majnūn runs to her grave and instantly dies. His death is also depicted as a mystic martyrdom,[69] since he dies innocently, protecting the purity of love. Before his death, for years, he lives with tame and wild beasts, a token that his pure love creates harmony in his surroundings. Another reason emphasised by Niẓāmī is that his love is not adulterated by lust as he does not touch Laylī, because any bodily contact would kindle "selfish intention" (*gharaż*), contaminating love's purity. At a certain point in the story Majnūn is identified with love itself, which is fire and will burn anything near it. Niẓāmī creates ambiguity in this story and allows different interpretations, but his emphasis is on Majnūn's pure intentions. Here, innocence, patient endurance and pure love are associated with martyrdom, and it is this very aspect of purity and love which is at the centre of the discourse on martyrdom in Iran.

Purity, innocence and love are among the qualities linked to the martyrdom of Imam Ḥuseyn, the grandson of the prophet Muḥammad (d. 632), who was killed by the forces of the Umayyad Caliph, Yazīd I (ca. 647–683), in Karbalā, Iraq, in 680 AD on the tenth day of the month of Muḥarram, called Āshūrā, in an unequal battle against the Umayyad army. In Shiite lore, Ḥuseyn is honoured with the epithet of "King of martyrs," and his courage in fighting against a mighty army is emphasised. Ḥuseyn became a model for Iranian soldiers for a number of reasons: first, he fought against unjust forces, as he (and with him the Shiites)

---

69 I have treated Majnūn's death in my book on *Laylī and Majnūn*, pp. 127–130. He refers many times to his desire to be killed by the beloved (*kushta-yi maʿshūq*), which is a favourite topos in Persian love poetry. Niẓāmī does not use the word martyr but the way he describes Majnūn as the "king of love," and his death, it could easily be interpreted as martyrdom. For a recent splendid English translation of this romance see Dick Davis, *Layli and Majnun*, Washington, DC: Mage Publishers, 2020, reprinted in Penguin Classics, 2021.

was of the opinion that his father ʿAlī ibn Abī Ṭālib (killed 661) and himself were the true heirs of the prophet Muḥammad destined to lead the Islamic community. He believed that the Umayyad dynasty (661–750) was usurping their rights, and therefore, he had no other choice but to fight against them, while being fully aware that he would be killed and his children and family would be taken prisoner in humiliating and shameful conditions. Shiite Iranians identify with Ḥuseyn for several reasons. First, they believe that Ḥuseyn is the rightful heir of the prophet Muḥammad. After Muḥammad's decease, there was a conflict as who was the right person to guide the Islamic community. By consensus, the first Caliph, Abū Bakr, was chosen, but the followers of ʿAlī ibn Abī Ṭālib, the son-in-law and cousin of Muḥammad, the Shiites, disagreed, offering several arguments to prove that Muḥammad had appointed ʿAlī as his successor, such as the event at Ghadir Khumm, an oasis between Medina and Mecca. Both Sunnite and Shiite sources report that Muḥammad appointed ʿAlī as his heir. In addition, ʿAlī was Muḥammad's confidant, playing a prominent role at several crucial moments of Muḥammad's life. ʿAlī carries the flag at the battle of Badr in 624, and in a war at Tabūk in 630, he appoints ʿAlī as his vicegerent in Medina. Muḥammad gives the hand of his daughter to ʿAlī, a marriage which gives the prophet his only two grandsons, Ḥasan and Ḥuseyn.

There are several allusions to Ḥuseyn's martyrdom in Persian poetry before the advent of the Shiite Safavid dynasty in 1501, but under the Safavids his martyrdom became a powerful icon of identity for Shiite Persians and recounting the martyrdom developed as a genre.[70] Ḥuseyn gained the status of martyr because he went to Karbalā knowing the fate that awaited him, but he sacrificed himself for his followers and God. To this day his martyrdom is widely and passionately celebrated annually, during the ten-day festival of Muḥarram. Ḥuseyn is seen as a paradigm of martyrdom, a unique model to be followed for his self-sacrifice in the face of a powerful and unjust enemy. The number of Ḥuseyn's followers is usually said to be 72, all of whom died in the battle against the mighty army of Caliph Yazīd ibn Muʿāvīya and all died for Ḥuseyn's cause. From the moment they came to power the Safavids encouraged people to commemorate Ḥuseyn's martyrdom in impressive public processions. This commemoration gave them political legitimacy, as the Safavids claimed descent from Imam ʿAlī, and it underlined the differences between their state religion of Shiism and the Sunni religion of the neighbouring powers. Generally speaking, although the Safavids used this commemoration of martyrdom as a political device, it gradually devel-

---

70 See W. Chittick, "Rūmī's View of Imam Ḥusayn," in *Papers From the Imam Ḥusayn Conference* (London, 6–9 July 1984), Norfolk: The Thetford Press Ltd., 1986, pp. 3–12.

oped into a quietist annual celebration of piety and suffering. This remained the situation for centuries, until the second half of the twentieth century, especially in the 1960s.

Political upheavals started in 1963, with the White Revolution initiated by Muḥammad-Rižā Shah Pahlavi.[71] The White Revolution was followed by far-reaching reforms, including land reforms and women's suffrage, which angered clerics, especially the young Khomeini. Ayatollah Siyyid Ḥuseyn Burūjirdī (1875–1961), who was a "source of imitation" for most Shiites in and outside Iran, died in 1961, leaving a gap in spiritual leadership. While Burūjirdī had advocated a separation between politics and religion, Khomeini argued that political leadership was one of the religious responsibilities of the *ʿulamāʾ*. His forceful response to the reforms, especially to women's suffrage, brought people onto the streets.[72] On 3 June 1963, at the annual commemoration of Ḥuseyn's martyrdom, Khomeini delivered a speech comparing the Shah to Caliph Yazīd. The demonstrations were violently repressed and Khomeini was arrested and sentenced to death. To prevent his execution, other high-ranking clerics such as Ayatollah Sharīʿat-Madārī and Ayatollah Mīlānī elevated Khomeini to the rank of *Ayatollah al-ʿUẓmā*.[73] In 1964, after his imprisonment, Khomeini was exiled. He went first to Turkey for a short period and then to the Shiite holy city of Najaf. Khomeini remained active in Iranian politics from a distance, commenting and issuing fatwas on socio-political matters such as the Family Protection Law (1967), which he considered an insult to Islam, and the Six Day War against Israel, which led him to issue a fatwa prohibiting all Israeli products.

In this period of turmoil and anti-western sentiment, several influential publications further intensified pro-religious and anti-western feelings. Among the most important were *Shahīd-i jāvīd* ("The Eternal Martyr") by Niʿmatullāhī Sālihī Najafābādī, published in Qom in 1968, and Āl-i Aḥmad's *Gharbzadagī* ("Westoxification").[74] In *The Eternal Martyr*, the author transforms the traditional

---

71 Fakhreddin Azimi, "Khomeini and the 'White Revolution'," in *A Critical Introduction to Khomeini*, ed. Adib-Moghaddam, Cambridge: Cambridge University Press, 2013, pp. 19–42; also see Amanat, *Iran: A Modern History*, pp. 652–616; Z. Shakibi, *Pahlavi Iran and the Politics of Occidentalism: The Shah and the Rastakhiz Party*, London: I.B. Tauris, 2020.

72 Azadeh Kian, "Gendered Khomeini," in *A Critical Introduction to Khomeini*, ed. Adib-Moghaddam, Cambridge: Cambridge University Press, 2013, pp. 170–192.

73 M. Momen, *An Introduction to Shi'i Islam: The History and Doctrines of Twelver Shi'ism*, New Haven, CT, and London: Yale University Press, 1985, p. 254.

74 For an analysis of *The Eternal Martyr* see Evan Siegel, "The Politics of Shahid-e Jawid," in *The Twelver Shia in Modern Times: Religious Culture & Political History*, ed. Rainer Brunner and Werner Ende, Leiden: Brill, 2001, pp. 150–177. An earlier draft of the book was published in 1963.

presentation of Imam Ḥuseyn as an oppressed martyr into that of a revolutionary with worldly political aspirations. The book generated a heated controversy among Shiite jurists. From this time onwards, the ʿĀshūrā paradigm is increasingly used as a prefiguration of contemporary socio-political events in Iran. The book went through many reprints.[75] Simultaneously, anti-western sentiments were spread through Āl-i Aḥmad's book, a fact which had a profound influence on almost all intellectual discourses on modernity. The politicisation of the holiest Shiite paradigm of Karbalā among the populace, combined with anti-western reflections among the intelligentsia, created fertile ground for resisting the Shah's westernisation programme.

In the 1970s, ʿAlī Sharīʿatī further politicised the narrative of Ḥuseyn's martyrdom in his struggle against the social injustice, falsehood and tyranny of the Pahlavi regime.[76] A combatant cult of martyrdom was born, which played a central role during the 1979 Revolution. In his lectures delivered at diverse venues, and especially at the Ḥuseyniyya Irshād in Tehran, Sharīʿatī introduced a new Islam in which classical figures such as ʿAlī, Fāṭima and Ḥuseyn represented a modern Iranian, who was true to his religious convictions and aware that they entailed political activism. Using a polemical rhetoric involving sweeping compounds and one-liners such as *marg-i surkh* ("the red death," i.e., martyrdom), Sharīʿatī was able to convince people of the value of dying in achieving one's ideals. His reading of the medieval Shiite narratives revivified the historical protagonists such as ʿAlī and Fāṭima as people that the common people could easily identify with. Fāṭima becomes an assertive, active and modern woman who helped her husband to fight injustice.[77] ʿAlī is portrayed as a political activist who fights injustice. To illustrate how Sharīʿatī enlivens these historical figures, I cite a few passages from his book *Shahādat:*

> Again from the silent and sorrow-stricken house of Fāṭima, this small house that is bigger than history, a man comes out. Fuming and determined, and with an appearance as if he wants to assault all the palaces of tyranny and centres of power. It is as if he is the peak of a

---

75 My edition is the 17th reprint dated 1382/2003. See Niʿmatullāhī Sālihī Najafābādī, *Shahīd-i Jāvīd*, Tehran: Fardā, 1382/2003.

76 On Sharīʿatī see Ali Rahnema, *An Islamic Utopian: A Political Biography of Ali Shariʿati*, London: I.B. Tauris, 1998; Amanat, *Iran: A Modern History*, pp. 695 – 700.

77 For a historical account of Fāṭima see C.P. Clohessy, *Fāṭima, Daughter of Muḥammad*, Piscataway, NJ: Gorgias Press, 2018, on Sharīʿatī's interpretation see pp. 5 – 6. Clohessy observes that Fāṭima's "image is not much changed since Safavid times, barring one major exception in the form of ʿAlī Sharīʿatī's celebrated book *Fāṭima is Fāṭima.*" Also see J. Afary, *Sexual Politics in Modern Iran*, pp. 240 – 242.

> mountain that houses a restless volcano in its heart, or he is the violent storm that God sent to the people of ʿĀd, which will now blow. A man comes out of Fāṭima's house, looking at Medina, the Prophet's mosque, the Mecca of Abraham, the Kaʿba chained by Nimrod, and at Islam, and the message of Muḥammad, and the green palace in Damascus and the hungry and the people in chains, ... A man comes out of Fāṭima's house; the heavy burden of all these responsibilities presses on his shoulders. He is the heir to the great suffering of human beings. He is the only heir of Adam, the only heir of Abraham, ... and the only heir of Muḥammad. He is a lonely man. No, shoulder to shoulder, there is a woman coming out of Fāṭima's house, walking step by step, carrying half of the heavy burden of responsibility on her shoulders.[78]

His lectures and pamphlets depict a type of martyr who corresponds to a national and religious hero, with the consequence that anyone who died directly or indirectly in support of the struggle against the Pahlavi regime was called a martyr. Sharīʿatī defines martyrdom in several of his writings. In these definitions he elevates the martyr to an ideal level that equates to a perfect human being, a person who has fully realised his human potential. Such a person is not an individual with specific personal traits, but rather a universal being who possesses a rich array of spiritual and mundane traits desired by many:

> The word martyr contains the greatest burden of meaning [...]. The martyr means "present" (*ḥāżir*), "overseer" (*nāẓir*), "witness" and "giving testimony" (*guvāh va guvāhī dahanda*), "messenger" (*khabar dahanda*), "sincere and trustworthy" (*rāstīn-u amīn*), it also means "conscious" (*āgāh*), "tangible and perceptible" (*maḥsūs-u mashhūd*), a person upon whom all eyes are transfixed, and, finally, it means "model" (*nimūna*), "paragon" (*ulgū*) and "archetype" (*sar mashq*).[79]

Sharīʿatī further defines how martyrdom functions in Iranian culture, emphasising that it is not a "bloody and unpleasant accident" (*ḥādithi-yi khūnīn va nāguvār*). While in other cultures and religions martyrdom is used for those heroes who have offered their lives and are killed by an enemy, in Iranian culture no enemy can impose such a death on a fighter (*mujāhid*); "Martyrdom is a voluntary death that the fighter chooses in full consciousness, with all logic and understanding, and with awareness." Afterwards Sharīʿatī refers to Ḥuseyn as an ideal martyr, interpreting his revolt in a politically charged sense. "Look at Ḥuseyn, he travels from his own city, he leaves his life, he rises to die! Because

78 ʿAlī Sharīʿatī, *Shahādat*, Tehran: Sāzmān-i Intishārāt-i Ḥuseyniyya Irshād, 1350/1971, pp. 61–62; it is interesting to note that Sharīʿatī created a new picture of Fāṭima in his famous book *Fāṭima is Fāṭima* (1980).

79 The compound *sar mashq* literally means words or sentences written down on the top of a page so that children can imitate them, learning how to write. See Sharīʿatī, *Shahādat*, p. 64.

there is no other weapon for his struggle to disgrace the enemy, and to tear apart the deceptive veils that are put on the ugly face of the ruling state. Indeed if he is unable to break the enemy, he can at least disgrace the state; if he is unable to defeat it, he can condemn it." For Sharīʿatī martyrdom is a last weapon to unveil injustice, to reveal the unfair treatment of the martyr. Natural death under an unjust tyrannical political system is disapproved of. He distinguishes between "black death" and "red death," which is martyrdom, stating, "Ḥuseyn teaches us that 'black death' is the destiny of the weak people who accept any disgrace to stay alive. However, for those who do not have the courage to choose martyrdom, death will choose them."[80] Sharīʿatī's ideas on politicised Shiism and martyrdom, together with the increasing popularity of books such as Āl-i Aḥmad's *Gharbzadagī*, were instrumental in creating a context in which political Islam could grow.

The cult of martyrs took such extreme forms that almost all streets came to be named after the martyrs of the Revolution. In the 1980s, when Iraqi soldiers invaded Iran, the concept of martyrdom was again called on to mobilise the people. A significant new element was that the graves of Imam Ḥuseyn and the first Shiite Imam, ʿAlī b. Abī Ṭālib's, are situated in Iraq. Iranians were called on to take revenge on the Sunnite Arabs, and the war offered them an opportunity to die on the "thresholds" of their beloved Imams. Shiite Persians call the tombs in Iraq *ʿatabāt-i ʿalīyāt* or *ʿatabāt-i muqaddasa,* "the lofty or sacred thresholds." Pilgrimage to these sites is second only to pilgrimage to Mecca.[81] The war slogans made it even higher: one mobilising call said that "Going to Mecca requires money while going to Karbalā requires blood" – a sharp criticism of Iranians who preferred to go to Mecca when other Iranians were sacrificing themselves in "Karbalā" (i.e., on the front with Iraq).[82]

Employing classical Persian love poetry and mystical concepts, Iranian soldiers were encouraged to identify themselves with lovers on their way to the shrines of the holy Shiite imams. These holy imams were the beloved, for whom soldiers were ready to offer their lives, so gaining immortality in the beloved's embrace. One of the differences between Shiite and Sunni daily prayers is that the former use a prayer tablet (*muhr*), made ideally from the clay of Karbalā (*turbat*). It is believed to be mixed with Ḥuseyn's blood. During each prayer cycle Iranians put their foreheads on this tablet several times out of respect for

80 Ibid., p. 63.

81 See H. Algar in *Encyclopaedia Iranica*, s.v. *ʿAtabāt. These holy places contain the tombs of six Shiite imams in the following* cities in Iraq: Najaf, Karbalā, Kāẓimayn and Sāmarra.

82 For an analysis of the role of pilgrimage to Mecca in this period see chapter seven of this book.

Ḥuseyn, and are continually reminded of their Imam.[83] In such a context, Persian mystic love poetry was used to refer to these Shiite saints, identifying the unnamed beloved of the poetry as a Shiite holy person. The war was not only about fighting Saddam Hussein as a puppet of the West and a heretic, but also about avenging the deaths of the Imams, especially Ḥuseyn. The individual's fight was experienced as exertion for the spiritual goal of perfection as a human being, which could be attained by dying as a martyr. It is in this context that in this book I analyse various instances in which the peaceful poetry of mystical love, essentially irreconcilable with war, was poetically transformed to become war propaganda.

2.2 Poems Celebrating Martyrdom

In what follows I will give a few examples of the poetry of martyrdom, its metaphors and imagery, themes and motifs, with an analysis to foreground the poems' aesthetics. Many of these poems are couched in the classical *ghazal* form. While originally the *ghazal* treats themes connected with love and the beloved, usually with a mystical connotation, after the 1979 Revolution *ghazal*s were often poems with a militant political message, often maintaining the mystical message and the theme of love.

The following *ghazal* by Qeyṣar Amīnpūr (1959 – 2007) is an example of how the theme of martyrdom is treated in Persian war poetry, playing on the emotions of the reader and connecting martyrdom to a mystical quest. Before analysing the poem, I give the full translation.[84]

---

83 See Jean Calmard in *Encyclopaedia Iranica*, s.v. Ḥosayn B. ʿAli. ii. In Popular Shiʿism; also see M. Ayoub, *Redemptive Suffering in Islam: A Study of the Devotional Aspects of in Twelver Shi'-ism*, The Hague: Mouton Press, 1978, for various aspects of suffering for the Shiite imams, especially Ḥosayn. Such prayer tablets (*muhr*) are also made from the soil of the grave of other Shiite saints but are regarded as less valuable than those from Karbalā. The word *turbat* denotes the grave of a saint in Shiism, but it can also mean earth or dust from the shrine of a saint, which has *barakat*, "blessing." The sacred and magical power is contained in every speck of dust. For a study of muhr see Helga Venzlaff, "Mohr-e Namāz: Das schiitische Gebetssiegel," in *Die Welt des Islams*, Vol. 35, Issue 2, 1995, pp. 250 – 275.

84 This poem is taken from the collection compiled by Muḥammad Ḥuseyn Ṣanʿatī, *Āshnā'ī bā adabiyyāt-i difāʿ-i muqaddas*, Tehran: Bunyād-i ḥifẓ-i āthār va nashr-i arzishhā-yi difāʿ-i muqaddas, 1389/2010, pp. 55 – 56. This poem is not included in Amīnpūr's collected poetry.

جوانه زد غزلی در دلم برای شهادت
دوباره کرده دلم گوییا هوای شهادت
طنین نبض مرا گوش کن چه می شنوی هان؟
به گوش می رسد از آن صدای پای شهادت
در این سرای دلم تنگ شد، خوشا پروبالی
کجاست پنجره ی باز و دلگشای شهادت؟
دلا برای پریدن ، نه یک دریچه، نه روزن
به جای حلقه به سر زن در سرای شهادت
لباس تنگ تعلق هزار پاره کن ای دل
به قامت تو بپوشند تا قبای شهادت
چه جای خواب سحرآفتاب عشق بر آمد
خروس دهکده سر میدهد صلای شهادت
به روی گونه گل بوسه نسیم سحر بین
به روی گونه دل بوسه صبای شهادت
به شوق وعده ی ادعونی استجب لکم ای دل
بخوان برای اجابت، بخوان دعای شهادت
دلا ز عهد الست این به جان خریده تو گویی
قبیله ی تو به قالوا بلی، بلای شهادت
شفا دهد دل و جان را، هزار جان جوان را
به یک اشارت خود پیر رهنمای شهادت
ز باغ لاله چه گویم ز داغ لاله چه مویم
که جای ناله و غم نیست در عزای شهادت
مگو مگو که چرا شد چراغ چشم تو خاموش
چه جای چندی و چونی است در چرای شهادت
اگر چه خانه به خانه تهی است جای شهیدان
مشام شهر پر از بوی آشنای شهادت
تو اوج شعر و کلامی، تو خود تخلص نامی
تو بیت حسن ختامی شهادت آی شهادت

A poem has bourgeoned in my heart, for martyrdom,
As if my heart longs once more for martyrdom.
Listen to my pulse! Aie! What do you hear?
It brings to the ear the footsteps of martyrdom.
My heart is constricted by this house; how pleased I would be with wings!
Where is the open and heart-rejoicing window of martyrdom?
O heart! To fly, you don't need an opening or a hole;
Instead of knocking on the door, knock at the house of martyrdom.
O heart! Tear the tight robes of attachment in a thousand pieces,
That your frame may be clothed in the mantle of martyrdom.
This is not the time to sleep at dawn: the sun of love has risen,
The village rooster is crowing the summons to martyrdom.
See the kiss of dawn's breeze on the cheeks of the rose,
the kiss of martyrdom that breathes on the cheeks of the heart.
O heart! In longing for the promise "call on Me, I will answer you,"
Recite, to have the response! Recite the prayer of martyrdom.
O heart! Imagine that at the time of the covenant "Am I not your Lord?"
your people's saying "Aye!" bought the trial of martyrdom.

With a single gesture, the venerable guide of martyrdom
has healed the heart and soul, a thousand youthful souls.
What can I say about the bed of tulips? What can I say about the brand-marks of the tulips?
For there is no place for lament or grief in commemoration of martyrdom.
Do not, O do not say, "Why has the light of your eyes been extinguished?"
There's no place for how and why, in the wherefores of martyrdom.
Although the places of martyrs in every house are empty,
The air of the town is filled with the familiar scent of martyrdom.
You are the climax of poetry and language, you yourself are the poet's signature,
You are the beauty of the closing verse, martyrdom, O Martyrdom!

By the critical standards of Persian poetry, classical or modern, this is an acceptable poem. It served the cause of mobilisation, but it is not doggerel. The impact of modernity, the 1979 Revolution and the demands of war have not separated it from the poetic tradition or the poetic sensibility of the people. It is written for a wide public for, as the previous chapter emphasised, "[p]oetry is to Iranian civilization what philosophy is to the Greek" – it permeates daily life. Persian readers would recognise the ghazal form and the vocabulary of images, and understand how this ghazal grows from the political poetry of the Constitutional Revolution that spoke of democracy and social justice.

The poem rhymes on the suffix *–ā-yi* and the refrain following the rhyme is "[…] *shahādat*" (martyrdom). Through this refrain Amīnpūr emphasises the ubiquity of martyrdom in Iranian society, yet this is a very personal poem in which the poet talks to his own desiring heart, advising it (couplets four and five), and reminding it of its elevated position (couplet nine). The poet tells of the desires of his heart, full of the beauties of martyrdom. Remarkably, there is no mention of dying or actual death, no allusions even to red flowers. Martyrdom is represented in each couplet in a different way through compound nouns. While martyrdom could be a desire, it is a living being with a pulse. One can hear its footsteps. It can be a mansion with open windows. Martyrdom is also depicted as a dress which could cover a person who desires it. Martyrdom has its own invitation, which is sung by a rooster. The rooster reminds people of the passage of time, and can also be a symbol for awakening from "the sleep of negligence" (*khᵛāb-i ghaflat*). By associating martyrdom with these and several other concepts, the poet accentuates martyrdom's living reality without directly defining it as death. All associations and metaphors are positive, referring to a new dimension of life.

While martyrdom is omnipresent in ordinary life, the poet reminds his heart of its spiritual and timeless dimensions by referring to two Quranic verses. The first allusion (40:60) in couplet eight, "call on Me, I will answer you," offers a sense of urgency and prepares the reader for the next couplet which refers to a primeval covenant between God and the souls of Adam's children. Dying is not merely for national defence; it is a call that can receive a response from the Creator himself. By putting death in this religious context the poet provides a new connotation of martyrdom, as a desire that cannot be fulfilled unless God grants it. The poet interprets the Quranic verse in terms of meeting God as the Beloved, without expecting any reward. If the poet truly wishes to achieve the state of martyrdom, it is God who honours him with such a position. Amīnpūr then introduces another Quran verse (7:172), which has become a cliché allusion in Islamic mysticism. The covenant of *alast* (*ʿahd-i alast*) or its variant *rūz-i alast* or *yaum al-alast* ("day of *alast*") alludes to the beginning of creation, when God created Adam's soul and asked Adam, "Am I not your Lord?" (*alastu birabbikum*). The souls of Adam's progeny answered, "Yes, we witness, Thou art" (*qālū balā shahidnā*).[85] Mystics interpret this moment as a covenant struck between man and his creator. They feverishly long to return to this moment of oneness.

The word "yes" is sometimes interpreted as *balā* or "affliction" in mystical literature. It is affliction in the sense that love afflicts the lover. Mystics have taught that Adam's offspring at that moment were filled with God's awesomeness (*jalāl*) and overwhelming beauty (*jamāl*) to such an extent that they felt inebriated by God. So to be drunk in this world is to be reminded of this overwhelming moment. Mystics interpret the affirmation/affliction of *balā* as spiritual love, a grace offered by the creator only to mankind. Love is tribulation because mystics burn in longing and painful separation before they can achieve union. The mystical path is an itinerary formed by a series of trials and exertions. This is a mysticism of suffering. The journey, with many impediments, is depicted in splendid allegorical stories such as the *Manṭiq al-ṭeyr* ("The Conference of Birds") or *Muṣībat-nāma* ("Book of Affliction") by Farīd al-Dīn ʿAṭṭār (d. 1221). *The Conference* recounts the journey of birds in search of their soul king, Sīmurgh. The journey starts with a large number of birds who fly through seven valleys, but many of them stop along the way, giving various reasons such as the difficulty of renouncing material, familial or emotional ties. Only thirty birds (*sī murgh*) with the encouragement and guidance of the Hoopoe, continue on to and reach their destination, the mythic Mount Qāf. Here, the more they call on Sīmurgh the less they hear, until finally they realise that they are themselves the *sī murgh*. So the tribulations connected with the souls' affirmative answer to God

85 The full verse runs as follows: "And when your Lord brought forth from the children of Adam, from their backs, their descendants, and made them bear witness against their own souls: Am I not your Lord? They said: Yes! We bear witness. Lest you should say on the day of resurrection: Surely we were heedless of this." (7:172) وَإِذْ أَخَذَ رَبُّكَ مِنْ بَنِي آدَمَ مِنْ ظُهُورِهِمْ ذُرِّيَّتَهُمْ وَأَشْهَدَهُمْ عَلَى أَنْفُسِهِمْ أَلَسْتُ بِرَبِّكُمْ قَالُوا بَلَى شَهِدْنَا أَنْ تَقُولُوا يَوْمَ الْقِيَامَةِ إِنَّا كُنَّا عَنْ هَذَا غَافِلِينَ

are exertions the mystic must embrace to achieve the goal, i.e., union with the immaterial beloved.

In this poem Amīnpūr argues that the moment Adam's progeny affirmatively answered God's question, it accepted the "tribulation of martyrdom." In this particular couplet the poet uses a commercial metaphor: man purchased this tribulation. The poet's heart is the agent in this commercial interaction. The poet reminds his own heart how it bought the tribulation of martyrdom by agreeing to give the soul a place. In Islamic mysticism the soul is housed in the heart. Such strong metaphors affect the reader's perception and the relationship with the Creator. As God has fulfilled his contract by offering man the soul, man is obliged to offer the soul back to God. Connected to this topic, the soldier-lover-mystic does not offer his life for the reward of Paradise, as this would spoil his exertions and would mean that he has commercially negotiated his life for Paradise. Rather, these mystics accepted dying as union with God or union with a Shiite saint.

As in ʿAṭṭār's allegory of the birds, the soldier mystics have a guide. The unnamed "venerable guide" is without doubt Ayatollah Khomeini who, through his words, will guide the soldiers to achieve martyrdom. References to and elaboration on the theme of martyrdom abound in Khomeini's speeches and writings. He depicts martyrdom as an ideal human achievement, a blessing, by connecting martyrdom to the ʿĀshūrā paradigm, in which Ḥuseyn as the prince of martyrs fought against infidels. In the couplets following the reference to Khomeini, the poet invites his reader not to mourn for martyrs, not to engage in logical deliberations about offering one's soul to attain martyrdom, and says that while each family has offered a martyr, the town is full of their presence.

The poem's ending is unusual. In the genre of ghazal, the poet usually contrives to include his pen-name (*takhalluṣ*) in the last verse. To respect the martyr who has offered his life, Amīnpūr effaces himself and instead uses the word *takhalluṣ*, which he connects to the martyr, "you yourself are the poet's signature." By this device the poet identifies himself with martyrdom, creating a new dimension in the longing for love-death. The poem begins with the floral metaphor of martyrdom as a bud opening or a seedling germinating. In the final line the plant of martyrdom has fully grown. The beauty of the closing couplet (*ḥusn-i khitām*) lies in using martyrdom as an embellishment for the poem and as a personal trait for the poet.

In Amīnpūr's poem the emphasis is on how vital – in both senses of the word – martyrdom is, avoiding any direct connection with ordinary death. The poet advises one not to deliberate about the loss of lives: in the context of martyrdom there is no room to ask why or how. He places martyrdom in the context of spiritual love, using the same vocabulary as medieval mystics such as ʿAṭṭār.

In matters of love discursive reasoning and deliberations are of no avail. Mystics have often referred to the dichotomy of love and reason. Reason's domain is land, the domain of love is the ocean, and the mystic secret is held in a shell in the depths of the ocean. By relying on such medieval mystical concepts, Persian war poets avoid direct references to death as death. They refer to death as the heart's desire to unite with the beloved.

Amīnpūr is by no means the only poet who relies on Persian mysticism. Each couplet of the following ghazal by Sāʾid Bāqirī (b. 1339/1960) makes a different allusion to mysticism. Before analysing the poem, I present the full English translation:

آفتابی دیگر
این سبکبالان که تا عرش جنون پر می کشند
آفتاب وصل را چون صبح، در بر می کشند
از دم تیغ شهادت باده جوی وصلتند
نیل اگر گردد بلا لا جرعه اش سر می کشند
هر مقام عشق را موقوف زخمی ساختند
بی سران در هفت شهر عاشقی سر می کشند
آفتاب دیگرند اینان که روز خصم را
تیره می سازند چون از کوه سربر می کشند
عرش با فریادهاشان همنوایی می کند
تا که از دل نعره الله اکبر می کشند
آذرخش خشم اینان آتش قهر خداست
بیشه زار بتپرستی را به آذر می کشند
فصل دیگر می گشایند از کتاب کربلا
عشق را با جوهر خون نقش دیگر می کشند

A singular sun
These light-winged ones who fly to the Throne of madness
    Embrace the sun of union like the dawn.
They receive the wine of union from blood on the blade of martyrdom
    If the Nile becomes affliction, they will guzzle it down.
They have dedicated each station of love to a particular wound.
    Without heads, they show their heads in the seven valleys of love[86]
They are a singular sun: they darken the enemy's day
    When they raise their heads from behind the mountain.
The Throne accompanies their cries
    When they shout "God is Great" from their hearts.
The lightening of their rage is the fire of God's wrath,
    They set fire to the thicket of idolatry.
They open a new chapter in the book of Karbalā
    They make a new drawing of love with the ink of blood.

86 This is an allusion to a poetic couplet that has become a proverb in Persian. It runs as follows: "ʿAṭṭār has traversed the seven regions of Love, we are still at the turn of one street."

In the first couplet the poet refers to the mystical union with the Beloved, through the compound "the sun of union." Other conspicuous elements in this couplet are the words *sabuk-bālān* and *junūn* or "madness." *Sabuk-bālān* is a variation on *sabuk-bārān* or "lightly-burdened," which Ḥāfiẓ (d. 1390) uses several times to refer to those who are at the shore of the sea of union, not daring to dive into it. Bāqirī has created a positive variant of this term, the "light-winged," and combines it with the compound "the throne of madness." Here the poet is describing the ascension of the mystic lovers to God's throne, following the example of the Prophet's *miʿrāj* (ascent to heaven). The "madness" is love-madness, which is required if the seeker is to leave worldly interests and attachments behind to attain union. God as the beloved is implicitly depicted as the Sun. The compound "the Sun of union" refers to how the mystic like dawn embraces the Beloved. The metaphors in this couplet are new. The poet has successfully combined several classical images into a new depiction of union. In the second couplet the poet immediately specifies how and why the mystic lover has longed for union. These mystics are yearning to die as martyrs. Martyrdom is connected to bacchic imagery, as the lover is taking wine. The hyperbole "If the Nile becomes affliction, they will guzzle it down" emphasises their strong embrace of suffering. On this mystic path, at each mystic station, they accept a wound, which prepares them to renounce the world. Classical mystic poets emphasise that one should offer one's head on the mystic path, referring to annulling the intellect and discursive thinking. The paradoxical phrase, "[w]ithout heads, they show their heads in the seven valleys of love," is an allusion to ʿAṭṭār's *Conference of the Birds* in which he depicts the seven valleys of mystical love.[87] The final station is the annihilation of one's identity in the beloved. The metaphor of journeying on the path of love is here connected to the path of war, which is explicit in the subject and the context of the poem. On the mystical journey the lover surrenders aspects of the human personality so that on reaching the final stage he or she is ready to annihilate self. Here the "wound" refers to this stripping off and renouncing of temporal existence.

The poet creates a paradox on the metaphor of the sun to describe how unique these mystic lovers are. While the sunrise puts darkness to flight, this particular sun exudes darkness over the plains when it shows its head. This is a rare allusion to the soldier's ability to use weapons, probably to firing missiles.

87 For an excellent essay on the structure of this poem see Dick Davis, "The Journey as Paradigm: Literal and Metaphoric Travel in Attar's *Mantiq al-Tayr*," in *Edebiyât: the Journal of Middle Eastern Literatures*, 4/2, 1993, pp. 173–183; also see H. Ritter, *The Ocean of the Soul: Man, the World and God in the Stones of Farīd al-Dīn ʿAṭṭār*, trans. John O'Kane with editorial assistance from Bernd Radtke, Leiden/Boston, MA: Brill, 2003.

In the next couplet the poet uses hyperbole, showing that the soldiers' aspiration derives from God, because as soon as they shout "God is Great," the Throne responds in their support. Having made this strong connection to God, the poet likens God's fiery wrath to the "lightening" of the soldiers' rage. It is not specified how their rage is lightening, but that has the connotation of a weapon that strikes from the air, such as a missile. This wrath sets fire to the thicket where idols are worshipped, a reference to Saddam Hussein as an unbeliever. Identifying the enemy with idolatry enables the poet to equate the soldier's weapons with God's wrath. God has two categories of names, Wrathful and Graceful. The specific word used here for fire is *ādhar*, a poetic word but also the name of Abraham's father. In Islamic lore Abraham is remembered as one who broke the idols, inviting people to worship one God. That image suggests an allusion to Ayatollah Khomeini, also called Abraham, who put an end to the "idol worshippers" of the Pahlavi regime, and was at war with Saddam Hussein. The last couplet relates all the elements of the poem to Shiism by referring to the Karbalā paradigm. All these soldiers' actions are a new manifestation of the "type" of Imam Ḥuseyn and his followers who offered their lives for God's love. This interpretation claims that Iranian soldiers, with God behind them, are re-enacting Karbalā and taking revenge on the Sunnites who humiliated and slew Ḥuseyn. The repetition of the word *dīgar*, meaning both "once again" and out of the ordinary ("singular") emphasises that the story of Karbalā never finishes; time and again a new chapter opens. In this poem Bāqirī appropriates religion and God as indispensable parts of the Iranian creation of the Iraqi other, who were depicted as Sunnites and idol-worshippers, while Saddam was presented as an irreligious puppet of Western powers.

Naṣrullāh Mardānī (1947–2003) is one of the widely cited poets of the Sacred Defence literature. His poetry is cited in schoolbooks to instill the doctrines of martyrdom, the teachings of Shiism, and altruism in children. The following poem, which is used in schoolbooks, refers to martyrdom, offering blood and the praise of Ayatollah Khomeini:

از خوان خون گذشتند صبح ظفر سواران
پیغام فتح دارند آن سوی جبهه یاران
در شط سرخ آتش، نعش ستاره می‌سوخت
خون‌نامه نبرد است آیین پاسداران
در کربلای ایثار مردانه در ستیزند
رزم‌آوران اسلام با خیل نابکاران
در شام سرد سنگر روشن چراغ خون است
ای آب دیده، تر کن لبهای روزه‌داران
در رزمگاه ایمان با اسب خون بتازند
تا وادی شهادت این قوم سربداران

گلگونه شهیدان با خون گل بشویید
تا سرختر نماید رخسار روزگاران
هابیلیان کجایید قابیل دیگر آمد
ننگ است جان سپردن در دخمه تتاران
در بادهای سوزان نیلوفران خاکی
چشم‌انتظار آب‌اند ای روح سبز باران
ای ابر پرصلابت، آبی ز دیده بفشان
با مرگ لاله طی شد افسانه بهاران
بی‌باوران عالم با چشم دل ببینید
آیینه زمان است این پیر در جماران

At victory's dawn, the riders passed from the feat of blood
Friends have the message of triumph from the other side of the front.
In the river of crimson fire, the corpse of the star was burning,
The Rule of the Guards is the bloody epic of battle.
At the Karbalā of sacrifice, the warriors of Islam
fight the army of ill-doers, courageously.
In the cold night of the trenches, blood is the light from the lamp.
O my tears, wet the lips of those who are fasting.
In the battlefield of faith, this tribe of Sarbidār
hurtles on steeds of blood into the valley of martyrdom.
Bathe the martyrs' faces in the blood of the rose
That the cheeks of Time may shade a deeper red.
People of Able, where are you? Another Cain has come:
It is a shame to entrust one's soul to a Tatar's grave.
O green soul of rain! The lilies in the dust[88]
wait avidly for water in the scorching wind.
O majestic cloud, pour some water from your eyes
For the myth of Spring ends with the death of Tulip.
Unbelievers of the world! See with the eye of your hearts
That this old man in Jamārān is the Mirror of Time.

As in many other war poems, blood (*kh^{v}ūn*) is a dominant theme. In the first couplet the compound *kh^{v}ān-i kh^{v}ūn* ("feat of blood") has two meanings. While the first meaning of *kh^{v}ān* reminds the Persian reader of Firdowsī's reference to the "seven feats" of the *Shāh-nāma* hero Rustam, the word also connotes "banquet."[89] The compound also suggests a natural scene, at dawn when the sun's red spreads along the horizon. Building on this sunrise scenery, the poet says that the star's corpse – or more literally, the bier with the body on it – is burning in the red river of fire. "Star" is not a precise term: it refers to heavenly bodies and in this image may be the sun reflecting on the river. This is, of course, not

88 This could also be interpreted as lilies grown on land in contrast to water-lilies.
89 The word *kh^{v}ān is also spelled khān in Firdowsī's Shāh-nāma.*

an ordinary river, as the word chosen, *shaṭṭ*, alludes to the water border between Iran and Iraq, which Iranians call *Kārūn* while the Arabs call it *Shaṭṭ al-ʿArab*. The emphasis on blood is again reiterated in the same couplet as the Rule of the Guards (*pāsdārān*) is the book of blood to battle. *Pāsdārān* means protectors, and is the name of the revolutionary guards, as distinct from the national army. In the third couplet the poet introduces the paradigm of Karbalā by referring to the locality and using the loaded term *īthār*, altruistic self-sacrifice, a key term in Shiism as a reference to Imam Ḥuseyn's followers who offered their lives for Ḥuseyn, knowing that they would be killed. The word *īthār* is one of the words used during the 1979 Revolution and the Iran-Iraq War to indicate the qualities of a devout revolutionary. This event at Karbalā cemented the breach between Shiite and Sunnite Islam, so this reference links Ḥuseyn's battle against the Sunnite Umayyad dynasty (661–750) to the twentieth century. Here the Iranians are Islamic warriors, while Saddam Hussein's army consists of ill-doers. In the fourth couplet the poet introduces a new metaphor of blood. The blood is a lamp shining and warming the cold dark night of the trenches.

We are also informed that it is the period of fasting, but this is probably not the month of Ramadan, since the faithful fast only from sunrise to sunset. Rather the "fast" is being deprived of provisions by conditions at the front. The warriors have no water, like the Shiite heroes at Karbalā. In the sixth couplet, blood is a steed that carries the warriors into the valley of martyrdom. It is here that the poet emphasises that the battle is not merely a physical fight but rather a spiritual terrain, and the warriors are not ordinary warriors but descendants of the Sarbidārān, alluding to the Shiites in the city of Sabzivār who fought against the Mongols in the fourteenth century. In the seventh couplet the metaphor of blood is combined with the rose. The first word is the compound *gul-gūna*, the "rose-cheeks" of the martyrs, which should be washed with the "blood of the rose." This is a figure of speech which classical Persian poets use frequently to conjure up other images. In this case, the face of the martyr is besmeared with blood and is washed with rose water. The rose's blood is nothing more than the essence of the rose. The poet invokes images working on several senses: colour, smell and touch. The rose cheeks of the martyrs suggest they are very young, with soft cheeks. Moreover, in the Persian poetic tradition the making of rose water is depicted as killing the petals in hot water.[90]

Couplet seven ends with the message that the accumulation of the red hue on the face of the martyr will affect the face of the world. "Time" here refers to

90 See, for example, the quatrain ascribed to the mystic Abū Saʿīd, included in the collection Ḥ. Āzād Tabrīzī, *Gulzār-i maʿrifat*, Leiden: Brill, 1906, p. 73.

the current of time today, to the world as it is and is becoming, and not, as in English, to a boundless antiquity. The next couplet contrasts the victim with the perpetrator by referring to Cain and Abel. It is a shame to be the victim, to lie in a Tatar grave. The Tatars in the Persian poetic tradition are associated with musk, archery and horsemanship, and bravery in battle. Tataristan is also a far-off country, so perhaps the suggestion is that there is honour in dying in Iraq, on the front. The poet employs natural imagery in the ninth and tenth couplets, revisiting the theme of water and thirst, and again invoking the paradigm of Karbalā. As Ḥuseyn, his family and followers were denied any water for ten consecutive days, the theme of water became an essential element in Ḥuseyn's martyrdom narratives. The poet depicts the setting through the natural imagery. In an area where rain does not fall often and scorching winds blow, plants long for water. Here the earthly lilies, the soldiers, are waiting for rain. In the next couplet the poet implores the clouds to shed tears because the Spring has proved to be a mythical epos, ended by the tulips' dying. The poet asks the clouds to rain, symbolising their weeping over the death of the tulips, a stock image for martyrs. These are unusual clouds, full of power. Perhaps there is a suggestion of a rain of missiles that avenges the death of martyrs. By saying that the myth of Spring has come to an end, the poet is using hyperbole to emphasise the intense grief his readers undergo. The poem ends with a tribute to Khomeini who is characterised as the "mirror of time" perceived only by those who look with the eye of their hearts.

Such poems have a strong propagandistic quality, and this is also why they are included in schoolbooks. Distinctions are made between dying and martyrdom, which is the most noble death. The value of the propaganda for society is not only to mobilise forces by offering recruits the prospect of meaningful death, but also to assure those left behind that their loss is meaningful. No doubt some of the children reading such poems at school found consolation in them for their own bereavements. A negative aspect of valorising death in war in this rich and religious way – much richer than mere patriotic war poetry – was that the martyr's family were supposed to be proud of their child, brother or cousin, and to receive congratulations rather than condolences. Lamentation for martyrs was considered shameful.[91] This practice was even exported to Leb-

---

91 H. Algar, in *Encyclopaedia Iranica*, s.v. Burial. There is nothing about funeral procedure in the Quran, but in prophetic traditions, there are chapters in which instructions to "bury the dead swiftly, to handle them gently and with respect and to refrain from excessive lamentation" can be found. See P. Chelkowski's opening story in his "All's is not Quiet on the western Front: Graphic Arts in the Iranian War effort," in *Moments of Silence: Authenticity in the Cultural Expression of the Iran-Iraq War, 1980–1988*, ed. A. Khakpour, M.M. Khorrami & S. Vatanabadi, New

anon.[92] In interviews with some Iranian mothers, they express their regret that they did not have more sons to offer to the cause of the 1979 Revolution and the war. I report this inexcusable development to show how the values of life and death were changing during and after the Revolution. It seemed that the more people were killed, the less life became valued. The Islamic Republic needed to give meaning to hundreds of thousands of deaths, and cherishing life and one's family was a victim of that need.

There are many poems dealing with the relationship between mothers and sons. For instance, Sīmīndukht Vaḥīdī writes about the relationship between a mother and her son at the frontline. Vaḥīdī was born in Jahrum in the province of Fars in March 1312/1923. She wrote poetry from the age of 17. After the 1979 Revolution, her poetry appeared in various publications related to war literature. She taught at the Centre for Education and the Teacher's Academy. She is hailed for her active participation in the 1979 Revolution, the war again Iraq, and later as an ambassador for culture in various governmental organizations, including the radio and television of the Islamic Republic. She is perhaps the most prolific female poet of the Sacred Defense, writing in the classical style, mainly ghazals.[93] Vaḥīdī's poetry covers a wide range of subjects related to Shiism, the Revolution and the War. Several of the poems are eulogies to Fāṭimat al-Zahrā, the daughter of the prophet and the wife of the first Shiite Imam ʿAlī ibn Abī Ṭālib, or poems devoted to the Return of the Twelfth Shiite Imam Mahdī, or other Shiite figures. Unfortunately, the poems lack a date to could link them to specific periods of the war. What makes her poetry invaluable is the inclusion of themes and perspectives often neglected by other female poets. The poetry itself is not comparable to the strong language, peerless metaphors, and intellectual vigour of female poets such as Bihbahānī. Its merits lie in the simple and plain language and how straightforwardly she communicates with her audience. The following poem depicts mother-son relationship:

آیا صدای من به صدای تو می رسد؟
اکنون دمای من به دمای تو میرسد؟
مادر بگو صدای روانسوز انتظار،

York: New York University Press, 2016, pp. 163–164, in which he talks to a taxi deriver who regrets that he could not die as a martyr. In those days, to die as a martyr was an honour.

92 J. Alagha, *Hizbullah's Identity Construction*, Amsterdam: Amsterdam University Press, 2011, p. 92.

93 Before the Revolution, she published one volume of poetry but after the revolution she authored several volumes of poetry, including *yik āsimān shaqāyiq* ('A Heaven Anemones'), and *mowjhā-yi bī-qarār* ('Restless Waves'). Her collected poetry (*Dīvān*) appeared in a single volume of 992 pages in Tehran in 2010.

همراه بادها به فضای تو میرسد؟
از لابه لای این همه موشک، تفنگ، توپ
برق سلام من به صفای تو می رسد
مادر مباد اشک بریزی برای من!
از سوی دوست، اجربرای تو می رسد
چشم انتظار آمدن این پسر مباش
صبری برای تو ز خدای تو می رسد[94]

Does my voice reach your voice?
Is my warmth now reaching your warmth?[95]
Mother, tell me, does the wind that blows into your room
carry the soul-scorching call of anticipation?
From among all these missiles, guns and mortars,
Does the lightning of my 'salām' reach your serenity?[96]
Mother, may you never shed tears for me!
From the Friend's presence, recompense will reach you.
Do not wait to see your son,
Patience will reach you from your God.

The poem, couched in ghazal form, is entitled 'Mother!' (*mādar!*), and is written by a mother from the perspective of her son, imagining that her son is talking to her about the violent situation at the front. The exclamation mark after the title *mādar* may allude to the soldier's voice, calling his mother. In the first couplet, the soldier asks rhetorically whether his voice or his warmth reaches his mother. Using the two senses, for hearing and embracing, in the opening couplet creates powerful metaphors to convey loneliness and separation. In the second couplet, the poet uses a classical metaphor in a new context. She wonders whether the wind could bring the soul-burning sound of the time of waiting, because the soldier is among loud weapons. The mother-poet is visualizing her son at the front, continually thinking of his mother. In the fourth couplet, the mother is implored not to shed any tears for the martyred soldier, because then God will reward her. The poet emphasizes how she should behave. She is setting the norm not only for herself but also for a generation of mothers who lost their sons. The last couplet shows that the son expects to be killed ('do not wait') and longs for it. By juxtaposing the perspectives, Vaḥīdī internalizes how her son would wish her to appreciate his fighting at the front and his wish to die as a martyr. The aesthet-

---

94 Sīmīndukht Vaḥīdī, *Dīvān*, Tehran: Vizārat-i Farhang va Irshād-i islāmī, 1389/2010, p. 223.
95 The word *damā* literally means temperature but here the poet is referring to warmth.
96 The word *ṣafā* has a wide range of meanings, including "purity, clearness, polish, brightness, pleasure," but I have translated here with serenity. The line may also be translated as, "Does the lightning of my 'salām' reach your purity." See F. Steingass, *Persian-English Dictionary*, London: Routledge, 1892, fifth print 1963, s.v. ṣafā.

ic value of such poems lies in the unexpected change of perspective and the ideological message the poem conveys. In common Persian poems with the title *mādar*, it is an individual who writes about the qualities of the mother and motherhood, but here it is a mother who imagines how her son would write about her. Through such juxtaposition, the mother is putting a heavy burden on her son's shoulder, by emphatically asking him to offer his life. Such poems show the commitment and resolve of Iranian mothers who were ready to offer the most precious things to defend the country.

Many poems by female war poets do not deal with female topics and gender issues. It is often not easy to find a female voice in individual poems, but in this particular poem, Vaḥīdī has chosen to cope with the relationship between a mother and son. Although the speaker is male, the poem is about a mother and how an ideal mother would behave towards an ideal son, who is ready to sacrifice himself for Islam and the country.[97] In government-sponsored Iranian media, Vaḥīdī herself is portrayed as an ideal woman who has devoted her talents to the Revolution. For many women, she is a model and inspiration. The poem also implies that the mother has brought up her son to be ready to offer herself for the Revolution, Islam and country. The ideal mother is one who has successfully raised a generation of martyrs.

Blood is a *leitmotiv* in Persian revolutionary and war poetry. The rich variety of images and metaphors that use blood to indicate a soldier's longing for death befuddles the reader. One example is the following quatrain by Ḥuseynī, describing soldiers in terms that are in turn antinomian, mystic and pious, each relating to blood:

این جرعه کشان مست از باده خون
معشوق شهادت اند و دل داده خون
با بانگ امام نور قامت بستند
هنگام قیام روی سجاده خون[98]

These drunken drinkers of the blood-wine:
Are the beloved of martyrdom and the lovers of blood.
They rose at dawn at the cry of the Imam of Light,
Now they stand in prayer on the prayer-mat of blood.

97 The theme of "mother" in Persian poetry could be traced back to medieval period, but from the end of the nineteenth century, poets gave increasingly more attention to mothers. See A. Karimi-Hakkak's discussion of Īraj Mīrzā's (1874–1926) *Qalb-i mādar* or "A Mother's Heart," in *Recasting Persian Poetry*, pp. 152–161.

98 Ḥuseynī, *Ham-ṣidā bā ḥalq*, p. 131.

Although the deaths of soldiers were celebrated in Iran, the Islamic government emphasised the positive and rewarding aspects of dying by connecting dying to Shiite martyrdom, especially the event at Karbalā and the martyrdom of Imām Ḥuseyn, which could be seen as the climax of the Shiite and Sunnite divide. This conflict is essential for the relationship between the Sunnites and Shiites in the modern times. To show their devotion to Ḥuseyn, people still celebrate his death during Muḥarram. People weep for the way Ḥuseyn died and in various ceremonies they beat their breasts with their palms, and strike their shoulders and backs with chains.[99] This love is intensified, as during these rituals a deep sense of guilt is evoked, guilt that they were not present during the events at Karbalā to support Ḥuseyn against the mighty Sunnite Umayyad army. The Shiites experience Ḥuseyn's decision to start an unmatched fight as an act of altruism, offering his own life for his ideology of truth against corruption, interpreting his death as a meaningful death and as martyrdom. This idea is stuffed with a rich collection of sayings and altruism, setting an example of how Shiite should behave.

Profound love of Ḥuseyn and a deep feeling of guilt generated intense hatred and vengeance. The hate was further fed by a wide range of ideas about the centuries-old animosity between the Arabs and the Persians, between the Sunnite and the Shiites, between the imperialist West and the oppressed East, etc. Finding themselves internationally in an underdog position, it was easy to identify themselves with Ḥuseyn, who became a stimulus to fighting the unequal enemy. While Saddam Hussein was supported by all Arab countries (except Syria) materially and morally and was backed by western countries in terms of supplying Iraq with advanced military equipment, including chemical weapons, Iran, which had alienated itself from the West by its Islamic revolutionary anti-western rhetoric, was isolated.

In this chapter I will examine a number of Persian elegies through which fallen Iranian soldiers were celebrated as martyrs. Such death on the battlefield was considered an exalted passing, which deserved to be praised rather than pitied and mourned. It is this particular paradox in such a context that makes poetry as an art form an appropriate means to convey a message, incorporating a wide range of interpretations through familiar motifs, metaphors and themes. As I will show, this poetry removes absolutist claims of certain factions of the Islamic government, who discouraged mourning for the deaths, emphasising the poetry's therapeutic function. In a number of cases soldiers or poets composed poetry to vent their feelings. In addition, a number of these elegies were made into

99 See M. Ayoub, *Redemptive Suffering in Islam*, pp. 142–158.

songs, sung by different revolutionary singers. Although these songs were, in the first place, a requiem to celebrate death, to cure the pain of loss, they also functioned as propaganda, conjuring up a sense of guilt in order to mobilise the soldiers, usually young people, to give their lives.

The following poem by Qeyṣar Amīnpūr (1959–2007) shows the brittle bridge between life and death:

فراخوان

مرا
به جشن تولد
فراخوانده بودند
چرا
سر از مجلس ختم
درآورده ام؟[100]

Invitation

I was
invited to
a birthday celebration

why
did I find myself
in a ceremony of death?

Although the poem could easily be a reference to a person in an ordinary situation, it is worthwhile referring to it as an example of reactions to human loss of life. The poem can, at least, be read on two levels. A second reading, which is less probable, is that the poet was invited to a birthday party, but the birthday person was killed and the ceremony was turned into a wake. Also, one can assume that the poet was invited to a ceremony in which the martyrdom of a soldier was celebrated but, to his astonishment, people were weeping and could not accept the loss of their loved one. This reading is probable as, during the Iran-Iraq War, to my knowledge it was not common to send convocation for a birthday party, but for a mourning ceremony.

Many poems were composed on the deaths of soldiers. In several of these poems the poet uses the rhetorical technique of "feigned ignorance" (*tajāhul al-ʿārif*) as if the dead are still alive. But there are also poems in which the deaths

---

100 Q. Amīnpūr, *Majmūʿa-yi kāmil-i ashʿār*, Tehran: Murvārīd, 9th printing, 1391/2012, p. 21.

of soldiers are accepted. In such poems the poet uses a wide range of metaphors, motifs and religious and historical allusions to rouse emotions. The following poem is by Parvīz Beygī Ḥabīb-Ābādī, who wrote many poems on the Iran-Iraq War and is still active in Iran, presenting his poetry to the leader of the Islamic state, ʿAlī Khamenei, during special annual sessions organised for conservative and committed poets at Khamenei's residence. The following poem does not have poetic merit but is a good example of variations of poems on mourning or celebrating martyrdom. The poem bears the title *Az Karbalā mīāyand* or "They Come Back from Karbalā":

بر دور دست این ره، چشمی در انتظار است
می آید اسبی اما، افسوس، بی سوار است
از لاله ژاله ریزد، از چنگ ناله خیزد
گویی به داغ یاران، این چرخ سوگوار است
تاب دلم ربوده است، محزو نترین سرود است
اشکی که می تراود، طفلی که بیقرار است
از کربلا می آیند، بی سر، ولی سرافراز
در مکتب حسینی، سرها طلایه دار است
از دیدگان بر در، خون می چکد سراسر
این آستان خاموش، پوشیده از غبار است
حلاج و دار معراج، خونین ترین حماسه است
ای خیل نابکاران، این قوم سربدار است
یاران ز پای افتند، اما بپاست رایت
این خطه را سراسر، مردان کارزار است
در فصل سبز رویش، این خاك ارغوانی است
گویی بهار این دشت خونین ترین بهار است
پا در رکاب بگذا ر ای یکه تاز موعود
کاین جا هوا هوای پرحجم انتظار است

At the far end of this road is a waiting and longing eye.
    A horse comes! Alas, it has no rider.
Dew drops pour from a tulip, a lament rises from the harp.
    As if the universe mourns the sudden death of loved ones.
My heart's rest has been stolen. The song is beyond sadness.
    One tear escapes. A restless child.
They are returning from Karbalā, headless, but heads held high.
    In the school of Ḥuseyn, the heads are the vanguard.
The eyes at the door are all dripping blood.
    This silent doorway is covered with dust.
The bloodiest epic is that of Hallāj's ascent to the gallows.
    O army of villains, this people has laid its head on the gallows!
Friends may fall but the flag still stands:
    All these lands have heroes for the battlefield.
In the green season of growth this dust is coloured purple,
    As if, on this plain, the spring is the bloodiest spring.

Put your foot in the stirrup, O champion, as promised,
For here, the air we breathe is the essence of longing and waiting.[101]

The poem is couched in the form of a classical ghazal, connecting classical motifs, imagery and allusions to contemporary events. The majority of the motifs are taken from religious poetry celebrating the third Shiite Imām, Ḥuseyn. According to popular Shiite lore, which is told during annual celebration of Ḥuseyn's death, when all of Ḥuseyn's followers were killed, he himself went to fight. His family were waiting at the opening of the tent and longing to see him come back, but tragically only his horse Zu'l-Jināh returned. The opening is strong but not original, yet functional in arousing emotions, especially when it refers to the contemporary situation, equating soldiers to the followers of Ḥuseyn at. The poet is apparently influenced by classical poets such as Saʿdī, whose elegies are universally known in the Persian-speaking world. As Siyyid Ḥasan Ḥuseynī (1956–2005) indicates, the imagery of "a lament rises from the harp" is borrowed from Saʿdī who says "a lament rises from the stone.". Another element from classical poets is the attempt to universalise mourning, in which even the Wheel is shedding tears for this loss. The poet connects this loss to the motif of offering one's head, as in the Karbalā paradigm this motif plays a central role. "Giving the head" or *sar dādan* symbolises an unconditional and absolute sacrifice to Ḥuseyn, which is here used to suggest that soldiers who return headless have voluntarily died for Ḥuseyn's cause. Here the poet succeeds in equating an event that happened some 1400 years ago to a contemporary event and hereby emphasises that the cult of martyrdom, like martyrs themselves, is a living being. While this motif of "giving the head" occurs here in a religious context, the poet adds a new mystical dimension to it by alluding to Ḥuseyn Manṣūr Ḥallāj, who was executed in Bagdad in 922 because of his illocutionary saying, "I am the Truth."[102] Although Ḥallāj was killed because he had built a Kaʿba in his house and walked around it, a blasphemous act according to orthodoxy, in Is-

101 S.Ḥ. Ḥuseynī, *Guzīda-yi shiʿr-i jang*, p. 183.

102 On the motif of "giving the head" in modern time see A.A. Seyed-Gohrab, "Martyrdom as Piety, Mysticism and National Icon in Iran," in *Der Islam: Zeitschrift für Geschichte und Kultur des islamischen Orients*, issue 1–2, 87, 2012, pp. 248–273. Also see idem, "'Martyrs of Love': Genesis, Development and Twentieth Century Political Application of a Sufi Concept," in *Martyrdom: Canonization, Contestation and Afterlives*, ed. I. Saloul & J.W. van Henten, Amsterdam: Amsterdam University Press, 2020, pp. 129–151; On the use of the motif in classical literature see Seyed-Gohrab, *Laylī and Majnūn*, pp. 131–134; C.W. Ernst, "On Losing One's Head: Hallājian Motifs and Authorial Identity in Poems Ascribed to 'Attār," in *'Attār and the Persian Sufi Tradition, the Art of Spiritual Flight*, eds. L. Lewisohn & C. Shackle, London/New York: I.B. Tauris Publishers, 2006, pp. 330–343.

lamic mystic memory he is commonly celebrated for his phrase, probably because of Farīd al-Dīn ʿAṭṭār's powerful and moving depiction of his execution on the gallows in his hagiography.[103] Apart from the religious and mystical dimensions he gives the motif of "giving the head," Beygī Ḥabīb-Ābādī introduces a political layer when he refers to the compound *sar-be-dār* or "head-on-the-gallows." In addition to its literal meaning, the term *sar-bi-dār* refers to a fourteenth-century movement of Shiites in the city of Sabzevār, who were ready to offer their lives to defend Persia and Shiism against the Mongol incursion.[104]In this way the poet builds up a heroic poem, celebrating the death of the fallen soldiers.

A more successful poem by Ḥabīb-Ābādī is *Gharībāna*, translated here as *Left Behind*. The word is connected to the Arabic verb *gharaba*. In Persian the word *gharīb* is commonly used to refer to a stranger, alone, an exile or a refugee. Although the word has a philosophical and mystical connotation, conveying the sense of being exiled from the spiritual world, in the following poem the everyday usage is predominant. The suffix *-āna*, attached to nouns, refers to a manner, here meaning loneliness, a sense of forlornness and left behind. Before starting an analysis of the poem, I give a full translation:

یاران چه غریبانه رفتند از این خانه
هم سوخته شمع ما، هم سوخته پروانه
بشکسته سبوهامان، خون‌ست به دل‌هامان
فریاد و فغان دارد دردی کش میخانه
هر سوی نظر کردم هر کوی گذر کردم
خاکستر و خون دیدم ویرانه به ویرانه
افتاده سری سویی گلگون شده گیسویی
دیگر نبود دستی تا موی کند شانه
تا سر به بدن باشد این جامه کفن باشد
فریاد اباذرها ره بسته به بیگانه
لبخند سرودی کو سرمستی و شوری کو
هم کوزه نگون گشته هم ریخته پیمانه
آتش شده در خرمن وای من و وای من
از خانه نشان دارد خاکستر کاشانه
ای وای که یارانم گل‌های بهارانم
رفتند از این خانه رفتند غریبانه[105]

103 Farīd al-Dīn ʿAṭṭār, *Tadhkirat al-Owliyā*, Tehran: Manūchihrī, 1991, p. 515; also see P. Losensky's translation, *Farid Ad-Din 'Attār's Memorial of God's Friends: Lives and Sayings of Sufis*, New York: Paulist Press, 2009, 394–407; A.T. Karamustafa, *Sufism: The Formative Period*, Edinburgh: Edinburgh University Press, 2007, p. 25.
104 C.P. Melville, in *The Encyclopaedia of Islam, Second Edition*, s.v. Sarbadārids.
105 S.Ḥ. Ḥuseynī, *Guzīda-yi shiʿr-i jang*, pp. 99–100.

The loved ones, how lonely, are gone from this house,
Our candle, and the moth as well, have burned to nothing.
Our drinking bowls are shattered, and the blood in our hearts.
The one who drinks the dregs in the tavern laments aloud,
"Wherever I look, in every street,
ashes and blood, ruin on ruin.
A head with rose-tinged locks in a corner:
no hand to comb its hair."
"As long as our heads are on our shoulders, our clothing is our shroud."
The battle cry of those like Abu Zarr has blocked the road to strangers.[106]
Where is the smile of cheerfulness, intoxication and excitement?
Both the wine jar and the cup have fallen over.
The sheaves piled high have caught fire: alas, alas,
Among the motherland's ashes is the outline of my house.
Alas, my loved ones, the flowers of my spring
They are gone from this house, departed in loneliness.

This poem was composed when the oil-rich city of Khurram-shahr fell to the Iraqi forces on 24 October 1980. Iranians fought to free the city sustaining a huge number of casualties. The casualties were so high that people changed the name of the city from Khurram-shahr, "prosperous city," to Khūnīn-shahr, "blood-studded city." The city was liberated on 23 May 1982. As in the previous poem, this elegy is also couched in the form of a ghazal, using various classical literary motifs to describe the horrors and atrocities of war. The powerful opening couplet immediately captures the attention. The strength of this couplet lies in the paradox and the change of a classical Persian motif. The word *yārān* denotes "friends," "comrades" or "beloved" and is usually used in classical Persian amatory poetry to refer to the beloved, who is haughty, indifferent and conceited, but here the poet conveys how humbly, self-effacingly and particularly reluctantly these loving friends have left the lover's home. The beloved's shining and handsome appearance is commonly compared with the light of a candle, which gives light to the assembly of lovers, but here the poet ably transforms the cliché image of the candle and the moth to the reality of war: the candle/beloved is burned, together with the moth/lover. The poet keeps the audience's attention by introducing a wine motif in the second couplet. In this house the

106 This is a reference to Abū Zarr al-Ghifārī (d. 652) who, according to Shiite tradition, together with ʿAmmār ibn Yāsir, Miqdād ibn ʿAmr and Salmān-i Fārsī was one of the first four individuals who supported ʿAlī's claim to be the prophet Muḥammad's rightful successor. See H. Reckendorf, in *Encyclopaedia of Islam, Second Edition*, s.v. ʿAmmār ibn Yāsir; G. Levi Della Vida, in *Encyclopaedia of Islam, Second Edition*, s.v. Salmān al-Fārisī; J. Robson in *Encyclopaedia of Islam, Second Edition*, s.v. Abū Dharr Ghifārī. See also M. Momen, *An Introduction to Shi'i Islam*, p. 20.

wine-bowls are broken, metonymically referring to hearts as containers of wine/ blood. The faithful visitor of the wine-house, who drinks the dregs from the cups, is shouting and lamenting as he has nothing to drink. The poet places himself from the outset as the subject. In the third couplet he searches in every direction, every dimension, but sees nothing save ruins and ashes. In these three couplets the poet has already depicted a ruinous home whose love, light and supplies are violently destroyed. In the fifth couplet the poet gives one gruesome example of this assault when he refers to a dead person whose hairs are blood-stained as he has no hand to comb his hair. In the sixth couplet the poet is outraged. Having seen these horrendous assaults, he is emboldened to fight, shouting a popular slogan of those days, "As long as our heads are on our shoulders, our clothing is our shroud," willing to fight the enemy. While dwelling on the destruction of the home and the death of its inhabitants, the last line emphasises again how the loved ones are gone. It is in this last line that the poet gives some clue about the age of these loved ones. They are compared to flowers of spring, pointing to their young age, who, without having experienced life, were forced to offer their lives to defend their home.

In addition to the elegy's content, the poem is constructed in such a way as to maximise the effect of motifs, metaphors and imagery through internal rhyme and parallelism. In the first couplet the suffix *-āna* in words *gharībāna*, *khāna* and *parvāna* establishes the poem's rhyme but also the internal rhyme. While the suffix *-āna* is maintained in the rhyme-scheme throughout the poem, an internal rhyme is inserted in the middle of each first hemistich. Furthermore, this poem is one of the favourite ghazals to be set to music and sung by singers.In the musical performance, the singer does not follow the poem from the beginning to end, but repeats, for instance, the first couplet twice, and the phrase *ham sūkhta parvāna* or "also the moth is burned" four times. The first couplet plays as a leitmotif repeated several times between various couplets. Before bringing the song to a close, the singer repeats the phrase *raftand az īn khāna* or "are gone from this house," followed by repeating the first couplet twice. In this way the poet fully exploits the beauty and emotionally laden metaphors of the first couplet to rouse emotions. While the first and the last couplets are repeated several times, other couplets such as six and seven are deleted in the musical performance. The couplet "Wherever I look, in every street, ashes and blood, ruin on ruin" is changed to "Whenever you look, you make a hundred of memories / from those who travelled with a heart full of delight from this house."

While Beygī Ḥabīb-Ābādī's poem is a typical means of celebrating martyrs publicly, the following poem by Sāʾid Bāqirī, an unknown poet, gives a personal and honest picture of the human loss. The poem is entitled "The Wound's Bloody Tears":

یادگار از تو همین سوخته جانی است مرا
شعله از توست ، اگر گرم زبانی است مرا
به تماشای تن سوخته ات آمده ام
مرگ من باد که این گونه توانی است مرا
نه زخون گریه آن زخم ، گزیری ست تو را
نه از این گریه یکریز ، امانی است مرا
باورم نیست ، نگاه تو و این خاموشی؟
باز برگردش چشم تو گمانی است مرا
چه زنم لاف و رفاقت ؟ نه غمم چون غم توست
نه از آن گرم دلی هیچ نشانی است مرا
گو بسوزد تنه خشک مرا غم ، که به کف
برگ و باری نبود دیر زمانی است مرا
عرق شرم دلم بود که از چشمم ریخت!
ورنه برکشته تو گریه روا نیست مرا

My only memory of you is of a scorched soul,
    The flame is from you, although I have warm words.
I have come to see your burnt remains,
    Better I were dead, than to come to this.
For you there is no escape from the wound's bloody tears,
    For me there is no escape from constant weeping.
I cannot accept this silence, or the way you are looking.
    I could almost believe your eyes will move again.
How can I boast of friendship? My sorrow is not like yours:
    There's no trace of your warm-heartedness in me.
May sorrow burn my dry stem: for a long time
    I have had no leaves or fruit.
The tears that flowed were as sweat, for my heart was embarrassed.
    Otherwise, no tears for your killing would be allowed.[107]

Also this poem is couched in the form of a *ghazal*. Unlike in the previous poems, the poet does not openly employ standard classical motifs and metaphors, but rather recounts his own moving personal account at seeing the "scorched" body of his friend, returned from the front line. The way the mourning poet depicts this horrific sight is based on the use of certain rhetorical techniques used in classical Persian elegies such as *tajāhul al-ʿārif*, "feigned ignorance," not willing to accept that the person has been killed.[108] One of the strong virtues of this poem and its innovative appeal certainly lies in the honest and personal vent to emotions. The poem exquisitely expresses that such ideas as congratulation for

107 S.Ḥ. Ḥuseynī, *Guzīda-yi shiʿr-i jang*, p. 185.
108 For the technique used in Persian elegies see J.T.P. de Bruijn, in *Encyclopaedia Iranica*, s.v. Elegy; also see C.E. Bosworth, "Farrukhī's Elegy on Mahmud of Ghazna," in *Iran: Journal of the British Institute of Persian Studies*, 29, 1991, pp. 43–49.

the death and happily celebration for the loss of human beings are vain constructions and propagandistic attempts to manipulate people. The poet becomes one with the grief of his lost friend. The rhyme *-ānist marā* "-x is not for me," which is unfortunately lost in translation, emphasises the first person vantage point, inviting the reader to share the poet's pain and loss. The syntax of the rhyme is constructed in the passive voice, underscoring the poet's powerlessness and foregrounding the loss of the friend, who is the centre of attention. Also the use of the long vowel /*ā*/ at the end of the rhyme gives a sound of bereavement. When recited or sung each vowel comes to life, transforming the text into a symphonic tone poem. The poetic person in Ḥabīb-Ābādī's poem emphasises his shortcomings compared to the friend's scorched body. Although the poem's words are warm, the friend is the flame, while he weeps the wounds in the friend's body are literally shedding tears of blood, the commotion in the poet is contrasted with the silence and motionlessness of the friend. The metaphors of the last two couplets powerfully display the relationship. The poet uses floral imagery, comparing himself to a tree which lost its leaves and fruits a long time ago. The last metaphor is strong. Here, the poet uses the word *koshte* or "killed" instead of various synonyms for martyr, alluding to the practice of not weeping for a martyr. The poet cleverly states that the tears are not from his eyes but sweat running from his embarrassed heart.

Another poem written in the same context is the following ghazal, entitled *A Ghazal to Decide* which is dedicated "to the patient family of martyrs." This is a short poem, in which Qeyṣar Amīnpūr celebrates the death of soldiers:

بیا به خانه ی آلاله ها سری بزنیم
ز داغ با دل خود حرف دیگری بزنیم
به یک بنفشه صمیمانه تسلیت گوییم
سری به مجلس سوگ کبوتری بزنیم
شبی به حلقه درگاه دوست دل بندیم
اگرچه وا نکند، دست کم دری بزنیم
تمام حجم قفس را شناختیم، بس است
بیا به تجربه به در آسمان پری بزنیم
به اشک خویش بشوییم آسمان ها را
ز خون به روی زمین رنگ دیگری بزنیم
اگرچه نیت خوبی است زیستن اما
خوشا که دست به تصمیم بهتری بزنیم

Come, let us visit the houses of the tulips
　　And speak in our hearts about something else, about the brand-mark;
To convey sincere condolences to a violet,
　　To attend the mourning for a dove,
To bind our hearts to the iron ring on the friend's door.
　　Although he did not open it, at least we have knocked.

We know every corner of the cage, it is enough.
    Come, for experience' sake, let us fly in the sky.
Although there's virtue in wanting to live,
    How pleasing it would be to decide on something better.

The imagery and metaphors used in this poem are mostly drawn from ordinary Persian. The flora and fauna metaphors are cliché images used for martyrs. The tulip has been a symbol of martyrdom from medieval times, but it became very popular as a symbol for martyrs from the Constitutional Revolution (1906 – 1911) when the poet and singer ʿĀrif from Qazvīn (1882 – 1934) composed a ballad, "From the Blood of the Homeland's Youth ...," in which he commemorated the martyrs of the Revolution, motivating people to continue their fight for freedom and democracy. The symbolism is based on the red colour of the tulip and the black colour of the tulip's heart. The opening two stanzas combine wine and floral motifs with a curse at destiny, embodied by the Wheel. This ballad is known to all Persians as it has been broadcasted frequently on radio and television. The first two stanzas are as follows:

هنگام می و فصل گل و گشت وچمن شد
دربار بهاری تهی از زاغ و زغن شد
از ابر کرم خطهٔ رشگ ختن شد
دلتنگ چو من مرغ قفس بهر وطن شد
چه کج رفتاری ای چرخ! چه بد کرداری ای چرخ!
سر کین داری ای چرخ! نه دین داری، نه آیین داری ای چرخ!

از خون جوانان وطن لاله دمیده
از ماتم سرو قدشان سرو خمیده
در سایهٔ گل بلبل ازین غصه خزیده
گل نیز چو من در غمشان جامه دریده
چه کج رفتاری ای چرخ! چه بد کرداری ای چرخ!
سر کین داری ای چرخ! نه دین داری، نه آیین داری ای چرخ!

It is the time of wine, the season of roses and wandering in the meadow
The court of the Spring has been emptied of crows and rooks.
Thanks to a generous cloud, Khotan is jealous of the region of Rey.
Like me, the caged bird sorrows for the homeland's destiny.
How crooked you are, O Wheel! How twisted you are, O Wheel!
You are intent on revenge, O Wheel!
You have neither religion, nor convictions, O Wheel!

Tulips grow from the blood of the homeland's youth
The cypress's tall form is bent in sorrow for cypress-tall youths
In the shadow of the rose the nightingale writhes in sorrow
The rose, like me, has torn her robe.
How crooked you are, O Wheel! How twisted you are, O Wheel!

> You are intent on revenge, O Wheel!
> You have neither religion, nor convictions, O Wheel![109]

Coming back to Amīnpūr's poem, in classical Persian love poetry the lover usually compares his heart to the red tulip; the black heart of the tulip stands for the lover's burned heart. In such contexts, as in, for instance, Niẓāmī Ganjavī's poetry, the tulip is associated with the death of the lover, who is characterised as a martyr of love.[110] Such associations between the tulip and martyrdom have classical roots, but the connection to a political context is certainly new. This application of classical concepts shows both the resourcefulness of Persian poets and the resilience of such concepts in Persian culture. In the cemetery of Bihisht-i Zahrā or "the Paradise of [Fāṭima] the Resplendent," which is the chief cemetery for the fallen of the 1979 Revolution and the Iran-Iraq War, the tulip is widely used to remind visitors of the martyrdom of the youth. Red water perpetually streaming from a huge fountain in the middle of this cemetery symbolises martyrdom.[111]

The violet is another flower which in medieval Persia was a symbol of mourning. The colour of mourning was dark blue or indigo, but in Amīnpūr's poem the poet identifies the martyr with violet flowers to which he conveys

---

109 For a full translation of the poem and an analysis see Seyed-Gohrab, "Of Poetry and Politics: Poetry as Awakening," in *Literature of the Early Twentieth Century: From the Constitutional Period to Reza Shah*, ed. A.A. Seyed-Gohrab, London: I.B. Tauris, 2015, pp. 103–110.

110 Seyed-Gohrab, *Laylī and Majnūn*, p. 137; R. Zipoli, "Poetic Imagery," in *History of Persian Literature*, ed. J.T.P. de Bruijn, London: I.B. Tauris, 2009, p. 190; A. Schimmel, *A Two-Colored Brocade: The Imagery of Persian Poetry*, Chapel Hill & London: University of North Carolina Press, 1992, pp. 161–176.

111 See Hamid Algar in *Encyclopaedia Iranica*, s.v. Behešt-e Zahrā'. On this cemetry and especially the poetry written on graves see F. Shams, "Dialogues with the Dead: Necropoetics of Zahra's Paradise," in *Iranian Studies*, Vol. 53, Nos. 5–6, 2019, pp. 893–909; there are a large number of articles written on Iranian celebration of martyrdom. Here I mention the following publications referring to the celebration of martyrdom in Iran. *Unburied Memories*, ed. Pedram Khosronejad (2012), is the title of a special issue of *Visual Anthropology* in which various aspects of Iranian martyrdom celebration are examined. In addition to the excellent editor's introduction (pp. 1–21), the article on the martyrs' museum is invaluable research: C. Gruber, "The Martyrs' Museum in Tehran: Visualizing Memory in Post-Revolutionary Iran," in *Visual Anthropology*, 25, 1–2, 2012, pp. 68–97; there are also several articles on the celebration of martyrdom in the form of mural paintings. See C. Gruber, "The Writing is on the Wall: Mural Arts in Post-Revolutionary Iran," in *Persica: Annual of the Dutch-Iranian Society*, 22, 2008, pp. 15–46. U. Marzolph, "The Martyr's Way to Paradise: Shiite Mural Art in the Urban Context," in *Ethnologia Europaea*, 33, 2, 2003, pp. 87–98. Also see Pamela Karimi, "Imagining Warfare, Imaging welfare: Tehran's Post Iran-Iraq War Murals and their Legacy," in *Persica: Annual of the dutch-Iranian Society*, 22, 2008, pp. 47–63.

his condolences. The association of the violet with suffering comes from its form and colour. As Riccardo Zipoli describes it, "The dark blue colour and curved stem lend it in the shape of a stooping blue-frocked ascetic or a person bent over in mourning and lament."[112]

It is noteworthy to see how the poetic persona is willing to die and to be united with the loved one. Although the poet is conveying his condolences, he also invites the audience to welcome death. The imperative "come" in the first couplet is explicit in the second and the third couplet, in which the audience is invited to visit, to convey condolences and to knock on the friend's door. Death is not depicted here; rather it is symbolised by a door, an opening to another world, the spiritual world. The word "friend" can mean either the lost friend or God in the Persian original, implying that the poet has exerted himself to enter the house but he is not allowed to enter. The closed door is used here to emphasise the exalted position of the dead person who in such poems is usually identified as a martyr. By using the metaphor of the closed door, the poet is implicitly exalting the martyr's position. The rejected guest does not give up, as in the next couplet he emphasises that he has experienced every corner of this cage, i.e., the world, and wishes to fly. In this experience of flight, he invites the audience to join him. The final couplet is a vibrant renunciation of life, the guest preferring a martyr's death, which offers eternal life, to a temporary life on earth. Amīnpūr's imagery of death as a door reminds me of my favourite medieval Persian poet Niẓāmī's description of death in his monumental poem *Leylī and Majnūn,* in which he depicts death as moving from one place to another:

گر مرگ رسد چرا هراسم
کان راه به تست می‌شناسم
این مرگ نه، باغ و بوستانست
کو راه سرای دوستانست
تا چند کنم ز مرگ فریاد
چون مرگ ازوست مرگ من باد
گر بنگرم آن چنان که رایست
این مرگ نه مرگ نقل جایست
از خورد گهی به خوابگاهی
وز خوابگهی به بزم شاهی
خوابی که به بزم تست راهش
گردن نکشم ز خوابگاهش
چون شوق تو هست خانه خیزم
خوش خسبم و شادمانه خیزم

112 For the symbolism of these flowers and their colour see R. Zipoli, "Poetic Imagery," in *History of Persian Literature*, pp. 172–232; on violets see p. 188; also see H. A'lam in *Encyclopaedia Iranica*, s.v. Banafša.

Why should I fear death?
    The road leads to you, I know.
This is not death, it is a garden and an orchard
    This is the way to the friend's hearth.
How long should I scream, because of death?
    Since death comes from Him, may death be mine too.
If I see with the eyes of reason
    This death is not death but changing places;
From an eating place to the place of sleeping,
    From the sleeping place to the banquet of the king.
It is a sleep that leads to your festivities,
    I will not hesitate to go to this sleeping.

As I long for you, I will rise from the house
    I will sleep sweetly and rise cheerfully.[113]

Amīnpūr wrote another poem with an activist and revolutionary message, very different from the above poem in which the poem's persona is a martyr, speaking in plural form. The title of the poem, *Going Is the Thing* (*Raftan, risīdan ast*), points to the poem's message. The title can be literally translated as "Going is Arriving," or "Going is achieving the goal," by which the poet means going to the front line and arriving at one's desired goal. Before analysing the poem, I give the full translation:

موجیم و وصل ما، از خود بریدن است
ساحل بهانه ای است، رفتن رسیدن است
تا شعله در سریم، پروانه اخگریم
شمعیم و اشک ما، در خود چکیدن است
ما مرغ بی پریم، از فوج دیگریم
پرواز بال ما، در خون تپیدن است
پر می کشیم و بال، بر پرده ی خیال
اعجاز ذوق ما، در پر کشیدن است
ما هیچ نیستیم، جز سایه ای ز خویش
آیین آینه، خود را ندیدن است
گفتی مرا بخوان، خواندیم و خامشی
پاسخ همین تو را، تنها، شنیدن است
بی درد و بی غم است، چیدن رسیده را
خامیم و درد ما، از کال چیدن است[114]

We are waves, the shore on which we melt is far away,
    The beach is an excuse, going is the thing.

113 *Leylī-u Majnūn*, ed. V. Dastgirdī, chapter one, pp. 7–8; also see A.A. Seyed-Gohrab, *Laylī and Majnūn*, pp. 130 – 131.
114 S.Ḥ. Ḥuseynī, *Guzīda-yi shiʿr-i jang*, p. 161.

So long as there's fire in our heads, we are the moth to the flame,
We are the candle whose tears run down within it
We are birds without feathers, of a different sort,
Our wing-beats pound in blood.
We fly up, our wings on the cloth of imagination;
The miracle of our vigour is spreading its wings.
We are nothing but our own shadows
It's in the nature of a mirror that it does not see itself.
You said, "call me." We called, but you were silent.
Your response is only to listen.
The plucking of ripe fruit entails no pain or sorrow,
We are unripe, our pain is that we're picked unripe.

The poet identifies the speaker using "we" as soldiers who would like to offer their lives, but towards the end of the poem this "we" is transformed into those who are mourning for the dead. In other words, the narrator changes from "we" as martyrs to "we" as mourners. What is significant in this poem is the poet's integration of classical imagery into a modern context. An innovative aspect of the treatment of, for instance, the maritime imagery is that the narrator identifies himself with the waves. In classical Persian mystic poetry, the mystery is described as a pearl in the bed of a shell in the depth of the ocean. To reach this pearl, the mystic has to dive into the ocean, bidding farewell to his head, a symbol of rationality. Another dimension of this image is how the sea is personified as a lover; the waters are taken as tears and the shore as the dry lips of the ocean, willing to drink more and more to quench its thirst. In this poem the union is described as divesting one's ego of oneself, comparing the journey towards annihilating oneself to waves that are dashing on to the shore. This dashing of waves is characterised as a pretext, because the true purpose is to arrive at union.

This journey, based on mystical imagery, is further buttressed by another metaphor, i.e., the candle and the moth. In the same way as in the nautical metaphor, the poetic persona identifies himself with both the flame of a candle and the moth. In classical usage either the candle or the moth is the lover, but here the poet is leaving behind the classical convention. The speaker has fire in his head, a symbol of extreme love, identifying himself with the moth. What happens here is that the speaker assumes all traits of both fire and moth, becoming one with them. To complete the imagery, the speaker states that he is a candle that is shedding tears. Normally the wax running from the candle is taken in Persian to be the candle's tears, but in this case the tears are running down within the candle, an allusion to the fact that the candle is consuming itself and is dying.[115]

115 On candle imagery see A.A. Seyed-Gohrab, "Waxing Eloquent: The Masterful Variations on

In addition, Amīnpūr wrote several poems in new poetic form to mourn the casualties of revolution and war. The following poem is an exquisite example, containing new imagery, parallelism and a suggestion that what happened need not have happened.

افتاد
آنسان که برگ
آن اتفاق زرد
می افتد

افتاد
آنسان که مرگ
آن اتفاق سرد
می افتد

اما
او سبز بود و گرم که
افتاد[116]

Incident

He fell
just as a leaf
– that yellow incident –
falls

He fell
just as death
– that cold incident –
falls

But
he was green and warm, who
fell

The poet is here mourning the death of a young person ("he" could also be "she"). Composed in 1358/1979, the poem may be referring to the youth killed during the 1979 Revolution. The poem relies on parallelism. The first two stanzas have exactly the same number of letters and syllables. There is an internal rhyme

Candle Metaphors in the Poetry of Hafiz and his Predecessors," in *Metaphor and Imagery in Persian Poetry*, Leiden Boston, MA: E.J. Brill, 2012, pp. 81–123; also compare J.T.P. de Bruijn in *Encyclopaedia Iranica*, s.v. Candle.

116 Q. Amīnpūr, *Majmūʿa-yi kāmil-i ashʿār*, p. 372.

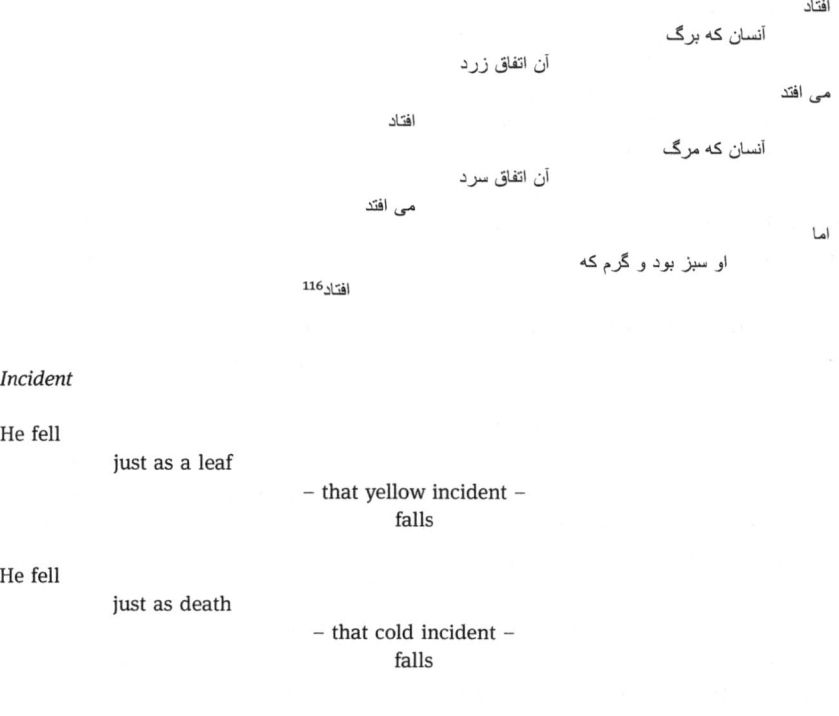

between *barg* / leaf and *marg* / death, which contrast with *zard* / yellow and *sard* / cold. Amīnpūr is inspired by classical Persian poets such as Firdowsī and Niẓāmī, who also use floral imagery to depict death. The falling of leaves when they become yellow anticipates the cold season. Yellow is the colour of decay, illness and death, but also of deep longing.[117] The last stanza tells us that while the leaves naturally turn yellow and death is by nature cold, what has happened in this "incident" is unnatural, as the person who died was green and warm. Green is often used in Persian poetry to indicate youth and vigour; it is also the colour of Paradise, the descendants of the Prophet and, together with red, signifies martyrdom.

The following poem by Ibrāhīm Bu'l-Ḥasanī describes how bombs or any other heavy weapon would wipe out any trace of the body of the fallen. During the war, the families of soldiers had to prepare themselves for the chance that their loved ones would die and the possibility that they would never see their sons again, dead or alive. The return of the dog-tag was the only evidence of death. In several writings of the "Sacred Defence Literature" (as the Iran-Iraq war literature is commonly called by the Islamic Republic) we see how graphic designers have used dog-tags to decorate the covers of books or pages within a book or a journal.[118] Bu'l-Ḥasanī's poem, *Dog-Tag*, refers to such a death, while pain, wonder and disbelief are foregrounded. The only solace for the author is that the soldier died a martyr's death:

و ناگهان خبری دردناك آوردند
ز رد پای تو يك مشت خاك آوردند
هنوز باورم این بود باز می‌گردی
برای باورم اما پلاك آوردند
به اشك و آه قسم، میهمان خورشیدی
که از تو خاطره‌ای تابناك آوردند
برای کوچه‌ی بی‌اسم و بی‌نشانی ما
به احترام تو يك اسم پاك آوردند

117 On the symbolism of colours in Persian poetry see R. Zipoli, "Poetic Imagery," in *General Introduction to Persian Literature*, pp.172–232. Schimmel, *A Two-Colored Brocade*, pp. 263–269.
118 On the various appellations used by the Iranian government to refer to the Iran-Iraq War see M.M. Khorrami, "Narratives of Silence; Persian Fiction of the 1980–1988 Iran-Iraq War," in *Moments of Silence: Authenticity in the Cultural Expression of the Iran-Iraq War, 1980–1988*, pp. 217–218. The war was called "the Battle of Islam Against Infidelity" (*jang-i islam u kufr*), "the Divine Test" (*imtiḥān-i ilāhī*), etc. Also see S. Gieling, *Religion and War in Revolutionary Iran*, London/New York: I.B. Tauris, 1999, examining how Iranian leaders sacrilized war, presenting Saddam as an unbeliever and Iranian soldiers as true Muslims, calling the war itself a blessing in the early years.

صدای زنگ درآمد دوباره می‌دانم
ز رد پای تو یك مشت خاك آوردند

Without any warning, they brought painful news,
    From your footprints they brought a handful of dust.
Still I was convinced, "he will return."
    To convince me, they brought me a dog-tag.
I swear through tears and sighs, you're the guest of the sun,
    For they brought a gleaming remembrance of you.
Our alleyway boasted neither name nor sign.
    Out of respect for you, they've brought a pure name.
The sound of the doorbell comes again, I remember again
    From your footprints they brought a handful of dust.[119]

Muḥammad-ʿAlī Mujāhidī, (pen-name Parvāna), composed the following powerful poem to commemorate the fallen. The poem is called *Memorial* and, as indicated by the poet in a footnote, the reason for writing this poem was therapeutic: "[i]n a meeting with a group of literati and contemporary poets in the town of Hoveyze to see the mass graves of anonymous martyrs, I was moved so deeply that I sought relief by composing this ghazal. I tried to paint the faithfulness of these dear souls, just as I felt it."[120] Another horrible aspect of the war was finding mass graves. Poems such as the one cited below are surely composed as a means to process pain and agony at seeing such shocking sights. Moreover, the poem shows that the regime's propaganda congratulating the parents and family of the dead person for an Islamic cause does not work. Before analysing the poem, I present it in translation:

سوخت آن سان که ندیدند تنش را حتّی
گرد خاکستریِ پیرهنش را حتّی
در دل شعله چنان سوخت که انگار ندید
هیچ کس لحظه ی افروختنش را حتّی
حیف از این دشت پر از لاله گذشت و نگذاشت
برگی از شاخ گل نسترنش را حتّی

---

119 S.Ḥ. Ḥuseynī, *Guzīda-yi shiʿr-i jang*, p. 175. Other couplets are added to his poem on the internet. The following two couplets appear after the second couplet of the poem cited here: "You were alive while they were speaking of your death / As evidence, they brought a frozen dog-tag. // Whatever had remained from your bones, Oh! / They had brought kohl for the eye of the wine rack."

تو زنده بودی و آن ها ز مردنت گفتند
پلاك یخ زده‌ای را ملاك آوردند
از آنچه آه! به جا بود استخوان هایت
برای سرمه‌ی چشمان تاك آوردند

120 S.Ḥ. Ḥuseynī, *Guzīda-yi shiʿr-i jang*, p. 81.

داغم از اینکه نمی خواست که گلپوش کنند
با گل سرخ شقایق بدنش را حتّی
داشت با نام و نشان فاصله آن حد که نخواست
بر سر دست ببینند تنش را حتّی
چه بزرگ است شهیدی که نهد بر دل تیغ
حسرت لحظه ی سر باختنش را حتّی
نتوان گفت که عریان‌تر از این باید بود
با شهیدی که نپوشد کفنش را حتّی
دل به دریا زد و دریا شد و اما نگذاشت
موج هم حس کند آبی شدنش را حتّی
بود وارسته‌تر از آن که شود باور پیر
جام می‌دید اگر می زدنش را حتّی
دوش می‌آمد و می‌خواست فراموش کند
خاطرم خاطره ی سوختنش را حتّی

His body so burned, one could see neither body
Nor the dust of the ashes of his shirt.
He burned so deep in the heart of the fire
That none could see when he dissolved in the flames.
It is not fair, he passed by this field of tulips,
But left us not one petal from the wild rose.
I burn, he would not allow us to deck his body
with flowers, with the poppy-red anemone.
So far detached from name and fame,
He did not wish to see his corpse carried on raised hands.
How great is the martyr who places the sword on his heart,
How great is the enviable moment of his death.
No-one could name a nakedness so bare:
A martyr wearing not even a shroud.
He threw his heart in the sea, became the sea,
Allowing not even the waves to feel his deliquescence.
With humility beyond the belief of the sheykh
He sees himself as a cup, even while draining the cup.
He appeals to me, longing to be erased from memory:
my memory, the memory of his burning.[121]

While the poet indicates in a footnote that he composed the poem on seeing the sight of the mass graves of anonymous soldiers, he has chosen in his poem to depict one soldier, exemplifying the rest. In the first stanza the poet captures the reader's attention by referring to the horrific way the soldier's body is burned so that only scorched remains can be seen. Choosing for this poem a ghazal form, which is commonly used for love and festivities, the poet uses familiar floral imagery not to celebrate sorrow, as we commonly see in a classical ghazal,

121 S.Ḥ. Ḥuseynī, *Guzīda-yi shiʿr-i jang*, pp. 81–2.

but rather to express sorrow in order to assuage pain. As in several other instances in such poetry, metaphors give way to reality. The poet imagines that the soldier, passing through the fields of tulips, did not leave even a sign of himself, indicated here by the wild rose. The wild rose may also metonymically refer to the fallen soldier. Torn flower petals are apparently the fallen soldiers. Afterwards, the poet connects the floral imagery with the dead body, complaining that there is no intact body to be covered with flowers, to be carried on raised hands. The poet soothes himself with the thought that the soldier has died as a martyr, envying such a death which, in his view, will be rewarded by martyrdom. In the last stanza the poet uses maritime imagery, implying that dying in such a way that nothing remains of the body is a sea. Using this imagery, the poet consoles himself with the thought that this death is so valuable that even the waves cannot feel deliquescence. The maritime metaphor rolls on to a wine metaphor in the next couplet. The fallen soldier is described as a wine cup that is consuming both the contents and itself. In the final couplet, while the poet conveys his affection, he interprets such a horrible death as an intentional way in which the soldier wanted to be erased from memory, to be physically erased in such a way that nothing of him would remain.

While the previous poems depict how war destroys soldiers, leaving nothing of their bodies behind, the following poem refers to another hard and horrendous reality of war. The poem is composed by the woman poet Zahrā Bīdakī and is called *The Anemone's Burnt Heart:*

باز امواج ملائک به تلاطم آمد
استخوانهای تو بر شانه‌ی مردم آمد
از حضور تو تمام سحر آکنده شده است
بوی گل در همه باغ پراکنده شده است
آسمان بار دگر داغ شقایق دارد
دشت در دشت زمین باغ شقایق دارد
دیدم امروز شقایق بدنی سوخته داشت
و شهیدی که به تن پیرهنی سوخته داشت
چه گذشته است گل من! خم ابروی تو را
و کدامین تبر انداخته بازوی تو را
ای که در غیبت خورشید دعا می خواندی
در فضا عطر تو پیچید خدا می‌خواندی
تو چه کردی که چنین صاحب سرمایه شدی؟
با خدای دل خود یک شبه همسایه شدی
کوچ کردند، کسی زآن همه ابرار نماند
غیر من هیچکسی لایق آوار نماند
روزگاری‌است اسیر غل و زنجیر شدم
من چه کردم که چنین خوار و زمینگیر شدم!
جان به لب آمده در خاک بمانم تا کی؟
و در این هی‌هی کولاک بمانم تا کی؟

شب یک پنجره را با تو سحر خواهم کرد
رو به خورشید از این شهر سفر خواهم کرد
ای کبوتر! تو بگوی آبی اشراق کجاست
و بگو سبزترین گوشه‌ی این باغ کجاست

Again the waves of angels are stirred in turmoil,
    Your bones are placed on the people's shoulders.
Your presence has filled the sunrise
    The scent of the rose permeates the garden.
Again the heavens mourn the anemone's burnt heart,
    For mile after mile the earth is spread with anemones
Today I saw an anemone, its body burnt
    And a martyr clad in a scorched shirt.
My flower, what has happened to you? Your face wears a frown,
    And whose axe has sundered your limbs?
You: saying prayers while the sun was concealed:
    When you called on the Lord the air was filled with perfume.
What have you done, that you have come into such wealth
    That you have become your dear God's neighbour, in one night.
They have all departed, none of those great men remain,
    None but I deserved these ruins.
For some time I have been in fetters and chains,
    What did I do, that I am so cast down, nailed to the ground?
My soul mounts to my lips: how long should I remain on this dust?
    How long should I remain in the tumult of the waves?
I will spend the window of a night with you; when dawn comes
    I will turn my face to the sun and leave this place.
O Dove, tell me, where is the azure of Illumination found,
    Where are the greenest corners of this garden?[122]

Using the form, themes and motifs of the classical Persian ghazal, Bīdakī starts her poem by a reference to the body of the killed soldier. Only the bones are put in the shroud to be carried on people's shoulders. Connecting this image with the waves of angels stirring in turmoil gives a double meaning to the opening line, as the killed soldiers can be the angels hovering in the town. It can also be the angels coming to greet the soldiers who died as martyrs. This is a cliché image, but the poet knows how to use this in the following lines to focus on martyrs. Having the same qualities as angels or being angels themselves, the martyrs have filled the horizons, giving a sweet smell to the garden. The poet accords a cosmic quality to the martyrs, assigning to them otherworldly powers. Afterwards, the poet refers to how the heavens are mourning for the anemone's burnt heart, an amatory motif from classical Persian, combined with elegy, i.e., the sun is mourning

122 S.Ḥ. Ḥuseynī, *Guzīda-yi shiʿr-i jang*, p. 85.

for anemones. In Persian dirges, heaven, the sun, the sky would usually mourn for the deceased.[123] The poet relies on this element and combines it with the symbolism of the anemone flower, i.e., martyrs. The image "mile after mile, the earth is spread with anemones," refers both to the field of anemones and to the boundless number of martyrs. After establishing this connection between flowers and martyrs, the poet continues to depict the martyrs in flower metaphors. This metaphor enables the poet to stress how innocently the powerless flower was injured by an axe and then was burnt. The phrase "saying prayers while the sun was concealed" refers both to the martyr's morning prayer before dawn as well as the early rise/opening of the anemones in the field. The poet continues in this fashion, but towards the end the focus changes from the martyr to the poet herself, her agonies and pains and her desire to be at the martyr's side.

Siyyid Ḥasan Ḥuseynī (1956 – 2005) is one of the prominent poets of the Iran-Iraq War. He has published several collections of poetry himself and has edited a volume of war poetry which has gone through several editions, the latest being from 2010. Many of his poems have been received positively among the revolutionary public. In the following forceful poem, the soldier's mute message becomes audible, expressive and touching through the poet's own interpretation of a soldier's death as martyrdom:

پیغام تو از وادی جانم گذرد
نامت چو زبانه برزبانم گذرد
شمعم که شبانه عابر یاد تو گرم
از کوچه مغز استخوانم گذرد[124]

The Martyr's Message
Your message passes through the valley of my soul.
Your name passes my tongue like fire.
I'm a candle. Your memory at night warms those who pass by,
Down the street of the marrow of my bones.

The poet is referring to an unspoken message that journeys through the valley of the poet's soul. By attributing a valley to the soul, the poet suggests a mystical context in which the soul develops through different stages/valleys to reach its destination, which is union with the Beloved. Using tactile imagery connecting "tongue" and "fire," the poet highlights how painful it is to have lost the soldier. This tactile imagery prepares the ground for the next cliché metaphor of the can-

123 See J.T.P. de Bruijn, in *Encyclopaedia Iranica*, s.v. Elegy.
124 Ḥuseynī, *Ham-ṣidā bā ḥalq*, p. 140.

dle and the moth. The absence of the moth, the perennial lover of the candle flame, highlights the soldier's absence, but the candle exists, giving light to and warming those around it. Likewise, only the memory of the soldier remains, warming the survivors. By comparing memories to a candle, the poet conveys how the memories arrive at night as a succour. The memory is both a solace and pain as the poet feels it even in his bones.

While these poems have poetic merits, deploying convoluted metaphors, some of Ḥuseynī's poems are mere propaganda for martyrdom, like the following:

بر عشق دوام میدهد خون شهید
از فتح پیام میدهد خون شهید
برخیز که با زبان گویای سکوت
پیغام قیام میدهد خون شهید[125]

The Message of Arising
The martyr's blood gives permanence to love;
The martyr's blood gives word of victory.
Rise! In the eloquent tongue of silence,
The martyr's blood gives word of rising.

2.3 Conclusion

While the cult of martyrdom remains a central icon of the Iranian Revolution and the Iran-Iraq War, and the Islamic Republic of Iran was successful in propagating this, the strategies exploited by the government to deal with death and the emotional impact of losing loved ones was certainly less effective as a random selection of the poetry of committed poets reveals in this chapter. As this poetry shows, dealing with the loss of human beings is hard and most of these elegiac poems have a therapeutic effects for the poets and families, rather than solely to celebrate the death of a martyr. Although it is hard to know through which specific channels committed poets were asked to compose poems for the funerals of dead soldiers, it is clear from poems such as the one by Parvīz Beygī Ḥabib-Ābādī that it is sheer propaganda to guide people's emotions in a certain direction, emphasising that these fallen soldiers are actually alive in heaven. This type of poem is certainly in praise of the cult of martyrdom, which does not always work to relieve pain, especially when such poems are compared to emotionally laden and personal poems such as the one by Sā'id Bāqirī. It is in such poems

125 Ḥuseynī, *Ham-ṣidā bā ḥalq*, p. 137.

that we read how the poet bursts into tears at seeing the friend's soulless body: "better I were dead, than to come to this," or "I cannot accept this silence, or the way you are looking."

3 Qeyṣar Amīnpūr on War

ای گل نه به سیم اگر به جانت بخرند
چون بر تو شبی گذشت نامت نبرند
گه نیز عزیز و گاه خوارت شمرند
بر سر ریزند و زیر پایت سپرند[126]

O rose! Not with silver, but with their souls, they purchase you.
When a night has passed over you, they will not even name you.
One moment they hold you dear, then they humiliate you.
[sometimes] they scatter you over heads, [at times] they entrust you under their feet.

3.1 Introduction

This chapter examines poetics forms, main themes and motifs in the work of Qeyṣar Amīnpūr (1959–2007), one of the poets of the Iranian Revolution and the Iran-Iraq War. Amīnpūr was born in Gotvand, a town near the city of Dizfūl in the southern province of Khuzistan.[127] After completing his education in Dizfūl, he went to Tehran to study veterinary science at Tehran University, but he abandoned this and moved into social sciences in 1978. During his studies he became increasingly involved with literary life on the campus, which inspired him so much that he abandoned social sciences and began a new study of literature. He completed his doctorate with a dissertation in literature under the supervision of the eminent scholar Muḥammad Riḍā Shafīʿī Kadkanī in 1988. After the 1979 Revolution, Amīnpūr and several other poets, writers and artists established the "Academy of Islamic Ideas and Arts" (*ḥowza-yi andīsha va hunar-i islāmī*), the aim of which was to promote Persian literature.[128] Together with Buyūk Malikī and Fireydūn ʿAmūzādih-Khalīlī, he founded the journal *surūsh-i now-*

126 The quatrain belongs to Sanāʾī and is cited by Ḥ. Āzād Tabrīzī, *Gulzār-i maʿrifat*, p. 56.
127 For a short biography of Amīnpūr see N. Farzad, "Qayṣar Amīnpūr and the Persian Poetry of Sacred Defence," in *British Journal of Middle Eastern Studies*, 34, 3, 2007, pp. 355–56; also see F. Shams, "From Revolution to Silence: The Political and Literary Life of Qaysar Amīnpūr," in *The Layered Heart*, pp. 551–588; idem, "Ideology of Warfare and the Islamic Republic's Poetry of War," in *International Journal of Persian Literature*, Vol. 1, 2016, pp. 5–58.
128 On the development of Persian literature after the 1979 Revolution see A. Karimi-Hakkak, "Introduction: Iran's Literature 1977–1997," in *Iranian Studies*, 30, 3/4, 1997, pp. 193–213; idem, "Revolutionary Posturing: Iranian Writers and the Iranian Revolution of 1979," in *International Journal of Middle East Studies*, 23, 4, 1991, pp. 507–531; also compare H. Yavari, *Encyclopaedia Iranica*, s.v. Fiction. ii(d). The Post-Revolutionary Short Story; K. Talattof, *The Politics of Writing in Iran*, pp. 108–134.

https://doi.org/10.1515/9783110748734-007

javān ("The Song of Youth") in 1988, aiming at discovering young literary talent who would produce poetry based on Islamic ideology. In the same year he continued his literary activities at the quarterly *Hunar* ("Art") and *Daftar-i shiʿr-i javān* ("The Young Poets' School"). In 1989 Amīnpūr first gained a position at al-Zahrā University for women, and two years later at Tehran University. He won several awards for his scholarly and artistic career, and was elected a member of the prestigious Academy of Persian Language and Literature in 2003. Despite his ill health he remained active in literary and cultural circles at various levels, but he died, aged just 48, on 30 October 2007.

Amīnpūr has a special place in the poetry of the Iran-Iraq War, which in Iran is called the "Poetry of Sacred Defence," due to the quality of his poetry written in classical forms such as lyric (*ghazal*) and quatrain (*rubāʿī*), and in new poetic forms (*shiʿr-i now*). Although his poetry is iconic among the poems of the Iran-Iraq War, he did not categorise himself as a poet of the sacred defence. Farzad says, "When asked for his opinion of the Poetry of sacred Defence, Amīnpūr commented recently that it is very difficult to sit in judgment on the literature or the arts of a fixed period and discuss the genesis of a genre, as these types of poetry or painting often emerge as an emotive response to a particular historical event."[129] Amīnpūr transcends the limits of a specific ideology, writing about a wide range of subjects within the broad context of Persian literature. His poetry in the ghazal form on love and longing, oscillating between profane and heavenly love, is as successful as his poetry about current social and political events. As an example, I cite the following ghazal entitled *One Letter from Your Name,* published in *Āyina-hā-yi nāgahān* ("The Mirrors of Suddenness") in 1993:[130]

حرفی از نام تو
ناگهان دیدم سرم آتش گرفت
سوختم، خاکسترم آتش گرفت
چشم واکردم، سکوتم آب شد
چشم بستم، بسترم آتش گرفت
در زدم، کس این قفس را وا نکرد
پر زدم، بال و پرم آتش گرفت
از سرم خواب زمستانی پرید
آب در چشم ترم آتش گرفت
حرفی از نام تو آمد بر زبان
دستهایم، دفترم آتش گرفت

129 N. Farzad, "Qayṣar Amīnpūr and the Persian Poetry of Sacred Defence," p. 357.

130 The poems in this collection were composed immediately after the war, between 1988 and 1992.

Suddenly, I saw that my head was on fire,
I burned, and my embers caught fire
I opened my eyes, and my silence melted
I closed my eyes, and my bed caught fire.
I knocked on the door, no-one opened my cage.
I fluttered, my wings caught fire.
Winter's sleep flew from my head,
In my running eyes water caught fire,
One letter from your name has come to my lips
And my hands and my book have caught fire.[131]

While this ghazal could effortlessly be read as conveying a mystic traveller's fiery longing for union with the beloved, it can equally be read as the poet's longing for a friend or a loved one. Its simplicity and the use of colloquial vocabulary, which speaks to readers of all walks of life, are conspicuous. The poet-lover is annihilated in the majestic presence of the beloved. The title of the poem, *One Letter from Your Name*, may refer to the Quranic scene in which Moses asked God to reveal Himself to him at Mount Sinai. This has been a favourite allusion for Persian poets from medieval times. Knowing that human beings, even the prophet Moses, could not bear to witness God's face, God bestowed no more than a glance on him so that Moses could perceive a small aspect of the divine, but this was enough to cause Moses to faint. Poets and Islamic mystics refer to this event in various ways. Jalāl al-Dīn Rūmī (1207–1273) says that in this scene Mount Sinai began to dance from longing and was reduced to dust.[132] This mystic undertone is present in much of Amīnpūr's poetry. He depicts contemporary social and political situations in Iran, but relies strongly on classical poetic and mystic traditions.

Amīnpūr became famous with his first collection of quatrains, *Dar kūcha-yi āftāb* ("In the Alley of the Sun," 1984), containing poems on a wide range of themes connected to the Iran-Iraq War. In this collection he included many quatrains of which the following is an example of his revolutionary sentiments.[133] In the following poem, entitled *Testament*, he depicts the last moments of a soldier, emphasising how content the soldier is to die. Dying is connected to love and the

131 Q. Amīnpūr, *Majmūʿa-yi kāmil-i ashʿār*, Tehran: Gulshan, 1391/2012, p. 299.

132 Jalāl al-Dīn Rūmī, *Dīvān-i Shams-i Tabrīzī*, ed. B.Z. Furūzānfar, Tehran: Amīr Kabīr, 1378/1999, Vol. II, p. 21–22, ghazal 562; Vol. I, p. 85, ghazal 130.

133 For a general overview of Persian quatrain see Seyed-Gohtrab, "The Flourishing of Persian Quatrains," in *A History of Persian Literature: Persian Lyric Poetry in the Classical Era 800–1500: Ghazals. Panegyrics and Quatrains*, Vol. II, ed. E. Yarshater, London: I.B. Tauris, 2019, pp. 488–568.

soldier is pleased to die for the beloved. As in many other poems, it is not clear who the beloved is: Imam Ḥuseyn, Khomeini or God himself. Each of these gives the poem a different meaning. With Imam Ḥuseyn as the beloved, the poem is placed in a Shiite context, and the soldier is offering his life to compensate for a centuries-old regret. When the beloved is identified with Khomeini, the poem becomes a political statement, showing the soldier's readiness to die for the ideals of the Revolution. Interpreting the beloved as God places the poem in a mystical context in which a metaphorical death, i.e., renouncing all worldly interests and attachments, is a condition for attaining union with the immaterial beloved. The last two verses emphasise the soldier's happiness as he dies with a smile. The title of the poem, *Testament*, creates expectations of some verbal self-justification, but here words fall short and only the gesture of a meaningful smile conveys the message:

وصیت
گفتم که چرا دشمنت افکند به مرگ؟
گفتا که چو دوست بود خرسند به مرگ
گفتم که وصیّتی نداری؟ خندید
یعنی که همین بس است لبخند به مرگ[134]

Testament
I said: "Why did your enemy throw you down in death?"
He said: "The beloved was pleased with death."
I said: "Do you have any last words?" He smiled,
Meaning, "It's enough to die with a smile."

Later he published *Tanaffus-e Ṣubḥ* ("Morning Breathing," 1984), a collection of poems on war in different poetic forms. These two volumes established him as a gifted poet, who was able to depict the horrors of war in new metaphors and imagery accessible to all people, and to draw on Islamic mysticism, the Shiite lore of martyrdom and sacrifice, and classical Persian poetry. Siyyid Ḥasan Ḥuseynī, a war poet and a historian of Iran-Iraq war poetry, opens his selection of Persian war poetry with the following poem, entitled *rāhī nā-tamām*, "Unfinished Road," by Amīnpūr:

راهی ناتمام
آن روز
بگشوده بال و پر
با سر بسوی وادی خون رفتی

---

134 Q. Amīnpūr, *Dar kūcha-yi āftāb* ("In the Alley of the Sun," 1984), as cited by Akbarī, *Naqd-u taḥlīl-i shiʿr-i difāʿ-i muqaddas*, p. 205.

گفتی
دیگر به خانه باز نمی گردم
امروز من به پای خودم رفتم
فردا
شاید مرا به شهر بیارند
بر روی دستها
اما
حتی ترا به شهر نیاوردند
گفتند
چیزی از او به جای نمانده است
جز راه ناتمام[135]

On that day
with wings open
you dived into the valley of blood
You said
I will not return home
Today I am leaving on my own feet
Tomorrow
People may carry me to the city
on their hands
But
they did not even bring you home
They said
Nothing remained of him
except an unfinished road.

The poem reflects the real willingness of certain Iranians to offer their lives, hoping to die in the front line to achieve the status of martyrdom.[136] Amīnpūr and other poets depict these volunteer soldiers who sought martyrdom using the metaphor of flight. In this poem the martyr has wings, which he has opened to dive down head first, to land in the valley of blood. Although the metaphors of flight are clichés – they have been used for more than a millennium in Persian poetry – when Amīnpūr transferred them to a war setting it had an enormous effect.[137] A metaphor of transcendence had been shifted to the gruesome setting of battle. Yet the force of such metaphors lies in their retaining mystic connotations which

135 S.Ḥ. Ḥuseynī: *Guzīda-i shi'r-i jang*, p. 23.
136 A.A. Seyed-Gohrab, "Martyrdom as Piety, Mysticism and National Icon in Iran," in *Der Islam*, pp. 248–273; also see M. Dorraj, "Symbolic and Utilitarian Political Value of a Tradition: Martyrdom in the Iranian Political Culture," in *The Review of Politics* 59, 3, 1997, pp. 489–521.
137 C.W. Ernst, "The Symbolism of Birds and Flight in the writings of Rūzbihān Baqlī," in *The Heritage of Sufism*, ed. L. Lewisohn, Vol. 2, Oxford: Oneworld, 1999, pp. 353–366.

are unspoken. In classical usage metaphors of flight are used in relation to the union of the lover with the beloved. The lover may fly to the end of the world to meet with and be absorbed in the reality of Truth, as in Farīd al-Dīn ʿAṭṭār's *Manṭiq al-ṭayr,* in which birds travel to meet their king and beloved one or, like the moth, fly into the light.[138] The term *wādī* or valley recalls the seven valleys of the journey depicted in ʿAṭṭār's *Conference of Birds.* Here, there is only "the valley of blood," and rather than giving concrete form to the abstract, the metaphor gives meaning to the concrete. Although "the valley of blood" is a new image concocted by Amīnpūr, classical poets, especially 'Attar, have emphasised that the road of love is filled with blood, implying that the lover should sacrifice everything, including his life, to achieve union with the beloved.[139]

The next section of the poem is narrated by the aspiring martyr, who is certain that he will not return home alive and that his death will be celebrated. The climax is towards the end of the poem when the poet indicates that the martyred soldier was not brought home, because nothing remained of him. This points to a new reality in modern warfare. Even thirty years after the war, families are still waiting for their loved ones, and occasionally soldiers' remains are found and returned, keeping the memory of the war alive. Some may interpret this as propaganda used by the regime to keep alive the memories of war, the cult of martyrdom and the image of the enemy, yet the fact remains that some families still live in hope of seeing their father or child again. While the poem starts as testimony to sacrifice and courage, the image of the unfinished road at the end has an element of an invitation to others to take up the task.

The idea of loss is imported by the references to flight and dying, and by the choice of verbs in negation, such as *bāz-nimīgardam* ("I will not return"), *nayāvardand* ("they did not bring"), *namānda* ("not remained") and the negated adverb *nā-tamām* ("unfinished"). The negations and disavowals are strengthened by the absence of the soldier, and the fact that his anticipation that he would be brought home and carried on the shoulders of the people is unfulfilled. In his short interpretation of the poem Siyyid Ḥasan Ḥuseynī sees this idea of loss in a positive sense. He states that when "travellers" go on a journey they leave behind many material things, which everyone can see, but it rarely happens that their spiritual remains are archived, "the spiritual weight of the

138 On the candle and the moth imagery see A.A. Seyed-Gohrab, "Waxing Eloquent: The Masterful Variations on Candle Metaphors in the Poetry of Ḥāfiẓ and his Predecessors," in *Metaphor and Imagery in Persian Poetry,* ed., A.A. Seyed-Gohrab, Leiden: Brill, 2012, pp. 81–123.
139 For an excellent analysis of ʿAṭṭār's story see D. Davis, "The Journey as Paradigm: Literal and Metaphorical Travel in ʿAṭṭār's Manṭiq aṭ-ṭayr," in *Edebiyāt: The Journal of Middle Eastern Literatures,* 4, 2, 1993, pp. 173–183.

poem *Unfinished Road* on this 'road' is a relic which creates responsibilities for the heirs."[140]

The choice of form is also noteworthy: not a classical form with a fixed metre and rhyme and conventional contents, but an arbitrary form. This allows him to insert pauses at specific places, creating astonishment, wonder and a feeling of forlornness. For instance, the word "but" is followed by a white space, indicating that the reader should insert a long pause before going on to the next line, "They did not even bring you home." This generates sadness in the reader, and at the same time makes the reader curious about why he was not brought home. The same technique is used in the next lines, when the poet puts the message in the mouths of others who report that nothing remained of the soldier. His only remains are his ideological legacy. The emphasis on the *unfinished road* is further underscored by a lack of punctuation marks, pointing to an on-going process. The poem finishes with the words of the title, completing a circle. The poet may be suggesting there is a closed loop of events from which one cannot escape. In this reading, "Unfinished Road" tells us that the road can never be finished.

3.2 A Poem about War (1)

Amīnpūr's reputation as a war poet centres on *A Poem about War*, which is certainly one of the masterpieces of Iran-Iraq war poetry in Persian, vividly depicting the horrors the war introduced into domestic lives. It was one of the first poems to describe the effects of war. I have translated it in full below, drawing on a translation by Narguess Farzad.[141] For this poem Amīnpūr adopted the loose form of "new poetry," which complements the poem's fractured subject, giving extra vigour to its colloquial language. Many of the shorter sentences below are a single word in the original. The empty spaces between unequal lines match the empty spaces in the bombed town.

شعری برای جنگ *A Poem about War*

می خواستم I set out
شعری برای جنگ بگویم to write a poem about war.

140 S.Ḥ. Ḥuseynī: *Guzīda-i shi'r-i jang*, p. 24.

141 Farzad, "Qayṣar Amīnpūr and the Persian Poetry of Sacred Defence," pp. 351–374; for an analysis of the poem see F. Shams, *A Revolution in Rhyme*, pp. 207–220.

142 Amīnpūr, *Majmū'a-yi kāmil-i ash'ār*, pp. 382–389.

دیدم نمی شود	I realised it cannot be.
دیگر قلم زبان دلم نیست	The pen is no longer the tongue of my heart.
گفتم :	I said:
باید زمین گذاشت قلمها را	"Pens should be thrown away."
دیگر سلاح سرد سخن کارساز نیست	The weaponry of words is no longer effective.
باید سلاح تیزتری برداشت	Sharper weapons are required.
باید برای جنگ	To speak of war, I must declaim
از لوله ی تفنگ بخوانم	about a gun and its barrel
- با واژه ی فشنگ -	– With words as bullets –
می خواستم	
شعری برای جنگ بگویم	I set out
شعری برای شهر خودم – دزفول -	to write a poem about war,
دیدم که لفظ ناخوش موشک را	A poem about my town – Dizfūl –
باید به کار برد	I realised I would have to use
اما	the unpleasant word "missile."
موشک	But "missile"
زیبایی کلام مرا می کاست	would reduce the beauty of my words.
گفتم که بیت ناقص شعرم	I said to myself that the deformed lines of my poem
از خانه های شهر که بهتر نیست	Are no better than the houses in the town.
بگذار شعر من هم	Let my poem
چون خانه های خاکی مردم	like the people's clay houses
خرد و خراب باشد و خون آلود	be shattered, ruined, soaked in blood.
باید که شعر خاکی و خونین گفت	What is needed is a poem filled with dust and blood
باید که شعر خشم بگویم	I must compose a poem of fury
شعر فصیح فریاد	An eloquent poem, full of clamour
- هر چند ناتمام -	– Even incomplete –
گفتم :	I said;
در شهر ما	In our town
دیوارها دوباره پر از عکس لاله هاست	the walls are again covered with pictures of tulips
اینجا	Here
وضعیت خطر گذرا نیست	The state of high alert never ends
آژیر قرمز است که می نالد	It is the red-alert siren that is howling.
تنها میان ساکت شبها	Lonely in the silences of night,
بر خواب ناتمام جسدها	over the unfinished sleep of corpses
خفاشهای وحشی دشمن	The enemy's savage bats
حتی ز نور روزنه بیزارند	are greedy, even for the light from a tiny opening.
باید تمام پنجره ها را	
با پرده های کور بپوشانیم	We must cover all the windows
اینجا	With heavy curtains
دیوار هم	Here,
دیگر پناه پشت کسی نیست	Not even the walls
کاین گور دیگری است که استاده است	shelter or support anyone.
در انتظار شب	Walls are graves standing upright,
دیگر ستارگان را	waiting for nightfall.
حتی	
هیچ اعتماد نیست	Even the stars
شاید ستاره ها	are no longer to be trusted.

شبگردهای دشمن ما باشند	They could be
اینجا	the enemy's night patrols.
حتی	Here,
از انفجار ماه تعجب نمی کنند	People were not astonished
اینجا	Even by the moon exploding!
تنها ستارگان	
از برجهای فاصله می بینند	Here,
که شب	only the stars,
چه قدر موقع منفوری است	from their distant watch-towers
اما اگر ستاره زبان می داشت	see how abhorrent night has become.
چه شعرها که از بد شب می گفت	But if stars had tongues
گویاتر از زبان من گنگ	What poems they would recite, on the evils of the night,
	more eloquent than my muted speech.
آری	
شب موقع بدی است	Yes,
هر شب تمام ما	The nights are bad.
با چشم های زل زده می بینیم	Every night, we all watch
عفریت مرگ را	with staring eyes
کابوس آشنای شب کودکان شهر	the demon of death.
هر شب لباس واقعه می پوشد	Every night, the familiar nightmare of the town's little children
	pulls on the garment of reality.
اینجا	
هر شام خامشانه به خود گفته ایم :	Here,
شاید	at every nightfall,
این شام ، شام آخر ما باشد	we silently tell ourselves:
	perhaps
اینجا	tonight will be our last.
هر شام خامشانه به خود گفته ایم :	Tonight
امشب	in the clay houses soaked in sleep
در خانه های خاکی خواب آلود	which wakeful mother will it be,
جیغ کدام مادر بیدار است	whose cry is dried out,
که در گلو نیامده می خشکد ؟	not even reaching her throat?

اینجا	Here,
گاهی سر بریده ی مردی را	we must sometimes bring
تنها	just the cut-off head of a man
باید ز بام دور بیاریم	from a far-off roof,
تا در میان گور بخوابانایم	to lay it to sleep in a grave.

یا سنگ و خاک و آهن خونین را	Or when we dig with our nails and claws
وقتی به چنگ و ناخن خود می کنیم	through bloodied stones, earth, and metal,
در زیر خاکِ گل شده می بینیم :	we see, under the muddied earth,
زن روی چرخ کوچک خیاطی	a woman silenced,
خاموش مانده است	leaning over a small sewing machine.

اینجا سپور هر صبح	Here, every morning, the dustman carries away
	The ashes of someone who was loved.

خاکستر عزیز کسی را
همراه می برد
اینجا برای ماندن
حتی هوا کم است
اینجا خبر همیشه فراوان است
اخبار بارهای گل و سنگ
بر قلبهای کوچک
در گورهای تنگ
اما
من از درون سینه خبر دارم
از خانه های خونین
از قصه ی عروسک خون آلود
از انفجار مغز سری کوچک
بر بالشی که مملو رویاهاست
- رویای کودکانه ی شیرین -
از آن شب سیاه
آن شب که در غبار
مردی به روی جوی خیابان
خم بود
با چشم های سرخ و هراسان
دنبال دست دیگر خود می گشت

باور کنید
باور کنید
من با دو چشم مات خودم دیدم
که کودکی ز ترس خطر تند می دوید
اما سری نداشت
لختی دگر به روی زمین غلتید
و ساعتی دگر
مردی خمیده پشت و شتابان
سر را به ترک بند دوچرخه
سوی مزار کودک خود می برد
چیزی درون سینه ی او کم بود.
اما
این شانه های گرد گرفته
چه ساده و صبور
وقت وقوع فاجعه می لرزند
اینان
هر چند
بشکسته زانوان و کمرهاشان
استاده اند فاتح و نستوه
- بی هیچ خان و مان -
در گوششان کلام امام است
- فتوای استقامت و ایثار -
بر دوششان درفش قیام است
باری

Here, there is not even enough air to stay,
Here, there is always plenty of news.
But
I have news from the heart,
From the heart in my mother's chest,
From the gleaming in my brother's moistening eyes.
I will give you other news:
News of pieces of mud and stone,
        on tiny hearts,
        in narrow graves.
News of blood-soaked houses,
the story of a bloodied doll,
of the bursting of a tiny brain
        on a pillow full of dreams
– sweet childlike dreams –
of that black night
that night of churning dust
when a man bent over the gutter,
with red and anxious eyes,
searching for his other hand.

Believe me,
Believe me.
I saw with my own two, bewildered, eyes
A child running swiftly in terror,
But he had no head.
A moment later, he rolled on the ground.
And soon after that,
A bent man came hurrying, carrying the head on the back of his bicycle
to the grave of his child!
Something was missing inside his chest ...
But
these dust-covered shoulders,
how artless and enduring
shook at the catastrophe.
Although
Their knees and backs are broken,
They are standing victorious and resolute
– without any house or shelter –
The Imam's words are in their ears,
a *fatwa* of resolution and sacrifice.
On their shoulders, they bear the banners of defiance.
Surely,
Even the walls could not bear to hear
these fiery words from my heart.

این حرفهای داغ دلم را	Can you bear to hear them?
دیوار هم توان شنیدن نداشته است	Walls?
آیا تو را توان شنیدن هست ؟	Cold, stony and moving walls!
دیوار !	Is it fitting that you remain dead,
دیوار سرد سنگی سیار !	Bound as you are to remain alive?
آیا رواست مرده بمانی	No!
در بند آنکه زنده بمانی ؟	So long as the cry "my child, my child" has not dried up,
نه !	we should burn our mothers' throats
باید گلوی مادر خود را	with the cry, "my child, my child
از بانگ رود رود بسوزانیم	We should take up a sharper weapon:
تا بانگ رود رود نخشکیده است	As the cold weapon of words is no longer effective."
باید سلاح تیز تری برداشت	
دیگر سلاح سرد سخن کارساز	
نیست[142]...	

The opening captures an Iranian reader's attention, as its new form breaks with the conventions, and because war is not one of the permissible subjects for classical Persian poetry. At the time this was written, in 1359/1980, Persian poets were just beginning to write about various aspects of war. Moreover, Amīnpūr is writing about a modern war, filled with guns and bullets. The poet realises that he will be required to use words that have not been considered suitable for poetry, such as "missile" (*mūshak*). And he will write in words that are also bullets. Each word is a bullet damaging the face of the poet's town and the people, destroying everything. Each word strikes the reader. The image of words that are bullets reverberates throughout the poem. As the subject is a town destroyed by missiles, bombs and bullets, it is only fitting that the poem's form is also fractured. The poet denotes the town several times using the adverb "here," usually followed by synonymous words such as *ḥattā* ("even"), *ham* ("also," "even") or *dīgar* ("no more") that emphasise the poet's bewilderment. The poet wishes to write a poem whose words are soaked in dust and blood like the town and its inhabitants. The poem also emphasises the people's resolve and commitment to resist the enemy, who are mentioned just once in the poem but are everywhere.

After an introductory section "saying" what type of poem the poet has committed himself to write, another "I said" marks the beginning of the poem within a poem, a physical description of the town. The walls are covered with pictures of "tulips" which are a metonym for photographs of the fallen, hung on the walls and decorated with flowers. But the same walls fall down, becoming people's graves, or threatening to do so at every bombardment. The situation in the town is so grave that sirens are continually howling the high-alert signal, telling people to take shelter immediately. Such shelters were not in fact available for ordinary people, so the sirens created mainly horror and confusion. This is the only sound people hear in the middle of the night, when Iraqi bombers come like voracious bats to feast on human blood. Paradoxically, these "bats" come looking for light, even a little light escaping from a carelessly hung blackout curtain.

The poem is set at night, a favourite setting in Persian poetry going back to the mesmerising descriptions of night by classical masters such as Firdowsī, Gurgānī (d. about 1039) and Niẓāmī. In classic poetry the night is not only an attribute of the story's setting, it is a symbol revealing the characters' feelings and moods.[143] The use of night as a setting in a poem on modern warfare was new for Persian readers, emphasising the emergency of the war situation. Although most of the bombardments took place during the day, cities were bombed at night, sometimes in the middle of the night. The falling of the night, the shimmering stars, the brilliance of the moon and the singing of the night-bird are elements originally used in Persian poetry to praise the beauty of nature and to lead to meditation on God's creation, but in this poem one cannot even trust the stars. They may be the lights of the engines of Iraqi Mirages, flying over towns and bombarding innocent civilians. In this way the poet adroitly highlights how war has changed reality: even nature can no longer be trusted. The nightmare of the little children is not a dream but reality, repeating itself every night. To emphasise this unbelievable transformation of nights from a time of serenity and peace to bustle and war, Amīnpūr changes the perspective by stating that "only the stars, from their distant watch-towers see how abhorrent night has become." The poet personifies the stars, enabling them to judge the night. These true stars are distant, unlike the lights of aeroplanes. If these stars had tongues to recite poetry, it would not be in praise of night. At this point the poet refers again to his inability to express what he sees during the night: the language of stars would be more eloquent than his "muted speech."

"The nights are bad" is a colloquial phrase Iranians repeated during the war, especially with regard to the city bombings. The nights were a time no longer for rest, but rather to escape from the houses, seeking a safe haven outdoors. The night becomes a demon of death visiting a different house every night, at random, and killing the innocent. This is exactly what happened in many families: every night at dinner people would think or say, "tonight will be our last night." The forceful simplicity of the description gives enormous vigour to the picture of people living with death hovering over them. Wakeful mothers in the clay hous-

143 See A.A. Seyed-Gohrab, *Laylī and Majnūn: Love, Madness and Mystic Longing in Niẓāmī's Epic Romance*, Leiden: Brill, 2003, pp. 314–319; D. Davis, *Epic and Sedition: The Case of Ferdowsi's Shāhnāmeh*, Fayetteville 1992, pp. 167–174.

es, watching to save their children from bombardments, are surprised by a death so sudden that even their cries die in their throats.

The picture of people at nightfall preparing themselves for death, or the death of a neighbour somewhere, is the first of several extended images of the detestable effects of the war, each heralded by the adverb "here," referring to the town. The second description is of the way body parts would be scattered in the town after a bombardment, and sometimes little would remain of a person: just a hand, foot or, in this case, a head. Amīnpūr conveys the emotional effects of finding such a body part and how respectfully people would bury it, "to lay it to sleep in a grave." The power of this image lies in the grotesque inversion of the night setting: someone was asleep, was a victim of random violence, and is again being put to sleep in a grave.

The next image is of people digging with their bare hands among the stones, earth and metal of destroyed houses, searching for the bodies of their loved ones. Death takes bizarre forms: not only the absurd violence of the head thrown onto a roof, but also the sudden stilling of the innocent: "we see, under the muddied earth / a woman silenced, / leaning over a small sewing machine." The terrors of war intrude into the most mundane daily activities. In Iranian towns the rubbish is collected every day from the streets. But in this poem, some of what a dustman collects would be the ashes of a body, burned during the night's bombardment. In such a horrible situation there is not even enough air to breathe. To remain in such conditions is inconceivable.

Having described a few horrific scenes from the war-stricken town, the poet says that there is always plenty of war news, but that he has news of a different kind. Not the news of war bulletins, but news from the hearts of mothers, news inferred from his brothers' moist eyes, news of the deaths of tiny children buried in narrow graves, of their dolls soaked in blood, of houses besmirched with blood and of a tiny brain burst "on a pillow full of dreams." These elements became the subjects of other poems, by Amīnpūr himself or by other Persian war poets. For instance, in a quatrain entitled *Qiṣṣa-yi jang* or "The Story of War," Amīnpūr refers to a doll:

قصه جنگ
موسیقی شهر بانگ "رودارود" است
خنیاگری آتش و رقص دود است
برخاک خرابه ها بخوان قصه جنگ
از چشم عروسکی که خون آلود است[144]

144 In Dizfūl and the Khuzestan province the word for child is *rūd*. Mothers would lament at

> The Story of War
> The music of the town is the shout "O my child"
> the fire plays music and the smoke dances.
> Read in the dust of the ruins the tale of war
> read from the blood-filled eye of a doll.

Amīnpūr is again using familiar metaphors in a new context to make his depiction forceful. The reference to the music of the town might point to Ābādān, which was a resort town before the 1979 Revolution, so that at the beginning of the war the city was still associated with leisure in the minds of Iranians. The poet effectively brings the connotations of pleasure into a war setting by personifying fire as a musician, a novel image, and by making the smoke a dancer. The next two lines surprise the reader with a direct and effective image: the reader is to read the story through the bloodied eyes of a doll, where the story is written in the dust produced by the destruction of houses. The poet does not need to tell the story of the war: the reader can fill it in from the doll, its eyes covered with blood. Other poets took up the image of the doll, and not only in admiration for the image of this poem which so captures the horrors of war: the fact is that thousands of small children were killed, some of them hugging their dolls.

Coming back to *A Poem about War*, the poet returns to his person experiences. The first is of seeing a man, in a shell-shocked state following a bombardment, searching with red and anxious eyes for his amputated hand, in a night of churning dust. Another horrible image is that of a child continuing to run, briefly, without his head. A little later he sees a man carrying the child's head for burial. At this point the poem takes an ideological turn, emphasising the solidity and resistance of the people and the leadership of Khomeini, the Imam, who preached fortitude, determination and sacrifice during the 1979 Revolution and during the war. Yet while the poet supports Khomeini's message, he does not allow it the last word: that goes to the lament of mothers for their children.

The poem is a powerful depiction of the horrors of war. A Persian reader is struck from the beginning by the colloquial language and new poetic form. It is as if the poet is pouring out his heart about all the traumatic events he has experienced. The colloquial form, without convoluted imagery and metaphors, is the strength of the poem, while its weakness is in the ideological turn, and the call to readers who are indifferent to the war, like "cold, stony and moving walls." He clearly feels frustration and anger here, but it is not clear who these "cold walls" are. He might be pointing to Western countries that did nothing,

---

their children's graves, calling *rūda, rūda*, "o my child, o my child." Amīnpūr, *Majmūʿa-yi kāmil-i ashʿār*, p. 441.

and even supported the Iraqi regime with conventional and chemical weapons.[145] In this poem Amīnpūr vividly describes what many Iranians, and not just those in the cities near the Iraqi border, experienced. Dizfūl could be a metaphor for the whole of Iran, the atrocities of this war are a universal metaphor for war. One of the poem's many virtues is how vigorously it persuades the reader that war in any form, at any time and place, should be condemned. The universalistic message of the poem is not thematised. Unlike the poetry on the Great War, in which British poets removed the sense of "us" and "them," interpreting all people involved in the war as victims, in this poem we do not see perspectives of the other, the doubts of the attackers, and the suffering and death of the enemy. While condemning war by depicting horrifying events, the poem still invites people to take up arms.

3.3 A Poem about War (2)

Most collections of Iran-Iraq war poetry do not mention a "sequel" to Amīnpūr's successful *A Poem about War.*[146] The second "Poem about War" is included in Akbarī's *Naqd*, in which the compiler indicates in a footnote that he has quoted the poem from Amīnpūr's poetic collection entitled *Tanaffus-i ṣubḥ* ("Morning's Breathing"), which appeared for the first time in 1984.[147] It is not in the subsequent editions that I have seen or in Amīnpūr's collected poetry. It is not clear whether Amīnpūr himself removed it from his collected poetry. Compared to the first part, the second part of *A Poem about War* is more about politics and its poetic flavour is reduced. In the first "Poem about War" the poet emphasises the atrocities of the war, suggesting that war should be stopped as it causes destruction, but in the second part the poet calls for action through slogans such as "It is time to perform the prayer 'death to the U.S.,'" alluding to the support of the West, and especially the United States, for Saddam Hussein, and to the slogans that revolutionary Iranians shouted at Friday prayers throughout Iran. While the strength of the first poem lies in revealing the poet's inability to depict the war, in the second "Poem about War" he comes to the fore as a determined person who wants to take action. Poetry is not enough. He uses phrases such as "Your poem is embarrassed to speak," and he desires to be "in the midst of

---

145 S. Taheri Shemirani, "The War of the Cities," in *The Iran-Iraq War: The Politics of Aggression*, ed. F. Rajaee Gainesville Florida: University of Florida Press, 1993, pp. 31–40.
146 See *Naqd-u taḥlīl-i shiʿr-i difāʿ-i muqaddas*, Vol. I, ed. M. Akbarī, Tehran: Sāzmān-i madārik-i farhangī-yi inqilāb-i islāmī, 1377/1998, pp. 117–122.
147 See *Naqd-u taḥlīl-i shiʿr-i difāʿ-i muqaddas*, Vol. I, p. 122.

events," i. e., the front line, in order to compose the poem. The first poem could be interpreted as being against war, as it suggests that its horrors and traumas should be avoided, but the second part stirs the reader to fight. But it is not a fight against Iraq, nor a struggle to obtain martyrdom and union with the beloved. It is a battle with the pen or anything else that comes to hand, perhaps a struggle to break a bubble of unreality, a deep questioning of the relevance of poetry itself.

The inclusion of the second poem in the volume *Naqd-u taḥlīl-i shiʿr-i difāʿ-i muqaddas* and its omission from the poet's collected works are significant, but we do not know whether the change stems from Amīnpūr's ideological shift to a more distanced poet shunning radical ideologies, or from the fact that he was not happy with its poetic quality, or a combination of the two. Its initial inclusion may reflect the swift pace of events after the Revolution, when poets wrote for a cause before they had the time to reflect and deliberate.

Although many of Amīnpūr's poems, and the war poetry in general, are widely available on the internet, this particular poem is not. I present the entire poem together with its translation, not only because it is a rare example in Amīnpūr's oeuvre of a poem that could be read as mobilising readers for war, but also because the text is hard to find:

شعری برای جنگ سرودم	I composed a poem about war
دیدم	I saw
حال و هوای جنگ ندارد	It does not have the air and temper of war
گفتم:	I said
شاید	Perhaps
ما هر چه گفته ایم	Whatever we have said
از جنگ بوده است	Was about the war
اما	But
ما جنگ را نگفتیم	We did not speak of war
ما جنگ را	We have only heard
تنها شنیده ایم	Of the war
یا از ورای فاصله ها	Or from beyond the voids
از دور دیده ایم	we have seen it from afar
اما	But
ما جنگ را نبودیم	We were not war
بودن	To be
یعنی میان حادثه بودن	Means to be in the midst of events
بودن	To be
نه گفتن و شنیدن و دیدن	is not to speak, or hear, or see.

148 The compound *namāz-i qaṣr* ("short prayer") refers to a shortened form of the obligatory daily prayer used by Shiites when travelling.

وقت حدوث حادثه باید بودن	To write a song
تا نغمه ای سرود	one should be in the midst of events
یک روز	One day
از باغبان شهرم پرسیدم	I asked the gardener of our town
اینگونه با شتاب چه می کاری	Why are you working with such haste?
خندید با دو چشم هراسان گفت:	He smiled with his two apprehensive eyes and said:
انسان	A human being
تازه نهال پرثمری را	A fresh sapling full of fruits
محصول عمر خود، پسرم را –	The harvest of my life, my son –
امسال	This year
محصول باغها همه لاله است	The gardens are yielding only tulips
امسال لاله زار " شهید آباد"	This year the tulip garden of "Martyr City"
آبادتر ز مزرع هر سال است	Is more productive than the fields of previous years
باور کنید	Believe me
اینجا	Here
هر چند خانه و وطن ماست	Although it is our home and our homeland
اما	Yet
ما هیچگاه قصد اقامت نکرده ایم	We never intended to stay
باید نماز قصر بخوانیم	We should shorten our prayers
زیرا مسافریم	For we are travellers[148]
جای نماز عشق همین جاست	The place to perform the prayer of love is this very spot
برخیز تا نماز بخوانیم	Rise, so that we may recite the prayer.
وقت نمازمرگ بر امریکاست	It is the time to perform the prayer "death to America"
تو از کدام حادثه می گویی؟	What event are you speaking of?
اینجا	Here
شعر تو شرم میکند از گفتن	Your poem is embarrassed to speak
آن قصه را که ورد زبانهاست	Of the story on every tongue
آن سیزده نهال بسیجی را	Those thirteen-year-old Basiji
که سبزناشده خط لبهاشان	With no dark down on their upper lips
-در خانه خدا-	–In God's house–
آنگونه سرخ گشت سراپاشان	They turned so crimson from head to toe
درشهر ما بلوغ	In our town, adolescence
آن میوه است	Is the fruit
که نارسیده شاخه رها کرده است	That falls from the branch unripe
مرز بلوغ مرز همین خاک است	The edge of adolescence is the beginning of dust.
هر کودکی به جنگ نرفته است	Every child who has not gone to war
بالغ نمیشود	Will not reach adolescence.
اینجا همیشه مرگ	Here, death always
در رفت و آمد است	Comes and goes
اما	But
رویین تنان عشق	Those champions of love
بی اعتنا به عابر مرگند	Pay no attention to death, the passer-by
اینجا	Here
این چیز دیگری است که می جنگد	It is another thing that is fighting
نه ساز و برگ و آتش و آهن	Not the soldier's kit, the fire and iron
جایی که عشق جاری است	Wherever love flows
ایمان یگانه حربه ی کاری است	Faith is the only thing to do

آری حدیث جنگ در اینجا حکایتی است	Truly the war's event is the story here
اما	But
دیوار سرد سنگ چه داند که جنگ چیست؟	How could the cold wall of stone know what war means?
شاید	Perhaps it thinks of the war
او جنگ را	As the scarcity of our daily bread
کمبود خواروبار بداند	But in this place
	The meaning of war
اما	Is the shortness of life
معنای جنگ اینجا	The shortage of souls, and the dearth of safety.
کمبود زندگی است	Although
کمبود جان و قحط امان است	Faith is abundant in all this
هرچند	Truly
ایمان در این میانه فراوان است	At the time of the event, one must be there
آری	To write a song.
وقت وقوع واقعه باید بود	What event are we talking about?
تا نغمه ای سرود	What event are we talking about,
ما از کدام حادثه می گوییم؟	When we are standing outside at a distance.
ما از کدام حادثه می گوییم	We should be in the midst of events
وقتی که در کنار گود ایستاده ایم	so we can see with our own eyes
باید میان حادثه باشیم	The flight of two detached hands.
تا با دو چشم خویش ببینیم	O child! O paragon of Dezful
پرواز دستهای مجرد را	What do you want to say with your speechless eyes
ای کودک، ای نجابت دزفولی،	To us
با آن نگاه گنگ چه می‌گویی؟	-this crowd of watching poets-
ما را	Surely
-این خیل شاعران تماشا را-	We have felt the pain of war
باری	Solely
ما درد جنگ را	where the rhyme pinches.
تنها	Now, enough of line and rhyme
در تنگنای قافیه حس کردیم	One must go to war
دیگر ردیف و قافیه کافی است	With any weapon that comes to hand
باید به جنگ رفت	With spears, with pens
با هر سلاح و حربه که پیش آید	With anything, with nothing
با نیزه، با قلم	One must go to war ...
با هیچ با عدم	To see with the eyes
باید به جنگ رفت ...	The tearing up of the soul
تا انتزاع جان را	The stripping of the spirit.
تجرید روح را	You must see it with your eyes
با چشم بنگریم	You must have felt the beating
باید تپیده باشی	In the pulse of the event
در نبض حادثه	You must see it with your own eyes
باید به چشم خویش ببینی	One shadow —one tiny movement—
یک سایه – یک تحرک کوچک را-	That is erased,
که محو می‌شود	Suddenly
ناگاه	On the way to school
در راه مدرسه	Then
آنگاه	With a strutting tongue you would say

با لکنتی غریب بگویی:	This bag
این کیف	This bag full of blood,
این کیف پر ز خون	Whose is it?
از کیست؟	And you would look at yourself
و بنگری به خویش	Seeing that you have no hands, no feet,
که دست و پا نداری	That you could bear the bag away.
تا کیف را از آنجا برداری	And you would look bitterly
و تلخ بنگری	At a mother who waits for it
به مادری که منتظر اوست	–A continuous waiting without end
یک انتظار ممتد بی پایان	In the empty frame of a ruin –
در چارچوب خالی ویران	

This unusual poem lacks the poetic flavour one expects from Amīnpūr. With phrases and sentences such as "We have felt the pain of war / Solely / where the rhyme pinches," he probably wants just to show how the horrors of the war render other aspects of life, including poetic activities, meaningless. The poem artificially breaks at each joint, preventing any momentum from developing. It is as if the poet is abandoning his job as a poet, describing the events he is witnessing without a narrative development. Compared to the first *Poem about War*, it lacks vivid imagery and a climax. For me, there is only one striking image, which recalls another story told by various Persian medieval authors. It is the story of the pre-Islamic Persian King Anūshīrvān who is passing through a village and sees that an old man is planting a young walnut tree. The king is surprised and asks him what the use of planting such a tree is, as the old man will not harvest the fruits in his lifetime. The old man says, "Others planted and we eat, we plant so that others eat." Amīnpūr transforms this story in his poem showing how a gardener is hastily digging to plant something. When the poet's persona asks why he is working in such haste, the gardener says that what he is planting is "a fresh sapling full of fruits / The harvest of my life, my son." Such shocking imagery focuses on the worst fears of war. Such events, such a loss, cannot be put into poetry. The inadequacy of poetry is indicated in several places: "Your poem is embarrassed to speak / Of the story on every tongue." This refers to the killing of 13-year-old boys who do not even have dark down on their upper lips. After the passage cited above, where the poet says that he has felt the pain of war only where the rhyme is difficult, he states, "enough of line and rhyme / One must go to war / With any weapon that comes to hand / With spears, with pens / With anything, with nothing." While such lines convey the inadequacy of speech and art for the situation of war, they also contain a mobilising element, calling diverse people to defend the country with weapons, pens and even with their empty hands. The aesthetic of this poem lies in the comparatively limited use of imagery and figures of speech to convey self-contempt, doubting the value of art and one's own life in a situation where dying has become an everyday event.

3.4 Chemical Weapons in War Poetry

On 28 June 1987 (7 Tīr 1366), Saddam's regime used chemical weapons against the Kurdish population in four neighbourhoods in the city of Sardasht which, according to several reports, resulted in 119 deaths and over 8,000 casualties. On other occasions he used mustard and nerve gas against civilians. Perhaps the most shocking attack, and one that received international media coverage, was against the Kurdish town of Halabja on 16 March 1988. The pictures of innocents murdered in the streets, sometimes holding their small children, dumbfounded media audiences around the world. Saddam Hussein was widely condemned. There is a rich documentation of these attacks, their effects and the international responses.[149] They have had a deep emotional impact on Iranians, and stories and poems have depicted the magnitude of the human losses. The following poem by Amīnpūr dresses the attacks in aesthetic attire, illustrating how poetry functions as a channel for registering such events, and demonstrating poetry's therapeutic values. As Farzad rightly indicates, Amīnpūr's poems "encompass more universal concerns" than simply a specific event.[150] Through this expansion of scope he depicts the human condition amid the atrocities of war:

باران زرد

اخبار تازه را نشنیدی
گفتند:
وضع هوا خراب است
گفتند: آسمان همه جا ابری است
گفتند:
از سقف های کاذب سربی
باران زرد
باران شیمیایی
می بارد

149 A Dutch company, *FCA Contractor* based in Switzerland, was one of the main suppliers of chemical material to Iraq. The person responsible who worked with the Dutch Ministry of Economy, Frans van Anraat, was arrested and sentenced to fifteen years' imprisonment in 2005, but in 2009 his sentence was changed to sixteen and half years.

150 See N. Farzad, "Qeysar Amīnpūr and the Persian Poetry of Sacred Defence," p. 360, which includes a somewhat different translation of this poem.

گفتند:
گل های شرحه شرحه ی مارا
با داغ های کهنه مادرزاد
تشریح می کنند
گفتند: ...
اما
با این همه خبر
در عصر شب
در عصر خستگی
در عصر بی عصب
در روزنامه عصر
از شرح حال ما اثری نیست
در عصر خواب و خلسه و خمیازه
در عصر آخرین خبر تازه
از نام ما
در روزنامه ها خبری نیست[151]

Yellow rain

Haven't you heard the latest news?
They said:
"The weather is terrible."
They said: "The sky is cloudy everywhere."
They said: "From the leaden false ceilings,
Yellow rain,
Chemical rain,
Is going to pour."
They said they will anatomise
Our torn and shredded flowers
With the ancient brand-marks they were born with.
They said: ...
Yet,
Despite all this news
In the evening of the night
In the evening of exhaustion
In the evening without nerves
In the evening newspaper
There is no sign of explanation for our condition.
In the evening of sleep, slumber, and yawning
In the evening of the latest news
there is no news,
in the papers,
of our names.

151 Amīnpūr, *Majmūʿa-yi kāmil-i ashʿār-i Qeyṣar Amīnpūr*, Tehran: Gulshan, 1391/2012, pp. 331–32.

This seemingly simple poem depicts the chemical bombardment, its effects, how it is covered in the media, and the reception of the news. The first part of the poem is a kind of dialogue in which the poem's persona tells another person about the news, but he continues in a monologue to describe waiting for more news, for something that will give meaning to their situation. He interrupts the poem five times with the verb *guftand*, "they said." This reported speech creates distance and an air of insecurity, as the poem's persona cannot verify the news. He tells his hearer about the bad weather forecast and the clouds covering the entire sky. The unusual nature of the clouds is depicted with the image of the "false" ceiling, which is leaden: this can refer to the aluminium skin of aeroplanes or missiles, or to the clouds of chemical weapons pouring down, or simply the foreboding associations of dark clouds. The word *kādhib* means "untrue" or "false" which, in combination with "ceiling," heightens the insecurity of the space the poet is describing, as well as the unreal nature of the clouds.[152] The strangeness of these clouds is conveyed by the compound "yellow rain," a new concept for Iranians, which the poet explains by adding "chemical rain." In the next three lines the poet uses the vocabulary of a newscast. The central word is *tashrīḥ*, which in a medical context is to "dissect," or in grammar is "to parse," but generally means to provide a detailed explanation. A related word is translated as "explanation" later in this poem. The news programme promises to "anatomise" the "our torn and shredded flowers," a metaphor for loved ones. The repetition of the word *sharḥa* ("torn and shredded") reminds the Persian reader strongly of Rūmī's famous opening lines in the *Mathnavī*, in which he refers to a torn breast. The word is rarely used in other contexts. In one line Rūmī puts the word in the mouth of the reed flute which is complaining of being cut from its original abode, "I want a breast, torn in pieces because of separation / so that I can explain the pain of longing."[153] This intertextuality is in line with Kristeva's understanding of a text's emergence from the ""social text" [and] its continued existence within society and history."[154] Rūmī's opening

152 The word comes from the Arabic root *kadhaba*, meaning to lie, to deceive, to delude or to mislead.

153 Jalāl al-Dīn Rūmī, *Mathnavī-yi ma'navī*, Vol. I, ed. M. Isti'lāmī, Tehran: Zavvār, 1372/1993, p. 9. For life and teachings of Rūmī see F.D. Lewis, *Rumi. Past and Present, East and West: The Life, Teachings and Poetry of Jalâl al-Din Rūmī.* Oxford: Oneword Publications, 2000. A poetic translation by Alan Williams would run as follows:

"I need the breast that's torn to shreds by parting, to give expression to the pain of heartache." See Rūmī, *The Masnavi of Jalāloddin Rumi Book 2 The Ending of the Self, A New English Translation with Explanatory Notes Alan Williams With the Persian Text Edited by Mohammad Este'lami*, London / New York, I.B. Tauris, 2020, p. 5.

154 Graham Allen, *Intertextuality*, London: Routledge, 2000, pp. 36–37.

lines are so interwoven into Persian culture that each of his words, in other contexts, evokes a new layer of meaning. In this poem the "torn, torn" is linked with flowers, implying that the petals are ripped.[155] The picture of torn petals conjures up fatal wounding.

The *tashrīḥ* ("dissection") will include the deepest parts of the flower, which might be an anemone, tulip or the poppy, whose heart is black. The black hue in a tulip is described in Persian as being "brand-marked," while the poppy is known as the *dāgh-dār*, the branded flower. The tulip is associated with the passion of love, which often goes with suffering, and the brand mark is referred to as scars left by love's fire, which burns the heart. The brand mark is also evidence of the lover's enduring suffering.[156] References to tulips in Persian poetry evoke several such connotations, which influence the interpretation here. By referring to a flower with a brand mark the poet is saying that soldiers died as martyrs, as the tulip is a symbol of martyrdom in Iran. Instead of using mundane words for a horrific death by chemical bombardment, the poet chooses to deploy floral imagery that reinforces the innocence and powerlessness of the victims. The last part of the reported speech trails off, as the ellipsis indicates. In the last part the poet emphasises the end of things by using the word *ʿaṣr*, translated here as "evening." The word means "afternoon," but also "epoch" or "era." The "evening without nerves" could also be "the evening without ligaments or bindings."[157] While the poet uses this word in different pairings, giving different associations, all the uses point to a dark, unfeeling and exhausted state in which the "we" implied in "our names" are forgotten. Despite this chemical attack, there is no news in the newspapers about "us." Perhaps the poet is referring to the silence of the international community, who supported Saddam Hussein, providing him with chemical substances. The penultimate line *az nām-i mā* ("of our names") highlights this idea of neglect. It may also refer to how isolated Iran was from the international community during the war.

---

155 The word *gul* means rose in classical Persian poetry but in modern usage *gul* refers to the general category of flowers.

156 For the symbolism of the tulip in Persian poetry see J.T.P. de Bruijn, "Some strip of Herbage: Gardens in Persian poetry," in *The Authentic Garden. A symposium on gardens*, ed. L. Tjon Sie Fat and E. de Jong, Leiden: Clusius Foundation, 1991, pp. 123–130, republished in *Pearls of Meanings: Studies on Persian Art, Poetry, Sufism and History of Iranian Studies in Europe by J.T.P. de Bruijn*, ed. A.A. Seyed-Gohrab, Leiden: Leiden University Press, 2020, pp. 137–147.

157 In combination with the connotation of *ʿaṣr* as the ending of an era, one thinks of W.B. Yeats, "The Second Coming": "Things fall apart; the centre cannot hold; / Mere anarchy is loosed upon the world..."

The tone of the poem is sad. Yellow in Persian is associated with decay, and the word *kharāb,* which I have translated as "terrible (weather)" also means ruined. The word *abrī* or "cloudy" is associated here with demoralisation.[158] I have already noted the "false ceiling of lead," the torn petals of the flowers and the brand mark. The last lines refer to the darkness of the night, exhaustion, sleep, slumber and yawning. Altogether the poem has a dejected and forsaken tone.

3.5 Poems on Peace

While Amīnpūr writes poems on the horrors of the war, several of his poems are on peace. His *Ṭarḥī barā-yi ṣulḥ I, II,* and *III* is a "plan for peace" in three parts, which he published in *Dastūr(-i) zabān-i ʿishq* ("A Grammar of the Language of Love"). The first of the three poems starts with an amiable image of Persian family life. The narrator is distanced and is only depicting what he sees:

طرحی برای صلح (۱)
کودك
با گربه‌هایش در حیاط خانه بازی می‌کند
مادر، کنار چرخ خیاطی
آرام رفته در نخ سوزن
عطر بخار چای تازه
در خانه می‌پیچد
صدای در!
- "شاید پدر"![159]

A child
is playing with the cats in the yard
Mother, before the sewing machine
is immersed in threading the needle
The evaporating smell of fresh tea
has filled the house
The sound of the doorbell
– "that could be father!"

158 Clouds and rain are usually positive in Persian poetry, associated with fertility and experienced as a grace from heaven, but here the poet has associated clouds with a desolate tone. See Seyed-Gohrab, *Courtly Riddles*, pp. 172–175, and see the index under Cloud.

159 Q. Amīnpūr, *Dastūr(-i) zabān-i ʿishq*, Tehran: Murvārīd, 1387/1999, pp. 16–18; also see Amīnpūr, *Majmūʿa-yi kāmil-i ashʿār*, p. 15.

The poem's date is unclear. The first edition of this volume was in 1386/2007, after the war, but the poem is probably set during or soon after the Iran-Iraq War. The phrase "that could be father" demands an interpretation by the reader. The peaceful homely scene is interrupted by the sound of the doorbell. The exclamation mark emphasises this. The conditional "could be" suggests that the family has been missing the father for a long time and has been longing to see him at any moment. Perhaps the father is a prisoner of war or is missing in action, someone about whom no official report is available, and the family is still hoping to see him alive, joining the warm family circle.

By putting the words "that could be father!" in the mouth of the child or the mother or some other person present but not mentioned, the poet reduces the distance between the reader and the characters. The direct speech and the brevity of the call, "that could be father!" is so powerful that the reader is forced to go back to the beginning of the poem and read it again, to construct a story about whom these final words apply to, and what has happened. The title "A Plan for Peace" then has new significance. On first reading, the homely family setting could be a plan for peace, but this peace is apparently illusory, for it is disrupted by the sound of the doorbell. The reader is also not informed about the plan and what it contains.

The second poem, *Ṭarḥī barā-yi ṣulḥ II*, must be read as a continuation of the previous poem:

طرحی برای صلح (۲)

شهیدی که بر خاک می‌خفت
چنین در دلش گفت:
"اگر فتح این است
که دشمن شکست،
چرا همچنان دشمنی هست؟"[160]

A martyr was falling asleep in the dust
saying in his heart:
"if victory means
that the enemy has been broken
Why should enmity remain?"

Again, the poem establishes an apparently familiar picture. The poem is written in a social context in which martyrdom is idealised and turned into an ideology, but here the martyr wonders why, even after victory, enmity, which is the essence of war, remains. The martyr who questions what is achieved by martyrdom and

160 Amīnpūr, *Majmū'a-yi kāmil-i ash'ār*, p. 16.

victory clearly has another agenda, and not one which would have been either expected or welcome in a mobilised society. The message of the third poem completes what is implied in the second:

طرحی برای صلح (۳)

شهیدی که بر خاك می‌خفت
سرانگشت در خون خود می‌زد و می‌نوشت
دو سه حرف بر سنگ:
"به امید پیروزی واقعی
نه در جنگ،
که بر جنگ!"[161]

A martyr was falling asleep in the dust:
dipped his finger into his blood,
and wrote
two or three words on a stone:
"In the hope of real victory
Not in war
but over war!"

The messages many Iranian soldiers left in expectation of their own martyrdom usually encouraged others to follow their example. It was also the policy of the regime to encourage people to lay down their lives. But here the martyr is emphatically censuring war and bloodshed. In all three poems there is a sharp antithesis between presence and absence. In the first poem the father is absent and the family and household are remembering him; in the last two poems the martyr wants to leave something important behind as a legacy. While in the second poem the poet allows us to share the martyr's thoughts, in the third poem they are written. Amīnpūr is clearly showing how ideas about war, peace, enmity and martyrdom changed in the course of the war and the following years. In the first years of the 1979 Revolution martyrs were living examples for other people, but here the futility of laying down one's life is underlined. In earlier war poetry martyrs were supposed to write slogans such as *jan, jang tā pīrūzī* "War, War, till victory!" in their own blood. But here the poet first questions the validity of such sentiments, and points to enmity as the root problem to be addressed, and then unequivocally bids farewell to arms all over the world.[162]

161 Ibid., p. 17.

162 For an alternative analysis of these poems see F. Shams, *A Revolution in Rhyme*, pp. 282–285.

A strong feature of this poem is its visual and emotive components and structure. As we arrive at the end of the third poem, we cannot help but think of the first poem, the peaceful atmosphere the poet has created and the sudden disruption of peace by the phrase "that could be father!," creating a sense, a reminder, of loss. The family can never be complete and at peace unless the father, for whom the mother and child are waiting, can return. In Shahrīvar 1365/August-September 1986, Amīnpūr wrote another poem on the theme of a missing father. It is entitled *Ey gulhā chirā nimīkhandīd?* ("O Roses, Why Don't You Smile?") and is published in his *mithl-i chishma, mithl-i rūd* ("Like a Source, Like a River") collection. This is a dialogue between a child and his or her mother, and the mother promises that the father will return from the front with the arrival of Spring.

ای گلها، چرا نمی خندید؟

"پس پدر کی ز جبهه می آید؟"
باز کودک ز مادرش پرسید
گفت مادر به کودکش که "بهار،
غنچه ها و شکوفه ها که رسید"

باز کودک ز مادرش پرسید:
"کی بهار و شکوفه می آیند؟"
گفت مادر که "هر زمان در باغ
غنچه ها لب به خنده بگشایند"

روز دیگر سراغ باغچه رفت
کودک ما به جست و جوی بهار
دید لب بسته است غنچه هنوز
بر لب غنچه نیست بوی بهار

گفت:" ای غنچه های خوب، چرا
لبتان را ز خنده می بندید؟
زودتر بشکفید و باز شوید
آی گل ها، چرا نمی خندید؟"

گاه با غنچه ها سخن می گفت
گاه خواهش ز غنچه ها می کرد
گاه گلبرگ غنچه ای را نرم
با سر انگشت خویش وا میکرد[163]

O Roses! Why Don't You Smile?

"So when will Papa come from the front?"
The child asked his mother, yet again.

163 Ibid., pp. 476–477.

The mother said to her child, "In Spring,
when the blossoms and buds open."

Again the child asked his mother:
"When will the Spring and blossoms come?"
The mother replied: "Whenever, in the garden,
The blossoms open their lips to smile."

Next day, he explored the little garden.
Our child was searching for the Spring.
He saw that the bud's lips were still closed;
That the scents of Spring were not on the bud's lips.

He said: "O, good buds, why
Do you close your lips and do not smile?
Be open and burgeon as soon as you can.
O roses! Why don't you smile?"

Sometimes he was talking to the buds
Sometimes he was telling them his wish.
And sometimes he would open the petals of a bud
Softly, with the tips of his fingers.

3.6 Conclusion

Several elements emerge from this appreciation of Amīnpūr's poetry. The first is his use of simple language in depicting the horrors of war, as in *A Poem about War.* Both parts of this magnificent poem express the doubts of a poet in time of war. While the first part creates an aesthetically unique artefact of war, displaying the fear, anxiety and destruction it generates even among ordinary people in big cities, the second part reflects on this aesthetic artefact. It conveys the poet's self-contempt, especially at his inability to capture and convey the emotionally laden moments of human loss: when young boys are killed or a father hastily plants his son. Amīnpūr's expressive and vivid poems could easily be regarded as critiques of the war. Direct condemnation appears in several of his poems, especially in *A Plan for Peace.* Amīnpūr departs from the ideologically committed and sometimes jingoistic "poetry of sacred defence," courageously following his own judgement on questions of life, war and love. It is significant that the dying soldier in his *A Plan for Peace* writes in his blood the words, "In the hope of real victory, not in war, but *over* war!"

4 Love in Persian War Poetry

من ندانستم که عشق این رنگ داشت
وز جهان با جان من آهنگ داشت
دسته گل بود کز دورم نمود
چون بدیدم آتش اندر چنگ داشت

I did not know that love had this colour,
that out of all the world, it longed for my life;
From a distance it showed itself to me as a bouquet of roses,
when I looked closely, it had fire in its claws.[164]

4.1 Introduction

In November 1983, the Persian daily newspaper *Iṭṭilāʿāt* published on its front page a picture of a ruined school in Bihbahān, which had just been struck by Iraqi missiles. The following sentence was visible on a wall that was still standing: *īnjā madrasa-yi ʿishq ast,* along with an English translation, "This is the school of love."[165] The image was used to show the world how Iranians viewed the war,[166] but the sentiment is significant for understanding the nature of love, for Iranians, in the Iranian war context. The newspaper also published the pictures of 74 teenagers and their teachers who were killed in this attack. The attack took place on 26 October 1983 (4 Ābān 1362), a day that is now commemorated annually in that city. Next to the picture, on the front page, the newspaper published the following ghazal by Fakhr al-Dīn Ḥijāzī entitled *Dars-i khūn* or "The Lessons of Blood":[167]

164 This poem is added to the preamble to Ghazālī's *Savāniḥ*, and is also the opening lines of a ghazal by the poet Khāqānī. See Aḥmad b. Muḥammad al-Ghazālī (d. 1126), *Sawāniḥ. Aḥmad Ghazzālī's Aphorismen über die Liebe*, Herausgegeben von Hellmut Ritter, Leipzig: Bibliotheca Islamica 15, 1942. Khāqānī, *Dīvān*, ed. ʿAlī ʿAbd ʾl-Raṣūlī, Tehran: Marvī, 2537/1979, p. 709.
165 Thursday, 3 November 1983 (12 Ābān 1362). In the picture, the English word "love" is out of the frame. It is unclear whether the Persian text was written before or after the bombardment. The translation was presumably added after the bombardment.
166 Thursday, 3 November 1983 (12 Ābān 1362). In the English translation of the phrase, the word "love" is out of the frame and it is not visible in the picture.
167 The author has also published this poem, and a few others, on the internet, but with some variants. The author has changed *dabistān* (primary school) to *rāhnamāʾī* (secondary school).

https://doi.org/10.1515/9783110748734-008

چو کودکان دبستان صلای خون دادند
به امتحان خدا خوب آزمون دادند
بیا به سرخی مدرسه نگر که این اطفال
بها به درس ز اجساد لاله گون دادند
ز بهبهان چو پریدند خیل چلچله ها
ز فیل ابرهه درسی به خصم دون دادند
کتاب عشق چو درسی ز کار عقل نداشت
عنان راحله را بر کتاب خون دادند
قلم به دفتر دنیا زدند با خط سرخ
رقم به هندسه ی چرخ واژگون دادند
نوشته گشت چو انشاء علّم الاسماء
غلط به دیکته ی درسیِ ذوفنون دادند
حساب زندگی دهر چون به صفر رسید
بها هزار به معراج فائزون دادند
از آن که زهره نوازد نوای نو به سماع
هزار نغمه به آهنگ ارغنون دادند
بقا ز قائمه ی خصم بدگهر بردند
فنا به عاصمه ی دشمن زبون دادند
ز کوبه ای که عدوشان به زنگ مدرسه زد
فغان به دایره ی چرخ بیستون دادند
هلا که فتح قریب است و نصر حق یاور
از این صلا که شهیدان دشت خون دادند

When the primary school children declaimed the call of blood,
 they performed well in God's exam.
Come! look at the school's redness, for these children
 gave tulip-hued corpses to increase the value of the lessons.
As the flock of sparrows flew from Bihbahān,
 they taught the enemy a lesson from [the story of] the elephants of Abraha.
Since the book of love had no chapter on affairs of the intellect,
 they pointed their mounts to the book of blood.
They drew a red line in the book of the world,
 giving the account to the geometry of the overturned Wheel.
When the writing exercise on "He taught the names" was done,
 they ascribed the spelling mistake to the dictation of the Master of Arts.
When the arithmetic of life's destiny came to zero
 they valued a thousand times the ascent of those who attain.[168]
Since Venus played a new melody at the *samāʿ*,
 they played a thousand strains to the tune of the organ,
Removing "survival" from the lesson plan of the ill-natured enemy;

168 The word *fāʾiz* means "overcoming," "overtaking," but it also means "reaching" and "attaining." In this context, the plural *fāʾizūn* means those who have experienced the ascension, referring to martyrs.

they offered annihilation to the capital mother of the fearful enemy.[169]
Thanks to the mallet their foe swung at the school bell,
their shout reached the rim of the Wheel of Bīsutūn.
Beware! The victory is near and God's aid is the succour;
due to this call, the martyrs offered a plain of blood.

The sentence "here is the school of love" is not a new slogan concocted to mark the deaths of these innocent children and their teachers. It derives from medieval Persian Sufism, in which educational metaphors are used to express the ethos of love. The lover should learn step by step how to become a worthy lover. The school of love is part of a rich arsenal of metaphors alluding to the "book of love," "teacher of love," "pen of love," etc., which were used in the medieval period to prepare the lover of God to embark on the mystic path. The final stage of the path is annihilation (*fanā*), through which the lover attains everlasting life in and with the beloved (*baqā*). The only thing the ideal lover longs for is union with the beloved and not any worldly reward or promises of Paradise. The union of God and man removes duality. The lover is dissolved in divinity or, as Ritter describes it, "room is made for divinity so that instead of two only one still remains, God. The lover must become part of the beloved, not the other way round."[170] Love is the essence of God as an omnipresent force. The lover usually suffers from separation and the beloved's indifference, yet he is ready to offer everything, including his life, to attain union. Elements of the school of love recur in the poem cited above. This poem contains several themes and motifs which constitute the cardinal qualities of love, which are limned in classical Persian amatory poetry. In what follows I will analyse a number of these motifs, concepts and doctrines to illustrate how Persian war poets incorporated classical mystic theories in the fabric of their poetry to depict the role of love, and how soldiers were characterised as mystic lovers, turning the battlefield into an arena of love. The essential concepts are the "school of love," "love-death" and the dichotomy between love and reason. I will also give some examples of the rich intertextuality between the poems of the war poets, and between the war poetry and later poetry that reflected on the love and sacrifice it had involved.

169 According to Steingass, *ʿāṣima* means (protected) Madina, but also a chaste woman, a matron. See F. Steingass, *Persian-English Dictionary*, s.v. *ʿāṣima*. Here I have chosen "mother" as the poet is probably referring to uprooting the enemy. This couplet may also be translated as follows: "Taking away 'living-in-God' from the steadfast of the ill-natured enemy / offering annihilation to the mother of the fearful enemy."

170 Ritter, *The Ocean of the Soul*, pp. 422 and 595.

4.2 School of Love (*madrasa-yi ʿishq*)

The doctrine of the "school of love" is a favourite topos in the Persian poetry of the Iran-Iraq War. It embraces a rich assortment of motifs, themes and imagery concocted by medieval masters such as ʿAṭṭār, Saʿdī (d. about 1293), Rūmī and Ḥāfiẓ, to name only the most famous. The modern war poets rely heavily on them and add their own elements to this repertoire. For instance, in the first couplet of the ghazal cited above, sitting an examination is added to the imagery. In this and similar poems, a successful exam means dying as a martyr. Innocent schoolchildren were killed by the enemy's missile, so their physical deaths are put in the spiritual context of the school of love. In other texts, returning from the front unhurt is depicted as failing an exam (*rufūza shudan*), and the soldier must take the test again.[171]

The soldier's death is also interpreted as love-death, which is martyrdom. The notion of love-death has a long history in Islamic mysticism and is an essential part of Persian war poetry. Historically, love-death goes back to the literary tradition of ʿUdhrite love (*al-ḥubb al-ʿudhrī*) during the Umayyad period (661–750), a love characterised by "passionate desire for an unattainable beloved, being chaste and faithfulness until death."[172] *ʿUdhrī* love became popular in Persian poetry in the genre of the ghazal, especially due to the widespread impact of Niẓāmī's epoch-making romance, *Laylī and Majnūn* (completed in 1188), which introduced a new ethos of love. Both in ghazals and in romances written in the *ʿUdhrī* tradition, faithfulness, spiritual aspirations, unrequited love and love-death are indispensable components of depicting love and the lover's yearning.[173] Mystics used elements of *ʿUdhrī* love to express their devotion to God.

Love-death is ubiquitous in Iran-Iraq war poetry, employed in a wide range of contexts and situations, expressing different shades of meaning, but essentially referring to union with God. Love-death enables poets and readers to interpret death as love in a modern military situation, as in the above ghazal. In many

---

171 For this specific topos see my article "Martyrdom as Piety, Mysticism and National Identity in Iran," in *Der Islam*, pp. 248–273.

172 R. Jacobi, in *Encyclopaedia of Islam, Second Edition*, s.v. ʿUdhrī; also see A.A. Seyed-Gohrab, in *Encyclopædia Iranica*, s.v. Leyli o Majnun; idem, *Laylī and Majnūn*, pp. 63–69; idem, "Longing for Love: The Romance of Layla and Majnun," in *A Companion to World Literature*, ed. Ken Seigneurie, Hoboken, NJ: Wiley Blackwell, Volume 4: 1771 to 1919, Vol. II, 601–1450, 2020, pp. 861–872.

173 The first Persian romance with such an ethos of love is probably ʿAyyūqī's *Warqa and Gulshāh*, but the romance never gained the popularity of Niẓāmī's romance. See Seyed-Gohrab, *Laylī and Majnūn*, pp. 69–78.

poems love-death is contextualised in the school of love motif, as in the following quatrain, "Prelude to love" by Siyyid Ḥasan Ḥuseynī. While the poet alludes to love-death, he also alludes to the mystic Ḥuseyn Manṣūr Ḥallāj:

تا خاک ز خون پاک رنگین نشود
این دشت برهنه لاله آذین نشود
تا لاله رخان بانگ انا الحق نزنند
دیباچه سرخ عشق تدوین نشود[174]

So long as the earth is not coloured by pure blood,
This naked plain will not be adorned with tulips.
So long as those with a tulip cheek do not shout "I am the Truth."
The red Preface of love will not be written.

In such poems blood is the ink used for writing the introduction to the book of love, as the conventional pen breaks when it wants to describe love.[175] The floral metaphor of tulips is a cliché in this poetry, pointing to martyrs who are expected to follow the path of Ḥallāj. What is new in this quatrain is the integration of the floral metaphor and Ḥallāj's blasphemous cry, "I am the Truth," into the book of love. Unlike in the previous ghazal, there is no direct mention of death or martyrdom in this poem, but from the opening line the poet suggests that the earth should be coloured by pure blood in order to adorn the plains with tulips. Blood turns into tulips and the tulips are related to faces who shout the cry "I am the Truth." All these constitute the "introduction" (*dībācha*) to the book of love. In other words, to be able to write one's book of love one must offer life itself.

This is one way of referring to the school of love, connecting it to Ḥallāj's death. As he was hanged high on the gallows, his death is interpreted as an ascension to encounter the divine. The death of the children in Bihbahān is also regarded as ascension. The poet states, "when the arithmetic of life's destiny came to zero, they valued a thousand times the ascent of those who attain." Death is characterised here as achieving union with the beloved through the metaphor of ascension. It is not strange at all that children's death is connected to ascension, because in Persian war poetry ascension provides space for poets to depict love-death as union with the immaterial beloved. The motif of ascension is linked to both the prophet Muḥammad's "night journey" and Ḥallāj's execu-

174 Ḥuseynī, *Ham-ṣidā bā ḥalq*, p 132.
175 See *Mathnavī*, Vol. I, p. 14, l. 114. Before and after Rūmī, many mystics have emphasised that the pen (a symbol of reason) breaks into pieces when it comes to write the word "love." See A. Schimmel, "Reason and Mystical Experience in Sufism," in *Intellectual Traditions in Islam*, ed. F. Daftary, London/New York: I.B. Tauris, 2000, reprinted 2001, pp. 130–145.

tion. In the following quatrain Ḥuseynī elaborates on the steed of love. This is not an ordinary steed. In the Prophet Muḥammad's ascension, the wondrous steed Būrāq, which has the face of an angel and flies as swiftly as lightning, takes him through the spheres to the throne of God. In the following quatrain Ḥuseynī creates a new metaphor. Būrāq becomes love. Such ideas are not new, as love is often depicted in early Persian poetry as a steed. Sanāʾī and Ghazālī refer to love as a steed that carries the soul to the Place of Return. Ḥuseynī combines the topos "the prelude of love" with ascension in the following quatrain. The soldiers' impatience to depart at dawn is depicted as mounting the steed of love as well as writing the prelude of love in red:

تا تیز سمند عشق را زین کردند
شب را به دم ستاره نفرین کردند
اوراق کتاب عمرشان گر چه گسست
دیباچه سرخ عشق تدوین کردند[176]

As they saddled the light-footed steed of love,
They cursed the night through the breaths of stars.
Though the pages of the book of their lives were scattered,
They wrote the red prelude of love.

While in the above quatrain he speaks of the "steed of love," in the next quatrain he introduces the compound the "steed of longing," which the soldier mounts to cross the boundary of the earth. A novel metaphor, the "gullet of the earth" designates the borderline between both life and death and this world and the Hereafter. The imperative "Return" is derived from the Quran (89:27–28) and is directed at the faithful at the time of death, inviting the souls to return to their original abode. The full verse, which many Muslims know by heart, reads as follows: "O soul that art at rest! Return to your Lord, well-pleased (with him), well-pleasing (Him)." In the war context, death is interpreted not as defeat by the enemy or being killed, but as a release from the material world. In order to hear God's cry, the soldier lover should bid farewell to this earthly domain. Death is then interpreted as a loving embrace of the beloved, marking the end of the long separation between the lovers:

آن خاطره سرخ که از یاد گذشت
با خرقه آتش ازدل باد گذشت

176 Ḥuseynī, *Ham-ṣidā bā ḥalq*, p. 134. Ḥuseynī bases himself firmly on the Persian mystical tradition.

زین کرد به بانگ "ارجعی" باره شوق
از حنجره خاک چو فریاد گذشت[177]

The red memory that passed the mind
With the cloak of fire, it traversed through the heart of the wind.
It saddled the steed of longing through the cry "Return,"
Passing like a shout from the gullet of the earth.

4.3 Love and Reason

To see the sun a foolish man lights a candle and goes outside, says the mystic poet ʿAṭṭār, referring to the relationship between love and reason.[178] Love is infinite while reason is finite; how can a finite entity fathom infinity? To indicate the great difference between love and reason, mystics often give the example of the prophet Muḥammad's ascension. During this journey he is guided through the spheres by the archangel Gabriel. When they approach the boundary of existence, Gabriel cannot fly further. When the Prophet asks him why he has stopped, Gabriel says that if he takes one step further, his wings will be burned. It is only the Prophet as a human being who can proceed further to be embraced by God's presence. In such stories Gabriel stands for reason who cannot fathom love in the way humans can.[179]

In the "Lessons of Blood" ghazal, written for the children of Bihbahān, the poet writes that the book of love has "no chapter on affairs of the intellect," and that they had "pointed their mounts to the book of blood." The poet Fakhr al-Dīn Ḥijāzī, here and in other parts of the poem, is referring to the dichotomy between love and reason and why love-death cannot be understood through reasoning. The poet is basing himself on medieval love theories in which innumerable allusions are made to love's transcendence and the restriction of human reasoning. There are also countless metaphors to depict the relationship between love and reason, which are widely known in modern Persian societies. In his influential treatise on love Aḥmad Ghazālī states: "What is the outer limit for knowledge, is the seashore for love. The lover on that shore may receive some little of love; if he goes one step further, he will drown. Who then can tell us of him,

177 Also see ibid., p. 140.
178 ʿAṭṭār, *Asrār-nāma*, ed. M.R. Shafīʿī-Kadkanī, Tehran: Sukhan, second print 1388/2009, p. 156, ll. 1582–1583.
179 The inability of angels to understand love is a *topos* in Persian poetry. See my analysis in "The Erotic Spirit: Love, Man and Satan in Hafez's Poetry," in *Hafiz and The School of Love in Classical Persian Poetry*, ed. L. Lewisohn, London: I.B. Tauris, 2010, pp. 107–121.

and how can one who has drowned have knowledge? […] Without a doubt, knowledge is the moth of love. Its knowledge relates to outward things. The first thing to burn in love, is knowledge, who then will return with news of love?"[180]

This inability to comprehend love was embraced by Iranian soldiers in a positive sense: like love – which they equated with martyrdom, God and the beloved – their actions could not be understood by human reasoning, but only through love and longing. Their strong longing would lead to madness and they themselves became mad. This madness is positively interpreted as love-madness, giving examples of frenzied lovers from the medieval period such as Majnūn, the perennial lover of Laylī. Before looking at some examples in the war poetry, I give an example from the classical theory of love to illustrate the poetic mystical culture from which war poets derived their ideas. In the following example Sanāʾī discusses the relationship between love and reason:

عقل عزم اِحاطت وی کرد
غیرت عشق پای او پی کرد
برگزیده دو مرغ بهر دو کار
عقل طوطی و عشق بوتیمار
قدم عقل نقدِ حالی جوی
شعله عشق لاابالی گوی
بالغ عقلها بسی یابی
بالغ عشق کم کسی یابی
حق پژوهان که راه دل سپرند
عقل را لاشه دبر شمرند
محدث از خلقت قدم که بُوَد
روز کور از سپیده‌دم که بُوَد
چون تو را نیست عشق، کم زانی
مزه نان نخورده، چون دانی
عشق را جان بلعجب داند
زانکه تفسیر شهد لب داند
صورت عشق پوست باشد پوست
عشق بی عین و شین و قاف نکوست
بنه ار هیچ عشق آن داری
در میان آنچه بر میان داری
بر تو چون صبح عشق برتابد
نه تو کس را نه کس ترا یابد
چون بترسی همی ز مردن خویش
عاشقی باش تا نمیری بیش
در جهانی چه بایدت بودن

180 Ghazālī, *Savāniḥ*, p. 11, faṣl 3/4. Here and in other parts of this treatise, knowledge stands for reason.

که به پنگان توانش پیمودن
که اجل جان زندگان را برد
هرکه از عشق زنده گشت نمرد
آتش بار و برگ باشد عشق
ملک‌الموت مرگ باشد عشق
هرکه را عشق آن جمال بود
درد بی‌دال و ری و دال بود
گرچه بیرون طرب فزون دارد
نوحه‌گر عاشق از درون دارد[181]

Reason intended to comprehend love
love's envy broke reason's feet.
Two birds are chosen for two jobs
reason is a parrot and love a heron.
The footsteps of reason search for the current cash
[while] the flame of love shouts: "I don't care."
Many men mature through reason
not many mature through love.
The seekers of Truth who take the path of faith
See reason as a corpse attracting hornets in a swarm.
How do created beings flow forth from pre-eternity?
how could the day-blind creatures be born from the dawn?
If you possess no love, you are even less than him,
how can you know the taste of bread, except by tasting it?
Only the wondering soul knows love
for the lips can describe the honey.
The form of love is the skin and nothing else
love is lovely without l-o-v-e.
If you cherish a love for something,
cast all you possess in the middle.
When the dawn of love shines on you
you can find no one, and no one can find you.
If you are constantly afraid of dying
be a lover, that you may die no more.
Why would you stay in a world
that you can measure with a gauge?
The hour of death takes the soul of the living;
he who has come to life through love does not die.
Love is the fire of all you possess
love is the angel of death.
For those who see that love has Beauty
pain is without p-a-i-n.
While outwardly, the lover is glad,
the lover's complaint lives in his heart.

181 Sanā'ī, *Ḥadīqat al-ḥaqīqa*, pp. 229–230, ll. 3925–3941.

Sanā'ī is here emphasising man's inability to perceive the reality of love. While reason is connected to the here and now, helping us to prosper in the world, love has nothing to do with this world or with comfort. All references to love are to its outward form, which is metaphorically the letters l-o-v-e. True love contains its attribute of loveliness even without the outward form. The approach to love is an individual quest, presupposing the renunciation of everything, including the body, so that the purified soul can taste love. At this stage, Sanā'ī refers to the notion of mystical death. Islamic mystics often use the phrase "die before you die," referring to a metaphorical death. The death of self in the beloved procures eternal life. The release of the soul from the material body, in death, is connected to complete detachment from material being, using metaphors such as bidding farewell to one's life. Sanā'ī states that death takes the soul of the living, but those who have experienced "die before you die" cannot die, as they have become part of love and are immune to mundane events.

The allusion to the dichotomy between love and reason in the "Lessons of Blood" ghazal is just one of dozens in a large body of Persian lyrical poetry that adopts the language of the mystics, with references to the lover's willingness to offer his life to the beloved. Such poetry is often deliberately crafted to allow for both secular-amorous and religious readings. The well-established vocabulary of self-sacrifice for love proved useful during the Iran-Iraq War, when it was abused to persuade soldiers to offer their lives. Dying for love, or in love, was such an elevated value that soldiers' motivations transcended any type of earthly love, whether it was love of the homeland or of their families or love of Khomeini as a leader. Self-sacrifice became a personal end in itself. Many modern Persian war poems give love an exceptionally elevated position, frequently related to love-death and martyrdom.

4.4 The Heart as an Intimate Companion

While reason and human intellectual activities are condemned, the heart attains the highest position in Persian love poetry. In fact, the rational thought of the intellect is rejected: thought should rise from the heart as a result of meditation. In Islamic mysticism, as observed by H. Ritter, occupying oneself with the sciences "which deal with the sources of knowledge is limited. A person who spends his whole life studying and learning these sciences has ultimately chosen a wrong, in fact a worldly, profession."[182] Ritter eloquently describes the mystic's relationship to knowledge:

> the mystic is far removed from effortlessly attaining possession of knowledge of God and the world-ground through *a priori* inner experience. Unquenched, tormented yearning for knowledge which one moment is directed to the riddle of the world and asks in vain about the meaning of existence, and the next seeks to penetrate to divinity which is hidden behind seventy thousand veils, drives the seeker restlessly forward and in all directions [...] until he finds what he is seeking at the source, within his own soul. Of course, here he is once more thrown back on his inadequate Ego, and God, after all, still remains transcendent! How mystics attempt to overcome this difficulty, namely by means of the idea of man's primordial affinity with God, a fundamental bond between the soul and the world-ground, and likewise by eliminating human subjectivity, the Ego, through extinction [...].[183]

Persian war poets connect the "heart" as perceived by Islamic mystics to war-stricken Iran, creating myriad metaphors and imagery to depict the soldiers' readiness to offer their lives. As in other topics, the majority of allusions to the heart are based on classical Persian poetry, in which the heart is usually personified as a love-stricken individual over whom the lover has no control. The lover commonly complains of the heart, that goes in the middle of the night to the street of the beloved or during the day to the "bazaar of heart sellers" (*bāzār-i dil-furūshān*) to visit the beloved. These classical tropes relate to the importance of the heart in mysticism.[184] Unlike reason (*ʿaql*), which is not mentioned in the Quran, the heart occurs frequently and is the seat of man's understanding, consciousness and personality.[185] Many Islamic traditions also underline the importance of the heart. Mystics elaborated detailed theories about the function of the heart in the existential encounter with the Truth, in union with the beloved, and as the seat of learning, understanding and consciousness. Abū Ṭālib al-Makkī's (d. 996) *Qūt al-qulūb* ("The Sustenance of Hearts") analyses various aspects of the heart in a mystical context.[186] The heart is the home of love's secret, gnostic knowledge (*maʿrifa*), and the reality of the Godhead.

---

182 Ritter, *The Ocean of the Soul*, p. 79.

183 Ibid.

184 L. Gardet and J.-C. Vadet, in *Encyclopaedia of Islam, Second Edition*, s.v. Ḳalb.

185 See Navid Kermani, in *The Encyclopaedia of the Qur'ān*, s.v. Intellect, ed. Jane Dammen McAuliffe, Leiden: Brill, 2001, Vol. I, pp. 547–549.

186 For an English translation see Aseko Yazaki, *Islamic Mysticism and Abu Talib Al-Makki: The Role of the Heart*, London: Routledge, 2013; also see A. Karamustafa, *Sufism: Formative Period*, pp. 87–90.

To give examples of how the heart is used in war poetry, I have selected some of Amīnpūr's poems. In the following poem, entitled *bugzār bigūyamat* or "Let me tell you," the poet wonders how he can recount what has happened In one quatrain, the heart is an intimate companion who listens to the poet's painful experiences:

این دل به کدام واژه گویم چون شد
کز پرده برون و پرده دیگرگون شد
بگذار بگویمت که از ناگفتن
این قافیه در دل رباعی خون شد[187]

This heart! With what word could I say what happened?
It happened outside the veil and the veil was all awry.
Let me tell you, because my not saying
Has made the rhyme bleed in the heart of this quatrain.

In a similar quatrain the poet complains of his heart filled with blood, a metonym for pain, agony and frustration:

نه از مهر و نه از کین می نویسم
نه از کفر و نه از دین می نویسم
دلم خون است، می دانی برادر
دلم خون است، از این می نویسم[188]

I am not writing out of love, or with hate.
I am not writing, out of disbelief, or with faith.
Do you know, brother, my heart is bleeding:
I am writing because my heart is bleeding.

The poet tells us that his poems are not (really) about love, hatred, apostasy and faith; they flow from him because his heart is in pain. His poems become synonyms for blood and pain. There is perhaps an implication that the pain is lessened by the composition of such poems.

In the following poem, entitled *O Heart*, the poet speaks to his own heart:

تو تنهایی، تو از تنها جدایی
غریبی، بی کسی، بی آشنایی
دلا گویی تو را من میشناسم
تو از اینجا نه ای، اهل کجایی[189]

187 Q. Amīnpūr, *Guzīna-yi ash'ār*, Tehran: Murvārīd, 12th edition, 2007, p. 162; Q. Amīnpūr, *Majmū'a-yi kāmil-i ash'ār*, p. 443.
188 Q. Amīnpūr, *Guzīna-yi ash'ār*, p. 165; Amīnpūr, *Majmū'a-yi kāmil-i ash'ār*, p. 460.
189 Q. Amīnpūr, *Guzīna-yi ash'ār*, p. 165.

You are alone, you are separated from aloneness
You are a stranger, having no one, no friend.
O heart! I feel I know you
But you are not from here. "Where do you come from?"

While in the previous poems the heart was a lover, a companion, here the heart is depicted as a stranger trapped in a foreign place, having no friend. The emphasis on the heart coming from a different realm gives a mystical colouring to the poem. According to Islamic mystics, the heart is the place where God has put his secret. Najm al-Dīn Rāzī (1177–1256) devotes one chapter to the importance of the heart in his *Mirṣād al-ʿibād* ("The Path of God's Bondsmen"), detailing how God created various layers of the heart and placing the mystical secret in the heart's deepest compartment.[190] It is the heart that connects man to the spiritual world. With this background, this quatrain, written in the early years of the war, could be interpreted as expressing a desire to abandon this material realm. Since the heart is exiled in this world, it is only natural that it longs to return to its original home. Because of the connotation of the heart in mysticism and poetry, there is a subtle suggestion of desire for mystical and actual death. The historical context suggests that the actual death worthy of being paired with mystical death would be death on the battlefield.

This reading is reinforced if we place *O Heart* alongside other quatrains, such as *Gum-karda-yi dīrīn*, "Lost long ago":

بیا ای دل از اینجا پر بگیریم
ره کاشانه دیگر بگیریم
بیا گم کرده دیرین خود را
سراغ از لاله پرپر بگیریم[191]

O heart! Come, so we may fly from here,
Let us take the road to a different homeland.
Come, let us search for the one we lost long ago
In the tulip, torn in pieces.

Although the obvious subject of this quatrain is the poet's desire to journey with the heart to another place, because he feels he is an exile where he is, the deeper meaning is to offer one's life like others, at the front. As in many other poems in this genre, the tulip stands for a martyr, torn apart in the violence of modern war. The martyr's example can point the way to something ineffable, lost long ago.

190 Najm al-Dīn Rāzī, *Mirṣād al-ʿibād*, ed. M.A. Riyāḥī, Tehran: ʿIlmī va Farhangī, 1371/1992, pp. 187–209.
191 Q. Amīnpūr, *Guzīna-yi ashʿār*, p. 164.

Many other quatrains express the poet's desire to leave this world. For example:

دگر این دل سر ماندن ندارد
هوای در قفس خواندن ندارد
چنان در دوزخ دنیا دلم سوخت
که دیگر بار، سوزاندن ندارد[192]

This heart has no intention to stay,
This heart has no passion to sing in this cage.
My heart has been so burned in the world's hell
It does not need to be burned again.

The poet's heart is impatient with the world, represented as a cage. It has been so badly burnt in this world that further suffering would be superfluous. As in the previous poems, the poet is using mystical (and gnostic) imagery. Man is trapped in the material world, which is ruled by time and place. The only way to free oneself from this world is through ascetic training, as outward suffering disciplines the self.

The heart can also be the fountain in which the poet-lover can make his ritual ablutions before performing his prayer. This image refers to a recurrent theme in classical mystic poetry, in which the lover's death is presented as a ritual purification in preparation for prayer. Prayer, in this context, stands for union with the beloved, since during a prayer the believer is expected to concentrate entirely on the object of prayer, i. e. God:

برخیز به خون دل وضویی بکنیم
در آب ترانه شستشویی بکنیم
عمر اندک و فرصت خموشی بسیار
تلخ است سکوت، گفتگویی بکنیم[193]

Rise, let us perform our ablutions in the heart's blood
Let us wash ourselves in the water of songs.
Life is short and the occasions of silence are many
Silence is bitter, rise, let's have a heart to heart.

The *topos* "performing ablutions in the heart's blood" often appears in Persian mystical poetry to indicate the purity of the mystic's intentions and his piety. The phrase appears in ʿAṭṭār's *Manṭiq al-ṭayr*, in the episode of Shaykh Ṣanʿān. In this story, the Shaykh, who was the most respectable divine of his

192 Ibid.
193 Ibid., p. 163.

time, having the key to the House of God, falls in love with a Christian girl and accepts all sorts of conditions the girl sets, to be united with her. These include drinking wine, burning the Quran, abandoning his faith and even herding her pigs. When his disciples see such humiliations, they ask the Shaykh to perform the ablution required after contact with unclean things, but the Shaykh replies that he has performed a hundred ablutions in his heart's blood.[194] By using such a *topos* in the first line of this quatrain, Amīnpūr connects war literature with classical Persian Sufism, in which the outward form of religiosity is commonly scorned while all attention is directed to the inward.

4.5 Love Poems as a Homage to Martyrs

Many poems have been written to commemorate the fallen in the context of love. Here I give one example, citing excerpts from Siyyid Ḥasan Ḥuseynī, who dedicated the poem "to the memory of the lover martyr Māshāllāh Sarhangī, killed during the Va-'l-Fajr operation in 1362/1983." It bears the title *Mathnavī-yi ʿāshiqāna* ('loving couplets'),[195] comprising twenty-five couplets.[196] Like many other poems, this has been put to music accompanied by videos from the frontline.[197] Before analysing the poem, I present several of these "Loving Couplets":

بیا عاشقی را رعایت کنیم
ز یاران عاشق حکایت کنیم

از آنها که خونین سفر کرده اند
سفر بر مدار خطر کرده اند
[...]

از آنها که پیمانه ی "لا" زدند
دل عاشقی را به دریا زدند

ببین خانقاه شهیدان عشق
صف عارفان غزل خوان عشق

194 ʿAṭṭār's *Manṭiq al-ṭayr*, p. 71, l. 1269.

195 The title can also be translated as "Romantic poem." The term *mathnavī* refers to a popular poetic form in Persian used to recount stories. It has the simple rhyming aa, bb, cc. etc. which allows the poet to elaborate on the subject.

196 The poem generated a response from Amīnpūr who composed a poem of 15 couplets in which he elaborates on the theme of mystic love referring classical masterpieces such as Shabistarī's *Gulshan-i rāz* ("The Rose-Garden of Mystery") and Suhravardī's *ʿAql-i surkh* ("The Crimson Reason"). Here the poet emphasises the communion between an individual and God, who is everywhere

197 https://www.didestan.com/video/p7KdqRdG (accessed 25.03.2021)

چه جانانه چرخ جنون می زنند
دف عشق با دست خون می زنند
[...]
به رقصی که بی پا و سر می کند
چنین نغمه ی عشق سر می کنند

"هلا منکر جان و جانان ما
بزن زخم انکار بر جان ما
[...]
بزن زخم، این مرهم عاشق است
که بی زخم مردن غم عاشق است

بیار آتش کینه نمرودوار
خلیلیم! ما را به آتش سپار
[...]
بیا در خدا خویش را گم کنیم
به رسم شهیدان تکلم کنیم

مگو سوخت جان من از فرط عشق
خموشی است هان! اولین شرط عشق
[...]
ببین لاله هایی که در باغ ماست
خموش اند و فریادشان تا خداست

چو فریاد با حلق جان می کشند
تن از خاک تا لامکان می کشند[198]
[...]

Come, let us honour loverhood
Let's tell the story of the friends in love,

Of those who made a blood-soaked journey,
a voyage to the turning heart of peril.
[...]

Of those who drank the cup of "No":
They threw the heart of loverhood into the sea.

Look at the monastery of the martyred lovers
The row of Gnostics who sing the ghazals of love,

How well they are whirling in insanity,
Striking the drum of love with their bloodied hands
[...]

[See] the dance they are performing without head or feet
Singing such tunes of love.

198 S.Ḥ. Ḥuseynī, *Ham-ṣidā bā ḥalq*, pp. 42–45.

> "Oh you who deny our souls and our beloved
> Strike the plectrum of negation on our soul.
> [...]"
>
> Strike with the plectrum, for this is the balm of lovers
> As dying without a wound is the lover's distress.
>
> Bring the fire of a rancour like Nimrod's,
> We are Abraham, God's friend, entrust us to fire.
> [...]"
>
> Come! Let us lose ourselves in God,
> Let us speak in the manner of martyrs.
>
> Don't say my soul has burned from love's intensity
> Surely, silence is the first requirement of love.
> [...]
>
> Look at the tulips growing in our garden:
> They are silent, yet their shout reaches God
>
> Since they cry with the throat of the soul,
> They carry their bodies from the earth to placelessness.
> [...]

This poem is a good example of the way poets deal with love in Persian war poetry. The soldiers are identified as lovers who are ready to offer their lives for a beloved. As in other cases, the beloved is unidentified, shifting from a friend to Khomeini as the leader, to Imam Ḥuseyn, to the twelfth Imam Mahdī, or to God. The opening line refers to the state of being in love (*ʿāshiqī*), and the friends, fellow soldiers, are identified as lovers. The word *yārān* (sing. *yār*) has different meanings ranging from the beloved, friend, God, or, in modern usage, a teammate in football or any other group. The context here is that the friend has reached the highest rung on love's ladder by dying as a martyr. Telling stories about such a lover-friend is a way to remember his heroism. The martyr's journey is not only physical death, it also points to the courage of going to the axis of danger. To arrive at that axis, the lover drinks the wine of *lā* or "No," which refers to the first word of the Islamic profession of faith, "There is no god but God." That in turn connects the lover to the execution of Ḥallāj in Bagdad in 922 on charges of blasphemy. He used to say, "I am the Truth" (*anna 'l-ḥaqq*), referring to his annihilation to God. It was God who was speaking the words through him. The following Quran verse (Sūra 3:163) is used to refer to Ḥallāj: "Do not call them dead who have been slain for God's sake, nay, they are alive." Mystics of various generations have commented upon such verses and Ḥallāj's execution. Relying on Rūmī, Annemarie Schimmel states that it is "the sword of *lā*, the first half of the profession of faith, that slays the lover, and then there remains nothing 'but God.'"[199] The graphic form of the word *lā* (لا) allowed poets to use the metaphor of a sword or scissors, cutting all attachments to the material world.[200] Such martyrs do not ask for any reward because they act purely for the Beloved, and if any reward is hoped for it is attaining union with God. When the great mystic Shiblī asked God about Ḥallāj's martyrdom, God spoke to him: "Whom my love kills, for him shall I be blood money."[201] The significance of the word *lā* in this militant mystic context was, for revolutionary Iranians, so central that it became part of the emblem of the *pāsdārān,* the "revolutionary guard," placed on the green uniform directly above the heart. Amīnpūr composed the following quatrain for this particular *lā:*

چون جامه سبز لا به تن میپوشد
چون جام شراب لا ز حق می نوشد
خون در رگ او چنانکه می در دل خم
با یاد شهید کربلا می جوشد[202]

When he pulls the green dress of *lā* on his body;
When he drinks the wine-cup of *lā* offered by the Truth;
Blood runs in his veins like wine in the heart of the wine-vat,
He boils on remembering the martyr of Karbalā.

Here, Amīnpūr connects the notion of *lā* with Imam Ḥuseyn's martyrdom. God is the cup-bearer, who pours wine in the body and the bubbling of wine fermenting in the vat is likened to the boiling of blood in the veins, a reference to the passionate engagement to fight and die like the third Shiite imam.

Another metaphor used in Ḥuseynī's poem is the sea, which connects the battlefield to the mystic path. The poet says, "They threw the heart of loverhood into the sea." In mysticism, land is associated with reason (*ʿaql*) which, according to Aḥmad Ghazālī, is the realm of the people of intellect, while the lover should throw himself into the depth of the sea to find the pearl of secret meaning. Through diving into the sea, accepting all perils and dangers and bidding farewell to all certainties gathered through intellectual reasoning, the lover

---

199 A. Schimmel, *Mystical Dimensions of Islam*, p. 136. The references to Rūmī are *Mathnavī* 3:4098 and 5:589.

200 For letter symbolism see A. Schimmel, *Mystical Dimensions of Islam*, p. 419; also see my introduction in, *The Mirror of Meanings: Translated with an introduction and glossary*, Costa Mesa, CA: Mazda Publishers, 2002, pp. xxiv-xxxi.

201 A. Schimmel, *Mystical Dimensions of Islam*, p. 136.

202 This quatrain is not includeed in the collected poetry of Amīnpūr but it is cited in many other sources. See Muḥammad Ḥuseyn Ṣanʿatī, *Āshnā'ī bā adabiyyāt-i difāʿ-i muqaddas*, Tehran: Bunyād-i ḥifẓ-i āthār va nashr-i arzishhā-yi difāʿ-i muqaddas, 1389/2010, p. 70.

can pursue his journey. In Ḥuseynī's poem, the martyr has done this. The Sufi monastery (*khānqāh* or *khānaqāh*), where mystics withdraw from the world has become a place where the martyrs of love live, they are in rows, singing songs of love, an allusion to the *samāʿ* or "mystic audition." The inclusion of the peaceful and ecstatic ritual of the *samāʿ* in a violent military context creates disconcerting imagery. These martyrs are depicted as being possessed (*junūn*), whirling like dervishes, drumming with their bloodied hands on the drum of love. The dancing imagery continues in the next line in which the classical imagery and terminology, which refer to the mystic's passionate dance, can also be taken literally. The phrase *raqṣ-i bī pā-u sar* or "a dance without feet and head," alludes to an ecstatic state of dancing, but when one thinks of a battlefield the idiom has a different meaning.

The double meanings of such phrases are intentional, because in several consecutive lines the poet elaborates on the *samāʿ* ritual, using the word *zakhm*, meaning "wound" but also poetically the plectrum of a musical instrument.[203] The first usage, "strike the plectrum of negation on our soul," can also be translated as "imprint the wound of negation on our life." The first interpretation refers to the soul as a musical instrument and God as the player, the second to the lover bearing wounds. In the next couplet *zakhm* is used twice, translated first as plectrum and then as wound. In the first case, the player is asked to strike with the plectrum or to infflict a wound on the body, because with either reading this is a healing balm for lovers. In mysticism, the heart is dead if it is not suffering, as only living hearts feel pain.[204] In the second usage, *zakhm* is depicted as necessary for the lover's sacrifice. Here *zakhm* means to inflict a mortal wound. A natural death, without a wound, would be the lover's shame.

Other metaphors relating to love concern fire. In the Persian literary tradition the physiognomy of love is fire, so there are innumerable images of love based on fire. Here the poet uses one of these cliché metaphors, of Abraham in fire, to refer to the martyr's pure trust in God and his determination. The metaphor refers to the story of Nimrod (Persian Namrūd) who, according to the Quran, wanted to throw Abraham into the fire, but God commanded, "O fire! Be cool!" (21:67–9). Abraham is referred to in Persian mysticism as *khalīl*, which means "friend," especially the friend of God. Confronted with the anger of Nimrod, who challenged Abraham's God, the martyr wholeheartedly accepted

---

203 The literal word for plectrum is *zakhma* but poets frequently use *zakhm* to create ambiguities.

204 Ritter, *The Ocean of the Soul*, pp. 257–258.

being entrusted to fire. Here again, the fire is ambiguous. At a metaphorical level, it refers to the Quran and mystic Quran exegesis, but the fire is also the modern weapons Iraq used. The reference easily creates a dichotomy, with Saddam as Nimrod and Iranians as God's friends. In medieval Islamic stories Nimrod's rancour was so intense that he built a high building to see God (28:38). Another story has it that he wanted to kill Abraham's God by sitting in a chest lifted to heaven by eagles.[205] With such negative references, the poet depicts the enemy as apostates while portraying the martyr as a holy man.

Having recounted how the soldier has achieved his status as a martyr lover, the poet invites the reader to follow the martyr's path with the imperative welcome *bīyā* ("Come!"). In this path, he who is annihilated in God becomes one with the creator. At this stage, words fall short. Although the poet invites the reader to speak in the manner of martyrs, this speaking is eloquent silence. Silence is an essential topic in Islamic mysticism. Rūmī used the pen-name "Silent" to emphasise the unspeakable. Here the poet stresses that one should not complain of being burned by love's fire, because silence is the first condition of being a lover. To illustrate this point, the poet refers to the mute tulips in the garden, whose existence is an eloquent cry reaching to heaven. As tulips stand for martyrs, the metaphor points to Iranian cemeteries in which thousands of Iranian youths are buried.[206] Just as the tulips with their red hue proclaim their presence, these martyrs cry with the throats of their souls, lifting their bodies beyond physical space. In addition to referring to martyrdom, this lifting points to the concept of the ascension of mystics who, like the Prophet Muḥammad, journey beyond time and place to perceive God's presence.

Poems such as the foregoing were well received in Iranian revolutionary circles and beyond, and they also invited ongoing responses from other poets long after the war had ended and revolutionary fervour had cooled. In 2007, Amīnpūr responded to Ḥuseynī's poem, commenting on the definition of love. In the following poem of nineteen couplets, entitled *Ikhvāniyya* ("Epistle"),[207] Amīnpūr refers to masterpieces of Persian mysticism such as Shabistarī's *Gulshan-i rāz* ("The Rose-Garden of Mystery") and Shihāb al-Dīn Suhravardī's (d. 1191) *'Aql-i surkh* ("The Crimson Reason"), emphasising the communion between an individual

---

205 See Heribert Busse, in *The Encyclopaedia of the Quran*, s.v. Nimrod (pp. 539–540). For a treatment of Nimrod in Persian poetry, especially Rūmī, see John Renard, "Images of Abraham in the Writings of Jalāl ad-Dīn Rūmī," in *Journal of the American Oriental Society*, Vol. 106, No. 4, 1986, pp. 633–640.

206 Ḥuseynī often refers to martyrs as eloquent mutes. See, for example, his poem *Qiṭ'a-yi shuhadā*, "The Martyrs' Corner," referring to a was cemetery: Ḥuseynī, *Ham-ṣidā bā ḥalq*, pp. 82–83.

207 This refers to the classical genre of *ikhwāniyyāt*, a letter addressed to friends.

and God, who is to be found everywhere. In this poem Amīnpūr focuses on mystic love, but he begins by changing Ḥuseynī's *ʿāshiqān* ("lovers") to *ʿāqilān* ("people of intellect"), and says that speaking of love should not entail anti-intellectualism:[208]

چرا عاقلان را نصیحت کنیم؟
بیایید از عشق صحبت کنیم

تمام عبادات ما عادت است
به بی‌عادتی کاش عادت کنیم

چه اشکال دارد پس از هر نماز
دو رکعت گلی را عبادت کنیم؟

به هنگام نیّت برای نماز
به آلاله‌ها قصد قربت کنیم

چه اشکال دارد که در هر قنوت
دمی بشنو از نی حکایت کنیم؟

چه اشکال دارد در آیینه‌ها
جمال خدا را زیارت کنیم؟

مگر موج دریا ز دریا جداست
چرا بر "یکی" حکم "کثرت" کنیم؟

پراکندگی حاصل کثرت است
بیایید تمرین وحدت کنیم

"وجود" تو چون عین "ماهیت" است
چرا باز بحث "اصالت" کنیم؟

اگر عشق خود علت اصلی است
چرا بحث "معلول" و "علت" کنیم؟

بیا جیب احساس و اندیشه را
پر از نقل مهر و محبت کنیم

پر از گلشن راز، از عقل سرخ
پر از کیمیای سعادت کنیم

بیایید تا عینِ عین القضات
میان دل و دین قضاوت کنیم

اگر سنت اوست نوآوری
نگاهی هم از نو به سنت کنیم

مگو کهنه شد رسم عهد الست
بیایید تجدید بیعت کنیم

208 Amīnpūr, *Majmūʿa-yi kāmil-i ashʿār*, pp. 63–65.

برادر چه شد رسم اخوانیه؟
بیا یاد عهد اخوت کنیم

بگو قافیه سست یا نادرست
همین بس که ما ساده صحبت کنیم

خدایا دلی آفتابی بده
که از باغ گل‌ها حمایت کنیم

رعایت کن آن عاشقی را که گفت:
"بیا عاشقی را رعایت کنیم"

Why should we admonish the men of intellect?
Come, we are speaking of love.

All our prayers are a habit
I wish we could get used to no habits.

What objection could there be, if we knelt twice
after each daily prayer, to worship a rose?

At the moment we form the intention, preparing for daily prayer,
Let us intend to be close to anemones.

What objection could there be, if each time we stand [in prayer]
We heard a little of "Listen to the reed"?[209]

What objection could there be, if in the mirrors
We made a pilgrimage to the beauty of God's countenance?

The ocean's wave is different from the ocean,
Why would we condemn "oneness" [with God] as multiplicity?

Dispersal is the fruit of multiplicity;
Come, let us do exercises on unicity.

Your "existence" is the essence of "quiddity"
Why should we again debate about "the origin"?

If love itself is the cause of the origin,
Why should we debate on cause and effect?

Come, fill the pockets of the senses and the intellect
With stories of love and affection,

Full of The Rose-Garden of Mysteries, The Crimson Intellect,
Full of the Elixir of Happiness

Come so that we, just like ʿAyn al-Qużāt,
May judge between the heart and the Faith.

---

209 This refers to the first line of Rūmī's *Mathnavī*.

If his Path was to innovate
We too should look anew at the path.

Do not say the rite of the covenant of "Am I not your Lord"
Is old; come, let us renew the bond.

Brother! What happened to the custom of the brethren writing letters?
Come, let us remember the promise of brotherhood.

Say, whether the rhyme is weak or false;
It is still enough that we speak in plain language.

O God! Bestow a heart, full of sunshine
So that we can protect the gardens of roses.

Consider the lover who said,
"Come, let us do honour to loverhood."

It is not clear why Amīnpūr recommends a mystical philosophy of love to his friend Ḥuseynī, bereft of any allusions to political issues, martyrdom or the war. Does he wish to separate love mysticism from contemporary politics? If so, why does he himself link the two in his poetry? Or is Amīnpūr simply suggesting to his friend that he might practise religion from an esoteric perspective? It is intriguing to see that the mystic martyr ʿAyn al-Qużāt al-Hamadānī (1098 – 1131) and his role in innovating religion is mentioned, along with works by other mystics. ʿAyn al-Qużāt was a genius of Persian intellectual history, who was "flayed, crucified, rolled up in a mat, and burnt alive" at the age of 33 for his unorthodox ideas.[210] While Amīnpūr only mentions the books of other mystics, he elaborates on the distinction ʿAyn al-Qużāt made in practising Islam, namely judging between the "heart" and "the Faith" (*dīn*). Amīnpūr here follows ʿAyn al-Qużāt's religious philosophy in which he cherishes another interpretation of Islam, considering the letters of the Quran as mere signs pointing to an ocean of meanings. "The Faith" refers to the exoteric aspects of Islam, while "the heart" points to esoteric aspects of the life of faith. What is also interesting in Amīnpūr's allusion is that he invites his friend to make innovations in religious traditions following ʿAyn al-Qużāt's example. If ʿAyn al-Qużāt brought in innovations in the eleventh century, Amīnpūr and his friend should critically scrutinise the tradition, bringing innovation into religion too. ʿAyn al-Qużāt's emphasis on the inner aspects of Islam, reading the Quran as a gate to a deeper reality, cost him his life, as his theological ideas were offensive to the *ʿulamā*ʾ (who were probably unaware of

210 On his life and thoughts see G. Böwering, in *Encyclopaedia Iranica*, s.v. ʿAyn-al-Qożāt Hamadānī; also see H. Dabashi, *Truth and Narrative: The Untimely Thoughts of ʿAyn al-Qudat al-Hamadhani*, Richmond, Virginia: Curzon, 1999.

his even more blasphemous philosophy in Persian). A few of his offences, as summarised by G. Böwering, concern "his theory on the nature of sainthood as a stage beyond reason, preparatory to prophethood; his interpretation of eschatological events as psychological realities experienced within the human soul; ... and his view that God, the source and origin of all being, is the All, that He is the Real Being, and that all other than Him is perishing and non-existent."

In addition to the doctrinal ideas of Persian mystics, Amīnpūr's allusion to ʿAyn al-Qużāt may be prompted by the letters he wrote to his friends. ʿAyn al-Qużāt's correspondence (*Mukātabāt*), especially with Aḥmad Ghazālī, is voluminous, addressing thorny issues of religion in elegant Persian prose.[211] The correspondence is also interesting because ʿAyn-al-Qużāt approached Aḥmad Ghazālī in 1122, after having carefully studied Muḥammad Ghazālī's *Iḥyāʾ ʿulūm al-dīn* ("The Revivification of the Religious Sciences"). While Muḥammad became a mystically-minded theologian after a crisis, he was different from his younger brother, Aḥmad, who followed ecstatic mysticism. Aḥmad introduced ʿAyn al-Qużāt to this mysticism, which contained *samāʿ*, erotic love, and unorthodox reading of Islam. They had a master and disciple relationship until Aḥmad Ghazālī's death. Amīnpūr's poem could be regarded as initiating an intellectual relationship with his friend Ḥuseynī, in which he assumes the role of Aḥmad Ghazālī, inviting his friend to love mysticism, in which God is seen as Absolute Love. Amīnpūr refers to God as Love, who exists in Eternity and desires to see his own beauty. He creates Adam in his own image as a mirror to admire his own face. In this philosophy God is the emanating source of creation and anything created contains a divine component.

In this poem Amīnpūr gives a different definition of love, removing it from the violent context in which Ḥuseynī had placed it. From the outset Amīnpūr adds a mystical construction, inviting the reader to look at religion from a different vantage point. The first lines, in which the poet connects daily obligatory prayer to floral metaphors, are inspired by Suhrāb Sipihrī's (1928–1980) famous poem, *The Sound of Water's Footsteps* (1964), which in Farzan's words "is of such unabashed ecstasy and abandon," directly praising nature, light, truth and love. Farzan compares this to Rūmī's mysticism of love. Citing some of its lines will give a good picture of how Amīnpūr's opening of the poem is based on Sipihrī, and why this poem has become very popular with Persians, who learn many of its lines by heart:

211 *Nāma-hā-yi ʿAyn al-Qużāt-i Hamadānī*, ed. ʿAlī-Naqī Munzavī and ʿAfīf ʿUsayrān, 3 Vols., Tehran: Asāṭīr, third print 1377/1998.

من مسلمانم.
قبله ام یک گل سرخ.
جانمازم چشمه، مهرم نور.
دشت سجاده من.
من وضو با تپش پنجره‌ها می‌گیرم.
[...]
من نمازم را وقتی می‌خوانم
که اذانش را باد، گفته باشد سر گلدسته سرو.
من نمازم را پی "تکبیره الاحرام" علف می‌خوانم.
پی "قد قامت" موج

کعبه ام بر لب آب.
کعبه ام زیر اقاقی هاست.
کعبه ام مثل نسیم، می‌رود باغ به باغ، می‌رود شهر به شهر.[212]

I am a Muslim.
My Mecca is a red rose.
My prayer-mat is a spring, my prayer-stone the light.
Fields are my prayer rug.
I perform ablutions with the heartbeat of the windows.
[...]
I perform my prayer when the wind,
from the minaret of the cypress tree, summons the faithful.
In my prayers, I follow
when the grass has pronounced the *takbīrat al-iḥrām*.
when the wave sits and rises (*qad-qāmat*).

My ka'ba lies at the edge of the water,
My ka'ba lies under the acacias.
My ka'ba travels like the breeze, from garden to garden, from town to town.

Amīnpūr's response to Ḥuseynī's poem illustrates that war poetry was still on his mind in 2007, and that the landscape of war poetry changed into a loving embrace of mysticism and a peaceful and serene interpretation of the war of more than two decades before. For Amīnpūr and also several other poets, Persian mystical tradition offered a way to process the traumatic experiences of the war, easily turning the military setting into a pacific context, which requires individual exertion to know oneself as part of God's creation. The poetry remains

---

212 My translation draws on those of K. Emami, "Water's Footsteps: A Poem," in *Iranian Studies*, Vol. 15, No. 1/4, 1982, pp. 97–116; and of M. Farzan, "Contemporary Poetry in Iran," in *Persian Literature*, ed. E. Yarshater, New York: Bibliotheca Persica, 1988, pp. 347–355. For Sipihrī's mysticism see my introduction in "'The Traveller' and the Sun's Companionship: Universal Mysticism in Sohrâb Sepehri," in *Writings and Writing: from another world and another era*, ed. R.M. Kerr & T. Milo, Cambridge: Archetype, 2010, pp. 393–447.

thoroughly religious but moves from revolutionary ideology to a spiritual dimension, allowing much room for individual growth.

4.6 Love as a Ubiquitous Being

The soldier's actions and thoughts are often interpreted within a definition of love and its effects. For instance, Amīnpūr has several poems in which he defines love. In his first collection, *Dar kūcha-yi āftāb* ("In the Alley of the Sun," 1984), Amīnpūr praises love in the "eulogy on love":

ای عشق زمین و آسمان آیه توست
بنیاد ستون بی ستون پایه توست
چون رهگذری خسته که می آساید
آسایش آفتاب در سایه توست[213]

O love! The earth and sky are your wonders
The primal foundation of the pillar is your footing
The sun, like an exhausted traveller,
takes a rest in your shadow.

Here, love is an all-encompassing entity that embraces the entire universe and holds it together. There is no mention of war, yet this quatrain can be read as a war poem: it was published in the midst of the war, and "love" was already a primary *topos* of the war poetry. The travelling sun can be regarded as the soldier who seeks rest, i.e., martyrdom, in the shadow of love. Such a description of love would motivate soldiers to aspire to martyrdom. Love is elevated to a supernatural force transcending even the sun. This love is God, the Absolute Love or Beloved, the generator and creator of the entire cosmos. The poet bases his idea on classical Persian mysticism, in the works of Shihāb al-Dīn Suhravardī, Niẓāmī, Rūmī and the like, in which love is an attractive force binding all the elements of existence, like gravity or magnetism. In Julie Scott Meisami's words, summarising classical Persian ideas on love, "The generative force that nourishes the world is love: 'if earth and mountain were not lovers, grass would not grow out of their breast.'"[214]

---

213 Q. Amīnpūr, *Guzīna-yi ash'ār*, p. 159.

214 P. 243: Julie Scott Meisami, "Allegorical Gardens in the Persian Poetic Tradition: Nezami, Rūmī, Hafez," in *International Journal of Middle East Studies*, Vol. 17, No. 2, May 1985, pp. 229–260. The quatrain, a eulogy on love, has a notably colloquial style, which is also used in the genre of *munājat* ("supplication to God") in classical Persian literature. This genre became famous through Sheykh ʿAbdullāh Anṣārī, whose *munājat* is a masterpiece and is still

In Amīnpūr's poetry the sun is often depicted as a traveller, and is connected to death. In another quatrain Amīnpūr starts with the journey of a grape as it is processed into red wine. The personified grape that becomes pregnant to the sun and is later cut off and crushed under foot to make wine is a common theme in classical Persian poetry.[215] Amīnpūr uses this familiar image to refer to the colour of martyrdom, i.e., crimson red, at the end of the grape's journey:

من همسفر شراب از زرد به سرخ
من همره اضطراب از زرد به سرخ
یک روز به شوق هجرتی خواهم کرد
چون هجرت آفتاب از زرد به سرخ[216]

The wine is my companion, we travel from yellow to crimson.
Anxiety is my companion, we travel from yellow to crimson.
One day I will leave my homeland, full of longing,
Like the sun going in exile from yellow to crimson.

In the next poem, entitled *Oh Love*, the poet depicts love as a concrete entity which may visit the soldier-lover:

دستی ز کرم به شانه ی ما نزدی
بالی به هوای دانه ی ما نزدی
دیری است دلم چشم به راهت دارد
ای عشق، سری به خانه ما نزدی[217]

---

used in Persian-speaking societies, often for night prayers. In this genre, the believer speaks to the Creator in an intimate and informal way, seeking salvation. In many such texts, and in Amīnpūr's poem above, love is interchangeable with God. For an excellent study on Anṣārī see M.R. Shafīʿī-Kadkanī, *Dar hargiz-u hamīshigī-yi insān: az mīrāth-i ʿirfānī-yi khᵛāja ʿAbdullāh Anṣārī*, Tehran: Sukhan, 1994/2015; also see B. Utas, "The Munājāt or Ilāhī-nāmah of ʿAbdu'llāh Anṣārī," in *Manuscripts of the Middle East*, 3, 1988, pp. 83–87; Seyed-Gohrab, "Life, Cult and Impact of Khāja ʿAbdullāh Anṣārī of Hirāt," in *Āshnāyān-i rah-i ʿishq: majmūʿa maqālātī dar muʿarrifī-yi shānzda ʿarif-i buzurg*, ed. M.R. Isfandyār, Tehran: Iran University Press, 2005, pp. 135–166.

215 Classical Persian abounds with such descriptions of wine-making, especially in the works of Manūchihrī from Dāmghān (d. 1040). See J.W. Clinton, *The Divan of Manūchihrī Dāmghānī*, Minneapolis, MN: Bibliotheca Islamica, 1972; also see Seyed-Gohrab, "The Rose and the Wine: Dispute as a Literary Device in Classical Persian Literature," in *Iranian Studies*, 47, 1, 2013, pp. 69–85. Also see K. Talattof, "What Kind of Wine Did Rudaki Desire? Samanids' Search for Cultural and National Identity," in *The Layered Heart*, ed. A.A. Seyed-Gohrab, Washington DC: Mage Publishers, 2019, pp. 127–171.

216 Amīnpūr, *Guzīna-yi ashʿār*, p. 160.

217 Ibid., p. 159.

You have not caressed our shoulders with the hand of grace
You have not come flying, desiring our grain.
For some time my eyes have been longing to see you.
O love! You have not visited our home.

Here, love may stand for martyrdom and the soldier longs to be touched by love. The reasons love has the connotation of martyrdom in Persian poetry, especially at this time, will be clear from the previous discussion. Although the imagery in this poem is concrete and there is an implication of violence, in the image of the bird coming to devour the seed, if the poem were removed from the historical context of the war it could easily refer to an ecstatic mystical experience in which the lover hankers for the beloved's presence. The intangibility of love allows the poet to use such depictions for a wide range of purposes. Bird imagery, used to depict love, is a familiar trope in classical Persian poetry. In the following excerpt, Sanā'ī depicts love as a bird whose original home is in pre-eternity. The more love is distanced from its original abode, the less powerful it becomes. It even becomes like a farmyard bird that cannot fly higher than the roof. This domesticated love is earthly love, trapped in conditionality. The only way to escape from this condition is by ascetic training, disciplining the body through vigils and fasting, and by avoiding associating with people. Through this disciplining process, love grows in strength so that it can be the steed that carries the soul up to its spiritual home in the presence of God:

عشق بی‌چار میخ تن باشد
مرغ دانا قفس‌شکن باشد
جان که دور از یگانگی باشد
دان که چون مرغ خانگی باشد
کش سوی علو خود سفر نبود
پر بود لیک اوج پر نبود
همتش آن بود که دانه خورد
قوّتش آنکه گرد خانه پرد[218]

Love is free from the four nails of the body;
    love is a wise bird, knowing how to break the cage.
Know that the soul which is far from unity
    resembles a farmyard bird,
She cannot make the journey to the heights,
    she possesses wings, but they cannot transport the soul
Her aspiration is to eat seeds,
    her power limits her to flying around the house [...]

218 Abu 'l-Majd Majdūd ibn Ādam Sanā'ī, *Ḥadīqat al-ḥaqīqa va sharī'at al-ṭariqa*, ed. Maryam Ḥuseynī, Tehran: Markaz-i Nashr- Dānishgāhī, 1382/2004, p. 228.

The four nails are the Four Elements (fire, water, earth and wind) out of which all material entities are created. Sanā'ī emphasises that love transcends corporal substance, which cannot be trapped in a cage.[219]

Love as a bird is also a recurrent *topos* in Persian war poetry. In the following poem Amīnpūr uses a similar metaphor, connecting this to the mystic doctrine of the renunciation of reason, but it receives a completely different meaning in the context of modern war:

آن مرغ که پر زند به بام و در دوست
خواهد که دهد سر به دم خنجر دوست
این نکته نوشته اند بر دفتر عشق
سر دوست ندارد آنکه دارد سرِ دوست[220]

That bird, flying around the roof and door of the friend,
wants to offer its head to the friend's blade.
This maxim has been written in the book of love
"He who loves the head of friend, does not love his own head."

In this quatrain the lover is a bird fluttering around the house of the beloved, ready to offer its life for the sake of union, in accordance with a maxim in the book of love. The maxim is the last couplet of a quatrain attributed to the eleventh-century mystic, ʿAbdullāh Anṣārī, which begins:

هر دل که طواف کرد گرد در عشق
هم خسته شود در آخر از خنجر عشق

Every heart that walks around the house of love,
will at last be wounded by the dagger of love.
This maxim has been written ...

The compound *dar-i ʿishq* "the door of love," is an allusion to the House of God around which the mystic's heart ritually walks seven times during the pilgrimage to Mecca. Anṣārī's poem says that the mystic must be ready to offer his life for the beloved. The lover must renounce everything, even his head, a symbol for the rational faculty. Amīnpūr has changed this to a bird and the house of a friend.

Another favourite love metaphor is that of the candle and the moth. In the following quatrain by Amīnpūr this metaphor is connected to the mystic idea of

---

219 Also see my chapter "'Martyrs of Love': Genesis, Development and Twentieth Century Political Application of a Sufi Concept," in *Martyrdom: Canonization, Contestation and Afterlives*, ed. I. Saloul & J.W. van Henten, Amsterdam: Amsterdam University Press, 2020, pp. 129–151.
220 Amīnpūr, *Guzīna-yi ashʿār*, p. 160.

concealing the secret of love. If the lover reveals the secret, showing he is a true lover, he will be destroyed. The addressee of the poem is not identified, but considering that this collection was published in 1362/1983 it may well be addressed to soldiers.

آهنگ و سرود لبتان سوختن است
اندیشه روز و شبتان سوختن است
این چیست میان تو و پروانه و شمع
کز روز ازل مذهبتان سوختن است[221]

The melody and song of your lips are of burning
Day and night you think of burning.
There's a secret you share with the candle and moth,
From the dawn of creation, your religion is to burn.

In the mystical context burning connotes the state of the ascetic, who is expected to burn and to conceal love's secret. The lover's lips burn with an intense longing to reveal his love. The burning is also a metaphor for the self-annihilation that unites the lover with the beloved, as a moth finds union in the flames of the candle. The lover shares in the intimate bond that exists between the moth and the candle flame. The word religion points to the innate nature of the moth, to be attracted to fire. In the same way the lover is attracted to the beloved, as God created Adam to love Him. Amīnpūr is probably referring to the physiognomy of love, which is fire and burns everything, turning it to love. Another aspect of the metaphor of the candle and the fire is that the candle flame is a window into the world of Non-existence. Moth and candle images have been used endlessly to depict aspects of the love relationship between the lover and the beloved. Commenting on Ghazālī's use of this metaphor in his theoretical exposition of love, ʿIzz al-Dīn Maḥmūd Kāshānī (d. about 1335) links the three stages of the moth's flight to the mystic's tripartite realisation of the Truth referred to in the Quran (102:5–7 and 56:95).[222] When the moth sees the light of the candle, it is *ʿilm al-yaqīn* ("certitude of knowledge"), when it draws near the fire and sees it, it is *ʿayn al-yaqīn* ("certitude of vision"), and when it is burned by the

221 Ibid. p. 160.
222 For more on the imagery of the candle and the moth see Seyed-Gohrab, "Waxing Eloquent: the Masterful Variations on Candle Metaphors in the Poetry of Hafiz and his Predecessors," in *Metaphor and Imagery in Persian Poetry*, pp. 81–123. See ʿIzz al-Dīn Maḥmūd Kāshānī, "Kunūz al-asrār va-rumūz al-aḥrār," in *Shurūḥ-i savāniḥ*, ed. A. Mujāhid, Tehran: Surūsh, 1372/1993, p. 24.

fire, it is *ḥaqq al-yaqīn* ("certitude of Truth").[223] The fire is a window on the world of Non-existence, where the lover is welcomed by the immaterial beloved. Connected to this division and also referred to in Amīnpūr's quatrain is the fact that mankind is destined to return to his creator. This world is commonly depicted as treacherous, a cadaver, or an old crone, showing herself as a bride but sharing her bed with one man after another. The true dwelling of the soul is in God's vicinity, a place acquired through meditation, contemplation and the annihilation of the ego. Such powerful metaphors, which are inseparable from Persian culture, inspired soldiers to apply them in the ferocious reality of war, offering themselves like moths to the fire of the enemy.

4.7 Conclusion

"Here is the school of love," a phrase on a bombarded school, was the departure point of this chapter, analysing how a wide range of violent realities are depicted through images of love. The poets used various mystical concepts and doctrines from medieval Persian Sufism and applied them to the war setting, justifying and praising death. The sort of love we encounter in this modern Persian war poetry is very similar to the notion of love in ʿAṭṭār's works, as eloquently described by Hellmut Ritter, with the marked difference that ʿAṭṭār's stories and anecdotes are metaphorical, written to ennoble human nature, while the Persian war poets move the metaphors to a violent reality. Ritter writes:

> His [ʿAṭṭār's] stories are allegorical and serve solely to proclaim a unique love which alone deserves the name, a love for which relief from the violence of emotion, deliverance from the fire of passion, is not a consideration, for which there is only the path forward, whose end, the annihilation of the ego, is not a limit to be avoided but the real goal, or not that either, but a transitional stage to a new form in which the ego is extinguished and after the command "Die!" a new existence arises on an entirely different basis.[224]

Persian poets depict the fight of Iranian soldiers as a mystical exertion to emancipate themselves from earthly existence, annihilating oneself and living eternally in the spiritual beloved. The Iranian soldier, like the lover in the Persian love tradition, sacrifices everything for the beloved's sake. As Ghazālī writes, the lov-

223 The Quran does not refer to the three stages in one place, but in two different contexts and without a mystical layer. However, mystics from the time of Ḥallāj applied these three phases to mystical illumination. See A. Schimmel, *Mystical Dimensions of Islam*, pp. 141–142.
224 Ritter, *The Ocean of the Soul*, pp. 382–383.

er's will should disappear in the beloved's will. Ritter points to a paradox that Ghazālī refers to, "On the lower level the lover is a subject that wills, he wants something. On the higher level he is the object of the beloved's will."[225] The war poetry encapsulates this mystical philosophy of love. Earthly existence is of less value, since man's urge and ultimate goal is to reach the Place of Return in and with the Beloved, beyond time and place. For the Persian poets and soldiers, God loved man first and man's love for God came in response, as indicated in the Quran (5:54): "He loves them, and they love Him."[226]

These soldiers did not expect any reward, as their compensation lay in the mystical aspirations, intentions and efforts that Iranian soldiers shared. The mystic layer also helped readers behind the front line to endure the horrors and material hardships of the war years. While classical Persian poetry usually turns on the ambiguity between earthly and heavenly love, in this war poetry there is always a drive to depict love in a spiritual context, extolling the dying soldiers as martyrs. One could even claim that the mysticism of this war poetry lies in making the object of love a superhuman being. As Amīnpūr elucidates in his poem *Dastūr(-i) zabān-i ʿishq*, published in a volume with the same title in 1386/2007, love remains a very effective weapon for Iranian soldiers:

دست عشق از دامنِ دل دور باد!
می توان آیا به دل دستور داد؟
می توان آیا به دریا حکم کرد
که دلت را یادی از ساحل مباد؟
موج را آیا توان فرمود: ایست!
باد را فرمود: باید ایستاد؟
آنکه دستور زبان عشق را
بی گزاره در نهاد ما نهاد
خوب می دانست تیغ تیز را
در کف مستی نمی بایست داد

May love's hand remain far from the hem of the heart!
    Can one give orders to the heart?
Can one really command the sea
    That its heart should not remember the shores?
Can one tell the waves, "Stop!"
    Or tell the wind; "Stop!"
He who put the grammar of love in our nature,
    without a conditional clause,
Knew full well He should not place
    a sharp blade in the hands of a drunkard.

---

225 ˡbid., p. 398.
226 See, for instance, Ghazālī, *Savāniḥ*, *faṣl* 1 and 8, pp. 4 and 21 respectively.

5 "In the Trenches of my Small Room..." Ideologically Committed Children's Poetry

ما گل های خندانیم   فرزندان ایرانیم
ایران پاک خود را   مانند جان می دانیم
ما باید دانا باشیم   هشیار و بینا باشیم
از بهر حفظ ایران   باید توانا باشیم
آباد باش، ای ایران   آزاد باش، ای ایران
از ما فرزندان خود   دل شاد باش ای ایران

We are smiling flowers, children of Iran
For us, our pure Iran is life
We must be wise, wakeful and seeing
We must be adept in protecting Iran
O Iran, may you thrive! Be free, O Iran!
May we, your children, gladden your heart, O Iran.[227]

5.1 Introduction

Children's literature is a genre introduced to Persia in the nineteenth century. Although several scholars have endeavoured to trace this genre back to the dawn of Persian history, a true children's literature with a specific theme, choice of vocabulary and language is a modern phenomenon. Before the nineteenth century, Persian children followed a more or less standard curriculum at traditional schools (*maktab*s) consisting of reciting the Quran, a selection of Persian poetry and prose.[228]Modern curricula are due to the efforts of several Persian intellectuals who modernised the education system based on western models and the needs of the changing Iranian society, achieving high standards in the twentieth century in terms both of innovative curricula as well as the production of high quality children's literature.

The 1979 Revolution changed almost every institutional sector which conveyed an ideology, trying to replace any ideological and conceptual models with a type of ideology fully committed to the principles of the Revolution.

---

227 This is the first poem that children in the first year of primary school before the 1979 Revolution had to memorise. Its secular nationalism contrasts to the poetry for children written by the Islamic revolutionary poets, preparing them to welcome martyrdom and process the loss of loved ones during the Iran-Iraq War.

228 For a description of the works commonly included in the curriculum see the editors of EIr in *Encyclopaedia Iranica*, s.v. Children vii. Children's Literature.

https://doi.org/10.1515/9783110748734-009

This ideological shift was very visible at all levels of society, including the education system. Not only did the space in classrooms and schools undergo drastic change, but the picture of the Shah was replaced by one of Khomeini, mixed schools of girls and boys were banned, the study books were thoroughly revised within two years to convey the Islamic revolutionary values, all pictures of women in the books, including painted pictures of unknown females, were covered with an Islamic cloth, fulfilling the norms of the hijab required by the newly established regime. As Mehran states, "In the new textbooks Persian society is said to be divided between self-sacrificing and moral Muslims and inhuman, oppressive Westerners, the former led by martyrs and revolutionary leaders, the latter influential among corrupt 'westoxicated' intellectuals."[229]

As part of preventing the western cultural invasion, the regime banned translations from western sources. The programmes of institutions that carried out translation projects were either abolished or combined with those of other institutions under "Islamic" guidelines. Authors tried to find new themes inspired by the social and political atmosphere of the time, devoting their attention to the "oppressed" (*mustażʿafān*) and the poor. In this new children's literature, themes, plots and allegories used in such books had to be aligned with the Islamic values set by the Ministry of Guidance. The majority of books published in the 1980s were devoted to themes related to religion, the revolution, martyrdom and support for the war with Iraq.[230]

As Golnar Mehran indicates, the changes in the education system happened in two phases, from the Revolution to the end of the Iran-Iraq War in 1988, and the period thereafter.[231] The first, commonly called the revolutionary period, concerned the regime's cultural and ideological revolution, aiming to replace a secular and western-modelled way of life with a religious model, both politically and culturally. To uproot any forms of secularism and western influence, the regime presented a plan explaining the principles of the educational system *Tarḥ-i*

---

229 Golnar Mehran, in *Encyclopaedia Iranica*, s.v. Education. xxiv. Education in Postrevolutionary Persia, 1979–95.

230 For a statistical table of the types of publications see ibid. For an Islamic revolutionary view of children's literature see Fāṭima Amīrī, "Chigūnigī-yi rushd va taṭavvur-i adabiyyāt-i kūdakān baʿd az pīrūzī-yi inqilāb-i islāmī," in *Majmūʿa-yi maqālāt-i simīnār-i barrasī-yi adabiyyāt-i inqilāb-i islāmī*, Tehran: Samt, 1373/1994, pp. 23–41. For a genral history of Persian children literature see Z. Ghaeni, "The History of Children's Literature (1900–1940)," in *Literature of the Early Twentieth Century: From the Constitutional Period to Reza Shah*, ed. A.A. Seyed-Gohrab, London/New York: I.B. Tauris, 2015, pp. 448–469; also see Shafīʿī-Kadkanī, *Chirāgh-u āyina*, pp. 102–203.

231 Golnar Mehran, in *Encyclopaedia Iranica*, s.v. Education. xxiv. Education in Postrevolutionary Persia, 1979–95.

kulliyyāt-i niẓām-i āmūzish u parvarish-i jumhūrī-yi islāmī-yi īrān. As Mehran indicates, the Islamic Republic focused on four ideological pillars, "inseparability of religion and politics, Islamic revival, cultural revolution, and creation of the new Islamic person," which had far-reaching consequences for the education system.[232]

The censor also plays an essential role in purging any ideas differing from the mainstream ideological channel directly provided by the Islamic government. While the state took control of the textbooks and any other texts used in schools, the Ministry of Culture and Islamic Guidance firmly monitored any activities at all levels for artistic production. It is hard, if not impossible, to obtain permission to publish books on the history of Persian children's literature and education, especially those related to the period after the 1979 Revolution. In addition, producing scholarly works on the change in the education system, the change in the content of textbooks is underplayed, yet a large body of state-sponsored literature is produced to propagate the principles of the Islamic government.

Creating a new Islamic person presupposed that that person had to embody a number of central traits including self-sacrifice, ready to die as a martyr, and and fighting the enemy of the Revolution. These points recur in all types of documents produced by various institutions and organisations related to the Islamic Republic. In this chapter I have chosen several poems written for children to inculcate the ideological Islamic principles. The value of these poems is huge as they are a type of guideline as to how children should think about the aforementioned ideological pillars. Moreover, choosing the point of view of a child to tell the horrors and consequences of war, the ideas on martyrdom and an ideal child makes these poems invaluable. Analysing these poems provides us with an exceptional vista into the psyche of the poet, the process of inculcating specific values into the youth and how youths are supposed to share their feelings with the reader.

The poems are composed by Ḥamīd Hunarjū in a collection entitled *Barf-i gul-i yās: majmūʿa-yi shiʿr-i kūdakān* ("Snow of Jasmine Petals: Collection of Poetry for Children"), published in Tehran in 1987. According to Hasan Anvarī's *Dictionary*, the word *kudakān* or "children" refers to people who are below the age of adolescence, usually between five and twelve years old. Ḥamīd Hunarjū is a committed poet propagating revolutionary values, involved in a literary festival organised by the regime called *Yār* and *Yādigār* which honours the founder of

232 For an analysis of this integration of revolutionary Islamic ideas see Golnar Mehran, in *Encyclopaedia Iranica*, s.v. Education.

the Islamic republic, Ayatollah Khomeini. In an interview Hunarjū refers to the goals of the fifth version of this festival: the festival's "main section is labelled 'Imam Khomeini, the father of all kindness,' which concentrates on 'Family being the basis of society,' 'Respect to parents' and 'Mutual respect between mothers, fathers and children.'"[233] Hunarjū has published several collections of poetry for primary and secondary schoolchildren. His book, *Kitāb-i firishtahā* ("The Angels' Alley") was acclaimed as the War Book of the Year (*kitāb-i sāl-i jang*) in 1999.

His collection *Snow of Jasmine Petals*, which is translated here in this chapter, consists of twelve poems. Most of these poems are written from a child's perspective. While a number of poems are apparently written from the viewpoint of a very young child, focusing on their experience and consequences of the war, other poems are written from the vantage point of a teenager. The language of these poems is colloquial and fits the way children express their feelings. There are no grammatical inconsistencies in the language, which one may expect from a child, and the contents of the poems are all meant to idealise concepts such as martyrdom, altruism, longing to go to Paradise, etc.

5.2 Dream of Paradise

The first poem, entitled *Dream of Paradise*, depicts a recurrent scene in which a young soldier volunteer (*basījī*) is killed and his sister is thinking and dreaming of him. The soldier's body is entirely annihilated and the only memory that has remained from the soldier is a *chafiyye*. This is a Palestinian shawl worn by many *basījī* forces during the war. It is this article of clothing that triggers sorrow in the sister in the first stanza, making her shed tears. The metaphor of buds for eyes is new, especially when it is used in connection with the verb *shikuftan* or "to bloom." The burgeoning of a bud is commonly used in Persian as a metaphor for a smile, but here the poet uses it for shedding tears. Normally when buds open they become flowers, but here the poet is metonymically referring to the red colour of the flowers. The poet uses positive imagery to express sorrowful emotions. In addition, while in the first stanza an omniscient narrator is at work, in the second stanza the girl is viewed from the perspective of a cushion, which is decorated with motifs of roses. The cushion is witness to the girl's love

---

233 See http://www.imam-khomeini.ir/fa/key/%22%D8%AC%D8%B4%D9%86%D9%88%D8%A7%D8%B1%D9%87%20%DB%8C%D8%A7%D8%B1%20%D9%88%20%DB%8C%D8%A7%D8%AF%DA%AF%D8%A7%D8%B1%22 (last accessed 25.03.2021).

for her brother: when she smells the *chafiyye* she is reminded of her brother. Here again the poet continues his floral imagery, using this powerful image to convey the girl's emotions. After this prelude, we see in the third stanza that the girl falls asleep. In her sleep the floral imagery is used again. She dreams of the gardens of Paradise, writing about her brother with the stem of a rose on a leaf. The floral imagery is so powerful that it points to the season of Spring, a season of renewal and of the return of green and flowers. This pleasant return of Spring flowers is contrasted with the brother's empty place. While this empty place is indicated through the return of Spring, the emphasis is on martyrdom. It is here that the reader understands that the brother was killed as a martyr and that martyrdom is a lesson that one should learn. This is certainly the core message of the poem, which is contextualised in an emotion-laden dream of a little girl, missing her brother. Having conveyed the message, the girl is awakened by the sound of her father, who knows how much his daughter is missing her brother, when he says, "It is morning. Enough of seeing your brother, it is the time for morning prayer … ." The father's call for morning prayer also indicates that the girl is nine years old or older, as the obligatory daily prayer for females starts at the age of nine. To emphasise the girl's feeling of missing, the poet ends his poem by stating that while the girl stands up to perform her prayer, her heart is still in Paradise with mobilising forces (*basījī*).

خواب بهشت	*Dream of Paradise*
باز هم چفیه او را برداشت	Again she took his chafiyye
با خودش چیزی گفت	She said something to herself
باز مانند دو غنچه، دَر اشك	Again, like two buds, the gate of tears
گونه هایش بشکفت	Opened on her cheeks.
بالِش گُل گلیِ زیبایش	Her beautiful cushion, decorated with rose motifs
باز دختر را دید	Saw the girl again
وقتی او چفیه داداشش را	Smelling the chafiyye of her brother
مثل گل می بویید...	As if it were a rose
دختر قصه ما خوابش برد	The girl of our story fell asleep
رفت تا باغ بهشت	She went to the gardens of paradise
باز با ساقه گل، بر تن برگ	She wrote a nice sentence
جمله ای خوب نوشت :	With the stem of the rose on a leaf:

234 *Barf-i gul-i yās: majmūʿa-yi shiʿr-i kūdakān*, first poem. My edition does not have any page numbers. I mention the poem number for an easy search.

ای که در درس شهادت ، ایمان "O you who in faith, in the lesson of martyrdom,
نمره تو شده بیست Were awarded the best grade,
فصل زیبای بهار آمده است The beautiful season of Spring has come
جایت امّا خالیست"... But your place is empty..."

باز پیچید صدای پدرش : Again the voice of her father resonated:
دختر کوچك و ناز! " "My small and lovely maid!
صبح شد، دیدنِ داداش بس است It is morning. Enough of seeing your brother,
شده هنگام نماز"... It is the time for morning prayer ..."

دخترك پا شد و خندید، ولی The little maid stood up and smiled, but
دل او آنجا بود Her heart was somewhere else
دل او توی بهشتی سرسبز Her heart was in a green paradise
با بسیجی ها بود[234]! With the mobilising forces (basiji).

5.3 Angels of the Town

The second poem in the collection has the title *Angels of the Town*. The term *firishta* or "angel" recurs in this type of poetry, referring to abstract forces that help soldiers. Here the poet associates the angels with martyrs, emphasising that death does not mean the end of life but is actually the gate to an eternal life. The poet emphasises that this is a promise made by the Quran. The notion of martyrdom as angels is particularly appealing for children, as many of them would have problems in accepting the loss of their fathers, brothers and other close relatives. Presenting martyrs as angels is a strategy for planting the seeds of the regime's ideological cult of martyrdom, brainwashing children about the value of martyrdom. Such a connection also enables the poet to link material life with the immaterial world, adding laudatory qualities to angels and stating that one can become an angel, i.e., by dying as a martyr. The impossibility of living eternally as a being who is loved and cherished by everyone has all of a sudden become an option. In addition, being in such a position, angels are protectors of the town, guarding people, bringing good news, living between the material and immaterial worlds in the presence of God:

فرشتگان شهر *Angels of the Town*

شما چقدر خوبید How nice are you!
شما چقدر پاکید How pure are you!
فرشتگانِ شهرید You are angels of the town
ستارگانِ خاکید You are stars of the dust

هنوز خنده هاتان	Still your laughter
به گوش باغ، جاری است	Is running in the ear of the garden
هنوز شهر ما با	Still our town is
صدایتان بهاری است	Hearing your voices
هنوز در دلِ شب	Still turns our town into Spring
سوار اسبِ نورید	
هنوز از دل شب	Still in the heart of the night
هزار شهر دورید	You are riders on horses
خوشا به حالتان، آه	Still from the village of night
	You are a thousand cities away
آه تا خدا پریدید	O, how happy you are
شما به قول قرآن	That you could wing so far to God
تمامتان شهیدید...	As the Quran says,
	you are all martyrs ...

5.4 Painting of War

The following poem depicts the effects of war on children, illustrating how they express their feelings and emotions in paintings. During and after the war, Iranian children used to paint horrible images of the war. These paintings were shown in children's programmes on television, which also affected and inspired other children to do the same. The poem translated below is written from the perspective of a girl who describes the interior of her room. It is striking to see that this child depicts her room in war terminology. She has a front line of war, comparing the room to trenches, a box of pens to a tank and pens to bullets. Although the poem is entitled *Painting of War*, which promises a painting, this is not the case, and the reader does not see a painting. The girl is painting flowers in trenches, emphasising that she has no missiles and mortars as she has no fight with her dolls. Her imaginary front line shows green Spring and Persian New Year on 21 March. Despite all of the war terminology and comparisons, the girl avoids painting a picture of war, and every time she paints, she tries to change the warlike material into components reminding the reader of peace, green Spring scenes, and festivity. The urge to include peace and festivity is an integral part of the poem. It is only towards the end of the poem that the reader is allowed to share in the girl's suffering at the loss of her two brothers. Here the poem is no longer about a painting, but the hard reality of the photos of the martyred brothers on the shelf in the room, smiling at the girl. The poet shows how preoccupied this girl is with war, the loss of her brothers and mundane daily life depicted through references to Spring and the New Year:

نقاشی جنگ *Painting of war*

من توی اتاقِ کوچك خود In my small room
يك جبهه خوب جَنگ دارم I have a nice frontline of war
اما عوضِ گلوله و تانك Instead of bullets and tanks
يك جعبه مداد رَنگ دارم I have a box of coloured pencils

در قلبِ سفيد دفترِ خود In the white heart of my book
نقاشی جنگ می کشم من I am drawing a picture about war
در باغچه بزرگ سنگر In the garden of the trenches
گلهای قشنگ می کشم من I am drawing beautiful flowers

در جبهه کوچكِ اتاقم In the trenches of my small room
خمپاره و موشکی ندارم I do not have mortars and missiles
چون خوبم و مهربانم و جنگ Since I am good hearted, I am not at war
با هيچ عروسکی ندارم With any of my dolls

در جبهه من، به قول مامان In my frontline, as mama says,
هر روز بهار سبز و عيد است Everyday is a day of green Spring and new year
بر تاقچه قشنگِ خانه On the special shelf in my room
عکس دو کبوترِ شهيد است There are pictures of two martyred doves

يك روز تمام شهر ديدند One day, the entire city saw
پرواز دو تا کبوترم را The flight of my two doves
مردم همه خوب می شناسند All the people know very well
لبخند دو تا برادرم را... The smiles of my two brothers ...

5.5 Rain of Kisses (Martyr Daddy)

The following is a strong poem written from the perspective of a child whose father is killed as a martyr. The title, *Rain of Kisses,* and the dedication “martyr daddy” gives an emotive tone to the poem from the start. In the first stanza the little child is missing the smell of her father and is searching for him among the photos in an album to smell him again like a rose, like the scents in Spring. The opening is strong, as the poet emphasises the sense of smell and how strongly the child associates her father’s smell with roses and Spring. Using this sense of smell, which melts away, the poet stresses the feeling of loss, which recurs in the second stanza. Here, while looking at a picture of the smiling father, the child keeps asking the mother about him. The child does not believe that he has died and asks her mother, “Mother! Where is Papa? When will he come to see us ...?” At this point, the poet allows the reader to enter into the child’s interior monologue in which she imagines that her father is softly knocking at the door, coming in, filling the child’s ears with his words, while the child floods his face with a rain of kisses. This fervent desire for contact with her father continues throughout the rest of the poem. In fact, the metaphors based on sense of smell magnify this physical distance. While the child longs to have physical contact with her father, this is not possible. At the end of the poem the child indicates that "traces of the hand of my martyred father remain on my head," which points to either the strong desire for and fixation of the child on her father, or the fact that the child has dreamt of the father and has just woken up, feeling the father's hand on her head:

بوسه باران (بابای شهید)	Rain of kisses (martyr daddy)
مثل گل، مثل بهار	Like a rose, like Spring
باز بویت می کنم	I will smell you again
لابه لای عکسها	Among the photos
جستجویت می کنم	I will search for you
باز هم صدها سؤال	Again I will ask mama
می کنم از مادرم	a hundred questions
شاد می خندد به من	The photo above my head
عکسِ بالای سرم	is cheerfully smiling at me.
مادرم! "بابا کجاست؟"	"Mother! Where is Papa?
کی به ما سر می زند...؟	When will he come to see us ...?"
ناگهان انگشت تو	Suddenly your finger
نرم بر دَر می زند	Knocks softly on the door
گوش ها پر می شود	My ears once more
باز هم از صحبتت	Are filled with your words
بوسه باران می شود	The sky of your face
آسمانِ صورتت	is filled with a rain of kisses
لای در وا می شود	When the door is ajar
خانه زیبا می شود	The house becomes pleasant
دَفترم با دست تو	You will sign my
باز امضاء می شود	book with your own hand.
این صدای خواهر است :	This is the voice of my sister:
که "ای بابا نرو! "	"O, Papa, do not go!
امشبی پیشم بمان"!...	Just one night stay with me
امشبی دریا نرو	Do not go to the sea tonight ...!"
خانه دیشب شد بهار	The house turned to Spring
شد پر از عطر امید	Filled with the scents of hope
بر سرم جا مانده است	Traces of the hand of my martyred father
دستِ بابای شهید...	Remain on my head

5.6 "When do you come back?"

The following poem, *When do you come back?*, belongs to the category of writings about soldiers who were lost during the war, and not knowing whether they were killed, taken as prisoners of war or for any other reasons had not returned home. These people were called *mafqūd al-athar* or "lost trace of." Writings on this tragic aspect of the war are prodigious, but the following poem is a distinctive piece as it is written from the perspective of a child who is observing his/her father and how hard s/he is finding it to deal with such a loss. The poem is dedicated to "Aḥmad Mutivassilīyān and all those who are missed" but the contents of the poem could be applied to the feelings that many soldiers who lost their comrades may have.[235] The poem consists of five stanzas, each comprising two couplets, that rhyme. The form is a type of traditional folk quatrain with colloquial and plain language. Before analysing the poem, I present the translation in full:

کی می آیی؟	When do you come back?
پدر همسنگرت بوده، دلاور	Warrior! My papa was your comrade in the trenches
اگر که خوب یادت مانده باشد	Surely you are remembered well.
کتاب خاطراتت را شب و روز	He reads your diary day and night,
هزاران بار شاید خوانده باشد	Perhaps a thousand times.
همیشه روبرویت می نشیند	He always sits beside you
سرود فتح می خواند برایت	Reciting the Song of Victory for you.
دوباره غنچه غنچه بوسه هایش	Again the buds of his kisses
شکوفا می شود بر گونه هایت	Bloom on your cheeks.
می آید باز عطر چفیه تو	The scent of your chafiyye is there
و نامت می چکد از خود نویسش	And your name trickles from his pen.
دل من می دود با کودك اشك	My heart runs with the child of tears
به دشت گونه های نرم و خسیسش	On the plain of his soft wet cheeks.
پدر از بس که از تو یاد کرده	My papa talks so much about you
دل من هم به سویت می کشد پر	My heart is also flying towards you.
تو باران بهاری، من زمینم	You are the rains of Spring, I am the earth.
تو باغِ آسمانی، من کبوتر	You are the gardens of the sky, I am the dove.
پدر گفته که تو حالا اسیری	Papa says you're a prisoner of war.
پرنده! سوی لانه کی میایی؟	Bird! When will you return to your nest?

235 Aḥmad Mutivassilīyān was a conservative militant figure fighting for the ideals of the 1979 Revolution.

آقا احمد! بیایی یا نیایی Mr. Aḥmad! Whether you come or not
برایت در دل من هست جایی I have a place in my heart for you.

War trauma inflicted on the father and its effect on the father-child relationship is the subject of the poem, which is about the loss of the father's comrade. The poetic persona speaks to the comrade in direct speech, drawing attention to this. It is as if the comrade is present and the child is pouring his/her heart out about the pain and agony of his father. In the opening stanza the reader sees a father who is emotionally attached to the comrade's diary and picture. He has read this diary a thousand times but keeps reading it to refresh memories. The child sees how the father sits next to the photo of the comrade, singing poems or reciting verses from the Quran. The compound *surūd-i fatḥ* means "song of victory," but it may also refer to verses from the Quran commonly read for the deceased. This recitation for the departed is called *fātiḥa khᵛāndan*. It is in this second stanza that the emotive aspect of the poem is strengthened when the poet likens the father's kissing of the photo to rosebuds which come into bloom as soon as the father's lips touch the comrade's cheeks. Using the rhetorical figure of *takrīr* or repetition in the word *ghuncha ghuncha* or "bud bud," the poet depicts how the father repeatedly kisses the photo. In the third stanza the child perceives two other emotive and traumatic effects of the war on the father and the child starts to identify him/herself with the father's pain and agony. The smell of the comrade's *chafiyye* is filling the space while the father writes down the comrade's name. The way the poet explains how the father writes the name is also significant as the father does not make any effort to write: the name trickles from the pen. This smell and the trickling of the ink are related to the father's tears. At this point, the child identifies with the father's pain by employing the metaphor of the heart running with a childish tear in the soft and moistened plains of the cheeks. Using this image, the child indicates the lack of control this situation has brought to the family.

From the fifth stanza we see how the child identifies himself with the father's agony, even surpassing his father's pain. The father's memories and his preoccupation with the comrade have such an enormous impact on the child that he is longing to see the comrade. Having exhibited this strong desire to see the comrade and feel the father's pain, the poet uses several metaphors of flight to convey the child's relationship with the comrade: the child's heart opens its wings to see him, the comrade is the sky and the child a dove and the comrade is identified with rain in Spring while the child is the earth generously receiving it. These images clearly have an ideological message as well, instructing children in such a situation how they should behave.

One of the dramatic results of missing those people is that people could not find closure and would think of any possible scenarios for death or disappearance. In the last stanza we see that the father thinks that the comrade is a prisoner of war, cherishing the hope that he has not been killed and that he will come back one day. Here the child compares the comrade to a bird, asking him directly when he will come back. The last couplet, in which the child says that s/he has a place for him in his/her heart whether this comrade comes back or not, forms a closure, indicating how the father's comrade and other memories and war reminiscences are part of his/her life.

5.7 Āmina

The next poem deals with the pain and emotions of a little girl called Āmina, whose father has become a martyr. The name is very significant as it refers to the prophet Muḥammad's mother. The small girl bears a historical name, loaded with piety and the birth of the Prophet.[236] The poet invites readers to the world of a small girl who has no companions to share her pain except baby fishes in a pool. The poet speaks in an illusory tone from the outset, introducing the little girl to the reader as a classmate of Bahār and Nasīm. These names connote "Spring" and "breeze" respectively. Setting this tone through an imagery of nature, the poet depicts how she writes her homework about flying, as she is the neighbour of a ring dove. The modern name for a ring dove in Tehrani Persian is *yā-karīm*, meaning literally "O Compassionate." After this illusory first stanza, the reader realises that this girl is preoccupied with her father. Every week, she writes her composition homework about her father in the calendar she has inherited from him. Āmina is depicted as a lonely and introvert girl, sitting every day on the stony edge of the pool, talking to fishes about her father, asking them to tell her about her father.

آمنه	Āmina
آمنه در کلاس بهار است	Āmina is in the class of Bahār (Spring)
آمنه همکلاسِ نسیم است	Āmina is classmates with Nasīm (breeze)
مشق پرواز را دوست دارد	She likes the homework of flying
چون که همسایه یا کریم است	As she's neighbour to a ring dove.
باز هم مشق های شبش را	She has written her homework
توی تقویم بابا نوشته	in her father's diary again

236 W. Montgomery Watt, in *Encyclopaedia of Islam, Second Edition*, s.v. Āmina.

مطمئنم که درباره او	I'm sure she has written
باز این هفته انشاء نوشته	This week's essay about him again
می نشیند لبِ حوضِ سنگی	She sits on the stony lips of the fountain
می چکد اشك او دانه دانه	Her tears trickling down, one by one.
با همان چند تا بچه ماهی	Like a child, she pours her heart out
درد دل می کند کودکانه	To the few baby fishes in the pool.
باز دیروز با گریه می گفت :	Yesterday she was sobbing and saying again,
"آی... بابای من را ندیدید؟"	"Aah ..., haven't you seen my father.
گفته بودم که مادر مریض است	I told you, my mother is ill.
راستی حال او را نپرسید؟	Why don't you ask me how she is doing?
می شناسید بابای من را؟	Do you know my father?
اوکه یك باره از پیش ما رفت	He left us alone all of a sudden.
او که با ساکی از عطر و لبخند	He went away from this village early one morning
صبح زودی از این روستا رفت	with a bag full of scents and a smile."
دختر کنجکاوی است، امّا	She's a curious girl, but
لهجه بچه ماهی بلد نیست	She does not know the language of fish.
دوست دارد بداند که غصه	She wants to know the definition of sorrow
در لغت نامه ماهیان چیست؟	In the dictionary of fishes.
نمره بیست دینی اش را	Last night she showed her best grade
باز دیشب به بابا نشان داد	In Religion classes to her father.
خانه از بوی گیلاس پر شد	When her father moved his lips
تا که بابا لبش را تکان داد	The house was filled with the scent of cherries.
آمنه دانش آموز خوبی است	Āmina is an excellent student
در دلش نوبهارِ امید است	The Spring of hope lies in her heart.
روی جلد کتابش نوشته :	On the cover of her book she has written
"آمنه دختر یك شهید است..."	"Āmina is the daughter of a martyr..."

5.8 My good father

The theme of the following poem is related to the previous one but the treatment of the subject of missing a father is different. In the first stanza the poet creates a childish atmosphere by letting the poetic persona, i.e., a child, ask the rains what conditions his/her father is under. By linking the father's absence to rain, the poet opens a new dimension: raindrops showering from the sky would suggest that the father is dead and that they are messengers conveying some news from the martyred father. Moreover, in an Iranian context rain is traditionally perceived as a grace, coming from heaven, turning deserts into green meadows. This child's simple question generates this symbolic level in the reader's mind. The last couplet of this stanza supports the idea of regeneration when the child says to the absent father that "You will not end in my heart / As your end is the beginning." This rain, the agent of regeneration and renewal, as a representation of the father reappears in the second stanza, in which the child refers to how s/he adopts the scent of Spring, of the New Year feast, of growing and blooming, and of the flower of the Sun. The father together with the rain reappears in the third stanza as a source of sorrow and delight, quenching the child's thirst. The final stanza commences by emphasising the father's empty place. There is also rain, but this time the rains are not from the sky but from the child's eyes for the good father who is the "season of kind reconciliation and light:"

بابای خوبم *My good father*

این روزها باران که می آید These days when the rain falls
حال تو را می پرسم از او باز I ask the raindrops how you are
تو در دلم پایان نمی گیری You will not end in my heart
پایان تو یعنی همان آغاز As your end is the beginning

من با مرور روزهای تو Thinking again of the days I spent with you
بوی بهار و عید می گیرم I find the scent of Spring, the New Year
بوی شکفتن، دوستی، لبخند The smell of green things growing, of friendship and smiles
عطر گلِ خورشید می گیرم I can smell the flower of the sun

من از تو دارم شادی و غم را My delight and sorrow are from you
من از تو دارم این پریدن را My flying is from you.
روی کویر تشنه شعرم In the thirsty desert of my poetry
نقاشی باران کشیدن را I draw a picture of rain.

امروز دیگر نیستی امّا Today you are no longer, but
با یاد تو چون ابر، می بارم I rain like a cloud when thinking of you.
ای فصلِ خوبِ آشتی و نور O season of kind reconciliation and light
بابای خوبم، دوستت دارم... O my father, I love you.

5.9 The Street of Angels

Many children's poems are devoted to the horrible day-to-day experiences during the war. In the poem *Angels of the Town*, the angels stand for martyrs, but the emphasis is on the destruction of the town by missiles. Here the poet uses the vantage point of a child to depict what the child is perceiving when a missile strikes in a street. In each of the stanzas the poetic persona depicts one event. In the first stanza a reference is made to ordinary ring doves, to be found in profusion in many Iranians cities, usually perching on roofs or the town's electricity wires. The sound of missiles exploding on the ground was so sudden and massive that the birds would become totally disoriented and some would simply die. Following this awful observation, in the second stanza the poetic persona, a child, sees a mother falling victim to a missile, rolling in blood and shattered glass. The atrocities of war are contrasted to regular peaceful activities in the third stanza, where the child tells of the butterflies in a garden and violets. Apparently the missile has destroyed all of these. Another event depicted here is a missile killing children. Images of dead little girls holding their dolls were exhaustively employed in the media to emphasise Saddam Hussein's war crimes and the innocent deaths of civilians. This killing of civilians helped to strengthen the cult of martyrdom. To be regarded as a martyr did not imply active participation in a fight and offering one's life, but innocent or untimely death is also a reason to characterise a person as a martyr. The cult of martyrdom was maintained through such losses. To ensure that people would remember the ruined sites, the victims were called tulips or angels: while the red colour of tulips and their short flowering season referred to martyrs, departure from the material world was indicated by angels:

کوچه فرشته ها	*The Street of Angels*
وقتی که موشك آمد	When a missile came
يك يا كريم اُفتاد	A ring dove fell
يك يا كريمِ زيبا	A beautiful dove
از روی سیم اُفتاد	From a wire
يك مادرِ بسیجی	The mother of a basiji
در خون و شیشه غلتید	Rolled in blood and glass.
انگار خون سُرخش	It was her red blood
توی حیاط پاشید	That was splashed in the yard.
آن روز، کوچه ما	In those days, our street
يك باغ شاپرك داشت	Had a butterfly garden.
مردی میان کوچه	In the middle of the street, a man was planting
عطر بنفشه می کاشت	the smell of violets.
وقتی که موشك آمد	When the missile came
دیدم عروسکی مُرد	I saw how a doll died
دیدم عروسکی در	I saw how a doll
آغوشِ کودکی مُرد	in the embrace of a child died
بچه کبوتر از ترس	On the roof, the child of a dove
در پشت بام، غش کرد	swooned away from fear.

مادر دوباره با بال Her mother was caressing her
گریان، نوازشش کرد With her wings, and weeping.

وقتی که موشك آمد When the missiles came
گلهای لاله وا شد The tulips bloomed
از آن به بعد، کوچه From that time on,
مال فرشته ها شد the street belonged to angels.

5.10 Memories of Spring

In the following poem, the poet regrets that he has reached the last stanza, revealing how sorrowful he is. He places himself in the position of the friend of a teenager who is killed, but cannot endure the pain of separation; he longs to see his martyred friend. Before analysing the poem, I cite it here:

خاطرات بهاری *Memories of Spring*
(دوستان شهیدم کجایید؟) (Where are you my martyred friend?)

گاه می آمد از سَمت کوچه Sometimes he would come down the alley
با کتابی که زیر بغل داشت With a book under his arm.
او که یك خانه از مهربانی With a house full of love
در دل پاك اهل مَحل داشت He was in the pure hearts of everyone around here.

راستی از همان روز اول Indeed from the very first day,
دوست من پریدن بلد بود My friend knew how to fly.
مثل یك شعر، خوب و صمیمی He was like a poem, a poem of kindness and intimacy
مثل یك قصه مستند بود Or like a narrative, he had a story to tell.

درس او بود یك چیز دیگر His lessons were something else,
غیر جبر و علوم و ریاضی Not algebra, biology or geometry.
بر لبش بود فعل شکفتن On his lips were the verbs of blooming,
حال او بود بهتر ز ماضی His present was much better than the past.

خوب فهمیده بودند مردم People knew well
او در آیینه ها خانه ای داشت That his home was in the mirrors.
دفتری از الفبای پرواز He had a book made of the alphabet of flying
در دل تنگِ پروانه ای داشت In the narrow heart of a butterfly.

گرچه در کوچه مان نیست دیگر Although we do not have his shadow
سایه اش در دلِ کوچه جاری است Running in the heart of our alley,
در زمستانِ سوزانِ هر سال Every year, in the hard winters,
کوچه با خاطراتش بهاری است The alley is turned to Spring by his memory.

عکس او را که می بینم انگار	When I see his photo, it's as if
می کشم سخت از خود خجالت	I am deeply ashamed of myself.
ای پرنده، پرنده، پرنده	O bird, bird, bird,
کاشکی مال من بود بالت	I wish your wings belonged to me.
باز پایان شعر من آمد	Once again, my poem has come to an end
آی غمها ! چه بی انتهایید	O sorrow! Why are you so endless?
خسته ام دیگر از این جدایی	This separation has exhausted me,
دوستانِ شهیدم، کجایید...؟!	Where are you, my martyred friend ...!?

Here poetry is used to give memories of the lost friend a place, yet poetry cannot contain the immense sorrow generated by the friend's departure. The penultimate stanza is revealing as it plants a deep sense of guilt in those who did not die, but in addition the poem is meant to generate a sense of desire for death, to be among the martyrs. More than the other poems we have discussed so far, this poem (written by an adult poet) inculcates in children a longing to die. Dying is valorised. What I personally can remember as a child from the Iran-Iraq War was that dying had become so much part of daily life that one was inclined to accept it, especially because people had lost so many loved ones. Especially with the start of the bombardments of cities, no-one felt safe and everyone was suddenly exposed to death. Moreover, media and street culture valorised death to such an extent that it was present everywhere in various ways, i.e., mural paintings of martyrs, songs on the radio, pictures on television, the voluntary mobilised forces (*basījīs*) who demonstrated their willingness to offer their lives in the streets by wearing shrouds, and the frequent returns of the fallen, whose remains in coffins were carried on people's shoulders through the streets, accompanied by slogans about the lofty position of martyrs.

War poetry contains hatred, demonisation and the culture of heroism, but there is little of this in Persian children's poetry. In these poems the poet does not appeal to patriotism and the ideals of valour, as is common in the poetry of a mobilised society, but to love and friendship, and guilt. It is this very aspect of such ideologically inspired poetry that makes these poems much more robust than the appeal to patriotism, which Wilfred Owen's *Dulce et Decorum est* propagates. While for Owen it was sweet and right to die for one's country, in these Persian poems one dies for the ideology of suffering to reach an elevated spiritual position. This poetry feeds on suffering rather than on the honour of one's homeland.

Having experienced what it was to lose friends during one's teenage years in the war against Iraq, this poet refreshes memories of how certain teenagers were totally ready to go to the front, as if they were hypnotised by love of the homeland and a feeling of adventure governing the early years of the war. The poem is not strong at all; it is actually a bad poem, lacking any original metaphor, simile and imagery, but it is successful in depicting the hypnotised way a teenager alienates himself from school, concentrating on only one thing, i. e., dying as a martyr. The poet emphasises how this teenager was different from the other children and that everyone expected that he would offer up his life. Although the poem depicts these aspects of a devoted youth who is ready to die, at the same time it is setting an example for other teenagers. The poem also manipulates young readers to feel ashamed that they have not followed in the footsteps of this martyr. Although the martyr's behaviour is unusual as he, for instance, neglects school, he is still portrayed as an ideal youth whose conduct should be imitated. The poem is an example showing how the Islamic regime promoted this type of martyr-focused behaviour among the youth during the war. Commitment to revolutionary ideals set by Ayatollah Khomeini had to override anything else, including when it came to choosing between school as a teenager and going to war.

What is also noteworthy in this context is that the Islamic regime depicted the war as a school. An example of this equation of the school and death in the front line is to be seen in the diaries published in the 1980s for basījīs. In such diaries or other types of publication such as the wills of the martyred, Ayatollah Khomeini's frequently-cited phrase "mobilisation is the school of love" (*basīj madrasa-yi ʿishq ast*) was printed to valorise a love that seeks no reward but martyrdom for love's sake.[237] The phrase was often combined with images drawn from the modern school system, such as examinations and re-sitting tests. The pages of some pocket calendars quoted phrases such as "[i]n the school of love, the pen is the weapon," "copy-books are lines of blood," "the front line is the classroom," "Imam Ḥuseyn is the teacher of the martyr," and "the mobilisation is the school of love and martyrdom is the diploma." The phrase *rufūza shudan* ("not passing one's exams") meant "to come back unharmed from the war."[238]For Persian readers, such phrases needed no explanation: love is synonymous with absolute devotion and willingness to die as a martyr, and when the youth chose between going to school and going to the front to defend "Islam" and the homeland, the choice was an easy one to make. Even today, over twenty years after the war, we see these phrases on the internet, often with horrible images of young soldiers cut down in battle.

---

237 For the relationship between the school of love and martyrdom see chapter four.
238 *Taqvīm-i madrasa-yi ʿishq (1381/2002)* (Qum: n.d).

5.11 You Are with us Again ...

The next poem, entitled *You Are with us Again ...*, shows how memories of martyrs were kept alive. While the ellipsis at the end of the title refers to the martyr's empty place, it also shows that his memory lives on. The smooth and child-like tone and rhythm, combined with a universalisation of the qualities of the martyr, offer a vivid picture. This martyr transcends human qualities, having a heart belonging to the children of cosmos, being a green garden, a forest, mountain, plains and a river. In this glorification of the martyr to the level of a supra-human being, the martyr becomes the source of all things growing. In this poetic universe the martyr is not merely a green garden, but he is also the rain. While deifying the martyr, the poet refers to memories of the martyr in the fourth stanza. It is here that the reader finds out that only a picture of the martyr is left. In the last stanza the poet refers to the desolation and loneliness the martyr's absence has created. "Without the martyr, no birds fly over the plains," but the martyr has become able to talk to clouds, sending his voice to the rest of the people:

باز بامایی...	*You Are with us Again ...*
چفیه ات رنگین کمان بود	Your chafiyye is in the colours of the rainbow,
سنگرت در آسمان بود	Your trenches are in the sky.
قلب تو از بچه های	Your heart belongs to the children
کوچه باغِ کهکشان بود	Playing in the lane of cosmos.
باغ بودی، سبز بودی	You were a garden, you were green,
جنگلِ انبوه بودی	You were a rich forest.
رود بودی، پاك و آبی	You were the river, blue and limpid,
دشت بودی، کوه بودی	You were the plain, you were the mountain.
عطر باران می تراوید	The scent of rain was streaming
از نگاهِ پر اُمیدت	From your hopeful eyes,
چون تو را بوسیده بودند	As your martyred companion
همسفرهای شهیدت	Kissed you before your journey.
خاطراتت هست اینجا	Your memories are here
مثل گلهای بهاری	Like spring flowers.
باز با مایی تو، امّا	You are with us again,
توی عکسِ یادگاری	But in a photo, as a memory.
دشت، بی تو بی پرستوست	Without you, no birds fly over the plains.
ابر می گوید برایت	The clouds speak to you.
توی گوش جبهه امّا	Your voice will resonate
باز می پیچد صدایت	In the ears of the trenches.

5.12 A Sparrow's Chatter

The next poem, entitled *A Sparrow's Chatter,* uses the context of children's experience of nature. The sparrow talks in the language of the children, so eloquently that the whole street is filled with commotion, longing to hear the sparrow's story. While the setting is an alley, the time is at dusk. The depiction of the sunset is typically Persian: the poet calls the Sun an auntie (*khāla khurshīd*) wearing a crimson veil (*chādur*). This sparrow, gathering the entire alley under his wings, is no ordinary bird, and has visited before. "Again" is a repeated motif in the poem. The neighbour's son, Murtażа, knows the bird and that he is coming to tell new stories. In the first three stanzas the poet uses suspension. We know the sparrow is a signifier, but not its connotation of a martyr. In the fourth stanza this bird is shedding tears. By giving human attributes to the bird, the poet gives away the sparrow's identity. Immediately, all the children on the street burst into tears, and the sound of their lamentation fills the entire space. The alley is also filled with the scent of roses. Both of these sensory elements are connected to the war: "[o]ur neighbourhood had the pleasant scent of the frontline" and "Abū Dharr, Salmān and Miqdād" are present again, in the weeping. It is not specified that they have died in the past, but it becomes clear that their bodies were brought back from the front. The three names are also significant, as they belong to champions of the earliest days of Islam. Such names were popular with revolutionary families who preferred them to pre-Islamic Persian names.

In the sixth stanza it becomes clear why the children are crying: the sparrow – speaking for the souls of the dead – says that it has heard a commander (perhaps to be understood as the Commander of Souls) approaching, heard the fervent silent prayer of a martyr, and flown to heaven. In this stanza we find out that the sparrow is a bird from paradise, coming to bring the message of martyrdom to children. It is not the first time such a message has been delivered, as the next stanza names several war operations such as Ḥajj Imrān, Fāv and Fakka. The final stanza makes it entirely clear that the sparrow flying at dusk is a harbinger of martyrdom and that this alley has offered several martyrs. Their destination is described as "the paradise of the sky" but is also in phrases such as "the pleasant village of rain" or "the ocean of freedom." Associating martyrdom with rain and the sea draws on the positive appreciation of water in Persian culture, in which rain is regarded as an agent of fertility and as God's grace. Linking martyrdom with the ocean points to God's love and the mystical secret in the depths of the sea. God's mystery is often depicted as a pearl held in a shell. Like an April raindrop, which has journeyed the entire world in different forms, it finally arrives at its origin, the ocean, but due to this travelling and transformation it is different from other waters. It drops into the sea but is not absorbed, so it can reach the heart of a shell, which holds it until it becomes a pearl. Likewise the martyr is the same as other people, but is transformed through a martyr's death, becoming exceptional, free from the dictates of the material world. The concept of freedom could also be interpreted as the release of the soul from this material world, joining the primordial abode.

حرفهای پرستو *The Sparrow's Chatter*

پرستوی قشنگی باز دیروز Once again yesterday a nice sparrow
برای کودکان تعریف می کرد Was telling a story for children.
میان کوچه غوغا بود وقتی When it began to tell the story
برای این و آن تعریف می کرد The whole street was jostling to hear.

غروبی ساده بود و خاله خورشید "It was just on dusk, and auntie Sun
دوباره چادری قرمز به سر داشت Had put a red veil over her head again."
پرستوی قشنگ قصه ما The nice sparrow telling our story
تمام کوچه ها را زیر پر داشت Had the whole street under her wings.

به قول مرتضی همسایه ما As Murtaża, our neighbour, says,
پرستو حرفهای تازه ای داشت The sparrow has new things to tell.
صدای بال می آمد دوباره The sound of the wings came again
محله شوِ بی اندازه ای داشت The whole neighbourhood was in ferment.

پرستو گاه گاهی گریه می کرد The sparrow shed a few tears
می آمد اشکهایش دانه دانه They fell one by one.
صدای گریه ها در کوچه پیچید The sound of lamenting arose in the street,
صدای گریه هایی کودکانه The sound of children weeping.

تمام کوچه ما بوی گل داشت All of our street smelled of roses
محله عطر خوبِ جبهه می داد Our neighborhood had the pleasant scent of the front line.
درون قابِ خیسِ چشمها باز Abū Dharr, Salmān and Miqdād were there again,
ابوذر بود و سلمان بود و مقداد In the sockets of moist eyes.

صدای پای یك فرمانده آمد "We heard the approaching steps of a commander,
مناجات شهیدی را شنیدیم We heard the prayer of a martyr,"
پرستو از بهشتِ آسمان گفت Said the sparrow of the heavenly paradise,
پریدیم و پریدیم و پریدیم "And we flew, we flew, we flew."

به یاد روزهای جنگ بودیم We were thinking of the days of war,
به یاد حاج عمران، فاو، فکّه Of missions such as Ḥajj Imrān, Fāv and Fakka.
دوباره آسمان چشمهامان Once again, the sky of our eyes was leaking,
به یاد لاله ها می کرد چِکّه We were remembering, thinking of tulips.

به یاد بچه های کوچه نور Remembering the boys from the alley of light,
که تا آبادی باران پریدند Who flew to the pleasant town of rain.

از این دنیای بی دریا گنشتند	We passed from this world with no ocean,
به اقیانوس آزادی رسیدند	Reaching the ocean of freedom.

5.13 You Became a Butterfly!

Another poem that uses the simple language of childhood is *You Became a Butterfly!*, which valorises a very young martyr's death. The dedication is to the war martyr Fahmīda, who was just twelve years old. As the title indicates, he is likened to a butterfly. An adolescent soldier would not be compared to this universal symbol of endearment and romanticism. The comparison points to the soldier's fragility and youth, implicitly emphasising that the place for such a young soldier was not the barren desert of the front line, but a green garden where petunias grow. His death is described as his transformation into a butterfly, and his receiving two small wings by which to leave the earthly abode.

The soldier is also compared to a fresh shoot, a seedling tree that is destroyed. The seedling's death makes the garden mourn. The queen of the garden, the rose, is clad in black out of sorrow. While the rose shows her sadness, she knows that the destiny of this shoot is rewarding. Using the antithesis of black and white, the poet emphasises the quandaries that parents of young children experience. While outwardly people are dressed in black to show respect for the family of the fallen, the dominant ideological culture asserts that these fallen have a promising future in eternity. The final stanza shows how a child, for whom this poem is written, recollects the young martyr, perhaps a friend, drawing his smile in "the blossom-laden garden." The ink the child uses is his own tears, in which he writes "I don't know anyone of better understanding (*fahmīda*) than you…!" This final line contains a double entendre, as at one level it refers to the young child's capacity to understand: i. e., he completely understands what he has to do at this critical moment in Iranian history, namely offer his life. At another level, this train of thought is further developed by the allusion to the twelve-year-old boy, Muḥammad Ḥuseyn Fahmīda, whom Ayatollah Khomeini called "our leader." The poet plays on the pun *fahmīda*, which means understanding, intelligible, thoughtful or sensitive, but it also refers to Fahmīda who as a boy offered his life under an enemy's tank to defend the city of Khurramshahr. The poem is also dedicated to Fahmīda and all other young boys who sacrificed their lives during the war.

The poem does not condemn such sacrifice; rather it encourages children to follow Fahmīda's path. As Karimi and Gruber rightly indicate, "In the wake of the Iran-Iraq war, the regime labored to create national heroes who might serve as role models for the country's youths, whose war efforts were needed to defend and ensure the survival of the newly established republic."[239] It was expected that selfsacrificial acts of boys such as Fahmīda would aspire other boys to go to the front. In this poem, it is implicitly suggested that if these children follow the path of martyrdom, they are thoughtful and can understand the essence of the crisis. They could even be praised by the supreme leader and become an example for all other soldiers. While the idea of patriotism is anchored in Fahmīda's daring sacrifice to defend the country, the uneasy aspect of this poem is its pliably manipulative character, which reassures children about what the right path is. From an early age they should know which road they have to travel:

پروانه شدی ...!	*You Became a Butterfly* ...!
برای شهید فهمیده و همه فهمیده ها...	(for Fahmīda the martyr, and all the Fahmīdas)
مانند کبوتری سبکبال	Like a lightly winged dove
از باغِ نگاه ما پریدی	You flew away, beyond the walled garden of our gaze,
دستی به علامت محبت	Caressing the face of the petunia
بر صورتِ اطلسی کشیدی	As a token of love.
پروانه شدی و سبز روییدِ	You became a butterfly and stirred into motion.
بر قامت تو دو بال کوچك	On your body were two small wings.
مانند بهار، سبز بودی	Like Spring, you were green,
ای سبزترین نهالِ کوچك	The greenest of all the little shoots.
در دفترِ آسمانِ جبهه	Your flight was simple homework
پرواز تو مشق ساده ای بود	In the heavenly book of the front.
در چشمِ زمانه قامت تو	In the eye of the world, your stature
چون قلهِ ایستاده ای بود	Was standing high like a summit.
با اینکه نهال بودی ای خوب	Dear one! Although you were a sapling,
سر سبزتر از درخت بودی	You were greener than a tree.
گل در غم تو سیاه پوشید	The rose donned black in sorrow,
یعنی آه سفید بخت بودی	Showing that your destiny was white.
با ساقه سبز، خنده ات را	With a green stem, I drew your smile
در باغ شکوفه ها کشیدم	In the blossom-laden garden.
با اشك، کنار آن نوشتم :	With tears I wrote beside it:
فهمیده تر از تو من ندیدم...!	"I don't know anyone of better understanding (Fahmīda) than you...!"

239 See Pamela Karimi, and Christian Gruber, "Introduction: The Politics and Poetics of the Child Image in Muslim Contexts," in *Comparative Studies of South Asia, Africa and the Middle East*, Volume 32, Number 2, 2012, p. 281; also see Shams, *A Revolution in Rhyme*, pp. 234–235.

5.14 Jasmine Petals Like Snow

The title of the last poem in this collection, *Jasmine Petals Like Snow*, is also the volume title. While the title promises a poem related to a blooming garden, it is a tragic poem, recollecting the bombardment of a school and the killing of classmates. The poet deploys the technique of suspense, confounding the reader with the peaceful quixotic title and the shocking contents of the poem. It is only in the last stanza that the reader finds out why the title refers to jasmine petals. It is set at Persian New Year, falling about 21 March, when Iranians traditionally reflect on the bygone year and hope for a better life in the coming year. The school has been bombarded and three girls, Parvanā, Ilhām and Hudā, have lost their lives. The setting is covered with jasmine petals, and red roses have been placed on the girls' empty seats. While this is the essential information the poem imparts, the air of the school is gloomy. The personification of the school and the chalk create a space to narrate what has happened. By giving soul to these objects, the poet amplifies the pain and anxiety that children feel. Even these inanimate objects feel the intensity of pain, trepidation and suffering inflicted upon children. The massacre is of such magnitude that even the pencil withdraws its cooperation. The blackboard is depicted as fertile ground by being compared to a garden. The school's walls have life. The walls embrace the pictures of the three girls. The poem is an elegy that universalises the pain of death:

برف گل یاس	*Jasmine Petals Like Snow*
(برای بچه هایی که در سنگر مدرسه پرواز کردند)	(for children who flew from the trenches of school)
باز هم مدرسه کوچکِ ما	Once more our small school
یاد غمهای بزرگش افتاد	Is remembering great sorrows.
دفتر خاطره ام غمگین است	The book of my memories is sorrowful
شده بی حوصله، کم حرف مداد	The pencil is not interested, has nothing to say.
باز در باغچه تخته سیاه	Again in the garden of the blackboard
می نویسد گچ کوچك بی تاب	The restless little chalk is moving.
توی گهواره آغوشم باز	In the cradle of my open embrace
می کند گریه عروسك بی تاب	My doll is restless, crying.
باز بر سینه دیوار شکفت	Once more, on the wall's chest,
عکس پروانه و الهام و هدی	Photos are like flowers, of Parvāna, Ilhām and Hudā,
یاد آن روز که بمباران شد	Reminding us of the day when our town
شهر ما، مدرسه کوچك ما	And our small school were bombed.

مثل يك دسته كبوتر، دلمان	My heart, like a flock of doves,
باز از شوِق پریدن پُر شد	Is once more brimming with longing to fly.
باز پرواز قشنگی کردیم	Once more we have taken a delightful flight
بالمان نیز همان چادر شد	Once more our veils have turned into wings.
یاکریم دلم آمد لبِ حوض	The dove of my heart alighted on the fountain's lip
نوکش از قصه پرواز پُر است	Its beak full of stories of flying.
آسمان ، مدرسه دوّم ماست	The sky's another school for us.
آه ، گرچه پرِ پروانه شکست! ...	Oh, but the butterfly's wing! It's broken!
باز هم برفِ گل یاس نشست	Once more, jasmine snowflakes
بر سر مدرِسه کوچكِ ما	Have covered our little school.
میز اول، گُلِ سرخی رویید	Red roses are growing in the front row,
جای پروانه و الهام و هُدی	In the places of Parvanā, Ilhām and Hudā.

5.15 Conclusion

By choosing one volume of poetry composed for children I wanted to demonstrate how the culture of martyrdom, war and Islamic revolutionary ideology is instilled in the minds of children. Such poems not only prepare children to deal with the loss of family members and classmates, they also deploy strategies to convince children that a martyr's death is justified. In addition, in several of the poems, these young teenagers are motivated to choose the path of martyrdom to join their martyred family members and friends, who are depicted as heroes whose moral and physical bravery is an example. They have achieved their goal of dying as martyrs, so as to live eternally, transformed into angels or sparrows soaring above the neighbourhoods. The martyr's death is depicted in positive terms. Metaphors and imagery limning martyrdom are linked to nature and to spring, which in Persian culture announces the New Year and a new beginning. The prevailing colours in these poems are red and green. While red refers to the blood of martyrs, green is the colour of eternal life, and together they stand for martyrdom.

The didactic layer of these poems transforms death from a sudden demise and the end of life to a positive turning-point that begins an eternal life. All these martyrs received respect from the community and were hailed as heroes who not only defended Islam and the country but also achieved the highest position a human being can achieve. These martyrs (*shahīd*) gave witness (*shahīd*) to their belief and are, therefore, eternal living beings (Quran 2:154; 3:169). Martyrs do not experience the tribulations of death, the torments of the grave, as they have an immediate passage to Eternity, because they died "in the way of God" (*fī sabīl Allāh*, Quran 3:157–8).[240] They enter Paradise directly (Quran 47:4–6 and 9:111), without suffering the torments of the grave and the ordeals of the resurrection, when the deeds of human beings are measured on the scales of justice (*mīzān-i ʿadl*). All the sins of martyrs are forgiven in the first flow of blood. Also, in the Iranian war context blood is positive. Although blood in Islam conveys ritual impurity, the blood of martyrs allows them to cross from this world to the Hereafter.[241]

These poems also create a collective identity during the war by magnifying familiar concepts from Persian Shiite culture. Although the poet does not use *in verbatim* the concept of *maẓlūm* or "oppressed," the poetic personas of these poems endure and accept what has been inflicted on them. Children are instructed to endure suffering. The concept of "oppressed" in Shiism denotes not only that Shiites are oppressed during the Greater Occultation of the Mahdī, it also connotes the virtue of enduring injustice. In fact, forbearing long-suffering is an essential element of Shiʿi piety, and this is wrapped up in the messages these poems convey to children.

A conspicuous aspect of these poems is the absence of mothers. No particular role is given to the mothers as parents. While one can assume that mothers are present as loyal wives and caring mothers, no attention is paid to the responsible role they fulfil, especially after the deaths of their husbands. In other poems mothers are depicted as ready and proud to offer their children to the Revolution and war. In fact, women and mothers are prominently present in the poetry and in Iranian visual culture of the Iran-Iraq War.[242]

---

240 See W. Raven, in *Encyclopaedia of the Qur'ān*, ed. Jane Dammen McAuliffe, Leiden/Boston, MA/Cologne: Brill, 2001, Vol. I, s.v. Martyrdom, pp. 281–286; also see Jacques Waardenburg in *Encyclopaedia of the Qur'ān*, Vol. I, s.v. Death and the dead, p. 506.

241 See Ze'ev, Maghen, in *Encyclopaedia of Islam, Third Edition*, s.v. Ablution; also see E.H. Waugh, in *Encyclopaedia of the Qur'ān*, s.v. Blood and Blood Clot, pp. 237–238.

242 See J.J. Elias, "Ultimate Sacrifice: Women and Motherhood in Iranian Visual Culture," in *The "Other" Martyrs: Women and the Poetics of Sexuality, Sacrifice and Death in World Literatures*, ed. Alireza Korangy & Leyla Rouhi, Wiesbaden: Harrassowitz Verlag, 2019, pp. 39–54.

6 Sīmīn Bihbahānī on the 1979 Revolution and Iran-Iraq War

ستاره دیده فرو بست و آرمید بیا
شراب نور به رگهای شب دوید بیا
ز بس به دامن شب اشک انتظارم ریخت
گل سپیده شکفت و سحر دمید بیا

The stars have closed their eyes and gone to sleep, come
The wine of light has coursed in the veins of the night, come
I have shed so many tears in waiting at night's hem,
That the rose of dawn has blossomed and day breaks, come.[243]

6.1 Introduction

Sīmīn Bihbahānī was born in Tehran in 1927 and died in 2014. Her father and mother were literary figures in the first decades of the twentieth century. Her father was ʿAbbās Khalīlī, a writer and editor, and her mother, Fakhr ʿUẓmā Arghūn, was a poet who also wrote prose pieces in defence of women's rights. Sīmīn started to write poetry when she was only fourteen years old. In this poetry she follows the style of the pioneer poet, Nīmā Yūshīj, who introduced "New Poetry," in which he chose to bid farewell to classical literary conventions about form, rhyme, metre and imagery. Later, Bihbahānī chose to write in classical forms, especially the ghazal. The ghazal has been used from the dawn of Persian literary history and came to full bloom in the hands of Saʿdī and Ḥāfiẓ in the thirteenth and fourteenth centuries respectively. A characteristic of the ghazal is that it sings the love of the beloved in both profane and mystical contexts, conveying the lover's pangs of love and separation, and passionate longing to attain union with the beloved. In the medieval period, ghazals were sometimes used to praise or criticise a person, usually a ruler or a vizier, in an indirect way. While Bihbahānī is heir to this rich tradition, she changes the form and the use of the ghazal. She contrives new metres based on classical prosody, and employs ghazals to depict everyday events, using new metaphors and imagery corresponding to socio-political events.

243 The translation is almost entirely based on Saeid Rezvani in *Encyclopædia Iranica*, s.v. Bihbahani, Simin ii. Poetry. The poem comes from the ghazal "Sharāb-i nūr" in *Majmūʿa-yi ashʿār*, Tehran: Nigāh, 2003, p. 294.

https://doi.org/10.1515/9783110748734-010

An established poet of twentieth century Iran, Bihbahānī is certainly a prominent war poet. The majority of her poetry is engaged with socio-political events in Iran. Following the 1979 Revolution she kept writing on political developments, often emphasising in her interviews that she was not a political activist but she wanted to voice her opinions about freedom of speech:

> I am neither a subversive, nor a militant. I do not seek to destroy. I am one who voices her opinion, which I feel is my right. I pay no attention to the Islamic Republic. If they now want to cut off my tongue, let them come and take it. If they want to blind me, let them do it. In both systems, we had and we have political prisoners. In those times too, despotism ruled our country. ... I hope that all political prisoners and those imprisoned for their opinions will soon be released, that peace and serenity will return to this country, that people will be at ease, and the people will no longer be subject to irrational pressure, for the people cannot endure this any more.[244]

Bihbahānī's pre-eminence among the war poets has already been mentioned. When the Iran-Iraq War broke out, Bihbahānī began writing poems that condemn violence and magnify the human and material losses of war. As Farzaneh Milani observes, Bihbahānī is an "advocate of individual rights, regardless of gender, class, religion, political affiliation, or ethnicity."[245] Bihbahānī believes that a poet should be engaged with his/her time, to voice the events of the time. She compares herself to the medieval Persian poet, Ḥāfiẓ, who in her view was also a man of his time. Yet Ḥāfiẓ's poetry is very much alive in today's Persian-speaking societies, because he actively lived in his time and the events of his time are identifiable by us. She writes, "The secret to Hafez's timelessness is his being current, his being with his time, and his movement toward eternity through the use of moments."[246] Taking Ḥāfiẓ as her model, Bihbahānī believes that a poet should actively participate in society and exert his/her impact on the current affairs of the time. According to Talattof, there are at least three literary discourses in which her voice is loudly heard: "[t]hese discourses encompass the pre-Revolutionary committed literary movement, the post-Revolutionary feminist literary movement, and in recent years (along with a whole new generation of writers), an emerging movement revolving around certain cultural exigencies

---

244 My translation, from a text online at http://www.rahman-hatefi.net/simin%20behbahani%20-125-850811.htm (retrieved 16.07.2019).

245 See Farzaneh Milani, "Sīmīn Bihbahānī: Iran's National Poet," pp. 3–17. On her biography see Saeid Rezvani, in *Encyclopædia Iranica*, s.v. Behbahani, Simin i. Life.

246 As cited by K. Talattof, "'I Will Rebuild You, Oh My Homeland': Simin Behbahani's Work and Sociopolitical Discourse," in *Iranian Studies*, 41, 1, 2008, p. 20; Ahmad Karimi-Hakkak, "Introduction: Iran's Literature 1977–97," in *Iranian Studies*, 30, 3–4, 1997, pp. 193–213.

of Iranian society. This new development indeed results from a discourse that strives for a renewed sense of literary modernity, in which feminist, reformist, and civil society movements find much common ground for concern." It is in this socio-political context that her poetry is an aesthetic representation of the politics of her country. Reading her poetry, we can see the socio-political history of recent Iran from the time of Muḥammad Riżā Shah, through the 1979 Revolution, the Iran-Iraq War and the fluctuating period until her death in 2014. Her poetry chronicles events in all these periods, preserving crucial moments of Iranian history. Bihbahānī is a poet of the people, and in this capacity her poetry voices the plea of both ordinary and intellectual, religious and freethinker, political activists and the apolitical, and their hopes and frustrations, aspirations and concerns, and security and vulnerability in a crucial period when Iran witnessed a change from monarchy to theocracy, the longest conventional war of the twentieth century, sanctions, floods of internal refugees, the Islamic cultural purification, emigration and the formation of a diaspora.

Profoundly aware of her position as a woman in a patriarchal society, she courageously participates in society. Calling herself "a beguiling Eve" and brandishing "a cup of wine in one hand and a red apple in the other," she bitterly mocks and challenges the image of woman in Islamic society.[247] Although in several poems she addresses gender issues, her poetry is a rich repository of life with all its private and public fluctuations. She writes passionate erotic poetry on love, but also addresses prostitution, the abuse of power, fanaticism and, above all, social justice.[248] In Iran, she is the poet of the people and people know several of her poems by heart, especially because some of them are sung by popular pop singers. Phrases from her poetry have also been used in political campaigns. Despite her reputation, she never received a distinction or official recognition in Iran. She was nominated for the Nobel Prize for Literature in 1999 and 2002.[249]

She started to compose poetry at an early age. From her *Chilchirāgh* ("Candelabrum" 1957) collection we see how, in addition to erotic love poems, she elaborates on socio-political subjects and the quandaries people face in a rapidly changing society. Although she has written poems in various poetic forms, it is in

247 The citation comes from Farzaneh Milani, "Sīmīn Bihbahānī," p. 3.

248 See also ibid., p. 4.

249 See Farzaneh Milani, "Sīmīn Bihbahānī," p. 6, where she refers to other prizes Bihbahānī received. Milani writes, "She also has been the recipient of several international prizes such as the Hellman/ Hammett Human Rights Award in 1998; the Carl Von Ossietzky Human Rights Award in 1999;7 the Latifeh Yarshater Book Award in 2004; and the Freedom of Expression Award by the Writers Union of Norway in 2007."

the ghazal that she shows her flair. The Persian ghazal has strict prosodic rules, specific themes and conventions, and a "conventional stock of imagery."[250] Her innovative contribution to Persian poetry lies in a unique treatment of the ghazal, in which she employs new metres or adjusts rarely used old metres, with new imagery and metaphors, dealing with topical subjects. This successful treatment appears first in *khaṭṭī zi surʿat u az ātash* ("A line of speed and of fire," 1981). In this collection she becomes a participating observer and commentator on gruesome events before, during and after the Revolution. In the following poem Bihbahānī treats the theme of injustice:

در خواب هول رفتم   با قصه یی ز بیداد
آری حکایتی بود   سرب از دهان پولاد
تکبیرگو به هر سو   فریاد خوان به هر کو
عرش خدا روان بود   بر موجهای فریاد
این تیر بود و آن، هم   تن را گرفت و جان، هم
این یک به عرش، بر شد   وان یک به کوچه افتاد
ناگاه، شیونی بود   بی چند و چون، زنی بود
کان کودک چو گل را   تا گور میفرستاد
رگبار مرگ پرور   آن گونه کرد محشر
کز هر ترنجی افتاد   بر خاک، صد پریزاد
من داغ داغ، از تب   گریان به نیمه شب
در سینه ظهر خورشید   در تن ظهور مرداد
چشمان بی فروغم   – هر سو نگر، هراسان –
چون لانه های خالی   در گاهواره ی باد
فریاد دادخواهی   حتّا ز مرغ و ماهی
وان داور شکیبا   داد کسی نمیداد.

وحشت فزا شبی بود   نفرین به هر لبی بود
کای مرگ و ننگ و نفرت   بر آیت ستم باد[251]

I fell asleep with horror by a tale of injustice.
    Truly, such a story, of lead from the mouth of steel:
crying to God on every side,[252] pleas for help in every alley.
    The throne of God was moving on waves of indignation
This was the bullet, it captured body and soul,
    One has gone up to the throne, the other fell in the alley.
The commotion was unexpected: a simple woman

---

250 De Bruijn, p. 354; Dominic Parviz Brookshaw, "Revivification of an Ossified Genre? Sīmīn Bihbahānī and the Persian Ghazal," in *Iranian Studies*, Vol. 41, No. 1, 2008, pp. 75–90.

251 Sīmīn Bihbahānī, *Khaṭṭī zi surʿat u az ātash*, Tehran: Zavvār, third print 1370, pp. 93–94; *Majmūʿa-yi āthār*, pp. 589–590.

252 The compound *takbīr-gū* literally means calling God by saying *allāhu akbar* or "God is Great."

had sent her budding child[253] – to the grave.
The rain[254] that nourishes death brought such a Judgement
that a hundred fairy-faced youths fell from every orange tree.[255]
I am burning up with fever, weeping at midnight.
The midday sun is burning in my breast, August is in my body.[256]
My eyes have no lustre, looking around in terror,
like two empty nests in the cradle of the wind.
Even the birds and fish are clamouring for justice,
But the patient judge gives no-one justice.

It was a night of terror, curses on every lip:
May death, disgrace and hatred light on the sign of oppression.

From the beginning, the poet captures the reader's attention by calling the event a "tale of injustice." The poet is stunned with horror at what she has heard. The story is cold; it is about lead coming from steel. The juxtaposition of the metals is striking, memorable – and then the listener also becomes stunned on realising that this mouth of steel is the barrel and story-words coming out are bullets. And the bullets are also the story, crying to God in every alley. The metaphorical mastery comes down to earth, for this innovative way of opening the poem is actually a description of what happened every day in the streets of Iran during the political protests. Shooting and cries for help to God are part of the one story. The next image has the Throne moving on waves of indignation. The throne of God is mentioned often in the Quran: before heaven and earth were created, it rested on the waters (Quran 11:7). In this image the Throne of God is again moving, such is the indignation aroused by this story. The bullets strike not only the body but also the soul. They are killing simple people's "budding children" without any warning. Bihbahānī depicts here the situation during the demonstrations against the Shah in 1978 when the army fired on protestors. The protestors looked for shelter in every alley, trying to hide in a house, but sometimes this was not possible and they were shot dead.

Even God seems unable to interfere in this injustice, for the bullet goes through both body and soul. It is certainly not God's appointed time of death. While the soul ascends to be near to the Throne of God, the body falls behind

253 Literally "the child like a flower/rose."
254 *Ragbār* is heavy rain, but also the rain of bullets from a machine gun.
255 The word *turanj* means literally sour or bitter orange, often referred to as "Seville orange."
256 Murdād is the fifth month of the Persian calendar, starting on 23 July and ends on 22 August. It is the name of one of the seven great angels in Zoroastrianism, meaning "Long Life on this earth or Immortality in the hereafter." See M. Boyce in *Encyclopaedia Iranica*, s.v. Amurdād. The poet literally says, "the manifestation of Murdād in the body."

in the alley. This seems to be a God's-eye view, for who else can see the soul ascending? This duality between the body and the soul is continued in the fifth couplet in which the poet uses the word *ragbār*, meaning heavy rain, but also the rain of bullets from a machine gun. Rain is very positive in Persian culture, symbolising life, grace and generosity, but here the rain brings death. In this couplet the poet connects this unexpected falling of young people to Firdowsī's *Shāh-nāma* (completed 1010) by mentioning the orange tree. In the opening of the story of *Rustam and Suhrāb*, Firdowsī refers to Suhrāb's innocent death, asking why he was killed and whether death is just or unjust. Firdowsī introduces the question, "If a gale should strike from a corner, knocking an unripe orange to the ground, would you call that justice, or injustice?" In this story, Rustam, the Iranian champion, kills his own son without knowing it. The gale in Firdowsī's poem refers to Rustam who knocks an unripe orange (i.e., Suhrāb) to the ground. In Bihbahānī's poem, it is the *ragbār* caused by the powers of Iranian society that are knocking down their own innocent children.

From couplet six, the poet speaks, and shares her pain and complaint. Experiencing this horrible event, she is burning with fever, cannot sleep and is crying. She depicts the burning in her heart, comparing it to the blistering sun at noon and the hottest month of the year in Iran. In couplet seven the poet moves to depict herself as a trauma-stricken person whose eyes have no light and lustre, looking everywhere in terror as if something horrible might happen at any moment. The simile used to describe the eyes is powerful. The eyes' dark rims are compared to empty nests from which young birds have been snatched. Given the allusion to Firdowsī's gale, one supposes that the birds were taken by a violent wind. Why then are the empty nests lying in "the cradle of the wind," a place of safety? It seems that this is not a description of the wind, but a striking epithet for a tree. The poet connects these original metaphors to another fauna figure, indicating how birds and fishes are shouting for justice. This is a cliché image from classical Persian poetry to indicate that the entire world, from the deepest areas of the earth to the highest heavens, is feeling the injustice done to the Iranian people. In the Persian worldview, the earth is held in the curve of a mythic fish, and the fish in turn is held between the horns of a mythical bull. The bull and the fish refer to the lowest imaginable part of the world, whereas fowls refer to the highest part.

One of Bihbahānī's most powerful poems depicts perhaps the bloodiest day before the 1979 Revolution, the day known as Black Friday. On 17 Shahrivar (8 September 1978), the Shah's soldiers openly shot people in Zhāla Square in Tehran. It is estimated that almost ninety people were killed and some 200 were injured. Michel Foucault (1926–1984), who went to Iran to cover the Revolution, wrote that some 4,000 people were shot.[257] The impact of the shooting was so enormous that ordinary people spoke of thousands of victims. It also brought protestors of different political backgrounds together to fight the Pahlavi regime. Basing himself on European journalists' reports, Ervand Abrahamian writes that Zhāla Square resembled "'a firing squad,' and that the military left behind 'carnage.' [...] A British observer noted that the gulf between Shah and public was now unbridgeable."[258] The carnage led to more demonstrations and also triggered strikes which, a few months later, led to the crumbling of the monarchy.

In "Black Friday," the poet pours out her sorrow about the massacre in a silent language, protesting against violence. Before analysing the poem, I cite it:

چه سکوت سرد سیاهی!

چه سکوتِ سردِ سیاهی!　　چه سکوتِ سردِ سیاهی!
نه فراغِ ریزشِ اشکی　　نه فروغِ شعله ی آهی
نه به چهره ی تو خراشی　　ز درون خسته، نشانی
نه به سینه ی تو، خروشی　　ز دل شکسته، گواهی
چه به جز دمیدن سرخی　　که شکفته از گل زخمی؟
چه به جز دویدن سربی　　که نهفته در خم راهی؟
به نسیم کوی شهیدان　　نفرستی از چه درودی؟
که غمین گذشته ز دشتی　　نه گلی در او، نه گیاهی ...
همه دیده بسته ز وحشت　　همه لب گزیده ز حسرت
نه بشارتی به کلامی　　نه اشارتی به نگاهی
چو فروغ نیزه ببینی　　ز گلوله بر حذرم کن!
که به شام گزمه جز این ها　　نه ستاره هست و نه ماهی
به حریم تربت مردان　　ز حریر پرده نظر کن
که به باد رفته چه سرها　　به لزوم پاس کلاهی!
من و بانگ نفرت و نفرین　　که نمانده چاره به جز این
تو و همنوایی "آمین"　　چو فغان کنم که "الاهی..."[259]

Such a cold black silence ...[260]

Such a cold black silence, such a cold black silence!
No end to the downpour of tears, no light from the flames of sighs,

257 See Ervand Abrahamian, *A History of Modern Iran*, Cambridge: Cambridge University Press, 2008, p. 159.
258 Ibid. Abrahamian compares Black Friday to Bloody Sunday in the Russian Revolution of 1905–06; also see Ahmad Karimi-Hakkak, *A Fire of Lilies*, p. 74.
259 *Khaṭṭī zi surʿat u az ātash, pp. 87–88; Majmūʿa-yi āthār*, pp. 583–584. *For a literary translation of this poem see Milani, A Cup of Sin, p. 91. The poem is dedicated to Arzhan Gharun.*
260 Literally, "What a cold black silence."

No scratch on your face as a sign of the inner wound.
In your breast, no clamour betrays a broken heart
What else but the appearance of the red, that burgeons from a wounded rose?
What else but the rush of lead that was hidden by a bend in the road.
Will you not send greetings to the breeze in the alley of martyrs,
which passes in sorrow over a plain, without any flowers, without any green?
They have all shut their eyes in horror, they bite their lips with shock.[261]
No good news on any tongue, no meaning in a glance.
When you see the gleam of the bayonet, warn me about the bullets,
because except these, there is no star or moon in the night watch.
From behind the silken curtain, gaze on the shrine of heroes:
How many heads have fallen to protect the crown![262]
Here I am with the cry of hatred and cursing, having no solution
But when I wail, "O my God...!" chant "Amen" together with me.

The poem bears the title "Such a cold black silence," referring to the shock the Iranian people experienced.[263] The title is repeated twice in the first line, stressing the despair and paralysis the poet experiences. By emphasising how the killings have stunned her, leaving her with no emotions and strength except silence, the poet shows how she is traumatised. To convey her condition, the poet uses the word "no" four times, giving a mood of helplessness and stupefaction. In this cold dark night the poet cannot stop shedding tears, no power to sigh any longer. In the third line she introduces a second person, who may be her interlocutor, who has also experienced the traumatic event. No wound is visible on the face, no sound is heard from the chest. These lines of stupefaction are followed by three lines in which the poet poses rhetorical questions. The first is wrapped in a floral imagery. The first phrase reads, literally, "what but the breathing of redness" in which "breathing" refers to the process of blooming, when the first signs of the red bud of the rose appear, but we are also informed that this bud is wounded.[264] How is this possible, the poet asks? Parallel to this

261 I have translated *ḥasrat* with "shock" here as I found this more fitting to the context, but the word literally means "sighing for grief; grief, regret; impatience, passion; strong desire, emulation, ambition; envy." See F. Steingass, *Persian-English Dictionary*, s.v. ḥasrat.

262 This line could also be translated as follows: "How many heads have fallen to protect their hats."

263 In her later poetry she uses the term *sīyāhī* ("blackness," "darkness") as a metaphor for repressive regimes. See Kamran Talattof, "'I Will Rebuild You...," p. 27.

264 An alternative reading is: "What else but red breathing, that flowers from the wounded rose" in the third couplet, the poet combines the image of a rose blooming with a wound bleeding. The word *damīdan* means to breathe, to blossom or the appearance of dawn. It is combined with *shikufta*, the "flourishing" of a flower, such as the opening of a rose. This floral image is applied to a vivid and violent situation to depict the bloody scene. There is bleeding, probably

imagery is the phrase "What else but the rush of lead," referring to a bullet, hidden in the curve of a road. Here it becomes clear that the bullet has wounded the fresh rose. The poet uses the rhetorical figure of *tarṣīʿ* or setting in jewels in which each syllable in the first line corresponds perfectly to the next.[265] The effect can be illustrated as follows:

chi bi juz damīdan-i surkhī,	*ki shikufta az gul-i zakhmī*
chi bi juz davīdan-i surbī,	*ki nahufta dar kham-i rāhī*

The final question is the revelation of what has happened. The poet asks the audience why they do not entrust their greetings to the breeze blowing in the martyr's quarter. The poet's bewilderment is emphasised in the immediately following line which ends with an ellipsis. The ellipsis points to the continuation of questions. The message in this line refers to the passing breeze, but it can certainly refer to the martyrs who passed over the plains, without any roses or green, in sadness.

Afterwards, the poet returns to her silenced mood, referring to the closed eyes and shut lips caused by horror and shock. This collective mood prevails in her world as she cannot find any good news or meaningful look. On the contrary, the possible visible news is the gleaming bayonet, a warning of bullets to come. The poet alludes to the night watch in this grim, starless and moonless setting. The word *gazma* means "a patrol" or "a watcher," but here the poet has made a compound of *shām-i gazma* or "the night of the watch or watchers," which in the following lines is linked to protection (*pās*). The poet integrates the Persian proverb *kulāh bi bād dādan*[266] (literally "giving one's hat to the wind"), meaning "to lose everything," into an image that exclaims "how many lost their heads in protecting hats!." But *kulāh* is not only a hat; it also means "crown." In classical poetic usage, the hat stands for material possessions and has a courtly signification,[267] so the line can be read "how many heads have gone to the wind, for the needs of the crown's protectors." The poem ends by emphasising that

fatal bleeding. The rose is metonymically used as a term of endearment, referring to a young person, who is compared to a new rose, but s/he has been shot and blood streams from the wound.

265 For a treatment of Persian rhetorical figures see E.G. Browne, *A Literary History of Persia*, vol. ii, Cambridge: Cambridge University Press, reprint 1956, pp. 44–79; also see E.J.W. Gibb, *A History of Ottoman Poetry*, London: Luzac, 1990, Vol. I, pp. 101–124.

266 Another variant is *kulāh bar bād dādan* or "entrusting one's hat to the wind."

267 In Persian Sufism the *kulāh* is the headgear of a Sufi master. The word *tāj*, "crown" is also used.

there is no way out from this trauma, except cursing the murderers and seeking refuge in God.

The poem is very bleak. The rhyme of the poem is *–āhī*. This is a suffix added to infinitival nouns, but on its own it means "a sigh." Choosing this word/suffix to create the rhyme scheme, the poet limns a saddened picture befitting the subject. Invoking the senses, the poet focuses on hearing: there is an eloquent silence, such that even no sigh can be heard. Paradoxically "a sigh" (*āhī*) is the rhyme. Lips shut out of fear, no tears escape. This silence continues to the end of the poem, where the poet implores God for aid. The sense of sight is also emphasised, through images related to dark, starless, moonless night and closed eyes, augmenting the gloomy time and setting. The barren backdrop of the poem is stressed through coldness, apprehension and the massacre of the living. The only flickering lights in this dark setting are the glints of bayonets. The anxiety is so intense that the individual introduced in the third line does not dare to pronounce anything, but the effects are visible. In this setting there are no sign of growth. The rosebud is wounded before it can open. A sense of paralysis is suggested through the holding of breath. There is no courage even to entrust a word to the breeze, to carry it to the martyrs' lane. The wind carries "heads," cut to protect the crown. The only thing that runs is the bullet in the road. The poem's desolate and decaying tone shows how injustice's dominion has created noxious anxiety.

Black Friday was the turning point, uniting all factions to fight against the Pahlavi regime. Bihbahānī wrote several other poems between this event and the completion of the Revolution in 1979. One written soon after the Revolution demonstrates her philosophy of non-violence. It is entitled *Nimītavānam bibīnam* or "I Cannot Look." Here, she ponders on man's ability to kill, and why one should have compassion even for the enemy. While criticising the gruesome act of execution, she condemns those responsible by problematising the nature of mankind, relating this to God's justice. The poet reveals her feelings at seeing the corpses of men executed after the Islamic Revolution. Given the date of the poem, Isfand 1357/March 1978, it may refer to the execution of several officials of the Pahlavi regime. Immediately after the Revolution, people such as Amir-Abbas Hoveyda, were swiftly sentenced to death by revolutionary courts, led by the low-ranking cleric, Ṣādiq Khalkhālī (1927–2003). Those convicted were immediately executed. Khalkhālī became known as the "hanging judge" or "executioner." The disturbing pictures of blood-soaked corpses were published on the front pages of many newspapers. On the internet this particular poem has been cited alongside the front page of the newspaper *Keyhān*, with photo-shopped pictures of Khalkhālī:[268]

نمی‌توانم ببینم   جنازه‌یی بر زمین است
که بر خطوط مهیبش   گلوله‌ها نقطه‌چین است:
حباب مردابِ چشمش   ز حفره بیرون جهیده
تهی ز اندوه و شادی   گسسته از مهر و کین است
ز سینه تا سیب آدم   نه بازدم هست و نه دم
گذرگهی سرد و خالی   ز ناله‌ی واپسین است
کسی که نقش نگینش   زخون نشان داشت، اینک
فضای خاموش چشمش   چو حلقه‌یی بی‌نگین است
نمی‌توانم ببینم   به خاک و خارا فُتاده
اگرچه خشمِ تو گوید: -"سزای دشمن همین است"
خدای داند که دشمن   اگر دمارم برآرد،
به کُشتنش دل ندارم   که مذهب من چنین است
خدای خوبم، خدایا!   چرا بدی آفریدی؟
کسی که خوبی پسندد   چرا بدی‌آفرین است؟
چه بود اگر آدمی را   فرشته‌خو می‌سرشتی؟
چه پاکی آید از آن گِل   که با پلیدی عجین است؟
به روح قابیل، نفرین!   گر آن یکی اولین بود،
به جان جبریل سوگند   نه این یکی آخرین است
"کتاب و میزان و آهن"،   اشارتی آسمانی‌ست
"عدالت" است این که تیغش   نهفته در آستین است!
زعدل هم می‌گریزم   که خود نمودار ظلم است
به عدل، آن‌جا نیاز است   که ظلم، مسندنشین است![269]

I cannot look, a corpse lies on the ground
    Over its horrific form, bullets have drawn a dotted line.
His moist eyeball has sprung from its socket.[270]
    Empty of joy and sorrow, cut off from love and hatred,
no breath rises or falls between his chest and throat:[271]
    a cold and empty passage for the last sigh.
He was one whose signet ring bore the sign of blood, now
    his lustreless eyes are like the bezel without the jewel.

---

268 http://tarikhirani.ir/fa/news/8402/%D8%AF%D8%A7%D8%B3%D8%AA%D8%A7%D9%86-%D8%A7%D8%B9%D8%AF%D8%A7%D9%85-%D8%A2%D9%86-%DB%B1%DB%B1-%D9%86%D9%81%D8%B1 (last accessed 25.03.2021); also see A. Karimi-Hakkak, *Fire of Lilies*, pp. 196–197; A. Amanat, *Iran: A Modern History*, pp. 779–783.

269 *Khaṭṭī zi surʿat u az ātash*, pp. 101–102; *Majmūʿa-yi āthār*, pp. 595–596. *For a literary translation see Milani, A Cup of Sin, pp. 89–90.*

270 A more literal translation would be "the swamp bubbles of his eyeball has sprung from its socket."

271 Literally "between his chest and Adam's apple."

I cannot look, how he has fallen on earth and flint.
Your anger might say, "this is what the enemy deserves"[272]
but God knows, even if the enemy wants to destroy me
I do not desire his death: such is my religion.
My good God, O Lord! Why did you create wickedness?
Why would one who loves the good make evil?
What would happen if you added an angelic nature into man?
What purity can come from clay that's mixed with evil?
A curse on the soul of Cain, for he was first.
I swear by the soul of Gabriel, this will not be the last.
The book, the scales, and iron are heavenly signs:
They stand for that justice whose blade is hidden in the sleeve,
I flee from justice as well, for it has oppression within it:
those places need justice, where injustice reigns.

Bihbahānī personalises the topic by using the first-person pronoun. She describes her deepest feelings on seeing such an abhorrent picture. After expressing her abhorrence, she nevertheless observes very closely: the bullet wounds form a dotted line, an eye has popped from its socket. The soulless corpse is beyond both love and hatred. The man's former power, signified by a ring with a precious stone, is now empty. The descriptive section ends with the repetition of the phrase "I cannot look," followed in early editions by "how he has fallen on earth and flint." In the third edition (1370/1991), this reads *chunīn bi khᵛārī fitāda* "fallen into humiliation in this way." The first part of the next line also reads differently. The edition cited reads, "Your anger might say," but the third edition (1370/1991) has *agar-chi farzāna gūyad* or "although the wise say," referring ironically to the judge and the revolutionary court as a whole. The word *farzāna* has positive connotations, even in an ironic context, and this may be why the poet has removed it.[273]

The poet emphasises that if even people say that these men of the old regime deserve to die, she would not accept killing other human beings as her faith does not allow it. By referring to her own religion, the poet is criticising the Muslim executioners as they put on a show of being good Muslims. By referring to an enemy who might want to destroy her, she shows that she is quite cognizant of the crimes of the old regime, but this does not give her the right to kill. The poet rejects anger, especially in judging whether to take the life of a human

272 In another edition it reads, "Although the wise says…," referring probably to the judge and the revolutionary court.

273 It is possible that the poet had to remove the word due to sensorship. On various ways the government applies censorship see A. Abiz, *Censorship of Literature in Post-Revolutionary Iran.* On the uneasy relationship of Bihbahānī and the regime see pp. 38, 93, 121, 155.

being. Bihbahānī states that people, in their anger, might well say, "this is what the enemy deserves," when they see the corpse, but she stresses that human life and dignity must be preserved. She condemns killing in general, even in self-defence. Bihbahānī points here to a dilemma of the 1979 Revolution, a time when almost all norms and values were changing. Should people kill others when they have been identified as the enemy? How have the Revolutionary times so changed people that they mimic the old regime's violent responses? What is the place of anger when weighed against human dignity? She does not answer these questions, but her focus on God and the citations from the Quran are explicit criticisms of the merciless events of this crucial period in Iranian history.

From the next line onwards she turns to God, and in a private conversation she asks God why He has created evil. Such conversations (*munājāt*) are a much-loved genre in Persian mystical and religious poetry. From this moment onwards, the poem becomes a religious and philosophical deliberation, pondering on the creation of mankind and God's justice. It is her religious conviction, her personal attitude, that encourages her to suppress her feelings of anger and revenge, not desiring death for the enemy. In this moral dilemma, she asks why men, who are capable of love, choose to do wicked deeds. Bihbahānī directly questions God for having created evil. What is the use and place of evil in creation, if God wanted men to do good? This question has long roots in Islamic theology and Sufism. Theologians and mystics tried to answer the question by pointing to God's names, which are divided into two categories: Merciful (*luṭf*) and Wrathful (*qahr*). At each moment, in each event, one of these categories prevails, but a lover of God embraces both because both come from the Beloved.[274]

While this is outside the scope of this analysis, it is worth mentioning here that mystics such as Ḥallāj (executed 922) and Aḥmad Ghazālī (d. 1126) question why God created Satan if he knew that he would remove him from Paradise and bruise him with His eternal curse.[275] Bihbahānī also refers to the dawn of creation, and to Cain as the first man to do evil by killing his brother. The central

---

274 See A. Schimmel, *Deciphering the Signs of God: A Phenomenological Approach to Islam*, New York: State University of New York, 1994, p. x; L. Gardet in *The Encyclopaedia of Islam, Second Edition*, s.v. Allāh; also see Ritter, *The Ocean of the Soul*, pp. 264–272.

275 F. Papan-Matin, *Beyond Death: The Mystical Teaching of 'Ayn al-Quḍāt al-Hamadānī*, Leiden: Brill, 2010, p. 160. Also see P.J. Awn, *Satan's Tragedy and Redemption: Iblis in Sufi Psychology*, Leiden: Brill, 1983; and A.A. Seyed-Gohrab, "The Erotic Spirit: Love, Man and Satan in Hafez's Poetry," in *Hafiz and the School of Love*, pp. 107–121; idem, "Satan as the Lover of God in Islamic Mystical Writings," in *The Beloved in Middle East Literature: The Culture of Love and Languishing*, ed. Alireza Qurangy, Hanadi Al-Samman and Michael Beard, London/New York: I.B. Tauris, 2017, pp. 85–101.

question is how we should interpret God's justice. Giving a philosophical turn to the killings relating to the 1979 Revolution, the poet ponders the mystery of creation, the responsibilities of God, and what the notions of good and evil entail. Bihbahānī's allusion to the Quran in the line "The book, the scales and iron are heavenly signs..." is another criticism of the executioners. She is not defending the Pahlavi regime, but based on her Muslim pacifist convictions she is trying to convince the reader that the executions are not what God has promised in the Quran. The verse (57:25) she alludes to reads, "Certainly we sent Our apostles with clear arguments, and sent down with them the Book and the balance that men may conduct themselves with equity; and we have made the iron, wherein is great violence and advantages to men, and that Allah may know who assists Him and His apostles, unseen; Surely Allah is Strong, Mighty." Afterwards Bihbahānī concludes that the Book, the scales and iron are God's signs, symbolising "justice" but its blade is "hidden in the sleeve." I am not sure what the poet means by this reference, but it parallels the equally cryptic "unseen" in the Quran verse. Does she mean that the Quran does not clearly specify the use of the sword in the service of justice, giving man the ability to choose vengeance or forgiveness? The association of the three things in the poem and in the verse is at least suggestive: iron performs great violence but it also has advantages for men; it is essential to use the Book; one must think of the Day of Judgment when all human actions are put on a scale before making such a grave decision. This strong condemnation of the executions forces her to "flee" from justice itself, because in her view justice is an example (*nimūdār*), a proof or model of "oppression" (*ẓulm*). The strong conclusion is that a strong desire and reliance on retributive justice is a sign of a fallen society: "those places need justice, where injustice reigns."

6.2 Bihbahānī as a War Poet

Bihbahānī is certainly one of the outstanding war poets. Her poetry on the Iran-Iraq War ranges from encouragement and emotional personal outbursts to depictions of the atrocities of war. The chief difference between her poetry and the poetry of the revolutionary committed poets is that she does not praise war. She neither tries to mobilise people to the front, nor does she elaborate on existing revolutionary concepts such as martyrdom. The title of her poem *shahīd qalb-i tārīkh ast* ("The Martyr is the Heart of History") is borrowed from the slogans used during the 1979 Revolution, in headlines and written on walls, often accompanied by the portrait of a martyr.

In the poem "He is the heart of history," Bihbahānī elevates the position of the martyr to the level of the Sun, depicting him as an individual who is imbued with light, even giving out light like the sun. Bihbahānī is connecting blood to light, a poetic strategy we also see in Amīnpūr's poetry. Bihbahānī negates the blood around the martyr, for that blood is light. In classical Persian poetry the dawn is sometimes depicted as if the disc of the sun cuts the head of the night and then the dawn is born. The crimson light of the dawn is associated with this sacrifice. Bihbahānī's association of blood and light may well derive from such imagery. Another image, also from classical Persian poetry, is the dust-mote and the sun. In classical usage, the mystical poet depicts how, with the rise of the sun, a symbol of the beloved, the lovers, who are dust-motes start to dance ecstatically in its rays. Such imagery refers to the elevated position of the beloved, the extreme longing of the lovers and their lightness, i.e., their freedom from attachments. Moreover it is possible to unite with the divine beloved only when the beloved draws them. In this poem the lover is united with the sun. The poet suggests that martyrdom has removed the duality of being the lover or the beloved, as the lover has become part of the beloved. In Persian mystical love theories, for example in Aḥmad Ghazālī's treatise, the lover becomes part of the beloved by shedding all personal qualities, so that there is nothing left that is not the beloved.[276]

Another topic Bihbahānī connects to martyrdom is the Quranic allusion "victory is from God" (48:1). The martyr is not only the way to victory; without him there would be no victory. The tender way Bihbahānī depicts the wounds on the martyr's head says a lot about the position of martyrs in Iranian culture of this period. The floral imagery compares the upright and tall stature of the martyr to a cypress tree, a symbol of eternity and of pure love. Red spots of blood are likened to the burgeoning of flowers on a Judas tree. This tree's blossoms appear on the tree's brown trunk in early Spring, when the tree does not have any leaves. The deep red blossoms later turn into green leaves. The blood spots are compared to jewels on a crown. Continuing the floral imagery in the last couplets, the poet refers to the scent of the garden. This scent is associated with the martyr who brings freedom:

او "قلب تاریخ است" محتاج دفتر نیست
او روح ایمان است جز عین باور نیست
خورشید میجوشد از سینه اش گویی
او غرقه در نور است در خون شناور نیست

---

276 Aḥmad Ghazālī, *Savāniḥ*, pp. 59 – 66, *faṣl* 39.
277 *Majmūʿa-yi āthār*, pp. 593 – 594.

شمعی میفروزید   بر خشت بالینش
کان چهره از خورشید   یک ذره کمتر نیست
او واژه "فتح" است   نزدیک شد – باری –
"نصر من اللّهت"   بی او میسر نیست
او معنی فضل است   آری "مجاهد" را
قدری عظیم ار هست   بی این مقدر نیست
شمشاد گلگون است   روییده در خون است
در هیچ باغ اینسان   سرو و صنوبر نیست
فرزند خورشید است   دلبند مهتاب است
روشنگر گیتی است   تنها ز مادر نیست
بر تارکش بنگر!   چون ارغنون، زخمی:
تاج شهیدان را   خون هست و زیور نیست.

امسال، فروردین   شاید توانم دید
باغی که آذینش   گلهای پرپر نیست
این عطر آزادی است   کز راه می آید
آری، نسیم اینسان   هرگز معطر نیست.[277]

He is "the heart of history," he needs no book.
    He is the spirit of faith, he is nothing else but the essence of faith.
You would think that the sun was boiling over in his chest.
    He is not swimming in blood, he is immersed in light.
Light no candle by his stone pillow,
    There's not a dust-mote of difference between him and the sun.
He is the word "victory." Is it near? Surely so.
    Without him there is no way to "victory is from God."[278]
He is the meaning of excellence. Even if the mujāhid is most worthy
    Without God, nothing is possible.
The boxwood is red, it has grown in blood;
    No garden has a cypress or greenwood to compare with this.
He is the son of the sun, the moon's sweetheart:
    The light of all the world is more than one mother's child.
Look at the crown of his head, wounded like the Judas tree.
    The crown of martyrs is blood, it needs no jewels.

Perhaps, this spring, I may see a garden
    whose glories are not shredded roses.
This is the attar of freedom, coming from the road,
    a breeze such as this is never perfumed.

* * *

Another war poem, written on 30 September 1980 (8 *mihr* 1359), is entitled "We didn't want it, but it exists." In a dedication, Bihbahānī writes, "a fragment of

---

278 Quran 48:1.

the heart, dedicated to the brave fighters of my country." The significance of the poem is that it was written shortly after the start of the war on 22 September 1980. It is an emotional outpouring emphasising how Saddam Hussein imposed the war on Iran by invading the country. The emphasis is on the presence and continuity of Iran as a country and culture. The rhyme is *-ā* followed by a *radīf* or refrain *hast*, meaning "it exists." Through the repetition of the present tense of the verb "to be" as a refrain to each couplet, the poet forces the reader to focus on the present and what is happening at this very moment. While encouraging Iranians to guard the country even with their souls, she refers to several emblematic localities, national poets, and to the elements constituting the homeland. She makes it clear that she is an Iranian, and the soil of Iran should be defended. The significance of the soil of Iran comes to the fore when the poet alludes to her father's bones resting in this soil, or her mother's body sleeping in the earth's chest. Through such allusions she invokes patriotism in the soldiers. Moreover, the poet refers to iconic cities of Iran such as Mashhad, Tus and Shiraz, to arouse individual readers' memories of the specific qualities of these localities and why they should be protected.

Towards the end of the poem, the poet turns to the homeland and renews her pact with it, emphasising that her soul belongs to the homeland for as long as she lives. This homeland has given her everything, such as poetry and excitement, and is also to be the place of her grave. In the last three couplets the poet speaks directly to the soldiers, wishing them victory. The enemy is characterised as Abū Lahab (literally "father of the flame"). Abū Lahab was a relative of the prophet Muḥammad who became his enemy. He is mentioned in the Quran (111:3) where he and his wife are consigned to "the flames of Hell."[279] Bihbahānī ends her poem with this religious allusion:

ما نمی‌خواستیم، اما هست
جنگ، این دوزخ، شررزا هست
گفته بودم که "هان مبادا جنگ!"
دیدم اکنون که آن "مبادا" هست
خصم، چون ساز کج مداری کرد
کی دگر فرصت مدارا هست؟
این وطن، جان ماست، با دشمن
مسپارید، جان ما، تا هست
آتش افزارتان – به نام ایزد -
آتش افروز و آتش‌افزا هست
خود گرفتم نبود، – گو که مباد! -
چنگ و دندان و سنگ خارا هست

279 W. Montgomery Watt, in *Encyclopaedia of Islam, Second Edition*, s.v. Abū Lahab.

دست یازید! تا توان باقی‌ست
پای دارید، تا که یارا هست
ای عقابان آهنین پر و بال!
خود ز پروازتان چه پروا هست؟
گر، به آبشخوری نیاز شماست
آبگیر سپهر مینا هست
رایتان گر شکار بحر و بر است
بره و ماهی‌اش مهیا هست
گر، گیاهینه خوردتان باید
توشه از خوشه ی ثریا هست
ای سمندروشان! خطا گفتم
آتش است آنچه‌تان گوارا هست
کوه آتشفشان جسته ز جا
دارد آن خشم و کین که با یا هست
بر سر دشمنان فرو بارید
هر بلا کز فرود و بالا هست!
ما نمی‌خواستیم جنگ و ستیز،
خواست، اهریمن و دریغا هست
لانه‌ی اهرمن نشاید داشت
خانه تا جلوه‌گاه مزدا هست
"آشنا" پوستین و پوست بکند
شرف اما هنوز با ما هست
آشنا را به غیر نفروشیم
عقلمان راهبر به سودا هست
نزل بیگانگان نشاید کرد
گرچه در خانه، خوان یغما هست
نام ایران بود شناسه من
اینچنینم جهان، شناسا هست
زنده و مرده‌ام بدین خاک است
غیر از اینم کجا پذیرا هست؟
استخوان پدر نهان اینجاست
تن مادر، به گور، تنها هست
خانه طفلیم، دبستانم
یادگاران خاطر آرا هست
همت‌آباد و باغ ملی و ارگ
دایه و بازی و تماشا هست
و آن نقاره که می‌زدند به شام
باز در گوش من به غوغا هست
و آن که اول کلام عشق، سرود
- گرچه اکنون دگرنه برنا – هست
توس و آن مشهد شریف امام
اشک خامش، زبان گویا، هست
دل که همچون کبوتران، به طواف
در تپش بود – و نیز حالا- هست
و آنگه آرامگاه فردوسی
- آن عظیم عزیز والا- هست
درد بسیار آن جذامی ی کور

شرم ناچیزی ی هدایا هست
شهر شیراز و موسم گل سرخ
سعدی و حافظ و مصلی هست
شب و کارون و آسمانی صاف
- که در او هرستاره پیدا – هست
طبرستان و بیشه‌ها انبوه
کوه و آئینه‌اش ز دریا، هست
خیل یاران- اگرچه رفته بسی -
بیشتر مانده پای بر جا هست
ای وطن! با تو بسته‌ام عهدی
جانم از آن تست، تن تا هست
شعر و شور و سرورم اینجا بود
تخت و تابوت و گورم اینجا هست
ای عزیزان! امید فتح شماست
در دلم هیچ اگر تمنا هست
شب اگر وهمناک و تاریک است
روشنی های صبح فردا هست
خصم اگر با نشان بو لهبی است
با شما آیت "سیصلی" هست[280]

We didn't want it, but it exists,
War, this hell, this inferno, exists.
I had said, "Oh, let it not be, the war"
Now I see that this "let it not be" exists.
As the enemy is determined to shoose a crooked way,
What other occasion could there be for fortitude?
This homeland is our soul. For as long as it is so,
Do not entrust it to the enemy.
Your fire machine throws fire,
In the name of God, the fire is burning.
I'm not imagining it – let it not be so:
Teeth and claws, the stone and flint, are so.
Stretch out your hand, so long as power remains
Stand and stay, to the limit.
O iron-winged eagles,
Why should you fear your flight?
If your need is for a place to drink,
There's the lustrous blue pond of heaven.
If your plan is to hunt the sea and plain,
There, there are rams and fish in plenty.[281]
If your appetite is for green herbs,
Take provisions from the Pleiades' cluster.
What am I saying? You are as salamanders,

280 *Majmūʿa-yi āthār*, pp. 613–617.
281 With an implied meaning: hunt in the heavens, where Aries and Pisces are found.

Only fire is food for you.
The volcano's been relocated,
Of course it is angered and vengeful.
Rain down every affliction in heaven and on earth
On the head of the enemy.
We didn't want war and enmity,
Ahriman wanted it and, more's the pity, it is so.
It is not fitting to possess Ahriman's nest
Where the house is Mazda's look-out tower.
The "acquaintance" may flay the shirt and skin from our backs,
But the honour will still be with us.
We do not sell the acquaintance to strangers
Our reason is the guide to passionate love.
The stirrup-cup should not be given to strangers,
Even when a banquet is spread within the house.[282]
The name of Iran is my identity:
know, O world, here am I.[283]
I live and die by this earth,
where else will I find a welcome?
My father's bones are concealed here,
my mother's body is alone in the grave.
The house and school of my childhood
are cherished memories, are here.
Himmat-ābād and the National Park and Citadel,
the wet-nurse, playtime, and great events to see are here.
That special music they played at night
still echoes in my ears.[284]
That one who first whispered the word of love
– who is no longer young – is here.
At Tus and the place where the noble Imam fell
there are silent tears and tongues that speak,
And the heart, like the doves, is circling, fluttering
and still it is so.
There stands the shrine of Firdowsī,

282 Probably an allusion to Ḥāfiẓ's *khᵛān-i yaghmā*, (see Ḥāfiẓ, *Dīvān*, ed. P. Nātil Khānlarī, Tehran: Khvārazmī, 1362/1983, p. 22, line 3) but in a completely different context. Avery's translation reads: "Alas that these saucy, jesting, city-ravishing gypsies / should, as Turks do the spoil's feast, pillage patience from the heart. *The collected Lyrics*, p. 21, line 3. Also see Dick Davis' elegant translation, *Faces of Love: Hafez and the Poets of Shiraz*, Washington D.C.: Mage Publishers, 2012, p. P. 128, line 3: "Alas, these rowdy, sweet-voiced gypsies have ripped out patience from my heart, / Like Turks who make off with a feast's leftovers when the guests depart."
283 Another translation could be: "In this way, the world knows me."
284 The poet is probably alluding to *naqāra* "kettle-drum and wind instruments," played at the shrine of the eight Shiite Imam Riżā (766 – 818) in Mashhad. In the next lines, the poet describes the shrine, the doves in the yard and the people walking around the Imam's mausoleum.

sublime and grand, and dearly loved.
Shame, at the inadequacy of our gifts,
Hurts like the many pains of that blind leper.[285]
Shiraz is here, and the season of the red rose
Saʿdī and Ḥāfiẓ and the garden of Muṣalā.
It is night: the river Kārūn,
In the limpid sky, every star shines out.
Tabaristān is there: densely forrested
And the mountain reflecting in the sea.
A company of dear friends is there:
True, many have departed, but most remain.
O my motherland! I have sealed a pact with you:
So long as my body exists, my soul belongs to you.
My poetry, fervour and delight have been here,
My bed and coffin and grave are here.
Dear ones, my hope is your victory,
is there any other desire in my heart?
If the night is dark and fearful,
there is still the light of tomorrow's dawn.
If the foe bears the sign of Bū-Lahab,
You have the verse of Sayaslā.

* * *

Perhaps her most famous war poem is "Once more, I will build you, my homeland" dating from Isfand 1360/March 1982. At a time when Iraqi attacks had intensified, the poem stirred patriotic sentiments.[286] While during the war the poem was cited by different hierarchies of society, after the war it became a poem with a nationalistic layer, sung by the famous pop singer, Dariush Eqbali. In this popular reception, the videos accompanying the song have different images depending on the maker's purpose and usage.[287] Although it is a war poem, alluding to the destruction of the country, it is also a poem of hope and peace, inviting Iranians to rebuild the country. The poem's continuing popularity is due to the positive orientation of building and progress. As K. Talattof rightly ob-

285 Probably a reference to Furūgh Farrukhzād's documentary of a leper coplony entitled *The House is Black* (1963).

286 The poem is also translated as "I Will Rebuild You, Oh My Homeland" by Kamran Talattof in "'I Will Rebuild You, Oh My Homeland': Sīmīn Bihbahānī's Work and Sociopolitical Discourse," in *Iranian Studies*, Vol. 41, No. 1 (Feb., 2008), pp. 19–35; Milani chooses "My Country, I will Build you Again," *A Cup of Sin*, p. 68.

287 For an analysis of the poem see Kamran Talattof, "'I Will Rebuild You…," pp. 19–35; idem, *The Politics of Writing in Iran: A History of Modern Persian Literature*, Syracuse, NY: Syracuse university Press, 2000.

serves, "the poem contains no clear references regarding the Iran-Iraq war itself. No airplanes, bombers, or missiles fly over Tehran in this poem. Tanks do not roll on the roads of the border cities. There are no war-martyr burial scenes, and the only corpses present are those in a state of resurrection. No external enemy occupies any city, and the enemy is fairly domesticated, in the form of Ahriman."[288] This is indeed a fascinating poem as it is used by different people for different purposes. My analysis of the poem aims to supplement Talattof's excellent examination. Before starting my analysis, I present the poem in translation. Sīmīn Bihbahānī dedicated it to the celebrated novelist, Sīmīn Dānishvar (1921–2012), whom the poet characterises as "the queen of the Persian novel":

دوباره میسازمت، وطن!　　اگر چه با خشت جان خویش
ستون به سقف تو می زنم　　اگر چه با استخوان خویش
دوباره می بویم از تو گل　　به میل نسل جوان تو
دوباره می شویم از تو خون　　به سیل اشک روان خویش
دوباره یک روز روشنا　　سیاهی از خانه می رود
به شعر خود رنگ می زنم　　ز آبی ی آسمان خویش
اگر چه صد ساله مرده ام　　به گور خود خواهم ایستاد
که بردرم قلب اهرمن　　زنعره آنچنان خویش
کسی که "عزم رمیم" را　　دوباره انشا کند به لطف
چو کوه می بخشدم شکوه　　به عرصه ی امتحان خویش
اگر چه پیرم، ولی هنوز　　مجال تعلیم اگر بود
جوانی آغاز می کنم　　کنار نوباوگان خویش
حدیث "حب الوطن" زشوق　　بدان روش سازمی کنم
که جان شود هر کلام دل　　چو برگشایم دهان خویش
هنوز در سینه، آتشی　　به جاست کز تاب شعله اش
گمان ندارم به کاهشی　　ز گرمی ی دودمان خویش
دوباره می بخشیم توان　　اگر چه شعرم به خون نشست
دوباره می سازمت به جان　　اگر چه بیش از توان خویش[289]

Once more, I will build you, my homeland,
though it be with the bricks of my soul.
I will raise pillars to your roof,
though they be of my own bones.
I will smell your flowers once more,
in the aspirations of your youth.
Once more, I will wash blood from you,
with the torrent of my flowing tears.
Once more, one bright day,
the darkness will pass from the house.

288 Kamran Talattof, "'I Will Rebuild You...,'" p. 29.
289 *Majmūʿa-yi āthār*, pp. 711–712. The poem comes from the *Dasht-i arzhan* collection (1360–1362/1981–1983).

I will dye my poem with the blue of my own heaven.
Even if I've been dead a hundred years,
I will stand again upon my grave.
Such will be my cry that I
will tear Ahriman's heart apart.[290]
Out of grace, the resurrector of "rotting bones"
Has given me a mountain of glory.
Although I'm old, if there's a chance to learn
I will return to youth, side by side with my children.
I'll recite the tradition about "love of homeland" with such passion
that every heart-felt word comes to life when I open my mouth.
I still have fire in my chest, and its burning
Assures me of the lasting warmth of my ancestors.
Once more, you give me strenth, though my poems are seated in blood.
Once more, I will build you with my soul, though it be beyond my powers.

This ghazal of nine couplets is couched in the metre *rajaz*, a flowing metre that several Persian poets have used, with variants. The word *rajaz* literally means "to roar" or "thunder" and in compounds such as *rajaz-kh^{v}ānī* "to swagger" or "using boastful verse or words at a time of contest." While the rhythm suggests a soldier's boast in war, proclaiming Iran's virtues to the enemy, paradoxically the poem is directed to the homeland itself. The poet's emphasis is on building rather than destruction. The rhyme is *-ān-i kh^{v}īsh*, for example, *jān-i kh^{v}īsh*, my soul (soul-of-me). The *radīf*-rhyme *-i kh^{v}īsh* is the first person possessive, and is repeated in most couplets. The word *kh^{v}īsh* in this prominent position emphasises the poet's active participation in the war. The Iranians are fighting in the front line, offering their lives to protect the homeland, yet the poet's persona emphasises that she is rebuilding the country. This determination to build the homeland is further emphasised through the word *du-bāra* or "once more," repeated five times, and the grammatical present continuous marker *mi-* added to many verbs in the poem. The central subject of the poem is homeland (*vaṭan*). Substituting the homeland for the beloved in a classical ghazal was a vogue in the literary movement of the Constitutional Revolution (1906–11). The trope was used by prominent ghazal writers such as ʿĀrif (1882–1934), Farrukhī-yi Yazdī (1889–1939) and Muḥammad Taqī Bahār (1886–1951), to name only a few, but that was not in time of war.[291] The difference between this ghazal

290 The last two couplets are not included in *Majmūʿa-yi āthār.*

291 Afsaneh Najmabadi, "The Erotic Vatan [Homeland] as Beloved and Mother: To Love, to Possess, and To Protect," in *Comparative Studies in Society and History*, Vol. 39, No. 3 (Jul., 1997), pp. 442–467; Mohamad Tavakoli-Targhi, "From Patriotism to Matriotism: A Tropological Study of Iranian Nationalism, 1870–1909," in *International Journal of Middle East Studies*, Vol. 34,

and other poems devoted to the homeland is that Bihbahānī writes a very optimistic poem at a time when Iraqi planes and missiles are bombarding Iran, and Iranian youths are offering their lives.

The poem's effectiveness lies in the assurance it offers that this sacrifice of lives is not in vain. The "I" of the poem, a persona in which the reader is invited to participate, will rebuild Iran. The compound *khisht-i jān-i khᵛīsh* (brick of my soul, brick of my life) in the first line is new. The word *khisht* refers to clay bricks, with the implication that the particles of dust together form a clay brick. The anatomical metaphor is extended in the second couplet, where the bones become pillars for the country's roof. Those killed at the front do not die in vain, for their sacrifice can be turned towards reconstruction. By foregrounding herself through first-person pronouns, verbs and the reflective or intensive pronoun "myself" (*khᵛīsh*), the poet makes the theme personal. Paradoxically, this smallness and subjectivity give the poem a collective and universal implication. The anatomic metaphors recur in the blood and tears of the fourth couplet, in which the poet repeats the "once more" of the first line. Two more repetitions follow. The connotation is not simply the repetition of past action, or a return to the past; "once more" contains within itself an openness to the future. The rebuilding is connected to the Quran by the compound *ʿazm-i ramīm*, corrupted or rotten bones, which occurs in the second Surah, verse 259, in connection with a question as to whether God could restore a ruined town.[292] God revives the bones, clothing them with flesh. The compound appears in classical Persian poetry in the context of Jesus reviving the dead on the Day of Judgement. The poet positions herself as a reviver of dead things who, with God's help, can breathe a soul into the dead body of her homeland. There is no explicit reference to the gender of the persona, but "Even if I've been dead a hundred years, / I will stand again upon my grave" suggests a woman, since it brings to mind the resurrection of the Sasanian princess in the opera "The Black Shroud" by Muḥammad Riżā Mīrzāda ʿIshqī (1893 – 1923). This opera takes place after the crumbling of the mighty Sasanian Empire (A.D. 226 – 652). A caravan arrives at nightfall at the former capital, Ctesiphon and, at seeing the ruins, the narrator is triggered to

---

No. 2 (May, 2002), pp. 217 – 238; for a historical meaning of the term *vaṭan* see Shafīʿī-Kadkanī, *Chirāgh-u āyina*, pp. 641 – 671.

292 In paraphrase: a man with a donkey passed by a ruined town and asked himself, "How could God restore this to life?." So God caused him to die for a hundred years, and then revived him. He said, "How long have you been like this?" The man said, "A day or part of a day." God said, "No, for a hundred years. Look at your food and your drink; it has not changed with time. But look at your donkey; ... and at the bones [of the donkey] – how we raise them and cover them with flesh." The man then concludes, "I know that God has power over all things."

think of Persia's forlorn glory and how the Arabs destroyed the Empire. Walking in this setting, he arrives at a graveyard where he meets a girl wrapped entirely in a black shroud. She introduces herself as a Persian princess, daughter of the Sasanian king, Khusrow Parvīz II. She laments Persia's declining conditions, demanding that Iranian women should remove the veil and participate in society, because so long as women are wrapped in black shrouds, half the Iranian nation is dead.[293] There are several elements in this story which are connected to Bihbahānī's couplet; the Sasanian Empire was defeated by Arabs, the ruins of the capital Ctesiphon are in present-day Iraq, and the resurrection and message of the Persian princess, who symbolises Iran's pre-Islamic culture and heritage. This woman becomes the symbol of Iranian woman in terms of participating in society, coming to life from death, and rebuilding the country to its ancient glory.

Bihbahānī's couplet could be interpreted as an answer to the Sasanian princess in which the poem's persona participates in the war against the Iraqi Arabs through her poetry, revives the history of Iranian heroes and is rebuilding the homeland even if it is reduced to dust.[294] Allocating the role of rebuilding the country to herself as a woman indicates that she has taken a leading role, reciting her poem as a war chant for the Iranian army. The leading role personified by the Sasanian princess in 'Ishqī's opera is now in the hands of Bihbahānī. Now it also becomes clear why the poet dedicated the poem to Sīmīn Dānishvar, characterising her as "the queen of the Persian novel." Bihbahānī is connecting to women who take a lead in Iran's socio-political developments. Her way of refashioning the homeland is different, as is emphasised in the line that refers to the Islamic tradition of *ḥubb al-vaṭan min al-īmān* or "the love of one's country is part of the faith." This tradition was widely used from the nineteenth century to create patriotism in Iranians, but in Bihbahānī's usage it turns into a life-giving invocation. Empowered, with God's help, to revive the dead, the poet turns the words of the tradition into *jān*, which means both life and spirit, as she speaks them. There is certainly a reference to Jesus' miracle of reviving the

---

293 Muḥammad Riżā Mīrzāda 'Ishqī, *Kulliyyāt-i Muṣavvar-i 'Ishqī*, ed. 'Alī Akbar Mushīr Salīmī, New York/Piedmont: Jahan Book Co, 1985, pp. 201–219; on using the past as a literary topos for the contemporary political context see B.S. Amoretti, "The Political Realm's Literary Convention: The Example of 'Ishqi and Iqbal," *The Necklace of the Pleiades: 24 Essays on Persian Literature, Culture and Religion*, ed. F.D. Lewis and S. Sharma, Leiden: Leiden University Press, 2010, pp. 281–293.

294 See Seyed-Gohrab, "Poetry as Awakening: Singing Modernity," in *Literature of the Early Twentieth Century: From the Constitutional Period to Reza Shah*, ed. A.A. Seyed-Gohrab, London/New York: I.B. Tauris, 2015, pp. 30–132.

dead and the biblical allusions to the "word." In the last couplets, the poet compares her courage, vigour and vitality to her pre-Islamic ancestors' and is ready to compete with them in fervour. The concluding couplet emphasises her passion for rebuilding the homeland by twice repeating "once more." The poet asks for strength from the homeland so that she can defend it. In the last line she renews her promise to rebuild the homeland even if it is beyond her powers.

6.3 A Poem on the Oil City of Khurramshahr

Another war poem Bihbahānī wrote is dedicated to "the brave defenders of Khunīnshahr and all the other blood-soaked cities of the homeland." The oil-rich city of Khurramshahr was one of the cities on the front which suffered the worst atrocities. Iraqi forces occupied the city for 578 days, from 24 October 1980 until the Iranian army liberated the city on 24 May 1982, in operation Beyt al-Muqaddas. This was one of the bloodiest periods of the war, during which many Iranians and Iraqis were killed, and women and children were assaulted. Due to the high casualties in this period, Khurramshahr received the sobriquet Khūnīnshahr, which means "the blood-soaked city," whereas Khurramshahr means "prosperous city." An iconic moment for the war was the action of the twelve-year-old boy Muḥammad Ḥuseyn Fahmīda, who threw himself with a grenade belt under an Iraqi tank and blew himself up. His deed is painted on the walls of buildings in various towns and cities, alongside Ayatollah Khomeini's praise, "Our leader is that twelve-years-old child who threw himself with his little heart against the enemy. He is worth more than a hundred pens and a hundred tongues."[295] Needless to say, dozens of artists and poets created artworks on Khurramshahr. Ḥuseyn Isrāfīlī composed an ode (*qaṣīda*) entitled "My City Khurramshahr" (*shahr-i man Khurramshahr*), in which he compares his hometown to "the minā of love," referring to pilgrims to Mecca.[296] One of the last rituals of the *ḥajj* is to sacrifice an animal such as a sheep as a re-enactment of Abraham's offering his son at God's command (Quran 37:102). This has

295 See C. J. Gruber, "The Message is on the Wall: Mural Arts in Post-Revolutionary Iran," in *Persica: Annual of the Dutch-Iranian Society*, 22, 2008, pp. 15–46, esp. pp. 31–33; also see Peter Chelkowski and Hamid Dabashi, *Staging a Revolution: The Art of Persuation in the Islamic Republic of Iran*, New York: New York University Press, 1999; J.M. Davis, *Martyrs: Innocence, Vengeance, and Despair in the Middle East*, New York: Palgrave Macmillan, 2003, p. 49.

296 For Isrāfīlī's use of this motif see M. Nematollahi Mahani, *'Do Not Say They Are Dead': The Political Use of Mystical and Religious Concepts in the Poetry of the Iran-Iraq War*, Unpublished PhD Dissertation, Leiden University, 2014, pp. 123–124.

become a festive day for Muslims, known as *yawm al-azhā*.[297] The analogy of Khurramshahr and Minā is that Iranian soldiers sacrificed themselves to free the cities.

Bihbahānī's depiction of the city concentrates on destruction, sacrifice and the horrifying anxiety overwhelming everyone, including animals. The poem was written in Ābān 1359/1980. The title of the poem emphasises the bloody events by repeating the imperative "Write!" followed by an exclamation mark:

بنویس! بنویس! بنویس!

(به مدافعان دلیر " خونین شهر"
و همه ی شهرهای خونین وطنم)

بنویس! بنویس! بنویس:　　　اسطوره ی پایداری
تاریخ، ای فصل روشن!　　　زین روزگاران تاری
بنویس: ایثار جان بود　　　غوغای پیر و جوان بود
فرزند و زن، خان و مان بود　　　از بیش و کم، هر چه داری
بنویس: پرتاب سنگی　　　حتی ز طفلی به بازی
بنویس: زخم کلنگی　　　حتی ز پیری به یاری
بنویس: قندان نوزاد　　　بر ریسمان تاب می خورد
با روز، با هفته، با ماه　　　بر بام بی انتظاری
بنویس کز تن جدا بود　　　آن ترد، آن شاخه ی عاج
با دستبندش طلایی　　　با ناخنانش نگاری
بنویس کانجا عروسك　　　چون صاحبش غرق خون بود
این، چشم هایش پر از خاك　　　آن شیشه هایش غباری
بنویس کانجا کبوتر　　　پرواز را خوش نمی داشت
از بس که در اوج می تاخت　　　رویینه باز شکاری
بنویس کان گربه در چشم　　　اندوه و وحشت به هم داشت
بیزار، از جفت جویی　　　بی بهره از پخته خواری
نستوه، نستوه، مردا!　　　این شیر دل، این تکاور
بشکوه بشکوه، مرگا!　　　این از وطن پاسداری
بنویس از آنان که گفتند:　　　یا مرگ، یا سرفرازی
مردانه تا مرگ رفتند　　　بنویس! بنویس! آری...[298]

Write, write, write!

(For the brave defenders of "Khūnīnshahr"
and all the other blood-soaked cities of my homeland.)

Write, write and write the legend of resistance,
[Write], O History, the luminous chapter of this dark time.

---

297 F. Buhl, in *The Encyclopaedia of Islam, Second edition*, s.v. Minā.
298 *Majmūʿa-yi āthār*, pp. 618 – 619.

Write: it was life-sacrifice,
It was a turmoil of young and old,
Women and children, house and home
Greater and lesser, whatever you had.
Write: to throw stones, even a child at play
Write: the wounds of the axe, even in old age coming to help.
Write: the new babe's swaddling clothes stay swinging on the line,
All day, all week, a month: hanging on the rooftop, restlessly.
Write: that brittle branch of ivory was cut from the body
With golden bracelet, painted nails.
Write: the doll, like her owner, submerged in blood:
The sight of one is full of dust, the eyes of the other besmirched.
Write: the doves had no desire to fly there,
so many armoured falcons were hunting in the skies.
Write: horror and grief in the eyes of the cat,
Wearied of looking for a mate, tired of cooked meat,
Courage, courage, O men! You lion-hearts, you chiefs.
Splendid, splendid, O death! You guardians of the homeland.
Write of those who said, "Death, or with head held high."
Courageously they went to die. Write, write: "Yes."

The poet shoots quick images of different scenes, like a camera lens, and so suggests the complete picture of what is happening in the war-stricken cities. The poet avoids a catalogue of atrocities, instead giving the telling details that show how the normal course of life has given way to horrors. She uses short phrases strung together in a long stretch, creating the effect of a panting breath. After referring to resistance and sacrifice, we see how women and children, young and old, are frantic and distressed, but taking part in the resistance. While little children are hurling stones instead of playing, old men are taking up the axe to aid the soldiers. The aberration is stressed through the image of a baby's swaddling clothes on the line, which shows how unexpectedly the enemy's forces have attacked the city. After these disturbing images, the poet depicts the deaths of innocent women through the metaphor of the "brittle branch of ivory cut from the body." Ivory in Persian poetry would often refer to the light colour of a courtesan's skin, but here it probably refers to the bone of an arm. Even the hand of the dead woman shows how ordinary life has changed: she had painted her nails, was wearing a gold bracelet. Another moving image is the murdered little girl who is soaked in blood together with her doll. The visual image of the girl's eyes and the doll's eyes, both covered in dust, highlights the war's indiscriminate ruthlessness. This is an image which appears again and again in Persian war poetry. Pictures of such events were also often printed in newspapers. To underscore the complete shock in the city, the poet describes how distressed the birds and animals have become. Either the doves stay away because of the warplanes above, or there are doves that are paralysed: the image works with either reading. The image refers to the sight and sound of warplanes, and to their predatory character, comparing them to the falcon. A cat serves as an example of the condition of abandoned domestic animals, with horror and grief in their eyes. Having depicted the terror, desolation and paralysis gripping the city and its inhabitants, the poet praises the Iranian soldiers who fight like lions, having no option except death to protect the homeland. The urge to record this in history is referred to in the last line.

6.4 Conclusion

Through such poems, which were widely read, poets offered a moral and philosophical dimension to the experience and the concept of war, calling on people to think about their emotions and actions, maintaining dignity and self-possession. Bihbahānī employs the classical ghazal form, but creates novel imagery and metaphors with a philosophical dimension, inviting her audience to think about the loss of life, the norms of good and evil, the place of God as a judge who should act justly and whether the deaths of the innocent can be called just.[299] While these poems deal with the intimate horrors of the battlefield, with individual deaths and a personal view of the destruction the war inflicted, there are several poems in which the poet places herself above the national and cultural domains, questioning the concept of war itself, why people kill one another, and showing compassion for the enemy's casualties, adroitly connecting this to her pacifist views. In such poems we see how poets reconcile conflicting ideals and personal moral dilemmas.

Bihbahānī's war poems usually lack the mystical tinge which is strongly present in many of the Islamic committed war poems. By disconnecting herself from the ubiquitous mystical tradition, she focuses all our attention on events as they are happening. Her poetry does not describe any connection with the other world or elevate death to union with God. Death is a great loss, which has great con-

299 In connecting death to justice, Bihbahānī is apparently influenced by Firdowsī, who eloquently questions the place of death in the creation at the beginning of his story of Rustam and Suhrāb: "If a fierce wind blows from a corner / It will throw down unripe citrus fruit. // Shall we call this tyranny or righteousness? / Shall we call this art or ineptitude? // If death is just, what is (then) unjust? / What is all this clamour and tumult (if) this is just. // Your soul is not aware of this mystery; / You have no way to penetrate into this curtain." See Firdowsī, *Shāh-nāma*, ed. J. Khaleqi-Motlaq, Costa Mesa, CA/New York: Mazda Publishers, 1369/1990, p. 117.

sequences. In her war poetry we see a narrator who loves people and her homeland, and abhors war, violence and death.

7 Nādir Nādirpūr on the 1979 Revolution

آن زلزله که خانه را لرزاند
یکشب همه چیز را دگرگون کرد
چون شعله جهان خفته را سوزاند
خاکستر صبح را پر از خون کرد

The earthquake that shook the home
turned everything upside down in one night:
like a flame, it burned the sleeping world,
it soaked the dawn's grey with blood.[300]

7.1 Introduction

With the advent of the 1979 Revolution and the Iran-Iraq War (1980 – 88), a new genre of poetry was born, depicting various aspects of the Revolution, agonies of the war, the cult of martyrdom and the ideology of political Islam. To this list we can add the poetry in praise and censure of the founder of the Islamic Republic, Ayatollah Khomeini (1902 – 1989), who played an essential role in these events.[301] As a political and religious leader, he served as a source of inspiration for his followers, but for Iranians in diaspora he was the person responsible for their voluntary or imposed exile, and they held him responsible for the deaths of thousands of Iranians. Several poets in dioaspora such as Hādī Khursandī, Ismāʿīl Khuʾī, Nādir Nādirpūr, and a host of others treated subjects such as 1979 Revolution, the Iran-Iraq War and the role of the Revolution in Iranian history. Some of the political literature of the decade after the Revolution rightly claims that the Revolution was not Islamic, but was appropriated by Islamists who imposed an idealistic Islamic form of government in which Ayatollah Khomeini secured the absolute power of the *Vilāyat-i faqīh* ("guardianship of the ju-

300 N. Nādirpūr, *Majmūʿa-yi ashʿār*, Los Angeles, CA: Kitāb Corp, 2002, Vol. 2, from "Blood and Ashes," p. 1275. For a full English translation of this poem see *False Dawn: Persian Poems*, Introduction and Tranlations by Michael Craig Hillmann, afterword by Leonardo P. Alishan, Austin, TX: Literature East & West, 1986, pp. 74 – 76. I have adjusted the translation.
301 On Islamic Revolution and Literature see K. Talattof, *The Politics of Writing in Iran: A history of Modern Persian Literature*, Syracuse, NY: Syracuse University Press, 2000, pp. 108 – 134; for an analysis of praise poems for Khomeini see F. Shams, *A Revolution in Rhyme*, pp. 260 – 272.

https://doi.org/10.1515/9783110748734-011

rist") for himself.[302] In this chapter I shall analyse several political poems of Nādir Nādirpūr in which he condemns the ideology of the Revolution, commenting on the events taking place in the first years of the Revolution and the Iran-Iraq War.

7.2 Nādir Nādirpūr's Life and Work

Nādir Nādirpūr was born on 6 June 1929 in Tehran to a family of artists.[303] His father was a painter and his mother a musician, and Nādirpūr was to become one of the most musical and pictorial poets of twentieth-century Iran. In his early education he read the works of classical Persian masters such as Firdowsī, ʿUmar Khayyām (d. either 1123 or 1132), Saʿdī, and Ḥāfiẓ, whose influence on his poetic genius is palpable. He admired these masters to such an extent that he imitated them in their own classical style. After finishing school, Nādirpūr went to France, spending five years at the Sorbonne, where he studied French literature. During these years he was active as a poet and translator. Modern French poetry had a strong influence on his poetry. Nādirpūr was also engaged with the political developments in Iran in the turbulent 1940s. He became politically active and started writing political poetry in a modern European style.

Nādirpūr published his poetry for the first time after the CIA-supported coup of 1953 in left-orientated journals. The removal of the reformist prime minister, Muḥammad Muṣaddiq (1882–1967), was followed by a tumultuous period in which many members of the Tudeh communist party were arrested. It was in that turbulent year, 1953, that Nādirpūr published his first collection of poetry, *Eyes and Hands* ("Chishmhā-u dasthā"). In 1955 he published *The Daughter of the Cup* ("Dukhtar-i jām"). His third collection appeared in 1958, under the title *Poetry of Grapes* ("Shiʿr-i angūr"). In 1960 he published *Sun's Kohl* ("Surma-yi khurshīd"). In 1957 Nādirpūr married, but the couple divorced in 1961.

In the 1960s Nādirpūr went to Italy where he translated Italian literature into Persian. Nādirpūr was one of the active literati of Iran, co-operating with other

302 See M.M. Khorrami, *Literary Subterfuge*, pp. 18–20; also see A. Keshavarzian, "How Islamic Was the Revolution?," in *Middle East Report*, No. 250, The Islamic Revolution at 30, Spring, 2009, p. 12.

303 For an overview of Nādirpūr's life and work see H. Yavari in *Encyclopaedia Iranica*, s.v. Nader Naderpour; also compare M.C. Hillmann's introduction to *False Dawn: Persian Poems*, pp. 1–28; also see *'Een schipper van was, kleiner dan God': Gedichten van Nader Naderpur*, translated by J.T.P. de Bruijn and A. Seyed-Gohrab, Leidschendam: Quist, 2006, pp. 7–12.

authors to establish the Writers' Association in 1968.[304] In this period he worked for Persian national radio and television, making programmes in which he introduced foreign poets, writers and artists. Just before the Revolution, in 1978, he published three collections of poetry, entitled *Not Plant and Stone, but Fire* ("Gīyāh va sang na, ātash"), *From Heavens to Nonsense* ("Az āsimān tā rīsmān"), and *The Last Meal* ("Shām-i bāz-pasīn"). After the 1979 Revolution, Nādirpūr left his homeland for self-imposed exile, since he opposed the religiously inspired Revolution and the political Islam it fostered. Nādirpūr expressed his opinions about the political situation in Iran in various Persian-language journals published abroad. In 1982 his collection *False Dawn* ("Ṣubḥ-i durūghīn"), in which he depicts his life as an exile, came out in France. During this period he was active, writing essays, poetry and other literary activities. He became a member of the French Writers' Association in Paris. In 1984 he married again. In 1987 he moved to the United States where he lectured on Persian poetry and the political situation in Iran at several universities. These lectures were well received by the Iranian diaspora. Nādirpūr published his last collections of poetry in California, under the titles *Blood and Ashes* ("Khʷūn-u khākistar," 1989) and *Place and Time* ("Zamīn-u zaman," 1996).

Nādirpūr is famous for his critical attitude to the political and social situation in Iran. His poetry has been translated into English, Dutch, French, German and Italian. He was nominated for the Nobel Prize for Literature in 1993. In the same year he received the Human Rights Watch Hillman-Hammet Award. He remained politically engaged until his death, condemning the political situation in Iran in his poems and essays. He died of a heart attack in Los Angeles on 18 February 2000 and was buried in Westwood Village Memorial Park and Mortuary. After his demise, "The Naderpour Foundation" was established to promote and protect his work and philosophy.

7.3 Nādirpūr's Poetic Genius

Nādirpūr is one of the renowned poets of Persian "New Poetry" (*shiʿr-i now*). His poems stand out from the work of other modern Persian poets for the way they are crafted, the way they are refined and polished, their sound and musicality and, above all, because of his unmatchable skill in contriving metaphors, image-

304 On the history of the Writers' Association see Ahmad Karimi-Hakkak, *A Fire of Lilies*, pp. 53–84.

ry and allusions.[305] It is not easy for modern poets to free themselves from a living poetic tradition that has existed for a thousand years, and contrive novel metaphors, but Nādirpūr is a master of casting old metaphors in a new mould. He follows in the footsteps of the pioneer of Persian "new poetry," Nīmā Yushij (1897–1960) and improves on his attempt to create a new style. Attempts to experience a new type of poetry, inspired by European examples started with the poetry of the Constitutional Revolution (1906–11), but it took several decades before people accepted new poetry. After Reza Shah's abdication in 1941 and World War II, new ideas streamed into Iran, also in the realm of poetry, which was closely connected to the social and political developments of the period. Nīmā believed that the classical Persian poetical forms and contents could not satisfy modern needs.[306] The rules of prosody required poets to use a single metre in all of the couplets of a poem, and a single rhyme-scheme for each poetic form, such as the panegyric, lyric, quatrain, etc. Moreover, the classical system of contriving imagery and metaphors did not resonate with the desires of the modern poet. Nīmā introduced a "new poetry" in which different metres were used in a poem depending on the poem's meaning. The rhyme had to be an organising principle, and the poet had to express his own feelings and ideas, rather than imitating old masters. Imagery and metaphor had to suit his purpose.[307]

Nādirpūr follows these basic principles, improving them to a sophisticated level. Ehsan Yarshater aptly compares Nīmā to the father of Persian poetry, Rūdakī (d. about 940), and Nādirpūr to the epic poet Firdowsī and the lyricist and panegyrist Farrukhī of Sīstān (d. about 1038): "[i]f Nima could be considered the Rudaki of the modern school of Persian poetry, I consider Nādirpūr its Farrokhi and Ferdowsi."[308] While Firdowsī and his *Shāh-nāma* are especially appreciated for saving the Persian language and culture after the Arab-Islamic invasion, Farrokhi is known for his lyricism and his inimitable simple style using a plethora of rhetorical figures such as parallelism, anaphora, antithesis, alliteration, etc.[309] Indeed, Nādirpūr has an epic inclination: he gives his poems a nar-

305 On Nādirpūr's skills in contriving metaphors and imagery see Riżā Barāhinī, *Ṭalā dar miss*, Tehran: Nashr-i zamān, 1992, vol. I, pp. 351–354.

306 On Nīmā's philosophy of a new type of poetry see *Essays on Nima Yushij: Animating Modernism in Persian Poetry*, ed. A. Karimi-Hakkak and K. Talattof, Leiden: Brill, 2004.

307 E. Yarshater, "A Star Ceases to Shine," in *Persica: Annual of the Dutch-Iranian Society*, vol. xvii, 2001, p. 137.

308 Ibid., p. 138.

309 On Farrukhī's life and work see J.T.P. de Bruijn, in *Encyclopaedia Iranica*, s.v. Farroḵī Sīstānī, Abu'l-Ḥasan ʿAlī. On Nādirpūr's lyrical style see Gh.H. Yusofi, "Dar jangal-i shab," in *Chishma-yi rowshan: dīdār bā shāʿirān*, 4th ed., Tehran: ʿIlmī, 1371/1992, p. 770.

rative form, telling a story, especially in poems denouncing the 1979 Revolution,[310] and his skill with imagery has already been remarked on.

Nādirpūr's fervent and unattainable desire to return to his homeland and his close monitoring of the suppression of Iranians in Iran inspired him to write patriotic and nostalgic poetry, to such a degree that he is one of the best exilic Persian poets. Despite his relentless criticism of the Islamic Republic, he is one of the most widely read poets in present-day Iran. A prodigious number of scholarly articles and books on Nādirpūr have been published in Iran in recent years. His poems criticising the Islamic Republic's policies are simply ignored. Although the Persian public has access to these poems clandestinely, mostly via the internet, they are not analysed in works published in Iran.

Nādirpūr refers in several of his poems to Ayatollah Khomeini, to how he was characterised by Iranians, and how he should be placed within the broader context of Persian history and culture. He also wrote articles and poems condemning the Islamic Republic of Iran. In the poems we see an emotional poet who blames Ayatollah Khomeini personally for Iran's deteriorating political situation, whereas his essays have a sober tone and a wider scope, analysing political developments in Iran. He condemns reformist insider politicians such as Mohammad Khatami (presidency 1997–2005). The title of one of his articles, "Khomeini on the Moon and Khatami on a Satellite," indicates the tone of his critique of the regime and of the people's gullibility, which has extended the life of the regime.

7.4 The Sermon of Perdition

The following poem, *Khuṭba-yi halāk* ("The Sermon of Perdition"), is perhaps the most famous of these political poems. It is dedicated to *imām-i ummat* or "the people's Imam," an ironic compound referring to Ayatollah Khomeini as the leader of the Muslim community. The word *umma(t)* is Arabic, deriving from the Quran. In the Quran it refers to a religious community as a whole.[311] The term was used to indicate that Khomeini was the leader of the whole Islamic community around the world. This idea corresponded with the policy of exporting the Revolution to other Islamic countries.[312]

310 See also E. Yarshater, "A Star Ceases to Shine," p. 148.

311 F.M. Denny in *Encyclopaedia of Islam, Second Edition*, s.v. Umma.

312 For a discussion about exporting the revolution to other countries, and how it became an incentive for Saddam to invade Iran see S. Gieling, in *Encyclopaedia Iranica*, s.v. Iraq. vii. Iran-Iraq War.

The title *imām* (Anglicised as Imam) is used in the Shiite context only for the twelve infallible Imams who succeeded the prophet Muḥammad (d. 632). It was not permissible to use this title for other people until the time of the Revolution, when it was applied to Ayatollah Khomeini. It is not clear who first did this, or why Khomeini, who knew that people were calling him Imam in their chants, did not stop this.[313] The term is also commonly used in adjectival phrases: the "Friday prayer leader," for example, is the *imām jumʿa*, but this was not the way people referred to Ayatollah Khomeini.[314] While the term Imam may be seen as innocent in such usages, other phrases applied to Khomeini were blasphemous by orthodox Shiite and Sunnite standards. For example, people used the chant *labbayk yā Khomeini*, "O Khomeini, we are here for you," a phrase based on *labbayk Allāh* ... ("O Lord, here I am for you ...") only used by pilgrims during their pilgrimage at Mecca, telling God that they have come to Him. These forms of address elevated Khomeini to a holy figure, next to God. While this would be simple blasphemy in the eyes of many Muslims, Khomeini's followers found so much inspiration in him that he was their immediate medium to commune with God. This sanctification grew significantly after Khomeini's death, and cast its aura on his successor, Khamenei: his home is called a *bayt*, Arabic for house, which in an Iranian context links to the *bayt al-ḥarām* or "holy house," a name for the Kaʿba in Mecca.

As we will see, Nādirpūr's poetry is composed for a broad audience, using metaphors, images and allusions that people from all walks of life can effortlessly understand. The first example is "The Sermon on Perdition," which appeared in February 1986.[315] It was instantly distributed in the Iranian Diaspora and was later translated. It became even more accessible with the spread of the internet.

خطبه هلاک
(برای امام امّت)

ای دوزخی سرشت! اگر ظلم آسمان
میراث سرزمین مرا بر تو عرضه داشت،
در زیر آفتاب دل افروز آن دیار

313 It is said that the first individual called Khomeini Imam was Hasan Rouhani, the contemprrary president of Iran.

314 Momen, *An Introduction to Shi'i Islam*, p. 289. Momen observes, "Khumaynī has also allowed the designation of *Nā'ib al-Imām* (Deputy of the Imam) to continue although it has been less used recently. If by this designation is meant the traditional Nā'b al-ʿĀmm (general representative) of the Imam, then it applies equally to all mujtahids and khumaynī is not even sole *marjaʿ at-taqlīd*."

315 See http://www.spectacle.org/0302/mafie.html (last visited 24.11.2014). I have drawn on Mafie's translation.

دست تو، غیر دانه ی نامردمی نکاشت
وقت است تا ز کِشته، ترا باخبر کنم.

زان پیشتر که پیک هلاک تو در رسد،
ای ناستوده مرد!
زان پیشتر که خون پلیدت فرو چکد
بر سنگفرشِ سرد
بگذار تا سرود فنای تو سر کنم:

در چشم من، تو باد سیاهی که ناگهان
چندین هزار برگ جوان را ربوده ای،
یا روح ظلمتی که پس از مرگ آفتاب
چندین هزار دیده ی پر اشتیاق را
بر بامداد بسته و بر شب گشوده ای.

شبهای بی ستاره، که چشمان مادران
بر گونه، اشک ماتم فرزند رانده اند
در دیدگان سرد تو، ای ناستوده مرد!
رحمت ندیده اند و ندامت نخوانده اند.

پیران مو سپید که بر تخته سنگ گور
نام جگر خراش عزیزان نوشته اند؛
خون گریه می کنند که در روزگار تو
آن را دروده اند که هرگز نکِشته اند.

گر نقش شیر و صورت مهر مُنیر را
از رایتِ سه رنگ دلیران زدوده ای،
یادش همیشه مایه ی جوش و خروش ماست
ور نام آن سخنور شهنامه گوی را
از لابلای دفتر و دیوان ربوده ای،
تنها ، سروش اوست که در گوش هوش ماست.

بگذار تا که ناله ی زندانیان تو
چندان رسا شود که نگنجد به سینه ها،
سیلاب اشک و خونِ کسان را روانه کن
تا بردَمد ز خاک، گل سرخ کینه ها.

بگذار تا سپیده دم روز انتقام،
وقتی که سر بر آوری ز خواب صبحگاه
پیر و جوان و خرد و کلان نعره برکشند
کای دیو دل سیاه!
مرگت خجسته باد بر انبوه مرد و زن،
نامت زدوده باد ز طومار سال و ماه ...

The Sermon of Perdition
O, infernal being! Although the heavens' oppression
Allowed you to inherit my homeland,
your hand has planted nothing under the mirthful sun of that land
save the seeds of inhumanity.
Now is the time to tell you what you planted.

Before the messenger conveys the news of your perdition
O, shameful man!
Before your impure blood trickles down
on the cold cobblestone,
Let me start singing the song of your death.

In my eyes, you are a black wind
suddenly taking thousands of young leaves.
Or a dark spirit, that after the sun's death,
Closes thousands of eyes full of longing,
Closes them to dawn and opens them to dusk.

In the starless nights, when tears of grief for their children
Flowed down the cheeks of mothers,
They did not see any compassion, or remorse,
In your cold eyes, O shameful man!

The elderly white-haired men, sitting at tombstones
have scratched the heart-rending names of their loved ones there.
They are shedding tears of blood,
They are harvesting what they never planted.

Although you wiped out the lion's image and the face of the shining sun
from the triple-coloured flag of champions,
their memories will always incite our passion.
Although you erased the name of Firdowsī the eloquent
from books and tomes,
only his heavenly voice resonates in the ear of our souls.

You will see: the cries of your prisoners
Will become so loud, they cannot be contained.
Let torrents of tears and blood run
That red roses of vengeance may bloom on the earth.

You will see the dawn of revenge
when you lift your head from your morning sleep.
Young and old, big and small, will shout:
"O, black-hearted demon!
May your death be a good sign, for men and women everywhere,
May your name be erased from the scroll of years, of months ..."[316]

In this poem Nādirpūr uses familiar images such as the heaven as an oppressor, planting seeds and harvesting the results. This familiar imagery makes the poem accessible from the beginning, although the expression is unusually direct and vehement. Iranians are suffering from the injustice of an oppressive heaven, or fate, and from fate's agent who is planting the seeds of inhumanity. In this

316 N. Nādirpūr, *Majmūʿa-yi ashʿār*, Vol. 2, pp. 1307–1309.

poem Ayatollah Khomeini is characterised by traits such as "shameful," "black wind," "infernal being," a person who sheds the blood of innocent youths. In the first stanza the poet conveys why he condemns Khomeini, and in the second stanza he sings the song of his death, as if to get revenge before Khomeini dies naturally. The poet's urgent desire to sing this curse while Khomeini lives accelerates the poem's pace and rhythm. The poet has actually started to sing this death song in the first stanza, by putting a negative loading on nature imagery that he links to Khomeini, for it is fate that allowed him to inherit the homeland and plant the seeds of inhumanity.

In the third stanza the poet builds on this natural imagery by comparing Khomeini to a black wind snatching fresh leaves from branches. Then Khomeini is compared to a dark spirit, a possible allusion to Khomeini's name, the "Spirit of Allah/God"' (*Rūḥ Allāh*), that takes the souls of thousands, not allowing them to see the dawn. There is also an antithesis here, as "the Spirit of God" is an appellation of Jesus, who is famous in Persian culture for his life-giving qualities, even quickening the dead to life. But here the opposite is the case: this "Spirit of God" seizes lives. Using the image of "the sun's death," the poet skilfully creates symmetry between the innocent people's destruction and the sun's death. The sun is among other things a reference to Iran under the Pahlavis, when its flag bore a gold lion and sun. All the positive elements in this stanza, such as the sun, the fresh leaves, eyes full of longing and dawn are associated with victims, whereas the negative associations belong to Khomeini. The horror of this cruel slaughter is augmented in the next stanza when the poet refers to the tears running down the mothers' eyes in starless nights while Khomeini shows no compassion, watching with cold eyes. This image of the grief of survivors continues in the next stanza, where fathers visit their children's graves where, in the desperate act of the powerless, they scratch the names of the dead on the stones. The metaphor of planting seeds recurs in the final line of this stanza, pointing to Khomeini, for these deaths are what he planted. Although simple, the imagery is strong as seeds are expected to come out of the ground, but here the seeds, i.e., young people, are placed in the chest of the earth.

In the last three stanzas the poet gives hope, emphasising that all of this destruction and all the changes will have no effect. The poet refers to actual events after the Revolution of 1979. First, he refers to the change to the Iranian flag by the removal of the image of the sun and lion and the substitution of the Arabic words *Allāh-u Akbar,* "God is great," repeated twenty-two times along the bottom of the green stripe and the top of the red stripe.[317] Nādirpūr emphasises that the

---

317 See A. Shapur Shahbazi in *Encyclopaedia Iranica*, s.v. Flags. i. of Persia. It is interesting that

memory of the lion and the sun will remain in people's hearts. The second change the poet refers to is the regime's hostility to Firdowsī and his monumental epic, the *Shāh-nāma*. In the first year after the Revolution, the Islamic government started to change the names of streets, schools, mosques and towns that showed any connection with the Pahlavi regime. One of these changes was the removal of the term Shah, which in some cases was simply replaced by the name of Khomeini. The historical port city of Bandar-i Shāhpūr in the Persian Gulf became Bandar-i Imam Khomeini. The Shah in this city's name and in many similar cases did not refer to the Pahlavi Shahs but to monarchs of previous Persian dynasties. Apparently the mere word Shah had such loaded connotations for the new Islamic government that even Firdowsī's millennium-old national epic had to give way to this relentless policy and be removed from bookshops and textbooks at schools. To my knowledge, there was not in fact any formal policy to ban the *Shāh-nāma*, as verses from this monumental epic were broadcast as part of the morning gymnastics on Iranian radio stations, and continued to be used in traditional martial arts (*zūr-khāna*) and in several other cultural domains.[318] Firdowsī's *Shāh-nāma*, some 50.000 couplets, contains legends, myths and the history of Iranian peoples from the dawn of history to the advent of Islam in the seventh century. For Persian-speaking peoples, it is a rich quarry of etiquettes, rites and traditions. Firdowsī and his epic proved to be too deeply rooted in Iranians' cultural memory to be affected by such politically motivated sentiments. Ayatollah Khomeini himself alludes in his poetry to several characters in Firdowsī's epic, which shows how integral the *Shāh-nāma* is to Persian

---

the lion and sun symbol is ancient and has been used by successive dynasties in different ways. In Safavid times (1501–722), the symbol was interpreted religiously, with the lion symbolising the first Shiite Imam, Ali, and the sun standing for the "glory of religion." Despite this and other Shiite interpretations of the lion and the sun, the symbol was removed from the Iranian flag after the 1979 Revolution.

318 Several articles and books have been written on Firdowsī's *Shāh-nāma* as Persia's national epic. Laina Farhat-Holzman, "The Shahnameh of Ferdowsi: An Icon to National Identity," in *Comparative Civilization Review*, 2001, p. 108, has concise coverage of the post-revolutionary events and A. Marashi, "The Nation's Poet: Ferdowsi and the Iranian National Imagination," pp. 93–111. On the censorship of Firdowsī during the early period of the Revolution see M.M. Khorrami, *Literary Subterfuge*, p. 20; see also M. Omidsalar, *Iran's Epic and America's Empire*, Santa Monica, CA: Afshar Publishing, 2012. For an elegant English translation of this epic see *Shahnameh: The Persian Book of Kings*, translated by Dick Davis, New York: Penguin Classics, 2006. On Firdowsī and *zur-khāne* see H.E. Chehabi, in *Encyclopaedia Iranica*, s.v. Zurḵāna; *idem*, "Wrestling in the Shāhnāmeh and Later Persian Epics," in *The Layered Heart*, pp. 237–282; for a more genral introduction see L. Ridgeon, "The Zūrkhāna between Tradition and Change," in *Iran: Journal of the British Institute of Persian Studies*, Vol. 45, 2007, pp. 243–265.

culture.[319] The Islamic government could not control Firdowsī's popularity and eventually lost interest in opposing the *Shāh-nāma*. But by the time the regime's interest had dwindled, Iranians had begun to use this animosity to Ferdowsi as a point on which the newly established government could be criticised. Nādirpūr's last two stanzas promise retribution and revenge, emphasising that the tyranny will not last long and that the oppressed people will rise against the regime and demand their freedom.

7.5 The Satanic Verse

The Sermon of Perdition speaks for and to the people: it is propaganda rousing people's emotions, especially those in the Iranian Diaspora who felt robbed of their homeland. The following poem, completed in September 1995, possesses more poetic vigour.[320] Before starting an analysis, I will cite the poem in its entirety:

آیه شیطانی
ساقی به نور باده برافروز جام ما
مطرب بگو که کار جهان شد به کام ما
ما در پیاله عکسِ رُخِ یار دیده‌ایم
ای بی‌خبر ز لذتِ شُربِ مُدام ما
هرگز نمیرد آن که دلش زنده‌شد به عشق
ثبت است بر جَریده عالَم دوام ما
مستی به چشم شاهد دلبند ما خوش است
زآن رو سپرده‌اند به مستی زمام ما[321] (حافظ)

The Satanic Verse
Cupbearer! Let our bowl glow with wine's light.
Musician! Sing how the world is just as we would wish.
O you, who do not know the joys of our endless drinking:
We have seen the beloved's face reflected in the cup!

---

319 See Khomeini's poetry in his *Dīvān*, Tehran: Mu'assissa-yi Tanẓīm va Nashr-i Āthār-i Imām Khomeini, 1998; see also A.A. Seyed-Gohrab, "Khomeini the Poet Mystic," in *Die Welt des Islams: International Journal for the Study of Modern Islam*, 51, 2011, pp. 438–458; B. Reinert, "Ḫumainī im Spiegel seiner Gedichte," in *Islamische Grenzen und Grenzübergänge*, Vol. 4, Bern: Peter Lang AG, 2007, pp. 191–293.
320 N. Nādirpūr, *Majmū'a-yi ash'ār*, Vol. 2, pp. 1485–1488.
321 Ḥāfiẓ, *Divān*, ed. P. Nātil Khānlari, Tehran: Khᵛārazmī, 1362/1983, p. 38, ghazal 11, lines 1,2,4,6. For a translation of Ḥāfiẓ's ghazals see *The Collected Lyrics of Háfiz of Shíráz*, translated by Peter Avery, Cambridge: Archetype, 2007. This particular ghazal appears on page 34, poem xi; my translation is based on Avery's.

He whose heart is made to live through love will never die:
our continuity's affirmed in the daybook of the world.
In the eyes of our heart-ravishing beloved, drunkenness is pleasing,
That's why our reins are in the hands of drunkenness. (Ḥāfiẓ)

آن کس که در ستایش می، عاشقانه گفت:
"ما در پیاله عکس رخ یار دیده ایم"
هرگز گمان نداشت که مستان بی خبر
تصویر جادوانه ابلیس را، شبی
در جام مه: "چهره دلبر" گمان کنند
وز شوق این مکاشفه فریاد بر کشند
کای آفریدگار! جهان شد به کام ما.

در آن شب شگفت
وقتی که از خشونت آن تصویر
جام ظریف ماه
مانند لوح آیینه، مو برداشت:
تاری ز موی عارض ابلیس را، نسیم
بر صفحه کتاب خداوندی
در نزد آیه های مقدس گرو گذاشت
مو، لای درز معجزه های کتاب رفت
وان صفحه بسته شد
اما صدای شاعر عاشق، به طعنه گفت:
– " ثبت است بر جریده عالم دوام ما".

در آن شب شگفت،
– بی اعتنا به وحشت نظارگان ماه-
– تصویر جادوانه ابلیس جان گرفت

و ز کتف او، دو مار گره خورده سیاه
بر خاستند و مغز جوانان خفته را
از میزبان خویش طلب کردند
ابلیس حیله گر، به امید شکار مغز
فنی به کار بست:
بر تخته سیاه افق، لفظ "مار" را
در نقطه مقابل تصویر وی نگاشت.
مستان بی خبر:
چیزی ز لفظ "مار" نفهمیدند
اما به نقش "مار" – که جویای طعمه بود-
مغز فریب خورده خود را فروختند.
ابلیس حیله گر، به خدای یگانه گفت
کای آفریدگار! کلام حلال تو
– بی آنکه راه در حرم آدمی برد-

دزدانه سجده کرد به نقش حرام ما.

آری، فریبکاری ابلیس و بیم مار
انبوه مرد و زن را بیمار کرده بود
تنها هنوز، سایه شاعر در آسمان

شعری نگفته را
با طنز تلخ خویش، بدین گونه می سرود
– شیطان به چشم مردم ایران زمین: خداست
زانرو سپرده اند به شیطان، زمام ما ...

He who in praise of wine lovingly said:
"We have seen the beloved's face reflected in the cup"
Could never guess that heedless drunkards
Would confuse the beloved's face
with Satan's conjured image
In the cup of the moon at night,
And that, transported by this discovery, they would shout:
"O Lord! The world is just as we would wish."[322]

On that wondrous night
When the violence of that image
Cracked the fragile cup of the moon.
It was like the face of a cracked mirror,
As if a breeze laid a strand of Satan's beard
On the page of the lordly book.
The strand of hair found its way,
Into the seams of the book's marvels
And the book closed.
Ironically, the voice of the love-struck poet has said,
"our continuity's affirmed in the daybook of the world."

On that wondrous night
– Without considering the fears of those admiring the moon –
The conjured image of Satan was ensouled,
And from his shoulders, two twisting black serpents rose
And demanded the brains of sleeping youths
from their host.
Satan the deceiver, employed a trick in his hunt for brains:
On the horizon's blackboard he wrote the word "serpent,"
Opposite to his image.
The heedless drunkards
Did not understand the word "serpent" at all,
But they sold their bewitched brains
To the image of the serpent, that was seeking prey.
Satan the deceiver said to the one true God,
"O Lord! Your pure words,

322 A similar image for the reflection of Khomeini's face in the moon appears in the poem *From Żahhāk to Fireydūn*, Vol. 2. pp, 1319–1322. In *bīmār-i bīdār* the image of Żahhāk and serpents appears in a different context. See p. 1141.

Rather than attaining to the human sanctuary,
Have surreptitiously bowed to our unclean image."

Surely, Satan's deception and the fear of the serpent
Had made the mass of men and women sick.
Still in his loneliness, the poet of heaven
Was reciting with bitter satire
A poem not yet composed, saying:
"In the eyes of Iranians, Satan is God
So the hands of Satan have seized our reins."

Immediately after the title, Nādirpūr cites four couplets from one of Ḥāfiẓ's famous ghazals of ten couplets, in which the poetic persona cheerfully tells the cupbearer to fill the cup, asking the musician to sing, "how the world is just as we would wish." The reason for this blissful delight and for the drinking is that the beloved's face can be seen reflected in the cup. Employing a bacchic motif, the speaker provocatively emphasises that those who condemn wine drinking do so because they cannot appreciate this happy situation. Ḥāfiẓ moves from the wine motif to the motif of love, adding that one whose heart has become alive and ensouled through love is destined to attain eternity. In the last couplet the reader sees how the beloved's drunken eyes have enthralled the lover, robbing the lover of self-control. Nādirpūr brilliantly integrates this erotic line into a modern context, changing the poem's message to be appropriate to the events of the Islamic Revolution. The lover symbolises Iran's revolutionary masses, who in a state of drunkenness have lost control of themselves and are carried away by the beloved.

After these lines, which function as a motto, Nādirpūr opens his poem by repeating one of the lines from Ḥāfiẓ, "We have seen the beloved's face reflected in the cup." The beloved's image in Ḥāfiẓ's poetry could be interpreted in both profane and transcendental senses. The cup is not merely a cup of wine through which the (mystic) lover is transported to an ecstatic state, contemplating the beloved, it is also a reference to the cup of the mythical Persian king, Jamshīd (*jām-i Jam*), in which he could see the entire world. As with the Holy Grail of Christian tradition, the lover searches for the cup all his life and, in the end, realises that this precious cup is his own heart.[323]

Nādirpūr uses this line with imagery that would be familiar to the Persian public to describe an absurd and confusing situation at the beginning of the

---

323 For more information on wine imagery see J.T.P. de Bruijn in *Encyclopaedia Iranica*, s.v. Hafez. iii. Hafez's Poetic Art.

1979 Revolution. Revolutionary Iranians *en masse* claimed to see Ayatollah Khomeini's face in the moon, and took it as a miracle and a sign of Khomeini's holiness. At the beginning of the Revolution, Khomeini's mystic character and even holiness were much emphasised, and he was called "Imam." Khomeini himself showed his ascetic and mystic propensities through his sober appearance and mystical interpretations of the Quran, broadcast on television. Some people believed that Khomeini was the twelfth imam, who had withdrawn from the eyes of men in 980 and had now returned to rescue Muslims from injustice.[324] This idolising context, and the uncertainty and anxieties of the time, led some people to see Khomeini's face in the moon.

Nādirpūr creates several parallels between Ḥāfiẓ's metaphor and his own: the cup of wine and the cup of the moon; the image of the beloved and the image of Khomeini who is loved by his followers: pesons who see Khomeini as their spiritual guide, and brainwashed Iranians. On top of these parallels, there is also the metonym of the moon-faced beloved in Persian love poetry, whose round and radiant face resembles the moon. Nādirpūr reinforces the effect of his opening lines by stating that Ḥāfiẓ himself could never have guessed that Persian readers would put a face in the moon in place of the beloved's face in a cup. Through this strong opening, the poet criticises the fervent desire of revolutionary Iranians to see Khomeini's image in the moon. Puzzled at this desire and faced with the fact that these Iranians are actually imagining Khomeini's face in the moon, Nādirpūr concludes that this is the work of Satan, who has bewitched people through black magic.

The second stanza consists of a chain of associations. The poet links the "wondrous night" when Khomeini's hook-nosed profile was seen in the moon with the jagged line of a crack or hair. The beloved's image in classical Persian love poetry is associated with haughtiness and violence, and we see the same violence here as the image causes the fragile cup of the moon to crack.[325] The face of the brilliantly shinning moon now looks like a cracked mirror. In Persian

---

324 Referring to this aspect of Ayatollah Khomeini, Arjomand says, "By 1982, Fakhr al-Dīn Ḥijāzī, perhaps the most important demagogue of the Islamic Revolution Party, would openly implore Khomeini to drop the veil if he indeed was the Mahdi himself. As is proper for such occasions, the Imam would of course observe nobly ambiguous silence." See Said Amir Arjomand, *The Shadow of God and the Hidden Imam: Religion, Political Order, and Social Change in Shi'ite Iran from the Beginning of 1890*, Chicago, IL/London: University of Chicago Press, 1984, p. 269.
325 For the beloved's image in Persian poetry see J.T.P. de Bruijn, in *Encyclopaedia Iranica*, s.v. Beloved.

culture a cracked mirror is a bad omen.[326] The poet then links this to another image, comparing the crack to a strand of Satan's beard. The hair has found its way into the seams of "the lordly book" and will stay there until eternity. Although Nādirpūr does not refer to the Quran explicitly, the title of the poem, *A Satanic Verse,* and other allusions point to the holy book, implying that Satan is present even in the Quran. This is certainly a reference to the "satanic verses" that are supposed to have entered the Quran.[327] It also refers to a popular superstition at the beginning of the Revolution that a hair of Khomeini's could be found in every copy of the Quran, showing his presence in every household. Here and in one other poem, Nādirpūr refers to this "miracle," and he sometimes connects Khomeini to mysterious forces as in this poem. Nādirpūr then cites Ḥāfiẓ again, "our continuity's affirmed in the daybook of the world." A daybook, *jarīda*, is here the book of destiny.[328]

The "satanic verses" are referred to in several Arabic and Persian sources, varying from Quranic exegesis to biographical epics and popular narratives. The story in brief is that the prophet Muḥammad once mistook the words of Satan for verses revealed to him to be included in the Quran. As Shahab Ahmed has stated, modern Islamic orthodoxy strongly rejects these accounts, threatening one who propagates it with excommunication (*takfīr*). By emphasising that this nocturnal theatre is the work of Satan, the poet connects Satan with Khomeini, an allusion that becomes stronger in the third stanza. The image of Satan is incarnated, it receives a "soul," an allusion to Khomeini's name, Rūḥ-Allāh. Khomeini is then compared to the tyrant Żahhāk, a tyrannical Arab king who kills Jamshīd and rules over Persia with crulty.

In Persian mythology, as recounted by Firdowsī in his *Shāh-nāma*, Ahriman, evil spirit and "God's adversary in the Zoroastrian religion," makes a plan to

---

326 On the symbolism of mirror in Persian poetry see R. Zipoli, "Poetic Imagery," in *History of Persian Literature*, ed. J.T.P. de Bruijn, London: I.B. Tauris, 2009, p. 214; also see idem, "Semiotics and the Tradition of the Image," in *Persica: Annual of the Dutch-Iranian Society*, 20, pp. 155–172; also see explanatory notes by Dick Davis to one of Ḥāfiẓ's ghazals, p. 248, *man dūstdār-i rū-yi khush-u mū-yi dilkisham* ("My love's for pretty faces, for heart-bewitching hair; I am crazy for good wine, a languorous, drunk stare ...)." See D. Davis, *Faces of Love*, pp. 122–123.

327 On the satanic verses see Shahab Ahmed, in *Encyclopaedia of the Qur'ān*, s.v. Satanic verses. Considering the date of this poem, in 1995, the title might also refer to Salman Rushdie's *Satanic Verses* and Khomeini's *fatwa* against the book and its author, but there is little textual evidence in this poem to support such a connection; also see his book *Before Orthodoxy: The Satanic Verses in Early Islam*, Cambridge, MA: Harvard University Press, 2017.

328 The word *jarīda* (pl. *jarāyid*) has different meanings. While it refers to the book of destiny, it also has the meaning of an account of receipts and expenses. In modern Persian, it means newspapers and periodicals.

destroy Persia and exterminate the Persian peoples by appearing first as a cook training Żahhāk to eat meat and to become a carnivore.[329] When Żahhāk wants to reward him for his excellent food, Satan says that he does not want anything except to kiss Żahhāk's shoulders.[330] As soon as he kisses the shoulders, two black serpents grow from them. Satan disappears from his sight and Żahhāk remains incurably sick. Żahhāk tries in vain to cut the snakes off his shoulders as they grow back each time. One day, Satan appears again, this time as a physician to the incurably ill tyrant. Satan cures him by asking Żahhāk to feed the snakes daily with the brains of two Iranian youths. For years, Żahhāk rules Persia until the blacksmith Kāve protests and helps Fireydūn to wrest the kingdom from him.[331] Nādirpūr suggests that Satan used almost the same device to deceive Iranians one again. In the story of Żahhāk Iranians had to offer the brains of their children as food for the serpents, and in this nocturnal scene Iranians are selling their "bewitched brains to the image of the serpent." Nādirpūr compares the crack in the cup of the moon to a serpent hunting people's brains, i.e., those who believe they have seen Khomeini's image in the moon are falling victim to the serpent. The strong ending of the poem commences with Satan's words:

> O Lord! Your pure words,
> Rather than attaining to the human sanctuary,
> Have surreptitiously bowed to our unclean image.

Satan's statement here implies that he has deceived Iranians so that they worship Satan while they think they are worshipping the one true God. The reference to the poet of heaven in the last stanza refers to Nādirpūr himself, who is not present in Iran but is watching and commenting on events from a distance.

Composed in September 1995, this is one of Nādirpūr's first poems criticising the idolisation and beatification of Ayatollah Khomeini. The poem's merits lie in the allusions to Ḥāfiẓ's poem, to Satan and the tyrant Żahhāk.[332] Each of these

---

329 On the evil nature of Ahriman see J. Duchesne-Guillemin in *Encyclopaedia Iranica*, s.v. Ahriman. For convenience's sake, I use Satan in my analysis instead of Ahriman.

330 Dj. Khaleghi-Motlagh in *Encyclopaedia Iranica*, s.v. Aždahā. ii. In Persian Literature.

331 See M. Omidsalar in *Encyclopaedia Iranica*, s.v. Kāva. idem., *Iran's Epic and America's Empire*, pp. 158–162, on the story of Żahhāk see pp. 140–141. A. Amanat, "Divided Patrimony, Tree of Royal Power, and Fruit of Vengeance: Political Paradigms and Iranian Self-Image in the Story of Faridun in the Shahnama," in *Shahnama Studies I*, ed. Charles Melville, Cambridge: The Centre of Middle Eastern and Islamic Studies, University of Cambridge, 2006, pp. 49–70.

332 On Ḥāfiẓ's allusions to Żahhāk see D.P. Brookshaw, *Hafiz and his Contemporaries: Poetry, Performance and Patronage in Fourteenth-Century Iran*, New York/London: I.B. Tauris, 2019, p. 185.

three elements gives a further dimension to the poem. The use of Ḥāfiẓ's well-known couplet contrasts his cultured audience, who could metaphorically see the beloved's image in a cup, or in other classical poetry, see the world in a cup, to the literal naïvety of Iranians who think they actually see Khomeini's image in the moon. Their longing to see the Beloved is so strong that their vision has been distorted. The image also presents an objective correlative between the cup as the beloved's image, the cup as the moon and Khomeini's image. Not believing that this event actually took place in twentieth-century Iran, the poet emphasises that it is satanic magic, so unscrupulous that the fragile cup of the moon cannot hold it. It cracks. The corrupt work of Satan and the form of the crack, resembling a serpent, inspires the poet to conjure up a new and strong allusion to Żahhāk. With this allusion, the poet finds a way to compare Iran's present political situation to the mythical moment when the Persian youths were murdered to feed Żahhāk's serpents.

Nādirpūr was not alone in using Żahhāk in this way. From the time of the 1979 Revolution, poets and writers employed the paradigm of Żahhāk to refer to an adversary. At first Muḥammad Riżā Shah was seen as Żahhāk and Khomeini as a rescuer, but later the paradigm was reversed. The following famous line by Ḥāfiẓ was on the lips of many Iranians during the first days of Khomeini's arrival and the Shah's departure. It even became the refrain of a popular revolutionary song, welcoming Khomeini home: *dīv chu bīrūn ravad firishta dar āyad* or "when the demon departs, the angel arrives."[333] Żahhāk commonly personifies an evil force, but the poet Shāmlū inverted the paradigm, presenting Żahhāk as "the leader of 'a popular movement against the atrocities of an insane and tyrannical king." In this reinterpretation, Kāvih was "a toiling man unconscious of his class situation, and Firdowsī is no more than a reactionary monarchist who deliberately transformed a historically obvious, determinate event, 'the suppression of a workers' uprising,' into 'a national liberation movement.'" This reversal shows that the Żahhāk paradigm is flexible enough to be used for different contexts to suit an author's purposes.[334]

---

333 Ḥāfiẓ, *Dīvān*, ed. P. Nātil Khānlarī, Tehran: Khᵛārazmī, 1362/1983, p. 472, ghazal 228, line 2.
334 Ahmad Karimi-Hakkak, *Fire of Lilies*, pp. 197–199. Also see his discussion of ʿAlī-Akbar Saʿīdī-Sīrjānī's *Żahhāk-i mār-dūsh* within the context of the 1979 Revolution. Sīrjānī's book was published in Iran and went through two printings in three months (January-March 1989) before it was banned in the same year. Several publications followed outside Iran, a 3rd edition was published in Los Angeles in 1990. Also see S. Gazerani's interesting analysis of the Żahhāk episode in Firdowsī's *Shāh-nāma* in the context of historiography, "Zahhak's Story and History," in *The Layered Heart*, pp. 199–235.

7.6 From Żahhāk to Fireydūn

Nādirpūr brilliantly combines ancient Persian poetic references and mythology to critique the political situation in Iran. The next poem, *From Żahhāk to Fireydūn*, uses the same category of allusions, but treats the coming of the 1979 Revolution and how Islamists dethroned Muḥammad Riża Shah (1919 – 1980). For convenience's sake, I first cite the entire poem before presenting my analysis: [335]

از ضحّاک تا فریدون

روزی که ناگهان
تاری ز موی عارض "بوجهل" در کتاب
دزدانه جای شهپر طاووس را گرفت
و آنشب که عکس او
در قاب تنگ ماه
آسوده تر ز مردمک چشم، جا گرفت
شهر غنوده را
دودی غلیظ چون شب دوزخ فرا گرفت:
از هر مناره، آتش طغیان زبانه زد
وز هر کرانه، لشکر طغیان شکن رسید
چندان که شهر، چهره نا آشنا گرفت.
جنگاوران سرخ
با نقش لاله ها به عَلَم های گونه گون
داغ شهید را همه جا تازه داشتند.
پیران موسپید
بر سینه برهنه دیوارهای شهر
دشنام ها به جای دعاها نگاشتند.
گلچهرگان، به پاس سکوت سپاهیان
گلبوسه بر دهان مسلسل گذاشتند.
آنگاه جملگی:
مشت دُرشت بر کمر آسمان زدند
فریادهای خشم به گوش جهان زدند ...

اما، خزان سرخ پس از نوبهار سبز
با جنگ، از کرانه مغرب فرا رسید:
وز موج خون، شراره ی طغیان فرو نشست،
باد ستیزه جوی، عَلَم های کهنه را
با نقش لاله های شهادت فرو شکست.
آنگاه، لاله های طبیعی، به رغم فصل
در کشتزار حادثه، سر برفراختند
وز شرم زندگان
چون شمع، بر مزار شهیدان ناشناس
ماندند و درحباب بلورین گداختند.

335 See N. Nādirpūr, *Majmū'a-yi ash'ār*, Vol. 2, pp. 1319 – 1322.

باران و آفتاب
دشنام های کهنه و خون های تازه را
بر سینه برهنه دیوارهای شهر
آمیختند و، رهگذران را هزار بار
زین بازوی دوگانه خود، خیره ساختند.

گل های آتشین
- بعد از کرشمه های زنان و سپاهیان -
از لوله های گرم مسلسل جدا شدند:
پایان گرفت الفت "گل ها" و "لوله ها"
آنگاه، این دو واژه ی از هم گسیخته
پنهان شدند در پس نام "گلوله" ها،
وز دیدگاه خویش:
راه هلاک آدمیان را شناختند.

امروز کودکان و جوانان و مادران
در دوزخی به نام "بهشت برادران"
- بر گرد روشنایی فواره های سرخ-
چون شمع، در سرشک ندامت تپیده اند
وز گوشه های چشم:
گل ها و لاله های پر از درد و داغ را
بر گور جنگیان نگون بخت دیده اند،
اما نگفته اند
کز لابلای دفتر اندیشه های خویش
آن تار موی را،
وز قاب ذهن، صورت آن فتنه جوی را
آیا ربوده اند و به آتش کشیده اند؟
یا با کلید وعده ی او، بردر بهشت
نوبت گرفته اند و به دوزخ رسیده اند؟

این "کاوه" های غافل اندوهگین، هنوز
مغز گرانبهای جوانان خویش را
قربانی قساوت "ضحّاک" می کنند،
اما کجاست روح "فریدون" نامدار
کز مرز شاهنامه اگر پا برون نهد:
"ضحّاک دیو" را همه در خاک می کنند
وانگه به پاس مقدم آن ایزدی سروش
آئینه ضمیر پشیمان خویش را
از نقش "ماردوش"،
وز جلوه های دوزخی اش، پاک می کند...

From Żahhāk to Fireydūn
One day, suddenly
A strand of hair from the beard of Abū Jahl, found its way into a book.
Furtively, it took the place of the peacock's flight feather,
And that night, when its image seated itself
In the moon's narrow frame
More comfortably than the pupil in the eye,
The sleeping city

Was overwhelmed with a thick smoke, like the night of hell.
From every towering building, fires of rebellion raged,
And from every corner, the rebellion-breaking army came.
So it was: the city assumed the mask of a stranger.
Fighters in red,
With images of tulips on multicolored banners,
Made mourning for martyrs fresh everywhere.

The white-haired elderly
Wrote insults instead of prayers
On the bare chest of the city walls.
The rose-faced ones
Placed rose-kisses on the mouths of machine guns
To respect the silence of the Revolutionary Guards.
Then all of them
Thumped a hard fist into the sky's kidneys.
They shouted angrily into the world's ears...

But, after the green Spring, the red Autumn arrived,
With war from the Western border,
And the waves of blood submerged the sparks of rebellion.
The belligerent wind
Broke the old banners with their images of tulips: martyrdom.
Then, despite the season, natural tulips raised their heads
In the seedbed of events.
Put to shame by the living,
They remained by the graves of anonymous martyrs
like candles, burning in crystal lanterns.
Rain and sunshine
Mixed the old insults with fresh blood
On the bare chest of the city's walls.
They made the passers-by stare
A thousand times at their double-edged game.

After the women had flirted with the Guards,
The fiery roses
Separated from the barrels of machine guns.
The intimacy between roses and barrels came to an end.
Later, these two words separated
They hid behind the name of "bullets."
And from that vantage point
They learned the path of people's ruin.

Today, in a hell called "The Brothers' Paradise,"
children, youths and mothers
Are fluttering round the red fountain's gleam
Like a candle, in tears of remorse.
And from the corners of their eyes
They have seen the roses and barrels

Full of pain and mourning
On the graves of the ill-starred fighters,
But they have not said
Whether they've ripped that strand of hair
From the book of their thoughts,
Or set fire to that quarrelsome face
In the frame of their memory,
Or whether they are waiting in line with a key,
Given with his promise of paradise,
And have found themselves in hell.

These sorrowful and ignorant Kāves
Are sacrificing the precious brains of their children
To Żahhāk's cruelty.
Where is the soul of the celebrated Fireydūn
Who, if he were to stand outside the *Shāh-nāma*
Would throw the demon Żahhāk in the dust.
Then, as beseems that heavenly lord's arrival,
He would wipe the image of that "Serpent King"
From the mirror of the mind's regret.

The poem consists of six stanzas, each depicting an event of the 1979 Revolution. In the first stanza the poet refers to the seeing of Khomeini's image in the moon, interpreting it as a victory for Khomeini, removing the Shah from Iran's "peacock throne." Abū Jahl is the familiar name of Amr ibn Hishām, one of Muḥammad's Meccan opponents.[336] His name means "father of ignorance." By linking his name to the appearance of Khomeini's face in the moon, Nādirpūr is saying very strongly that the people have adopted an irreligious superstition, but also that Khomeini is the opponent of true religion. The book in which Abū Jahl's hair falls is not specified, but in *The Satanic Verses* and *From Ahriman to Tahmtan* the book is identified as the Quran. The reader is expected to think here of the supposed presence of a hair of Khomeini's in every copy of the Quran: this is a dark inversion of that miracle. The poet refers to "peacock's flight feather," s symbolism of affluence and monarchy, which is now replaced by a lock of Abū Jahl's beard.

Nādirpūr emphasises that this event took place in a hideous time. The sleeping city connotes people's slumber and their divorce from reality. The dark and depressed night is like the night of hell. The angry demonstrators set fire to cinemas and shops and blockade the streets. Fire rises from many places. As the police were unable to stop these demonstrators, the Shah's regime set the

336 On Abū Jahl see W. Montgomery Watt in *Encyclopaedia of Islam, Second Edition,* s.v. Abū Djahl.

army to stop them with tragic consequences, the killing of hundreds of innocent people. It is in this context that people feel alienated from the familiar city. It is as if it wears "the mask of a stranger."

The poet continues in the second stanza to depict the events during the bloody days of the Revolution. The stanza commences with an emphasis on demonstrators' readiness to offer their lives to topple the Shah and establish a democratic state. During the Revolution (and during the Iran-Iraq War), one could see demonstrators wearing shrouds, and holding banners with slogans, to emphasise their willingness to die. Here we see how images of tulips, a symbol of martyrdom, are on demonstrators' banners.[337] Elderly men are writing insults on the walls. The poet is surprised at seeing white-haired men writing such slogans on the wall, instead of praying or writing prayers. The insults may refer to the slogans shouted by demonstrators and inscribed on walls and banners against the Shah and foreign powers such as the United States, England and Israel. The walls are like bare chests – bared to show readiness for bullets. While the elderly are writing slogans, women with graceful faces like red roses are convincing the Shah's guards not to shoot, putting roses in the barrels of the machine guns. Nādirpūr's imagery of placing "rose-kisses on the mouths of machine guns to respect the silence of the Revolutionary Guards" is effective as it shows how demonstrators respect the inactive guards, who eventually side with demonstrators, but it also emphasises how peace is achieved in the middle of the fight. Instead of fighting each other, they unite and thump a hard fist into the sky's kidneys, shouting so hard that the whole world can hear their voices.

The poet depicts the start of the war against Iraq in the third stanza. Red autumn refers to the time when Iraqi soldiers invaded Iran, i. e., 22 September 1980. Nādirpūr subtly refers to the effects of the war and how it gave a pretext for the newly-established Islamic Republic to ban free political activities and to consolidate and centralise its power. From this time onwards the Islamic Republic imprisoned and later executed a large number of dissidents, or prompted them to flee Iran. Nādirpūr emphasises that all the sparks of rebellion and the ideals for which people were prepared to die were immersed in the war's waves of blood. This is a vivid imagery. This atypical situation is further amplified by the poet's allusions to tulips flowering out of season. The colour of blood invokes the red hue of the tulips. During the early fighting against the invading Iraqi army, waves

---

337 On martyrdom during the Revolution see Seyed-Gohrab, "Martyrdom as Piety, Mysticism and National Icon in Iran," in *Der Islam: Zeitschrift für Geschichte und Kultur des islamischen Orients*, issue 1–2, 87, 2012, pp. 248–273; also see M. Dorraj, "Symbolic and Utilitarian Political Value of a Tradition: Martyrdom in Iranian Political Culture," in *The Review of Politics*, 59, 3 1997, 489–521.

of Iranian youths sacrificed themselves to defend the country. These youths were commonly compared to tulips in popular songs, on mural paintings, in news items, etc. Tulips became symbols for the fallen.

The tulips are then connected to the candles which families would place beside the graves of the fallen. They were placed in glass vases shaped like tulips and often called "tulips." While candles give light, keeping memories alive, they are consuming their souls. The image of the candle consuming its own substance is a familiar one in classical Persian poetry.[338] The candles therefore are a metonym for the families who come to light them. They placed pictures of the deceased and light candles on their graves. The pain of loss was so unbearable that mothers would come to the cemetery and stay all day long, talking to their lost sons as if they were alive. I know from my own experiences how cemeteries became mournful picnic places where families gathered to keep the memories of their loved ones alive. But in this image we have tulips beside the graves of anonymous martyrs, whose graves are not visited by family members since their remains could not be identified. Many soldiers were lost in action or were so severely wounded that they could not be identified. A special section of the cemetery was assigned to them, and we are asked to imagine the tulips as candles, and the family sitting at the graveside.

In the fourth stanza the poet reflects on the time during the Revolution when women flirted with the guards, giving them roses, bringing an end to violence.[339] Nādirpūr makes a pun on the Persian word *gulūla,* "bullet," which Nādirpūr reads as a compound of *gul,* "rose," "flower," and *lūla,* "pipe" or "tube," by artificially doubling the consonant /l/. While harmony between women and guards, or "roses" and "pipes," brought peace, the separation of the two caused war and destruction.

The fifth stanza foregrounds the cemetery, "The Brothers' Paradise," which the poet characterises as a hell. This is the outcome of the slogans, protests and war: an emotional hell where children, youths and mothers have gathered and are hopelessly mourning the loss of their loved ones, and lamenting their own fate. To commemorate the fallen, the Islamic state had built a huge fountain with red water in the cemetery. People would gather around it to respect the fallen of the war and the Revolution. At the end of the fifth stanza the poet alludes to the motto at the beginning of the poem, "A strand of hair from the beard of Abū Jahl, found its way into a book." Here the poet asks whether the mourners

---

338 For various candle imagery see A.A. Seyed-Gohrab, "Waxing Eloquent: the Masterful Variations on Candle Metaphors in the Poetry of Hafiz and his Predecessors," in *Metaphor and Imagery in Persian Poetry*, Leiden/Boston, MA: Brill, 2012, pp. 81–123.

339 People placed flowers, especially carnations (*mīkhak*), on the barrels of the soldiers' guns.

have "ripped that strand of hair / from the book of their thoughts" and rejected the "quarrelsome face" they have seen, or whether on the contrary they are still "waiting in line with a key (to paradise)." In the latter case, their disillusionment is still to come, for they will find themselves in hell. This is the "miracle" of Khomeini's hairs projected into the psychology of individuals: what matters is not whether there is a hair in a book, or even whether there are traces of ignorance even in the Quran, but whether the hair of ignorance, superstition and idolisation is in the mind. Both the hair image and that of the quarrelsome face point directly to Khomeini.[340] The poet does not believe in the promises of paradise, as what he observes is a hell in which people are burning both physically and emotionally.

In the last stanza the poet links the current situation to the mythological period in Persia, when the tyrant Żahhāk fed his two serpents with the brains of Persia's children. The brave blacksmith, Kāva, who rose against Żahhāk's tyranny, has now become sorrowful and ignorant Kāvas. Kāves stand for all the mothers and fathers who have ignorantly sacrificed their children's brains to Żahhāk. The poem ends with the wish that the hero, Fireydūn, who joined with Kāva, defeated Żahhāk and became a legendary king, might appear in the world to throw Żahhāk in the dust and erase the hellish images of Iran's recent past.[341]

* * *

Similar sentiments are found in Nādirpūr's poetry long before the revolution and war, and it will be worth exploring the earlier poems to get a sense of how much his condemnation of Khomeini and the Islamic Republic, and the ways he expresses these, are interwoven with a sensibility shaped by Persian epic poetry, a nativist approach to Persian identity, anti-clericalism, rejection of Islam and the frustrated viewpoint of the exile.

---

340 See also J. Matini, "Nādir Nādirpūr Shā'ir-i chīra-dast (1308–1378)," in *Irān-shināsī*, 1379/2000, 46, pp. 402–403.

341 For a completely different rearticulation of the myth of Żahhāk and Kāve by Aḥmad Shāmlū see Ahmad Karimi-Hakkak, *A Fire of Lilies*, pp. 29–52. Karimi-Hakkak discusses Shāmlū's "ideal of a classless society in contrast with Ferdowsi's notion of Iranianness" (p. 52) presenting the reign of Żahhāk in a different light: "[i]n the new version, then, Żahhak undergoes a complete reversal and emerges as the hero who, having destroyed the monarchical order, is engaged in a protracted battle for the creation of the classless society. Similarly, Feraydun's image is re-versed completely. He is no longer the just, liberal possessor of divine glory, but rather a vestige of the old regime, waiting for a chance to return to power. Meanwhile, Kaveh, the popular leader of Ferdowsi's story, turns into the unknowing accomplice of the forces of reaction, eventually coopted against the interest of his social class into the unholy alliance of the monarchy, the army, and the clergy." See pp. 49–50.

Nādirpūr refers to myth, Persian history and the struggle of good and evil in poetry that is contemporary in style and subject matter to frame the events as so surreal that the poet feels he is in a reality mixed with myth and fiction. In *The Guamata of Heaven* (*Gaumātā-yi Āsmān*), published in 1958, he tells how Gaumātā ruled the ancient Persian Empire, having disguised himself as the brother he had murdered. This story gives Nādirpūr an opportunity to say that the world appears to be governed by the Devil. I quote the first two stanzas of this poem, which contains several elements that were to reappear in his later poems denouncing the Revolution and Khomeini:

یک شب ز تخت عرش فرو می کشم ترا
ابلیس، ای کشنده ی پنهانی خدا
گر در گمان خلق، تو ابلیس نیستی
من دانم ای خدای پلیدان، تو کیستی (...)

هشدار، ای کسی که جز ابلیس نیستی
خلق جهان هنوز نداند که کیستی
هر چند تکیه بر سر جای خدا زدی
در گوش خلق، بانگ خوش آشنا زدی
یک شب ز تخت عرش فرو کشم ترا
ابلیس، ای کشنده ی پنهانی خدا

One night, I will drag you down from the throne of heaven,
O Devil, O secret murderer of God.
You are not the Devil in the mind of men,
But I know who you are, O god of the foul!

Beware! O you who are none but the devil,
–The people of the world do not yet know who you are –
Although you have propped yourself up in the place of God,
And have sung a pleasant song in the people's ear,
One night I will drag you down from the throne of heaven,
O Devil, the secret murderer of God![342]

A number of poems composed in this period, while refraining from political comment, can be read as social criticism. Nādirpūr enrolled at the Sorbonne in 1950 to study French language and literature, and returned to Iran during the period of political unrest after the 1953 *coup d'etat.*[343] Nādirpūr was disappointed by the

---

342 The translation is taken from Ehsan Yarshater, "A Star Ceases to Shine," in *Persica*, pp. 149–150.

343 H. Yavari, in *Encyclopaedia Iranica*, s.v. Nader Naderpour; also see afterword of L.P. Alishan in *False Dawn: Persian Poems*, pp. 92–93; Mark J. Gasiorowski, in *Encyclopaedia Iranica*, s.v. Coup d'Etat of 1332 š./1953. On Nādirpūr's view on committed poets see M. Khushnām,

frustration of democracy, and concentrated on poetry. Still, stanzas such as the one cited above, in which words such as "devil" and "god" could refer to agents in the political battle, display his concerns with social and religious matters. Another reason for integrating Persian mythology into his poem is Nādirpūr's desire to present current socio-political events in such a way that they acquire a timeless character. The hardships are not only personal and present; this is something that has befallen the Persian peoples many times. In a prose introduction to his collection of poetry entitled *Place and Time*, Nādirpūr comments on the way classical Persian masters used ancient mythological figures to depict events of their own time.[344] He especially praises Ḥāfiẓ for the way he incorporates historical elements into his poetry, giving the following couplet as an example of how Ḥāfiẓ represents his personal experiences in a purely poetic way:

شاه ترکان سخن مدعیان می شنود
شرمی از مظلمه خون سیاووشش باد

The king of the Turks listens to the words of calumniators;
May some shame be his for the complaints of the blood of Siyāvash.[345]

Nādirpūr explains that Ḥāfiẓ coins "the king of Turks" to refer to Tūrān-shah, a Minister during Ḥāfiẓ's time, and contrasts him to Afrāsiyāb, a character from Firdowsī's *Shāh-nāma*. Here Ḥāfiẓ equates his situation, having been unjustly imprisoned by the Minister twice, to that of Siyāvash who was innocently imprisoned and finally murdered. Siyāvash was the estranged son of the Persian king Key Kāvūs, who sadly listens to calumniators of his son. Siyāvash exculpates himself in an ordeal of fire, and later deserts his cruel father to serve with Afrāsiyāb, the enemy of Iran, whose daughter is married. They begat Key Khosrow, who became the king of Persia and avenged the murder of his father. Ḥāfiẓ's couplet can be interpreted at different levels, referring to different figures during his lifetime. Nādirpūr underlines how Ḥāfiẓ mixes his own experiences with the widely-known lives of the heroes in the *Shāh-nāma*.[346] Nādirpūr seeks to connect modern issues to ancient Persia in the same way.

"Nigāhī gudharā bar shiʿr-i Nādir Nādirpūr," in *Irān-Nāma*, 1378/1999, issues 68–69, pp. 839–848.

344 N. Nādirpūr, *Majmūʿa-yi ashʿār*, Vol. 2, p. 1363.

345 Ḥāfiẓ, *Dīvān*, ghazal 101, line 4; Avery, p. 144, poem ci. For an interpretation of this couplet see D.P. Brookshaw, *Hafiz and his Contemporaries*, pp. 178–179.

346 Peter Avery says, "Hafez was doubtless alluding to royal inability to resist the prompting of jealous slanderers against people such as an apprehensive tyrant's own sons and kinsmen, or against the poet himself. Hence the "King of the Turks" stands for Shah Shuja." See Avery's comments in footnote 2, p. 145.

A number of Nādirpūr's poems and prose works reveal his aversion to islamist ideology and Islamic clerics, and his distrust of Islam itself. He expresses his pain at seeing Iran in the hands of religious ideologists. Part of this aversion stems from his doubts that Shiite Islamic culture is compatible with pre-Islamic Persian culture. In this he echoes the ideas of nineteenth-century Persian nationalists, and of anti-Islamic and anti-Arabic figures such as Fatḥ-ʿAlī Ākhūndzāda (1812–1878) and Mīrzā Āqā Khān Kirmānī (1854–1896).[347] Both these intellectuals dismissed Islam and blamed the Arab Other for Persia's "backwardness" in comparison to Europe. Nineteenth-century European scholarship on the Indo-European languages and theories about race had made the Iranian peoples more aware of being different from their Semitic and Turkic neighbours. Iranian nationalists used racial theories and emphasised additional cultural differences between Iranians and Arabs, blaming Islam and the Arabs for Persia's backwardness. Such nationalistic sentiments became a prominent element in the intellectual landscape of the time, especially when the Pahlavi dynasty made Aryanism one of the cornerstones of its modern nationalism and emphasised the Aryan origin of Iranian peoples and the splendour of the pre-Islamic Persia.[348] Muḥammad Riża Shah even called himself Āryā-Mihr, meaning "The Sun of the Aryans." Ahmad Ashraf is right when he says, "Race is rarely taken up as the main element of identity by Iranian intellectuals."[349] Yet a limited number of intellectuals played with this, including Nādirpūr. Ashraf summarises the way Nādirpūr combines territorial and cultural ties to define an Iranian nationality in which religion, especially Shiism, plays no role: "Nādirpūr believes that blood ties (Indo-European origin, Aryan race, and Iranian stock), territorial ties (Iranian

347 Nader Naderpour, "Une contradiction: L'āme iranienne et l'esprit islamique," in *Die Welt des Islams*, vol. 23/24, 1984, pp. 129–135; also see Nādirpūr's essay on the Persian language and how he categorises Iranian intellectuals through the Islamic history in two groups: those defending and praising the Persian language and culture, and those who prefer the Arabic language as the vehicle for intellectual exercise and an icon for Islamic culture. "Irānīyān yikka savārān-i du-gānigī (andīshihā'ī dar bāra-yi milliyyat va farhang-i īrānī va peyvandishān bā zabān-i pārsī," in *Irān-nāma*, 1373/1994, issue 47, pp. 439–472. Here Nādirpūr equates Ayatollah Khomeini with Muḥammad Bāqir Majlisī (1627- about 1700) and Abū Ḥāmid Muḥammad Ghazālī (d. 1111) who, preferring Arabic to Persian, stand in contrast to Firdowsī, ʿUmar Khayyām and Ṣādiq Hidāyat. On Ākhūndzāda and Kirmānī see H. Algar, in *Encyclopaedia Iranica*, s.v. Āḵūndzāda, and M. Bayat in *Encyclopaedia Iranica*, s.v. Āqā Khan Kermānī.

348 See A. Marashi's chapter two, "Nationalizing Pre-Islamic Iran," in *Nationalizing Iran: Culture, Power, and the State, 1870–1940*, Seattle, WA: University of Washington Press, 2008, pp. 49–85; also see R. Zia-Ebrahimi, "Self-Orientalization and Dislocation: The Uses and Abuses of the "Aryan" Discourse in Iran," in *Iranian Studies*, Vol. 44, No. 4, 2011, pp. 445–472.

349 A. Ashraf, "The Crisis of National and Ethnic Identities in Contemporary Iran," in *Iranian Studies*, Vol. 26, No. ½, 1993, pp. 163, footnote 10.

history, the Iranian plateau, and the Iranian state), and cultural ties (the Persian language, Persian arts, and Persian customs) are the pillars of the 'glorious palace of Iranian nationality.'"[350] Nādirpūr's criticism of Shiism is part of his othering of Islam and the Arabic language, which are combined with attempts to highlight Iran's great contribution to Islamic civilisation.[351]

Nādirpūr's lack of sympathy for Shiism is to be seen in many of his poems, among which his bleak and depressing depiction of the city of Qom, one of the centres of Shiite learning. The poem was composed in 1953, but it is still one of the popular poems in the Persian language:[352]

قم	Qom
چندین هزار زن	Several thousand women,
چندین هزار مرد	Several thousand men
زنها، لچک به سر	Women wearing veils,
مردان، عبا به دوش	Men wearing cloaks.
یک گنبد طلا	One single gold dome
با لک لکان پیر	With old storks
یک باغ بی صفا	A garden bereft of joy
با چند تکدرخت	With lonely trees
از خنده ها تهی	Bereft of laughter
وز گفته ها خموش	Silent, without words,
یک حوض نیمه پُر	A pool half full.
با آب سبز رنگ	With greenish water.
چندین کلاغِ پیر	Some old crows
بر توده های سنگ	On some piles of stones.
انبوه سائلان	Beggars at every step
در هر قدم به راه	along the road.
عمامه ها سفید	Turbans white,
رخساره ها سیاه	Faces black.

Like a camera, the poet pictures what he sees from a distance, with brief descriptions of people, their characteristic dress and the golden dome of the tomb of Fāṭima al-Maʿṣūma, the sister of the eighth Shiite imam, ʿAlī ibn Mūsa al-Riżā (d. 818).[353] The birds in this city are old storks and crows. The stork is a symbol

350 See ibid. pp. 163, footnote 10. Ashraf bases himself on N. Nādirpūr, "Huviyyat-i millī va zabān-i mushtarak," in *Kitāb-i Nīmā*, no. 3, 1990, pp. 19–37.

351 On the Persian contribution to Islamic culture see *The Persian Presence in the Islamic World*, ed. Richard B. Hovannisian & Georges Sabagh, Cambridge: Cambridge University Press, 1998.

352 N. Nādirpūr, *Majmūʿa-yi ashʿār*, Vol. 1, pp. 187–188. For a literary translation see *False Dawn: Persian Poems*, p. 34.

353 The analysis of this poem is based on my earlier publication, "The Tuin Qom," in *ZemZem: Tijdschrift over het Midden-Oosten, Noord-Afrika en Islam*, Issue 15, No. 1, 2019, pp. 34–7.

of worshiping God. In Iran the stork is associated with the prophetic tradition, *al-mulk lak, al-amr lak, al-hamd lak* or "Yours is the kingdom, Yours is the command, Yours is the praise." The stork is considered a devout bird who constantly praises God with his clattering *lak lak* sound. The gardens have no soul and the trees in the gardens are here and there, lonely. Poets usually describe the garden using roses and nightingales, but their absence is very marked here. The nightingale has given way to the intimidating crow, an ill-omened symbol in Persian culture, associated with the winter and earthly existence.[354] There are many cemeteries in Qom and perhaps the poet refers to these cemeteries rather than to finely designed courts, which are sometimes referred to as gardens. When Nādirpūr wrote this poem (1953), the water of Qom was notorious for its salty taste. In this poem, the water in the pond is stagnant and turning green. The pond is the centre of Persian gardens from which the water feeds the four geometrically designed parts of the garden. People sit around the pond to celebrate life, but here the stagnant water does not invite people to celebrate life. The poem's tone is grim, sad and lifeless. Although the town has gardens and a gleaming golden dome, it does not lure people to enjoy the city. The short lines indicate the poet's rush, as if he wants to leave the city quickly. By using a pejorative word for the headscarf (*lachak*), he reveals his disapproval. The poem ends with an allusion to the many beggars at every step and the white turbans of the clergy, and their black faces.

Nādirpūr also praised pre-Islamic Persia in his earlier works, evoking the symbols of light and fire used in Zoroastrian texts and worship, and denounced Islam as a force of darkness. This preference for pre-Islamic Persia and aversion to Islam inspired the poet to contrive metaphors and imagery for Iran that are bereft of Islamic elements. This has led scholars such as J.B. Saad to characterise Nādirpūr as an anti-Arab and anti-Islamic poet.[355] The frustration and bitterness of exile only increased Nādirpūr's resentment of Islam. From his point of view as an exile, he saw the situation in his homeland deteriorating quickly due to political Islam and a deliberate ideological neglect of ancient Persian culture. He was not alone: many modern Persian poets, writers and intellectuals have voiced their emotional discomfort with Islam. Nādirpūr's poetry from exile emphasises his bitter experiences, his rage at the policies of the Islamic regime, and his re-

354 See Seyed-Gohrab, *Laylī and Majnūn*, pp. 322–328.

355 J.B. Saad, *The Image of Arabs in Modern Persian Literature*, Lanham, NY, and London: University Press of America, 1996. See also F.D. Lewis's review in which he rightly states that when a classical Persian poet such as Firdowsī refers to an Arab poet, it is not a concrete Arab but a type. "Review of Joya Blondel Saad's The Image of Arabs in Modern Persian Literature," *Iranian Studies*, issue 32, No. 1, 1999, pp. 163–167.

luctance to accept exile. These themes are usually expressed within a setting framed by oppositional pairs: nostalgic feelings of the cherished past versus the sentimentality of unattainable desires; the uncertain future versus the cherished past; longing for union with his beloved Iran versus the pain of separation; longing for the sun in a land without sun. In a note on the translation of three of Nādirpūr's poems, in which the poet depicts moments of "thoughtful peregrinations in exile," William L. Hanaway eloquently observes:

> As exile, Nādirpūr inhabits two places at once: an inner, remembered place, now evoked in ever more nostalgic images, and an outer, physical place where he dwells and passes his days. These places are quite separate, but related. Were he still in pre-revolution Iran his inner and outer spaces would probably resemble each other closely: the inner overlaying the outer and providing the map that makes it coherent. The inner place would have been tinged with nostalgia for his lost childhood, the outer still perceived through the overlay of the inner one and coloured by his daily concerns in familiar territory. Nowadays, the inner and outer places have been forcibly separated and the experience of the outer place seems to have worked its effect on the inner vision.[356]

The displaced poet holds the Islamic regime responsible for his situation. He comforts himself by comparing his own time and situation with events during Persian history and even mythical periods. By framing his poems through pre-Islamic myths and stories, Nādirpūr creates a dichotomy between Islamic and pre-Islamic values, putting Islamic forces and characters in the category of evil. In his attack on Ayatollah Khomeini he compares him to the serpent king, Żahhāk, and thus an enemy to authentic Persian culture.

7.7 Conclusion

Several conclusions can be drawn from the poems analysed in this chapter. First of all, while Nādirpūr's political poems analysed here are not representative of the merit of his entire work, these highly engaged poems do reflect his poetical flair and virtuosity. They make interesting use of Persian myths and legends and reveal his views in relation to Islam and his ideas on a national state based on pre-Islamic archetypes.

---

356 See William L. Hanaway, "The Cross and the Clock," in *Iranian Studies*, Vol. 30, No. 3/4, 1997, pp. 301–303. The poem are "A Spring Tale" (written in Paris in 1982), "The Cross and the Clock" (written in Los Angeles in 1988), and "A Leaf in Rain" (written in Los Angeles in 1988).

The theme of exile, an integral part of Nādirpūr's poetry, was present even in his early poetry composed in Iran. Themes such as exile and alienation are so much part of the experience of human beings that they can be found in all types of poetry. Exile is a ubiquitous theme from the beginning of Persian poetry in the ninth century, whether referring to the mystical exile of the soul from the spiritual abode or missing one's birth place, as in Ḥāfiẓ's famous ghazals, or experiencing imprisonment, as in the poetry of Masʿūd Saʿd Salmān (d. about 1131), or expressing exile in propagandist religious terms, as in the poetry of Nāṣir-i Khosrow (d. about 1071).[357] In all these types of exile, the poet laments being far from his cherished ideals. In Nādirpūr's poems written outside Iran the theme of exile encapsulates alienation, estrangement and loneliness, and is used to generate rage against the Islamic Republic of Iran, whose leaders the poet dehumanises.

Another conspicuous element of his poetry is his use of dualities, such as his frequent references to the mythical struggle between Ahriman and Ahūrā Mazdā. In ancient Persian mythology Ahriman personifies evil forces coming from darkness that attack Ahūrā Mazdā. The forces of good are locked in an incessant fight against the dark forces of Ahriman. These elements can also be found in his earlier work, but take a more concrete form in his poetry in exile, especially when the mythological figures are associated with specific modern historical figures. The oppositional pairs enable the poet to voice his opinion unequivocally. Nādirpūr often implores God to remove injustice and to fight evil forces. In the poems analysed above Satan is equated with evil and negative forces in history, but in other poems Satan also appears as a rather mischievous figure standing for realities commonly censured by religion. Houra Yavari appositely refers to Nādirpūr's "A poem for God," in which the poet presents Eblis/Satan as the creator "of woman, love, music, wine, and pleasure," while God is sympathetically portrayed "as a poet, whose only poem as well as masterpiece, 'sorrow,' he celebrates."[358] L.P. Alishan sees this fascination with the diabolic as a concern of the Romantics, to be detected from the first period of his poetic career:

> After being deprived of God, of hope in a secular paradise, of nature and of woman's love as means of transcendence, faced with himself as a prisoner of Schopenhauerian "Will," Nādirpour attampts one last desperate effort before he concedes that nothing is left to him but

357 Sunil Sharma, *Persian Poetry at the Indian Frontier: Masʿūd Saʿd Salmān of Lahore*, Delhi: Permanent Black, 2000; A.C. Hunsberger, *Nasir Khusraw: the Ruby of Badakhshan, a Portrait of the Persian Poet, Traveller and Philosopher*, London/New York: I.B. Tauris, 2003.

358 H. Yavari, in *Encyclopaedia Iranica*, s.v. Nader Naderpour.

> his imagination, i.e., the world of art. This last refuge for Nādirpūr in the first period of his poetic career appears as an obsession with evil and with Satan himself.[359]

In his poetry written in exile, the evil force, personified in Satan, usually loses its positive mischievous attributes to become an icon of wickedness, viciousness and barbarity. Identifying Satan with the clergy who, in Nādirpūr's view, were responsible for the 1979 Revolution and the sufferings and loss during the Iran-Iraq War, the poet recognises the power of religion in society. This realisation and his frustration as an exile are expressed by depicting the actions of the evil forces within the tradition of Persian epic poetry. The poet's enemies are placed in Persia's legendary history, so that they can be interpreted in an additional dimension. Often, at the end of these poems, the poet implores God to hear his voice and to revise the course of the history.

In Nādirpūr's view, even during his early career, a poet is part and parcel of his generation. Everything he writes, whether on private or public issues, should be understandable by his readers as if it is part of their own lives.[360] In the introduction to *Sun's Kohl* ("Surma-yi khurshīd"), published in 1960, the poet comments on his own position in society:

> If I, during my life as a poet, have attained any honour (*iftikhār*), I see this honour as part of being a travelling companion of others in my generation. I swear by the serenity that I have not yet felt that I have never stopped being part of my generation's story. Shoulder to shoulder I have battled, attaining the highest and lowest points together with my generation. Standing in the ranks of my generation, I fought against "corruption," rolling on the ground of "corruption." My purity lies in this contamination. Contrary to many others, I was not made of stone or iron, I was not unaffected by my generation's pollutions. If there is any honour, this lies in my fight. Sometimes we are conquerors and sometimes the conquered. Surely, honour does not lie in remaining "in a paradisiacal state" and "making no mistakes," not entering the arena because of fear.
>
> If I am good or bad, if I am a competent or incompetent poet, whoever I am, and whatever I am, I am the poet of my generation, the poet of my time. I gamble the cash of my existence in this play. I have no way back as I have broken all the bridges behind me.[361]

---

359 *False Dawn*, p. 91.

360 On the poet's literary commitment and his participation in society see M.R. Ghanoonparvar, *Prophets of Doom*, pp. 88–96.

361 Nādirpūr, *Majmūʿa-yi ashʿār*, Vol. 1, p. 461.

8 Iran and Saudi Arabia

با کاروان بگویید از راه کعبه برگرد
ما یار را به مستی بیرونِ خانه دیدیم
لَبّیکْ از چه گویید ای رهروان غافل
لَبیّک او به خلوت از جامِ می شنیدیم

Say to the caravan: “Turn back from the road to the Kaʿba,
In our drunkenness we saw the beloved outside the house.”
O heedless travellers, “Why do you cry ‘I am yours’ (*labbayk*)?
In our private retreat we heard His *labbayk* from the wine-cup.”[362]

8.1 Introduction

Part of the Persian Iran-Iraq war poetry relates to Saudi Arabia’s support for Saddam Hussein’s war against Iran and the consequences of Iran’s attempts to export the Revolution to neighbouring countries, especially to Saudi Arabia during the ritual pilgrimage (*ḥajj*). In many historical analyses, authors focus on the Shiite and Sunnite divide with little or no attention for other essential factors. For instance, in his analysis of the Iranian *ḥajj* and protests during the 1980s, Martin Kramer states that “the pilgrimage ritual itself is not an issue about which Sunnis and Shiites have conducted an elaborate polemic.”[363] He then focuses on the differences between the two schools, examining various aspects of the international relations between the two countries. It is to a certain degree true that *ḥajj* rituals are similar for both the Shiites and Sunnites, but there are at least three cardinal elements that constitute the experience of *ḥajj* for Iranian Muslims which explain the animosity between Iran and Saudi Arabia.[364] Firstly, ethnicity, nationalistic sentiments and stereotypes employed to construct the image of an “other” play a central role. The imagery is often built on medieval stereotypes. Hostilities between Sunnite Persians and Arabs are recorded in literary debates dating back to the eleventh century, and this literature is still widely read and cited. In such debates there is no reference to Shiism: the discussions revolve

362 Khomeini, *Dīvān*, Tehran: Muʾassisa-yi tanẓīm-u nashr-i āthār-i imām Khomeini, 16th edition, 1377/1998, p. 164, ll. 2–3.
363 M. Kramer, *Arab Awakening and Islamic Revival: The Politics of Ideas in the Middle East*, New Brunswick/London: Transaction Publishers, 1996, p. 162.
364 For the experiences of a Shiite pilgrim to Mecca see *A Shiite Pilgrimage to Mecca 1885–1886: The Safarnāmeh of Mirzā Moḥammad Ḥosayn Farāhāni*, edited, translated, and annotated by Hafez Farmayan and Elton L. Daniel, London: Saqi Books, 1990.

https://doi.org/10.1515/9783110748734-012

around ethnicity. In addition to the role of ethnicity in the *ḥajj* rituals, Islamic mysticism plays a central role. Persians have been extremely prone to Sufism from at least the tenth century, to the extent that mystical ideas, doctrines and vocabulary have become part and parcel of Persian culture, leaving traces even in aspects of Persian life that are far removed from mysticism.[365] Although Sufism greatly honours the first Shiite Imam ʿAlī, most Sufi brotherhoods and most of the Persian Sufi poets were Sunnites.[366] These Sufis and poets created transgressive doctrines in which central Islamic appellations such as Islam and Quran, and central rituals such as the *ḥajj*, are given pejorative connotations, while directing attention to opposing interpretations. "Islam" was placed in opposition to *kufr* ("unbelief"), and while *kufr* was praised, Islam had the connotation of hypocrisy. In one of the central Sufi stories, the Quran is burned because one should focus on the Beloved and have no distractions.[367] The ritual *ḥajj* was seen as worshipping an idol, while the true *ḥajj* was to worship the Owner of the House. What is more, as Persia converted from Sunnism to Shiism in the sixteenth century, these deep-rooted mystical ideas and ethnic identity were profoundly mixed with Shiism in the Persian experience of *ḥajj*. Neglecting any of these components would lead to misunderstanding of the relationship between Iran and Saudi Arabia in modern politics. In what follows I will analyse the consequences of the Saudis' support for Saddam Hussein, the demonstrations of Iranian pilgrims in the holy cities of Mecca and Medina, and the poetic responses of Iranian revolutionaries, taking these three dimensions into account.

---

365 A term of endearment used often by Persian speakers is *ilāhī qurbūnat bigardam*, literally "God, may I be walking around you," which places the loved one in the position of God, while the lover is performing the ritual circumambulation (*ṭavāf*). Phrases with similar meanings abound in Persian pop songs, which are often based on classical Persian lyrical poetry.

366 Sufism was so much part of the lived culture in the thirteenth century that in discussing Saʿdī's work E.G. Browne states that Sufism was "at this time so much in the air, and its phraseology was –as it still is –so much a part of ordinary speech, that the traces of it is in Saʿdī's writings are neither few nor uncertain." See Browne, *A Literary History of Persian*, Vol. II, p. 526. J.T.P. de Bruijn states that it is hard to distinguish a poem as mystical or profane, as this depends to a great extend on the poet and whether he had mystical affiliations or was known as a court poet. See *Persian Sufi Poetry*, p. 55.

367 See ʿAṭṭār, *Manṭiq al-ṭeyr*, ed. Siyyid Ṣādiq Gowharīn, Tehran: Shirkat Intishārāt-i ʿIlmī wa Farhangī, 1368/1989.

8.2 Demonstrations in the Holy Cities of Mecca and Medina

There are abundant references in Persian war poetry to the Saudis' support for Saddam, the *ḥajj*, and how Iranian pilgrims were treated in Mecca and Medina. Before the 1979 Revolution Iran had a better diplomatic relationship with the Saudis, yet from time to time the relationship suffered from ideological incongruence between Shiism and Wahhabism, especially when some Shiite clerics wrote treatises against Wahhabism. In 1943 an Iranian pilgrim was executed on charges of disrespecting the holy shrine, and the Iranian government decided not to send any pilgrims to Mecca until 1948.[368] The relationship between the two countries was respectful for most of the Pahlavi period. The situation deteriorated with the 1979 Revolution. Khomeini considered monarchy to be incompatible with Islamic government, and he regarded Iran's Arab neighbours as agents of the western powers. These countries worried about the effects of the Revolution among their own populations. To awaken the Saudi population and Muslims around the world, Khomeini appointed the cleric Muḥammad Mūsavī Khuʾīnīhā, a leader among the students who seized the American Embassy in Tehran for 444 days, as Iran's pilgrimage representative in 1982.[369] He was a key figure in the demonstrations in Mecca and Medina, but following clashes he was expelled from the country. As a staunch supporter of Khomeini, Khuʾīnīhā firmly believed in the politicisation of the *ḥajj*. He wrote several articles interpreting Khomeini's messages on the *ḥajj*. In one analysis, Khuʾīnīhā cites the following sentence by Khomeini: "*Beyt al-ḥarām* ('the Sanctified House') is the first house built for human beings; it belongs to all people, and no individual, no regime, and no tribe[370] can feel supremacy." Khuʾīnīhā emphasises that no political regime has the right to act on behalf of other Muslims, alluding here to the Saudi government.[371] One of his articles, in which he provocatively politicised *ḥajj*, bears

---

368 See D. Farhosh-van Loon, *Of Love and Longing*, pp. 86–87.

369 Khuʾīnīhā studied jurisprudence under Khomeini's supervision in Najaf from 1966 to 1967. At his return to Qum, the book *Eternal Martyr* was published, which was praised by Khomeini and Ḥuseyn ʿAlī Muntaẓirī (1922–2009), while other ayatollahs with much higher positions were critical about a political reading of Shiism. It is said that Khuʾīnīhā visited the grand Ayatollah Gulpāyigānī voicing his angry protest against him. Such an act is extremely disrespectful in Persian Shiite culture. It is reported that Gulpāyigānī raised his staff in the air to express his disapproval of such behaviour. For more information see Farīd Mudarrisī, "Rāzhā-yi Āyatollāh," *Shahrvand*, 1386/2007, Ābān, No. 23. On Muntaẓirī see S. Akhavi, "The Thought and Role of Ayatollah Hossein-ʿAli Montazeri in the Politics of Post-1979 Iran," in *Iranian Studies*, 41, no. 5, 2008, pp. 645–666.

370 The word used here is *ṭāyifa*, which can also mean ethnic group, kinfolk.

371 Khuʾīnīhā, "Ḥajj az dīdgāh-i imām," in *Pāsdār-i islām*, No. 5, Issue 55, 1365/1986, p. 34.

the title *Hamrāh bā imām ba sū-yi ḥajj: pāygāh-i inqilāb-i jahānī-yi islām* or "With the Imam to Ḥajj: The Headquarters of Islam's International Revolution." The article explains why politics is an integral part of pilgrimage.[372] Among Khomeini's sayings that Khu'īnīhā further politicises are "Turn the honoured Mecca into a centre of protest against the oppressors by orchestrating harmony (*ham-āhangī*) amongst the pilgrims from all over the world, as this is one of the secrets of *ḥajj*."[373] Or "when Muslims go on *ḥajj*, this must be a lively *ḥajj*, a pounding *ḥajj* (*ḥajj-i kūbanda*), a *ḥajj* that denounces this criminal Soviet Union and that criminal United States, then such a *ḥajj* is accepted."[374] The reception of Khomeini's views on pilgrimage requires a separate study, but these brief reflections suffice to show how persuasively the leader and the revolutionary Iranians wanted to politicise the ritual.

This was not the first time that Iranian revolutionary pilgrims had politicised the *ḥajj*. On 6 February 1971, Khomeini, who was in exile in Najaf, sent a message to the Iranian pilgrims stating that this annual gathering was not merely for pious purposes. "The people of each country should, in effect, present a report concerning their own state to the Muslims of the world, and thus all will come to know what their Muslim brothers are suffering at the hands of imperialism and its agents."[375] Khomeini's message is full of political statements, urging Iranian pilgrims to demonstrate. It is mainly a criticism of the White Revolution and the celebrations of 2,500 years of Iranian monarchy. Many Iranian pilgrims who distributed this message were arrested.[376]

While Khomeini's 1971 message was not directed at the Saudis directly, he expressed his concern that they had permitted the publication and distribution of an anti-Shiite pamphlet[377] by the staunch Wahhabi Muḥibb al-Dīn al-Khātib (1886–1969), published in Jeddah in 1960, which argued that Shiism does not "constitute a school of thought within Islam, but rather an entirely separate religion."[378] Khomeini writes, "It is surprising that the authorities in the Hijaz would permit such misleading material to be distributed in the land of revela-

372 Khu'īnīhā in *Pāsdār-i islām*, No. 6, 67 Issue, 1366/1987, pp. 27–43.

373 Khu'īnīhā in "Hamrāh bā imām...," p. 32.

374 Ibid., p. 42.

375 *Islam and Revolution*, pp. 196–197.

376 Hamed Algar writes that they were kept in leg-irons for over two years until they were set free through the intercession of the Saudi ambassador in Tehran: *Islam and Revolution*, pp. 195–199.

377 *al-Khūtūt al-ʿarīża li al-usūs allatī qāma ʿalayha dīn al-shīʿa al-imāmiyya al-ithna ʿashariyya.*

378 Such Wahhabi pamphlets were translated into several Islamic languages to depict the Shiites as heretics. See, for instance, a discussion of such works in Indonesian in Zulkifli, *The Struggle of the Shiis in Indonesia*, Canberra: Australian National University Press, 2013, pp. 245–250.

tion. The Muslim peoples must shun such divisive and imperialist-inspired books and publications, and reject those opponents of Islamic unity."[379] In many of his messages Khomeini tries to downplay the Sunnite and Shiite division, concentrating on the socio-political conditions of Muslims around the world.

Khomeini wrote another message from Najaf to pilgrims on 27 September 1978, just before he left Iraq for France. The core of the message is to invite Muslims around the world to sympathise with the Iranian people's fight against the Pahlavi regime. As Algar indicates, the message was distributed among pilgrims, but the Saudi authorities arrested several Iranians. Before presenting a report of the conditions in Iran, Khomeini opens his message as follows:

> Now that it is the season of pilgrimage to the sacred House of God and Muslims have come from all over the world to visit God's House, it is necessary that they pay attention to one of the most important aspects of this great gathering while they are performing the noble rites of the hajj, and examine the social and political circumstances of the Islamic countries. They must inform themselves of the hardships that their brothers in faith are suffering and strive to relieve those hardships, in accordance with their Islamic and moral duty. To concern oneself with the affairs of the Muslims is one of the significant duties of Islam.[380]

The message is rhetorically strong, lashing out in one-liners at the superpowers and their puppets in the Islamic world. Khomeini refers to the violence the Shah inflicted on Iranians with sweeping statements such as "[w]ith the support of America and with all the infernal means at his disposal, the Shah has fallen on our oppressed people, turning Iran into one vast graveyard." He also pays attention to the ways western powers exploited Iranian resources, picturing the Shah as a puppet of the Western powers, "[h]e [the Shah] has given oil to America; gas to the Soviet Union; pastureland, forests, and part of the oil to England and other countries."[381] At the end of the message he turns again to the Muslims of the world and cites the following prophetic tradition, which leaves Muslims no option but to answer his call: "[h]e who arises in the morning and gives no thought to the affairs of the Muslims is not a Muslim."[382]

Another message Khomeini wrote to pilgrims dates from 24 September 1979, when he was in Qom immediately after the 1979 Revolution. In this exhortation Khomeini again urged Muslims around the world to unite and fight imperialism. His opening differs from the previous messages as it is direct and authoritarian:

---

379 *Islam and Revolution*, p. 196.
380 Ibid., p. 237.
381 Ibid., p. 237.
382 Ibid., p. 238.

> It is undeniable and requires no reminder that the great religion of Islam, the religion of divine unity, destroys polytheism, unbelief, idolatry and self-worship. It is the religion of man's essential nature, which liberates him from the bonds and fetters of material nature and from the temptations of demons in jinn and human form, both in his inner being and in his outward life. It is a religion that provides guidance for conducting the affairs of state and a guide to the straight path, which is neither Eastern nor Western. It is a religion where worship is joined to politics and political activity is a form of worship.[383]

Given Khomeini's beliefs about monarchy, the first sentence's reference to "polytheism ... and self-worship" probably hints at the Saudis, whom he would not consider a truly Islamic government. In the second sentence he underscores the spiritual layer of the pilgrimage. Such a journey is a means to discover one's inner potential by divesting oneself of material interests and possessions for a period. In the fourth and fifth sentences Khomeini connects Islam with politics, highlighting that political activities are acts of worship. Afterwards, he directs his attention to male and female pilgrims, imploring them to oust the western powers from their country:

> Dear sisters and brothers, in whatever country you may live, defend your Islamic and national honour! Defend fearlessly and unhesitatingly the peoples and countries of Islam against their enemies – America, international Zionism and all the superpowers of East and West. Loudly proclaim the crimes of the enemies of Islam.[384]

Khomeini reiterates that western powers are "plundering" all "material and other resources," making the Islamic world dependent on the West economically, militarily and culturally. He then continues to condemn Israel and the problems the creation of the state of Israel caused for Muslims:

> Come to your senses; rediscover your Islamic identity! Endure oppression no longer, and vigilantly expose the criminal plans of the international bandits, headed by America! Today the first *qibla* of the Muslims has fallen into the grasp of Israel, that cancerous growth in the Middle East. They are battering and slaughtering our dear Palestinian and Lebanese brothers with all their might. At the same time, Israel is broadcasting dissension among the Muslims with all the diabolical means at its disposal. Every Muslim has a duty to prepare himself for battle against Israel.[385]

The gist of Khomeini's message in all of his exhortations regarding the pilgrimage to Mecca is that politics is an integral part of the ritual ordained by God, and

383 Ibid., p. 275.
384 Ibid., p. 276.
385 Ibid., p. 276.

Muslims are bound to engage with the political conditions of other Muslims.[386] Moreover, he repeatedly states that sectarian issues within Islam should not play a role. In his message to pilgrims on 12 September 1980, he urges Muslims all over the world to "repel the treacherous superpowers from your countries and your abundant resources"[387] and to abandon ethnic and sectarian splits and return to the culture of Islam:

> More saddening and dangerous than nationalism is the creation of dissension between Sunnis and Shi'is and diffusion of mischievous propaganda among brother Muslims. Praise and thanks be to God that no difference exists in our Revolution between these two groups. All are living side by side in friendship and brotherhood.[388]

Although in such messages Khomeini subtly condemned the regimes of other Muslim countries, his main focus was the Shah's regime, which he described as "a military base for Israel, which means, by extension, for America."[389] For Khomeini, *ḥajj* was a setting for unmasking the imperialist policies of the West and their collaborators. A *ḥajj* without the condemnation of the US and its allies such as Israel was unacceptable. In Shiism, the sayings of an Ayatollah have consequences for the people who take their mujtahid as their source of imitation (*marjaʿ-i taqlīd*). With such sayings, Khomeini forced even the apolitical believers among his followers to participate in the protests, lest their pilgrimage have no merit in the eyes of God.[390] Khomeini attacked the Saudis several times in his speeches.[391] His treatment of the Saudis also differs from his speeches on international relations, in which he emphasises respectful engagement. As Kamrava has shown, Khomeini's "deep-seated resentment for all things Western was tempered by the exigencies of the times."[392] Khomeini saw himself as the leader

386 In his writings Khomeini has repeatedly said that religion has a political dimension. See, for instance, his interview published on 2 January 1980: "As you know from your studies, Islam is a religion whose divine precepts have a political dimension. Sermons given at Friday prayer and on the occasion of festivals; congregational prayer; the pilgrimage with its vast assemblies at Mecca, Muzdalifa, Mina, and 'Arafat— all these are political matters. Of course, they are acts of worship, but politics and worship are intermingled in them." See ibid., p. 341.
387 Ibid., p. 304.
388 Ibid., p. 302.
389 Ibid., p. 197; see also Khuʾīnīhā, "Ḥajj az dīdgāh-i imām," in *Pāsdār-i islām*, 5, issue 55, p. 35.
390 On the development of the views on Iranian pilgrimage to Mecca see R. Ekhtiari Amiri, K. Hasnita Binti Ku Samsu and H. Gholipour Fereidouni, "The Hajj and Iran's Foreign Policy towards Saudi Arabia," in *Journal of Asian and African Studies*, Vol. 46, No. 6, 2011, pp. 678–690.
391 Ibid., pp. 680–681.
392 See Kamrava, "Khomeini and the West," in *A Critical Introduction to Khomeini*, ed. A. Adib-Moghaddam, Cambridge: Cambridge University Press, 2014, pp. 161–162.

of all Muslims around the world. He also created the "day of unity" among Muslims (*rūz-i vaḥdat*). He considered it his religious duty to guard the rights of all Muslims against the imperialist West. This principle was so important for him that it was anchored in the new Constitution of the Islamic Republic. The constitution rejects "any kind of domination, both its exercise and submission to it," and emphasises the defending of the "rights of all Muslims."[393] His views on international relations and foreign policy evolved, until in 1979 he could say, "Whoever treats us with respect, we will be their friend."[394] But this did not apply to the Saudis as he condemned them until his death, as we shall see.

The first protest during the *ḥajj* took place in 1981, leading to one death and many injuries. In the last two years of the war, the relationship between Iran and Saudi Arabia deteriorated further due to two incidents.[395] In 1987 Iranian pilgrims held demonstrations during the *ḥajj*, leading to the deaths of 402 pilgrims and security forces, and on 22 July that year the US reflagged Kuwaiti ships in response to Iran's attacks on ships in the Persian Gulf.[396] Although many Western countries, with the US in the lead, had supported Saddam Hussein, this reflagging achieved the internationalisation of the Iran-Iraq War. The US was actively aiding Arab states in the Persian Gulf.[397] The Saudis had banned any political demonstrations, but Iranian pilgrims organised protest meetings, shouting slogans such as "death to America, death to Israel," implying that the Saudi government was an ally of Israel and the US. The bloody demonstrations resulted in the banning of Iranian pilgrims and the breaking off of diplomatic relations between the two countries for three years.[398]

---

393 See Article 152: "The foreign policy of the Islamic Republic of Iran is based on the rejection of any kind of domination, both its exercise and submission to it; the preservation of the all-inclusive independence of the country and its territorial integrity; the defense of the rights of all Muslims; non-alignment in relation to the domineering powers; mutual peaceful relations with non-aggressive states." For the translation see "The Constitution of the Islamic Republic of Iran," (1989 Edition), translated by Firoozeh Papan-Matin, in *Iranian Studies*, 47:1, 2014, pp. 159–200; also see R. Ekhtiari Amiri et al., "The Hajj and Iran's Foreign Policy towards Saudi Arabia," p. 679; also see E.P. Rakel, "Iranian Foreign Policy Since the Iranian Islamic Revolution: 1979–2006," in *The Greater Middle East in Global Politics*, ed. M.P. Amineh, Leiden: Brill, 2007, p. 148.

394 Kamrava, "Khomeini and the West," p. 155.

395 E.P. Rakel "Iranian Foreign Policy...," pp. 157–158; idem, "Factional Rivalries and Iranian Foreign Policy," pp. 153–154.

396 E.P. Rakel, *The Iranian Political Elite, State and Society Relations, and Foreign Relations Since the Islamic Revolution* (PhD thesis, University of Amsterdam, 2008, pp. 153–154).

397 Eric Hooglund, "Iran and The Persian Gulf," in *Twenty Years of Islamic Revolution: Political and Social Transition in Iran Since 1979*, Syracuse, NY: Syracuse University Press, 2002, pp. 164–167.

398 See M. Kramer, *"Khomeini's Messengers in Mecca," in Arab Awakening and Islamic Revival: The Politics of Ideas in the Middle East, New Brunswick/London: Transaction, 1996, pp. 161–187.*

This violent incident exacerbated the situation to such an extent that the influential Iranian politician ʿAlī Akbar Hāshimī Rafsanjānī (1934–2017) declared, "the Saudi rulers have chosen an evil path, and we will send them to hell."[399] This fierce condemnation opened the gate for revolutionary poets to write invectives against the Saudi King Fahd and the ruling family.

The deaths of Iranian pilgrims stirred anger that was expressed in poems of little poetic merit. They should be read as an emotional outburst from revolutionary Iranians who were reflecting on their sacred pilgrimage. These poems cannot be overlooked when mapping a period of modern Iranian history in which poems were composed for internal use, to channel the emotions and steer the political dimension. Such poems depict an Arab other, highlighting differences between the two peoples. While in the nineteenth century Iranian intellectuals such as Mīrzā Fatḥ ʿAlī Ākhūndzāda (1812–1878) blamed Arabs and Islam for the stagnation and even backwardness of Persian culture, relying on Aryan racial theories, at the end of the twentieth century conservative revolutionary Shiites were condemning Arabs for failing to realise how they are used by the West to humiliate Islam and Muslims, even allowing themselves to be Western puppets in killing their fellow Muslims. In such poems the arrows are directed against the reigning family of Saud, who have become a symbol of evil. As in Nādirpūr's use of Persian myths in chapter seven, we see how stereotypical characterisations of Arabs and the Wahhabis are used to mobilise political forces. The poem is by Muḥammad Kāẓim Yūsufpūr:

حج خون
خسته از زخم خسته بر گشتند
قمریان پر شکسته بر گشتند
زائران در هوای خانه شدند
میهمان خدای خانه شدند
شهد ناب حضور نوشیدند
باده از جام نور نوشیدند
خانه حق مطاف آنان بود
کعبه جان طواف آنان بود

بر خود احرامی از خطر بستند
کربلا را به مکه پیوستند
مکه با نینوا قرین کردند
کربلا را حرم نشین کردند

399 M. Mohaddessin, *Islamic Fundamentalism: The New Global Threat*, Washington, DC: Seven Locks Press, 1993, pp. 94–95; Ten years later Rafsanjani visited Saudi Arabia, as the head of the Expediency Council, staying for 15 days. He was warmly received by the King and the Crown Prince. See E.P. Rakel "Iranian Foreign Policy...," p. 163.

سرخ شد در پی جواب حسین
ورقی دیگر از کتاب حسین
در حریم پناه کشته شدند
به کدامین گناه کشته شدند
کعبه از خونشان جلایی یافت
مروه از سعیشان صفایی یافت
خونشان جوششی خروشان داشت
در دل کعبه بذر طوفان کاشت
جوششی یافت مکه در جانش
خون حق ریخت در خیابانش
چشمش از ابر سینه بارانیست
کعبه ارام نیست طوفانیست
[…]
سفره از خون میهمان رنگین
در کجا رسم میزبانست این
مکه در کام آل سفیان است
کعبه اینک اسیر شیطان است
روی خود جانب حریم کنیم
خیزتا رجم این رجیم کنیم
مکه از زخم ها اثر دارد
مکه تاریخی از خطر دارد
مکه سنگ ستم فراوان دید
بارها مکه زخم عصیان دید
کعبه از خون عشق رنگین است
حج مقبول نزد ما این است
گردن ما به تیغ ارزانیست
کمترین رسم عشق قربانیست
جان به مردی سپردن عادت ماست
گوش مشرک کر از برائت ماست[400]

Pilgrimage of Blood
They returned fatigued, weakened by wounds
Ring doves with broken wings have returned.
Pilgrims longing for the house
Entered as guests in God's house.
They drank the pure nectar of the Presence,
Drinking wine from the cup of light.
They circled round the house of truth,
They circled round the Ka'ba of the soul.
They put on the pilgrim's garb,
Joining Karbalā to Mecca.
Aligning Mecca with Nineveh,
Making Karbalā a sanctuary.

---

400 Manūchihr Akbarī, *Naqd va taḥlīl-i adabiyyāt-i inqilāb-i islāmī*, Vol. I, Tehran: Sāzmān-i Madārik-i Farhangī-yi Inqilāb-i Islāmī, 1371/1993, pp. 333–335.

In answering Ḥuseyn, another page
of Ḥuseyn's book was coloured red.
In the sanctuary of refuge, they were killed:
For what sin did they kill them?
Their blood made the Kaʿba shine,
Their efforts made Marva pure.
There was a tumultuous boiling in their blood,
Planting the seed of a storm in the Kaʿba's heart.
The soul of Mecca was boiling
As the blood of truth was shed in her streets.
The cloud in Mecca's chest filled her eyes with rain,
The Kaʿba is not calm, but in a storm
[...]
The table spread with food is coloured with guests' blood!
Where in the world is this the custom?
Mecca is subject to the will of the Family of Ṣufyān
Kaʿba is now a thrall of Satan.
Let us turn our faces towards the sanctuary.
Rise, to throw stones at this execrable evil.
Mecca has traces of wounds,
Mecca has a history of dangers.
Mecca has felt many stones of oppression,
Mecca has felt many wounds of transgression.
The Kaʿba is coloured by love's blood:
Surely this pilgrimage is accepted.
Our necks for the blade: a little thing.
The first rite of love is sacrifice.
We are used to risking our lives for manliness,
A true pilgrim's repentance leaves the polytheist deaf.

A similar poem with a poetic flair is by Ḥuseyn Ḥuseynī in which he promises that the Islamic community will rise and revolt against the Saudis. He uses the parallel terms *āl-i Saʿūd,* "family of Saud" and *āl-i islām* or "family of Islam," presenting the entire Muslim community as a family who will rise against the Saudis. This poem must date from the beginning of the war when Saudi Arabia declared its support for Saddam. It is a straightforward poem, depicting the Saudi government as a slave to the United States. The initial references to the prohibition on kissing the prophet's grave points to the Shiite practice of kissing the tombs of their saints to show their love, which is strictly forbidden by the Wahhabis. Ḥuseynī mocks the Saudis who kiss the hands of the Americans, referred to as Satan here, while kissing the holy tomb of the prophet is forbidden. Through this allusion to kissing, Ḥuseynī sharpens his reader's consciousness of differences between Shiism and Wahhabism, as well as the differences in piety and sincerity between the two:

آل اسلام به پا می خیزد

بوسه بر قبر پیمبر ممنوع!
بوسه بر پنجهٔ شیطان مشروع!
چهره منحوسان آل سعود!
ننگ بر زشتی قاموس شما
دین‌فروشان هم‌آواز جهود
زود باشد که بگیرد ناگاه
شعله در خرمن سالوس شما

گوشتان هست اگر گوش کنید:
بغض شب می‌ترکد
در سحرگاه قیام
آل اسلام به پا می‌خیزد
و فرو می‌میرد
آخرین پت پت فانوس شما![401]

The family of Islam will rise to its feet

Kissing the Prophet's grave is banned!
Kissing the claws of Satan allowed!
The cursed faces of the family of Saud!
Shame on you, for your repulsive nature;[402]
Sellers of religion, singing harmonies with Jews.
Soon and suddenly
Flames will consume the harvest of your hypocrisy.

Do you have ears to listen?
The resentment of the night will be no more
In the dawn of the uprising.
The family of Islam will rise to its feet
And inflict death
On the last splutter of your lantern.

Another related poem condemns the US presence in the region. The poet, Muḥammad Khalīl Jamālī, laments the Saudis' close ties with the US:

شیطان بزرگ
چارده قرن از قیام خون گذشت
باز خون گوید که بر خون چون گذشت
حاجیان خونین خضابی کرده اند

---

401 Siyyid Ḥasan Ḥuseynī, *Ham-ṣidā bā ḥalq*, p. 57.
402 *Qāmūs* commonly refers to the titles of reference works. Here it means essence, constitution or nature, which is a modern Persian usage. The poet has chosen it to rhyme with *fānūs* ("lantern") in the last line.

عشق حق را فتح بابی کرده اند
موسم حج بود و روز اتفاق
روز دوری جستن از کفر و نفاق
آمدند از هر دیاری فوج فوج
همچو دریا فوج ها بر داشت موج
بر لب حجاج در گفت و شنفت
غنچه سرخ برائت می شکفت
سیل آسا لشگر عشق و امید
در خم شعب ابو طالب رسید
آفتاب مردمی مهر و فاق
آتشی افکند بر جان نفاق
خیل دژخیمان به فرمان فهد
معبر آزادگان کردند سد
ناگهان از پشت هر دیوار و بام
سنگ و آتش ریخت در دارالسلام
یر سر مردم فرو بارید تیر
خاک خون آلوده شد با هر صفیر
داستان کربلا تکرار شد
چشمه چشم جهان خونبار شد
در غباری لاله گون گردون نشست
چشمه زمزم به موج خون نشست
روزها شد روز عاشورای دوست
کربلای دیگر از سودای دوست
بتگران از نو شرر انداختند
خون اسماعیل ها ریختند
در حریم کعبه شیطان بزرگ
کسوت چوپان سپرده دست گرگ
گر به دست مصطفی بت ها شکست
باز بو جهلی به جای بت نشست
خا ئنی چون فهد در کسب مقام
شد به ظاهر خادم بیت الحرام
چون یزید و ابرهه این دیو مست
احترام کعبه را در هم شکست
در لباس میزبانی شد پدید
میهمانان خدا را سر برید
در حریم حضرت پروردگار
شرک پنهان ناگهان کرد آشکار
حج گزاران را به خاک و خون کشید
در حریم حق حقیقت را ندید
کعبه گر امروز در زنجیر اوست
می شود آزاد از الطاف اوست
صبح صادق سر کشد از شام تار
چهره خورشید گردد آشکار[403]

403 Manūchihr Akbarī, *Naqd va taḥlīl-i adabiyyāt-i inqilāb-i islāmī*, pp. 336 – 338.

The Great Satan
Fourteen centuries since the blood rose up.
Once again, blood says, "What has happened to blood"?
The pilgrims have dyed their beards with blood.
They have opened the gate of victory in their love for Truth.
It is the season of pilgrimage, the day of occurrence,
The day of turning away from hypocrisy and apostasy.
The pilgrims came in groups from every land
Like a sea, full of waves.
The sun of fellowship, love and sincerity
Set fire to the soul of hypocrisy.
The army of the executioner, led by Fahd,
Blocked the path before free men.
In the house of Islam, without warning,
Stones and fire fell from every roof and wall.
Arrows were raining on the heads of the people,
At every shaft, the earth was stained with blood.
The story of Karbalā was retold,
The spring of the eye of the world was full of blood.[404]
The Wheel sat to mourn in the tulip-coloured dust,
The spring of Zamzam was under the waves of blood.
The days become the ʿĀshūrā of the Friend,
It is another Karbalā, for love of the Friend.
Once more, the idolaters have struck sparks,
They have shed the blood of many Ishmaels.
At the sanctuary of the Kaʿba, the Great Satan
Has granted a wolf a shepherd's garb.
Where Muṣṭafā's hands shattered the idols,
The Father of Ignorance sits in their place.
To win a position, the traitor Fahd
Pretends to serve at the Holy House.
This drunken demon, like Yazīd and Abraha,
Has breached the respect due to the Kaʿba.
He appeared in the dress of the host,
And cut off the heads of the guests of God.
In the court of God's presence, abruptly
He revealed a hidden polytheism.
He dressed the pilgrims in dust and blood,
Unable to see the truth, in the sanctuary of Truth.
Today the Kaʿba is in his chains,
But it will be freed, by the grace of the Friend.
True dawn will appear from the dark night
The face of the sun will be revealed.

404 This is an allusion to universal mourning for the third Shiite Imam.

The poet compares the bloodshed at Mecca to events at Karbalā, when Ḥuseyn and his followers were brutally massacred by the Umayyads. By comparing Fahd to the second Umayyad Caliph Yazīd ibn al-Muʿāviyya (r. 680 – 683), who was responsible for slaying Imām Ḥuseyn, the poet places the Iranian demonstrators in Ḥuseyn's camp.[405] History is repeating itself. Linear time plays no role in such poems. Current events are connected to past wrongs in ways that are so tangible for the audience that 1400 years ago seems like yesterday. The poem contains references to the pagan period of the Arab people. Allusions to pre-Islamic Arabia and how the prophet Muḥammad announced his messengership are popular in the Shiite anti-Sunnite and anti-Arab literature. The poet alludes to the Kaʿba before the advent of Islam, when it housed Arab tribal gods, and how the Prophet (Muṣṭafā) cleansed the House of idols, inviting people to worship One God.[406] Another reference is to Abraha, who appears in the Quran (105:1–5). There are several stories about Abraha, a Christian King of South Arabia who led an expedition against Mecca in 570, the year of Muḥammad's birth.[407] Popular sources say that he was jealous of the Kaʿba and wanted to destroy it so that his church at Ṣanʿa would be unrivalled as a place of pilgrimage. A short Surah in the Quran is devoted to this event, running as follows: "Have you not considered how your Lord dealt with the possessors of the elephant? Did he not cause their war to end in confusion, and send down upon them birds in flocks, casting against them stones of baked clay? So he rendered them like straw eaten up?"[408]

---

405 G.R. Hawting, in *Encyclopaedia of Islam, Second Edition,* s.v. Yazīd (I) b. Muʿāwiya.

406 The most important venerated deities in pre-Islamic Arabia were al-Lāt, Manāt and al-ʿUzzā. See T. Fahd, in *Encyclopaedia of Islam, Second Edition, s.v.* al-Lāt; also see A.J. Wensinck and J. Jomier, in *Encyclopaedia of Islam, Second Edition*, s.v. Kaʿba.

407 A.F.L. Beeston, in *Encyclopaedia of Islam, Second Edition*, s.v. Abraha.

408 Rūmī also refers to this event in his *Mathnavī* (book six, pp. 195 – 197). See R.A. Nicholson's translation: "Abraha came with the elephant to dishonour the House (of Allah), that he might throw down the living (and leave them lying) as though dead, // and destroy the holy Kaʿba and cause all (the inhabitants) to wander forth from that place, // in order that all the pilgrims might gather round him and might all turn in worship to his Kaʿba, // and that he might take vengeance on the Arabs for the injury (inflicted by them), for "why," said he, "should they set my Kaʿba on fire?" // His efforts only turned to glory for the Kaʿba: they caused the (holy) House to be glorified." See specifically M. Istʿlāmī, Vol. 6, p. 197, ll. 4389 – 4499; and the translation by R.A. Nicholson, *The Mathnawí of Jalálu'ddín Rúmí*, Vol. VI, Cambridge: University of Cambridge, 1934, p. 500.

8.3 Shiite versus Wahhabi

Khomeini's antipathy for the Saudis probably stemmed not so much from political considerations as from their Wahhabi convictions, which have been the subject of several Shiite polemical treatises.[409] Wahhabism refers to the teachings of Muḥammad ibn ʿAbd al-Wahhāb (1703–1791), a preacher and activist who defined what is proper Islam and who is a good Muslim, concentrating on the literal word of the Quran, and condemning any other readings as un-Islamic. He considered the majority of Muslims to be apostates and those who did not strictly adhere to his ideology heretics. He severely criticised several practices that are, for Shiites and mystics, a central component of religiosity: building mausoleums, visiting the shrines of saints or imams; paintings and artworks, making sculptures, and wearing talismans.[410] Considering these and many other things as apostasy, he found it necessary to "destroy tombs, shrines, and art works."[411] As Michael Sells rightly observes, many of the Wahhabi claims are unfounded and cannot be found even in a literal reading of the Quran. For instance, instructions on levelling graves or destroying images of animals and humans cannot be found in the Quran.[412]

Wahhabism revived at the beginning of the twentieth century under the leadership of ʿAbd al-ʿAzīz ibn Saʿūd who in 1918, when asked about the Shiite shrines in Iraq, said, "I would raise no objection if you demolished the whole lot of them, and I would demolish them myself if I had the chance."[413] In the cemetery of Baqīʿ near the city of Medina lie the graves of the prophet Muḥammad's

---

409 There are many Shiite treatises written to condemn Wahhabism. One famous book is by Siyyid Muḥsin Amīn Ḥuseynī ʿĀmilī, *Kashf al-irtīyāb*, which is also partially translated into Persian by ʿAlī Akbar Tihrānī, in Tehran: Bītā, 1357/1978. A recent book is *Dībācha'ī bar zīyārat: pāsukh ba shubahāt-i vahhābiyyat az dīdgāh-i dānishmandān-i shiʿa va ahl-i sunnat*, Qumm, Payām-i Imām Hādī, 1394/2015, written by a research group called Payām-i Imām Hādī. They do not give the names of individual authors. See also the essay by H. Algar, *Wahhabism: A Critical Essay*, New York: Oneonta, 2002, which refers to the "elegantly and courteously worded treatise" by Shaykh Jaʿfar Kāshif al-Ghitā' (d. 1813), entitled *Manhāj al-Rashad li man arada 'l-sadad*. Algar gives an extract of this treatse in his book showing how the author drawing "exclusively on Sunni books of hadith, [...] to refute the many accusations of *kufr* and *shirk* that Wahhabis were levelling against the Muslims-including par excellence the Shiʿa." See pp. 81–83.

410 See the excellent article by Michael Sells in *Huffington Post* entitled "Wahhabist Ideology: What It Is And Why It's A Problem" (published 20 December 2016, https://www.huffpost.com/entry/wahhabist-ideology-what-it-is-and-why-its-a-problem_b_585991fce4b014e7c72ed86e, last accessed 25.03.2021).

411 Ibid.

412 Ibid.

413 As cited by Kramer, p. 164.

daughter Fāṭima (604 – 632) and four of the twelve Shiite imams. Iranians visited these tombs out of devotion and for intercession, but Wahhabis interpret such caring devotions as idolatry and largely erased the structures in 1806.[414] They were later restored for a short period, but the Saudis demolished them again. Iranian Shiites regard these tombs as sanctified, paying much attention to the graves and also the surroundings, just as one can see at the similar shrines in the Iranian cities of Mashhad and Qom.

In both Shiism and Sufism, it is essential to visit the shrines of the saints. The Sufi shrines in India and the Shiite shrines in Iran and Iraq are visited by millions of pilgrims annually. Ayatollah Khomeini despised the Saudi regime until the end of his life. In his Will he curses the Saudis as lackeys of the superpowers. The passage appears in a section in which Khomeini deals with Shiite cursing of the Ummayads who killed the Shiite Imams:

> It is necessary to preserve these curses, and it is necessary to include elegies in the memory of the Imams (A.S.) and also the condemnation of the oppressors of each epoch. The present era, which is the epoch of the oppression against the Muslim world by America, the Soviets and their lackeys, such as the Saudis, may God's curse go to them, these conspirators against the House of God: they should be condemned firmly. We should all know that what will unite Muslims is this political ceremony [the Friday prayer], which will protect the dignity and preserve the identity of Muslims, particularly the Twelver Shi'is.[415]

In addition to his speeches, Khomeini wrote several ghazals in which he expressed his mystical aspirations and referred to the House of God in a spiritual sense. As we shall presently see, such poems show the mystical appreciation of

---

414 For a description of this famous cemetery by Mīrzā Muḥammad Ḥuseyn Farāhānī see *A Shiite Pilgrimage to Mecca 1885 – 1886*, pp. 267 – 269; on the role of women in Shiism see Aghaie Kamran Scott, "Fatemeh, Zeynab, and Emerging Discourses on Gender," in *The Martyrs of Karbala: Shi'i Symbols and Rituals in Modern Iran*, Seattle, WA: University of Washington Press, 2004, pp. 113 – 130.

415 Translation from https://www.al-islam.org/printpdf/book/export/html/39086 (last accessed 25.03.2021). It is worth mentioning that reproaches directed at the Umayyads are part of *Nahj al-Balāgha*, compiled by Abū 'l-Ḥuseyn Siyyid Muḥammad al-Rāzī (c. 970 – 1053), which is believed to consist of documents written by ʿAlī ibn Abī Ṭālib, the first Shiite Imam. The ritual cursing of the first three caliphs has a long history in Shiism, as a reaction to the Umayyads' cursing of ʿAlī. Although this ritual cursing was discouraged after the 1979 Revolution, it remained a popular ritual in some circles. For ritual cursing during the Safavid era see R.J. Abisaab, *Converting Persia: Religion and Power in the Safavid Empire*, London/New York: I.B. Tauris, 2004, pp. 34, 42 – 50; also see H. Anṣārī, "Dar bāra-yi ziyārat-i ʿāshūrā," in *Barrisī-hā-yi tārīkhī dar howza-yi islām va tashayyuʿ*, Tehran: Kitāb-khāna, 1390/2011, pp. 675 – 679.

the *ḥajj*, and why Khomeini and revolutionary Iranians experience the pilgrimage ritual as a means for political change.

8.4 Khomeini vs Arabism

Another area of tension that plays a role in the poetry of the Iran-Iraq War is Khomeini's rejection of ethnic nationalism as a unifying principle for the modern state. This points to the Saudis to some extent, but also to the Baʿth party of Iraq and Syria, the Arab league and, of course, Iran's war enemy, Saddam's Iraq. In Khomeini's view, Islam alone is the unifying principle that will strengthen the Muslim world and confound the plans of the western powers, and true Islam is found in the period of the Prophet Muḥammad's life. With the coming of the first three caliphs, and the Umayyad and the Abbasid dynasties, Islam was distorted. This contrasts with the paradigmatic role of the first three generations of Muslims for the Wahhabis, and for most Sunni Muslims. Khomeini blames the distortion of Islam primarily on the Umayyads who followed a Sunnite path in which a successor to the Prophet was chosen by consensus among influential individuals. Khomeini says that the Umayyads "changed the nature of government from divine and spiritual to worldly."[416] In Shiism, the successor to the Prophet should be appointed by God himself (in practice, by designation by his predecessor). Shiites are rationalistic and even scholastic on the matter of succession. They believe in the Quran and the traditions of the prophet, but they also believe in the words and deeds of the twelve imams, each designated in succession as normative. The fact that succession to the prophet was a divine matter is discussed in a wide range of literature. The "change" Khomeini referred to is the usurpation of ʿAlī's position as the true successor of the Prophet who could safeguard Islam and lead the Islamic community. But Khomeini also argues that Umayyad "rule was based on Arabism, the principle of promoting the Arabs over all other peoples" and that it distorted Islam completely "by reviving the Arabism of the pre-Islamic age of ignorance."[417]

Khomeini emphasises that the prophet Muḥammad wanted to abolish "nationality and unite all mankind in a single community, under the aegis of a state indifferent to the matter of race and colour."[418] By referring to "the age of ignorance" (*jāhiliyya*) as a pillar of Umayyad politics, Khomeini triggers strong

416 *Islam and Revolution*, p. 332.
417 Ibid.
418 Ibid.

negative associations with the supposed brutality and backwardness of the Arab tribes before Islam. Few readers would have asked themselves whether Arabism could have been a feature of the pre-Islamic era, given that the Arabs then were tribally organised and less developed compared to the Byzantian and Persian empires. Khomeini is not deprecating Sunnism here, but rather the supremacy that the Arabs claimed as kin to the Prophet. After depicting the Umayyads as betrayers of the ideal of equality among all Muslims in one community (*umma*), Khomeini links the leaders of certain Arab countries to the Umayyads. He states, "The same aim is still pursued by the leaders of certain Arab countries, who declare openly their desire to revive Arabism."[419] Algar surmises that Khomeini is probably referring to the Baʿthist regime in Iraq that believed in the "primacy of race over religion as the proper focus of loyalty and identity," but in his addresses Khomeini commonly treats the Baʿthist regime and Saddam as unbelievers, while the Saudis are characterised as Wahhabi Muslims, who wish to return to the first days of Islam. It is interesting that Khomeini is not discussing the doctrinal divide between Wahhabism and Shiism, but rather attributing the problem to a historical ethnic issue, which in his view has consequences for Muslims to the present day. The modern Arabism he is referring to is undoubtedly related to the treatment of the Shiites in the holy cities of Mecca and Medina, especially when they visit the holy graves of the Prophet, his daughter and the Imams. It is particularly during these rituals that Shiite (and often Iranian) identities are revealed.

8.5 Mystical Dimensions of the Ḥajj

In the Persian cultural domain *ḥajj* has historically had mystical Sufi connotations. Generations of theologians such as Abū Ḥāmid Muḥammad Ghazālī (d. 1111), as well as leading poets such as Ḥāfiẓ (1315–1390) and Rūmī (1207–1273), have emphasised the importance of the mystical experience of *ḥajj*. In modern Persian war poetry, poets rely on this mystical appreciation, which they then connect to current political dimensions. The way modern Shiite Iranians look at *ḥajj* differs considerably from the understanding of most Arabs. Suf-

419 Ibid. Algar gives an example of Arabism in his footnote (p. 345): "A striking example of the 'Arabism' of the Umayyads was provided by Ḥajjāj ibn Yūsuf, governor of Iraq, when he forbade all non-Arab Muslims to lead the prayer in the cities under his jurisdiction." Khomeini and his readers would also have been aware that Arabism in the Abbasid era was resisted by the Shuʿūbiyya movements of the ninth and tenth centuries, in which Persian Muslims played a leading role.

ism made a distinction between the Kaʿba of the heart (*Kaʿba-yi dil*) and the Kaʿba of clay (*Kaʿba-yi gil*), and the distinction became a rich topos in Persian mystical poetry from the tenth century on. Great mystics, such as Muḥammad Ghazālī, Mustamlī of Bukhara, Rūmī and many others, prefer the Kaʿba of the heart to the physical Kaʿba, advising their readers to scrutinise the mysteries of the heart where God's intimate knowledge (*maʿrifa*) is harboured. The physical house is usually despised because it is associated with outward religiosity, showing off one's economic affluence and superior piety. *Ḥajj* is one of the five pillars of the faith that every Muslim should go on pilgrimage to Mecca once in his/her lifetime, provided s/he is physically fit and has the financial means to do so. By taking the journey to Mecca, everybody sees that the pilgrim is taking the trouble to cross the desert and to perform the *ḥajj* rituals. Mystics believe that going to Mecca may create hypocrisy, as it is a show of one's piety, while the true piety is only between the believer and the Creator. God dwells in one's heart, and the spiritual Kaʿba is in the believer's heart. A pious Muslim should first learn about the mysteries of the heart, investigating all of the heart's qualities, before embarking on a pilgrimage to Mecca. The heart is the central site of human consciousness, and for mystics it is a repository of God's intimate knowledge, where God has placed his love. Mystics have written many treatises on the mysteries of the heart, identifying several compartments and layers. The mystic Abū 'l-Ḥuseyn al-Nūrī (d.c. 907–908) believed that the heart has four layers, whereas others, such as Ghazālī, identify seven layers. Nūrī refers to the breast (*ṣadr*), the heart proper (*qalb*), the inner heart (*fu'ād*) and the heart's core (*lubb*), allocating a different feature to each layer.[420] The breast harbours Islam; the proper heart is the place of faith; the inner heart holds gnosis; and the heart's core is for God's unity (*towḥīd*). Nūrī describes the heart in his *Maqāmāt al-qulūb* ("Stations of the Heart") as follows:

> Know that God created a house inside the believer called the heart. He then sent a wind of His magnanimity and cleansed this house of idolatry, doubt, hypocrisy and discord. Afterwards, he directed clouds of His favour to rain over the house, and there grew in it all kinds of plants such as certainty, trust, sincerity, fear, hope and love. Then he placed in the centre of the house a couch of unity and covered it with the rug of contentment. And He planted the tree of knowledge opposite the couch, with its roots in the heart and its branches in the sky (Quran 14: 24), below the throne. He also placed on the right and left sides of the couch armrests of his laws. Then He opened a door to the garden of His mercy and sowed there many kinds of fragrant herbs of praise, glorification, exaltation and commemoration. He made waters of the ocean of guidance flow to these plants through the river of kindness.

420 Ahmet T. Karamustafa, *Sufism, the Formative Period*, Edinburgh: Edinburgh University Press, 2007, p. 15.

> He hung a lamp of grace high on the door and lit it with the oil of purity and the light of the lamp gleamed with the light of piety. Then He locked its door in order to keep out the wicked. He held on to its key and did not entrust it to any of his creatures, neither Gabriel, nor Michael, nor Seraphiel, nor others. He then said, "This is My treasure on My earth, the mine of My sight, the home of My unity and I am the resident of this dwelling." What an excellent resident and what a wonderful residence![421]

God is present in the believer's heart. Therefore he should cultivate his heart to come to a full realisation and knowledge of the Creator, fighting the negative forces of the "lower self" (*nafs*), an enemy of the heart. While *nafs* constantly tempts man to rely on his own ego by foregrounding the importance of the outward, the heart directs man towards the inward, finally showing the way to God's path through gnosis. Any activity other than concentrating on the heart is seen as a distraction from God. As Karamustafa rightly observes, "The Sufis thus directed their energies to the cultivation of the heart, and to the extent that preoccupation with legal and theological scholarship tended to distract one from this central exercise, it was inevitable that they would view the increasingly 'professional' scholarly enterprises with a mixture of caution, suspicion, alarm and, at times, even disdain."[422]

As early as in the tenth century we find detailed scrutiny of the heart. One of the first comprehensive mystic manuals is *Qūt al-qulūb* ("The Sustenance of Hearts") by Abū Ṭālib al-Makkī (d. 996), who analyses how gnosis is housed in the heart.[423] Karamustafa cogently describes the essence of the book as follows, "In *The Sustenance*, Makkī tapped into this 'knowledge of hearts.' Since knowledge that is the province of hearts was the fruit of both outward and inward deeds of devotion, he carefully drew a veritable topography of the pious life, paying attention not only to such acts of piety as invocation, litany and the prescribed rituals of daily prayer, fasting, alms-giving and pilgrimage, but also to questions of social life such as poverty, earning a living, marriage, visiting public baths, travelling, companionship and political leadership."[424] Abū Sa'd al-Khargūshī (d. about 1016) also wrote on the secrets of the heart in *Tahdhīb al-asrār* ("Refining the Secrets").[425]

421 The translation is taken from ibid., p. 11.

422 Ibid., p. 21.

423 Ibid., pp. 87–91.

424 Ibid., p. 88.

425 Pūrjavadī, "Manba'ī kuhan dar bāb-i malāmatiyyān-i Neyshābūr," in *Ma'ārif*, 15, No. 1–2, 1377/1998, pp. 3–50; Hassan Ansari and Sabine Schmidtke, "Abū Sa'd al-Ḫargūšī and his Kitāb al-Lawāmi' A Ṣūfī Guide Book for Preachers from 4th/10th century Nīšāpūr," in *Arabica*, 58, 2011, pp. 503–518; A.J. Arberry, "Khargūshī's Manual of Ṣūfism," in *Bulletin of the School of Oriental*

The preference for the Kaʿba of the heart is purely religious, but it also has a political and cultural motivation, which to my knowledge has not been examined. The rise of antinomian mystical movements such as Malāmatiyya, Karrāmiyya and Qalandariyya, to name a few, from the ninth to the twelfth centuries created new norms in interpreting religious laws. What all these movements have in common is the tendency to challenge the norms of piety set by the religious scholars, the *ʿulamāʾ*, so pushing the centre to the periphery. The champions of these mystical movements questioned the piety of religious scholars by problematising a wide range of central religious tenets, showing the limitations of a literal interpretation of the Sharia. These movements interpreted the laws as referring to the outward things of Islam, while mystics were seeking the core of the Quran's meanings, the traditions and lives of the Prophets and the early Islamic ascetics. In other words, these mystics interiorised Islam, which generated a wide range of critical discussions on who is a good Muslim. It is also essential to mention that most of the Persian mystics and poets before the sixteenth century were Sunnites. Their emphasis on the Kaʿba of the heart worked to personalise the mystic development in individuals.

Khomeini placed himself in this mystical tradition, in which orthodox tenets with regard to pilgrimage were censured in favour of mystical interpretations.[426] In his poetry Khomeini identifies with the qalandars, a category of antinomian mystics who censure the mosque, going instead to the wine-house, preferring the Kaʿba of the heart to the Kaʿba of clay. In several of his ghazals Khomeini laments his inability to find the Beloved in the mosque or Kaʿba, and goes instead to the tavern where he finds union with the cup-bearer, who stands for the mystic guide and the beloved. As in classical Persian poetry, Khomeini concocts new compounds and metaphors to censure the physical Kaʿba, emphasising the greater significance of the heart. Khomeini employs the compounds the Kaʿba of Love (*Kaʿba-yi ʿishq*),[427] the Kaʿba of the Goal (*Kaʿba-yi maqṣūd*),[428] and

and African Studies, 9/2, 1938, pp. 345–349; Christopher Melchert, "Khargūshī, *Tahdhīb al-asrār*," in *Bulletin of the School of Oriental and African Studies*, 73, 2010, pp. 29–44.

426 See Vanessa Martin, *Creating an Islamic State: Khomeini and the Making of a New Iran*, London/New York: I.B. Tauris, second print 2003, pp. 29–47; H. Algar, "Imam Khomeini, 1902–1962: The Pre-Revolutionary Years," in *Islam, Politics and Social Movements*, ed. E. Burke & I.M. Lapidus, Berkeley, , CA: University of California Press, 1988, pp. 263–288; S.A. Arjomand, *After Khomeini: Iran under His Successors*, Oxford: Oxford University Press, 2009, pp. 16–25; L. Ridgeon, "Hidden Khomeini: Mysticism and Poetry," in *A Critical Introduction to Khomeini*, pp. 193–210; Alexander Knysh, "*ʿIrfān* Revisited: Khomeini and the Legacy of Islamic Mystical Philosophy," *Middle East Journal*, 46, 4, 1992, pp. 631–653.

427 *Dīvān* (16th edition, 1377), *ghazal* 108.

428 Ibid., *ghazal* 147.

the Kaʿba of the Heart (*Kaʿba-yi dil*)[429] for different purposes in his *Dīvān*.[430] Suffice it here to give one example:

خار راه منی ای شیخ! ز گُلزار برو
از سر راه من ای رند تبهکار! برو
تو و ارشاد من؟ ای مُرشد بی رُشد و تباه!
از بَرِ روی من ای صوفی غدّار! برو
ای گرفتار هواهای خود، ای دیر نشین!
از صفِ شیفتگانِ رُخ دلدار برو
ای قلندر منش، ای باد به کف، خرقه به دوش!
خرقه‌ی شر ک تُهی کرده و بگذار برو
خانه‌ی کعبه، که اکنون تو شدی خادم آن
ای دغل! خادِم شیطانی از این دار، برو
زین کلیسای که در خدمت جبّاران است
عیسیِ مریم از آن خود شده بیزار، برو
ای قلم بر کفِ نقّادِ تبهکار پلید!
بنه این خامه و، مخلوق میازار، برو

O Sheikh! You are a thorn on my path, get out of the rose-garden;
You felonious rogue! Get out of my way.
Unrighteous, corrupted, *murshid!* You want to lead me to the straight path?
O deceitful Sufi! Get out of my sight!
O you, secluded in a cloister! O prisoner of your passions!
Here lovers in ranks are enraptured by the heart-ravisher's face! Get out!
O you with the Qalandarī manners! O you with wind under your feet and a Sufi robe on your shoulders! Empty the robe of polytheism, let it go, and go!
The House of Kaʿba, where you now serve:
You servant of Satan, you double dealer, get out of this House.
Jesus, son of Mary, is weary
of these churches that pander to tyrants. Get out!
O pen in the hand of the foul and criminal caviller,
Put down the pen, do not harm people, and go.[431]

This ghazal is modelled on those of classical Persian masters such as Sanāʾī, ʿAṭṭār and Ḥāfiẓ and is brimming with mystic symbolism. As in Ḥāfiẓ's ghazals, the poet distances himself from organised Sufis (led by the "sheikh" and "*murshid*" in the first lines) and those theologians who show their outward piety to

429 Ibid., *ghazal* 164.
430 Ibid., *ghazal* 176. In the NWO-funded project *Of Poetry and Politics*, my team and I analysed many such poems. An excellent example is the unpublished PhD dissertation by D. Farhosh-van Loon, *Of Love and Longing: A Study of Ayatollah Khomeini's Mystical Poetry and its Reception in Iran and Abroad*, Leiden: 2016; see also A.A. Seyed-Gohrab, "Khomeini the Poet Mystic," in *Die Welt des Islams: International Journal for the Study of Modern Islam*, 51, 2011, pp. 438–458.
431 *Dīvān* (16th edition, 1377), p. 176.

gain respect. In the Persian antinomian mystical tradition, mystics provoked the religious hierarchies and the organised Sufis by flouting social and religious norms, walking half-naked, shaving all facial hair, using piercings, engaging in homo-erotic love, and praising other religions such as Christianity and Zoroastrianism. They were severely criticised for such behaviour. The mystics used the criticism as a shield for their inner piety, which they concealed. True piety was between God and the mystic. As soon as any sign of piety was revealed, it would lead to hypocrisy and pretension. In this context, even the holy ritual of the *ḥajj* receives a different meaning: the mystic should concentrate on the Owner of the House, rather than the house itself. It is interesting that Khomeini even dismisses the qalandarī way of religiosity which in his view could lead to polytheism, the greatest sin in Islam. Moreover, the poet includes Christianity in his personal approach to religion by presenting Jesus as disowning the churches that serve tyrants.

On the Jamārān website, a name alluding to Khomeini's former residence, this ghazal is presented with a footnote at the end of the fifth couplet stating that the line refers to Saudi Arabia's leader who is outwardly serving the holy house while inwardly serving the "Great Satan." He composed this poem on 24 Bahman 1365 /12 February 1986, two days after the annual celebration of the Revolution, but we do not know what occasioned it. The editor's footnote seems over-specific, given that Khomeini is writing in a tradition in which condemning the outward forms of religion is the norm.

Persian ghazals usually do not have a title. Khomeini's ghazals do, but it is not clear whether he contrived them himself or they were added by his posthumous editors. The heading of the poem above is "The Kaʿba in Chains" (*Kaʿba dar zanjīr*), an image which is, to my knowledge, new. It has probably been concocted to politicise the poem by connecting all of the ghazal's motifs, themes and images to Saudi Arabia. The ghazal is one of the most transgressive poems in Khomeini's *Dīvān*, as it rejects all religious hierarchies, ranging from religious scholars, Sufis, Rinds ("libertines"), to the guardianship of one of the holiest symbols of Islam, the Kaʿba.[432] By connecting this to the Saudi government, the editors steer the reader to interpret the poem in a political context, without its original antinomian message about inward piety and rejecting outward religiosity. Yet it is possible that Khomeini is combining the antinomian motifs with political condemnation of the Saudis and the United States. It is fas-

---

432 On the *rind* of "rogue" or the "inspired libertine" in Persian ghazals see "Prolegomenon to the Study of Ḥāfiẓ: 2- The Mystical Milieu: Ḥāfiẓ's Erotic Spirituality," in *Hafiz and the Religion of Love in Classical Persian Poetry*, London/New York: I.B. Tauris, 2010, pp. 31–36.

cinating to see how medieval literary motifs are utilised in a modern political discourse to arouse enmity. The critique of outward piety easily slides into othering, while inward piety is appropriated by the poem's persona.

Khomeini's poetry employs many antinomian qalandarī motifs and themes. The following poem, which he wrote in the last year of his life on 17 February 1989 (28 Bahman 1367), alludes specifically to the Kaʿba and Hijaz. Although the entire ghazal is modelled on classical Persian masters in terms of metre, imagery, motifs and themes, the allusions to the house of God and Hijaz are possibly influenced by his aversion to outward religion and the Saudis, especially because he wrote this ghazal six days after the tenth annual commemoration of the 1979 Revolution:

ساقی! به روی من درِ میخانه باز کُن
از درس و، بحث و، زهد و، ریا، بی نیاز کُن
تاری ز زلفِ خم خم خود، در رهم بنه
فارغ ز عِلم و، مسجد و، درس و، نماز کُن
داوود وار، نغمه زنان ساغری بیار
غافل ز درد جاه و نشیب و فراز کُن
بر چین حجاب از رُخ زیبا و زلف یار
بیگانه‌ام ز کعبه و مُلک حجاز کُن
لبریز کن از آن مِی صافی، سبوی من
دل از صفا، بسوی بُت ترکتاز کُن
بیچاره گشته‌ام ز غم هجر روی دوست
دعوت مرا به جام می چاره ساز کُن

Cup-bearer! Open the gate of the tavern to me,
    Make me independent of lessons and debates, asceticism and hypocrisy.
Drop a lock of your curly hair in my path;
    Relieve me of learning and the mosque, attending classes and prayers.
Bring me a goblet while playing a tune like David,
    Make me forget the worries of status, high or low.
Remove the veil from the beloved's comely face and tresses;
    Make me a stranger to the Kaʿba and the kingdom of Hejaz.
Fill my jug to the brim with that pure wine;
    turn the heart from Ṣafā towards that enchanting idol.
The grief of separation from the face of the Friend has made me forlorn,
    invite me to the wine-cup that is the remedy.[433]

In this poem Khomeini uses the motifs of *Khamriyyāt* ("wine-poetry"), *qalandariyyāt* ("poems with antinomian themes") and *zuhdiyyāt* ("poems of abstinence"). The persona of the poem asks the cupbearer to open the wine-house, which he prefers to the lessons and discussions at Islamic schools and mosques. The wine-

433 *Dīvān*, p. 171, which is composed in mużāriʿ metre - - 0 / -0 – 0 /0 - - 0/ -0- .

house is filled with sincerity while the people in mosques and schools show off their superior piety and knowledge. They are focused on outward religiosity and not on their true selves. In such wine motifs, the cup-bearer usually stands for God, the prophet or a Sufi saint, but in Khomeini's poetry this character is unidentified. Khomeini was not linked to the contemporary or classical Sufi brotherhoods. His mysticism was mostly private, an eclectic system built on Ibn ʿArabī and Mullā Ṣadrā's mystical philosophy, combined with the Persian mystical love tradition represented by poets such as Sanāʾī, ʿAṭṭār and Ḥāfiẓ. In Persian poetry the cupbearer is often a graceful young man who serves wine in the tavern. In the second couplet the poet asks him to place a lock of his hair on the path so that he will be distracted from formal obligations and outward appearances. In the classical context the cupbearer was not only a pleasing figure who entertained the guests, he was also an able musician.[434] The poet builds on this trait and prays him to bring a goblet while playing a song like the prophet David, who is legendary in Islamic culture for his attractive voice. Where a strand of hair was to distract the poet in the second couplet, here he refers to the cup. The poet combines the senses of touch, hearing and taste, while seeing is also explicit. These sensory references imply that the poet-lover is concentrating deeply on the beloved. In the fourth couplet the poet implores the cupbearer to remove the veil from the beloved's face, because then the poet will leave the physical Kaʿba and Hejaz. It is not clear whether the poet asks the cupbearer, as the beloved, to remove his veil, or the cupbearer is to remove the veil of another person who is the poet's beloved. Does the beloved represent a verse from the Quran, a couplet from Ḥāfiẓ, or something else? It remains unclear. In the fifth couplet the poet asks the cup-bearer to fill the cup with pure wine so that his heart will be entirely directed to the beloved. Here the poet is using the motif of the Kaʿba of the heart, Ṣafā and Marva being two small hills within the grand mosque at Mecca, adjoining the outward Kaʿba. In the concluding couplet the poet provocatively asks the cup-bearer for more wine as he has become desperate in his separation from the Beloved.

These poems, which were privately produced, contribute to our knowledge of Khomeini's personality, his religious views on pilgrimage and how he connected such ideas with politics in his speeches. We know from a large body of poetry written in praise of Khomeini and his role during the Iran-Iraq War, and from

434 In classical Persian poetry the cup-bearer is the same as the beloved. See Julie Scott Meisami, *Medieval Persian Court Poetry*, Princeton, NJ: Princeton University Press, 1987, chapter six; E. Yarshater, "The Theme of Wine and Wine-drinking and the Concept of the Beloved in Early Persian Poetry," in *Studia Islamica*, Vol. 13, 1960, pp. 43–53.

commentaries on his legacy, that his mystical ideas were widely known. Their relevance to the Islamic Republic's relationship with Saudi Arabia was also recognised.[435]

8.6 The Persian and Arab Rivalries

One reason why the Saudis unreservedly supported Saddam was the historical rivalry between the Persians and the Arabs. Saddam framed the war within the context of this rivalry. To motivate Iraqi soldiers, Saddam used the Muslim Arabs' victory over Persian forces at the historical battle of al-Qādisīyya (AD 636).[436] He called his fight against Iran a second Qādisīyya:

> It is the immortal heroic epic led by the Iraqi people in the defence of Iraq and the Arab nation with a great victory over the racist Khomeini Persian enemy. It was named "the kadissya of Saddam" after the great leader Saddam Hussein who led the wonderful heroic battles ... as had done the leader Saad Bin Abi Wakass in the first Kadissya ... about fourteen centuries ago. The Kadissya of our Arab ancestors has returned thanks to the hero of Arabism and Islam, the leader Saddam Hussein, against the same Persian enemy ...[437]

Distorted stereotypical images have been constructed on both Persian and Arab sides, through the ages and especially with the rise of nation states in the Middle East in the nineteenth century. Most Arab countries today, including Saudi Arabia, were once part of the Ottoman Empire. The new Arab states defined borders and fresh identities to legitimise modern rule and culture.[438] During the Iran-Iraq

---

435 In several of his publications the hardliner cleric, Mūsavī Khu'īnīhā, interprets Khomeini's views on the *ḥajj*, and his commentary includes the mystical aspects of the pilgrimage.

436 See Talal Atrissi, "Arab and Iranian Images of Each Other," in *Imagining the Arab Other: How Arabs and Non-Arabs View Each Other*, ed. Tahar Labib, London: I.B. Tauris, 2008, pp. 316–356; Amanat, *Iran: A Modern History*, pp. 828–839; D.G. Lewental, "'Saddam's Qadisiyyah': Religion and History in the Service of State Ideology in Ba'thi Iraq," in *Middle Eastern Studies*, Vol. 50, Issue 6, 2014, pp. 891–910; A. Moosavi, "Stepping Back from the Front: A Glance at Home Front Narratives of the Iran-Iraq War in Persian and Arabic Fiction," in *Moments of Silence*, p. 126; on this battle see D. Gershon Lewental, in *Encyclopædia Iranica*, s.v. Qādesiya, Battle of; A.H. Zarrinkub, "The Arab Conquest of Iran," in *The Cambridge History of Iran*, Cambridge: Cambridge University Press, 1975, Vol. IV, pp. 10–13.

437 Talal Atrissi, "Arab and Iranian Images of Each Other," p. 325.

438 As Dankwart A. Rustow states, "Since the end of the Second World War, the Muslim countries have fully participated in the world-wide transition from colonialism to sovereignty. At the end of the First World War, there were only six independent Muslim states (Albania, Turkey, Persia, Afghanistan, Yemen and Sa'udi Arabia—the latter formed in 1925 through the annexation of the Hejaz to Najd). In the inter-war period, Egypt (1922) and Iraq (1932) were recognized as in-

War, it was not easy for the Iranian side to define the Arabs who were allegedly Iran's enemy. Saddam however presented himself as the leader of the Arabs by pointing to Iran as an ancient enemy, inviting Arab countries to join forces in fighting the Shiite Iranians. In this eight-year war Saudi Arabia supported Saddam. After Saddam's removal from power, Saudis positioned themselves as leaders of the Arab nations and Iran as the enemy. In addition to supporting Iraq in the war, the Saudis hosted American forces and were a close ally of the US, which Khomeini called the Great Satan. The Saudis' monopolisation of Arab identity has increased since the US government commenced the war on terror and intensified its support for the Saudi government. The Saudis had also turned against Saddam Hussein after his invasion of Kuwait in 1990, which shows how fluid the monopolisation of "Arab power" can be. A modern Saudi poet wrote the following invective:

> Saddam, O Saddam,
> Of our flesh are you not.
> Claim not to be a Muslim,
> For you are truly a Jew.
> Your deeds have proved ugly,
> Your face is darkest black.
> And we will yet set fire
> To your bottom and your back.[439]

While Saddam used the ethnic rivalry between Persians and Arabs to mobilise Iraqi soldiers to fight the Iranians, Iranian poets made many allusions to the superiority of the Shiite Iranians over the Arabs – without mentioning that the majority of Iraqis are also Shiites! Polemical superiority contests can be traced back to the ninth century, when non-Arab Muslims, mostly Persians, claimed equality in the Shuʿūbiyya ("confessors of equality") movement. This movement, flourishing mainly in the literary field, started in Bagdad and resonated in the following centuries in Persian cultural areas. Its chief aim was to establish equality among Muslims, irrespective of their descent, and especially to resist the Quraysh family's claim to leadership. In several Shuʿūbī texts, the authors emphasise the superiority of Persians by referring to their ancient culture and splen-

---

dependent, although their sovereignty remained in fact rather restricted until the 1950s." See "The Political Impact of the West," in *The Cambridge History of Islam*, ed. P.M. Holt, A.K.S. Lambton and, B. Lewis, Cambridge: Cambridge University Press, 1977, p. 696.

439 As cited by Christian Lange, *Justice, Punishment, and the Medieval Muslim Imagination*, Cambridge: Cambridge University Press, 2008, p. 165, footnote 182.

dour.[440] Even poets who wrote in Arabic, such as Bashshār ibn Burd (about 714–783) and Abū 'l-Ḥasan Mahyār Deylamī (d. about 1073), boast of the sophisticated pre-Islamic Persian courtly culture.[441] The champions of this movement were from the Persian bureaucratic and administrative class, usually known as secretaries (*dabīrs* or *kuttāb*). These secretaries were central in administration and also in the scientific and cultural growth of the Islamic empire. They played a key role in the translation movement of the eighth and ninth centuries, during which a wide range of texts were translated from various languages into Arabic. Political debates provided them with the opportunity to foreground Persian culture in its literary, religious, scientific and political aspects. These Persians did not turn their backs on Islam; rather they integrated Islam into Persian culture. Richard N. Fry assesses that Islam developed within the continuity of Persian culture, becoming "a truly universal culture and religion."[442] The Islam which

---

440 The term Shuʿūbiyya comes from the Quran (49:13): "O you men! Surely We have created you of a male and a female, and made you tribes (*shuʿūb*) and families (*qabā'il*) that you may know each other…"; see Shakir N.D., p. 773. In some Quran translations such as that of M. Pickthall, *shuʿūb* is translated as "nations" and *qabā'il* as "tribes," which becomes politically loaded. I have relied mainly on Ignaz Goldziher's translation. There are a large number of studies on this topic. See H.A.R. Gibb, "The Social Significance of the Shuʿubiya," in *Studies on the Civilization of Islam*, eds. S.J. Shaw and W.R. Polk, Boston, MA: Beacon Press , 1962, pp. 62–73; L. Richter-Bernburg, "Linguistic Shuʿūbīya and Early Neo-Persian Prose," *Journal of the American Oriental Society*, 94, 1, 1974, pp. 55–64; R. Mottahedeh, "The Shuʿubiyah Controversy and the Social History of Early Islamic Iran," *International Journal of Middle Eastern Studies*, 7, 1976, pp. 161–182; D.A. Agius, "The Shuʿūbiyya Movement and its Literary Manifestation," *The Islamic Quarterly*, issue xxiv, 1980, pp. 76–88; H.T. Norris, "Shuʿūbiyya in Arabic Literature," in *Cambridge History of Arabic Literature: Abbasid Belles-Letters*, ed. J. Ashtiany et al., Cambridge: Cambridge University Press, 1990, pp. 31–47; S. Enderwitz,, in *Encyclopaedia of Islam, Second Edition*, s.v. al-S͟huʿūbiyya; I. Goldziher, "Die Śuʿūbijja unter den Muhammedanen in Spanien," in *ZDMG*, liii, 1899, 601–620; P. Pourshariati, "The *Akhbār al-Tiwāl* of Abū Ḥanīfa Dīnawarī: A *Shuʿūbī* Treatise on Late Antique Iran," in *Sources for the History of Sasanian and post-Sasanian Iran* (collection *Res Orientales* 19), ed. R. Gyselen, Bures-sur-Yvette: Groupe pour l'Étude de la Civilisation du Moyen-Orient, , 2010, pp. 201–289. The most recent studies I know of are G. Dabiri, "Historiography and the Shoʿubiya Movement," in *Journal of Persianate Studies*, 6, 2013, pp. 216–234; P. Webb, *Imagining the Arabs: Arab Identity and the Rise of Islam*, Edinburgh: Edinburgh University Press, 2016, pp. 246–249; S.B. Savant, "Shu'ubis" in *The Princeton Encyclopedia of Islamic Political Thought*, ed. Gerhard Böwering, Princeton, NJ: Princeton University Press, 2013; ʿA-Ḥ. Zarrīnkūb, *Tārīkh-i Īrān baʿd az islām*, Tehran: Amīr Kabīr, 1368/1989, pp. 384–387.

441 See Ḥuseyn-ʿAlī Mumtaḥin, *Nihzat-i Shuʿūbiyya: junbish-i millī-yi Irāniyān dar barābar-i Khalāfat-i Umavī va ʿAbbāsī*, Tehran: Kitābhā-yi Jībī, 1354/1975, second print 1370/1991.

442 R.N. Fry, *The Golden Age of Persia*, London: Phoenix, 1975, reprinted 2003, p. xii.

was created during the tenth and eleventh centuries was an "Iranian Islam using the Arabic language."[443]

The genre of debates allowed Persian poets to catalogue in an imaginary setting the praiseworthy qualities of a Persian Muslim as compared to an Arab Muslim. These poems emphasise the dominance of Persian culture and Persian Muslims' piety. In the oldest example of a Persian debate between an Arab and a Persian, by Asadī from Ṭūs (ca. 1000 – 1072), part of the Persian narrator's criticism centres on the Arabs' mistreatment of Persian pilgrims who made a long journey through the desert to visit the house of God:[444]

فرسنگ هزاراز پی حج ما بگذاریم
آییم به کعبه ز حد بلخ و ز بلخان
بوسیم به دل سنگش و گردیم به گردش
گرییم و بخوانیم گنه ز ایزد دیّان
[...]
حاجی ز ره دور چو در بادیه آید
گیرید و کنیدش تهی از جامه و از نان
ایمن نبود گر کند از پای برون کفش
زیرا که بدزدید اگر دست دهدتان

For the sake of pilgrimage, we journey a thousand leagues
To come to the Kaʿba from the borders of Balkh and Balkhān.
We kiss her [the Kaʿba's] stones with our hearts and we walk around her;
We weep and ask forgiveness from the exalted God.
[...]
When a pilgrim comes to the desert from a far off place,
You seize him and strip him of clothing and bread.
He's not safe if he takes off his shoes,
For you'll steal his shoes as soon as you can.[445]

443 Ibid., p. 165.

444 On these debates see Seyed-Gohrab, "The Rhetoric of Persian Verbal Contests: Innovation and Creativity in Debates between the Persians and the Arabs," in *Disputation Literature in the Near East and Beyond*, ed. Enrique Jiménez and Catherine Mittermayer, Berlin: De Gruyter, 2020, pp. 261 – 282.

445 Khaleghi-Motlagh, "Asadī Ṭūsī," in *Majalla-yi Dānishkada-yi Adabiyyāt va ʿulūm-i insānī-yi dānishgāh-i Firdowsī*, issue 14, 1, 1357/1978 p. 74, ll. 64 – 65, 67 – 68. Asadī's allusion may refer to the unsafe Baghdad route which Persian pilgrims used to take. After a while they chose the Jerusalem rout which was much safer. I am grateful to P. Webb for this specific information. See his chapter, "Fragmentation and Integration: A Response to the Contributions by Hugh Kennedy and Walter Pohl," in *Empires and Communities in the Post-Roman and Islamic World c. 400 – 1000 CE*, eds Walter Pohl and Rutger Kramer, Oxford University Press, 2021, pp. 76 – 88.

Such debates extend to over a hundred lines. They preserve for us the cultural characterisation of the "other" by magnifying differences. These debates are still used in Persian popular culture from Los Angeles to Tehran, in social media and television, to censure the Arabs. Such catalogues of ethnic characterisations help to construct an imaginative picture of what an "Arab" is, making no distinction between contemporary Arabs and those living 1,000 years ago. In this example the Arab emphasises his culture's hospitality, courage, the language of the Quran, the Arab descent of the Prophet Muḥammad, the Arabian horse and camel husbandry. The Persian, who is the narrator, attacks the Arabs for mistreating the prophet and his family, alluding to the Prophet's forced migration from Mecca to Medina, pointing to instances in which the Arabs insulted the Prophet, and even broke his teeth. Instead of accepting the Prophet's new religion, the Arabs called him a demon and a sorcerer. The Arabs killed the third and fourth caliphs, ʿUthmān (d. 656) and ʿAlī Ibn Abī Ṭālib (c. 600 – 661). The poet then rejects the assertion of Arab hospitality, complaining about the ill-treatment of pilgrims to Mecca. Out of sheer love for the House of God, the Persians cross deserts and mountains to reach the Kaʿba, to kiss and circumambulate the House, asking for God's forgiveness in tears, while the Arabs lie in ambush, ready to steal the pilgrims' clothes, provisions and shoes. In such poems even the eating habits of the Arabs become an important ground for disparagement. The following lines inserted in the Persian epic, *Shāh-nāma* or *The Book of the Kings*, composed in 1010 by Firdowsī, are still widely used to humiliate the Arabs:

زشیر شتر خوردن و سوسمار
عرب را به جایی رسیده ست کار
که ملک عجم شان کند آرزو
تفو باد بر چرخ گردان، تفو![446]

From feeding on camel's milk and lizards,
the Arabs' hopes have come so far
as to grasp at the Persian Empire,
spit on you, O revolving Wheel, spit on you!

Although scholars of Persian literature have shown that such passages are later interpolations in this mammoth poem (some 50,000 couplets), this does not discourage modern Persian speakers from using them in their anti-Arab cam-

446 Abū 'l-Qāsim Firdowsī, *Shāh-nāma*, Vol. 8, ed. J. Khaleqi-Motlaq, Tehran: Markaz-i Dāyirat 'l-Maʿārif-i Buzurg-i Islāmī, 1386/2007, p. 423, in the note

paign.[447] The lines are interpolated in the section in which Firdowsī depicts the fall of the Sasanian Empire (224–650 CE). Before the battle the Persian general, Rustam Farrukhzādān, writes a letter to his enemy, Saʿd b. Vaqqās, seeking to intimidate him with Persian power.

Examples of such debates from the eleventh century indicate that anti-Arab sentiments existed from an early period. One should of course be wary of generalising, because the examples above are not repeated throughout the vast Persian cultural areas. An example of an anti-Shuʿūbiyya text is Ibn Quteyba's (828–889) *Excellence of the Arabs*. He descended in the "second or third generation from an Arabicised Iranian family" whose culture was probably Persian. He tried to allay the Persians' sense of superiority by extolling the qualities of the Arabs.[448]

In modern Persian war poetry myriad historical references highlight the Persian identity and recall how the Arabs harmed Persians and Iranian culture when they invaded Iran 1,400 years ago. A study on this topic would go beyond the scope of this book. It is certainly a desideratum to investigate how pre-Islamic Persian motifs and themes are wedded to a modern Shiite ideology to support the struggle against an Arab enemy. It is noteworthy that the majority of these allusions are contextualised within a strongly Shiite framework. The references range from allusions to legendary and heroic figures in Firdowsī's *Shāh-nāma*, to imitations of the marching rhythm and metre of Firdowsī's poem, and historical hints labelling Arabs as cruel enemies. In a ghazal of sixteen couplets by Qādir Ṭahmāsbī (b. 1952), the poet refers to a popular story in which Khālid ibn Valīd, an Arab commander during the invasion of Iran in 633, killed so many Persians that he could run a nearby watermill by their bloods to grind wheat for bread.[449] The event is known as "the Battle of Blood River" and it is

---

447 See T. Daryaee, "Food, Purity and Pollution: Zoroastrian Views on the Eating Habits of Others," in *Iranian Studies*, 45, 2, March 2012, pp. 231–232, and the literature Daryaee refers to. Also see Abbas Jamshidi, "Lizard as Arab Food: Representation of Arabs and the Shāhnāmeh scholarship," in *Persian Language, Literature and Culture: New Leaves, Fresh Looks*, ed. K. Talattof, London/New York: Routledge, 2015, pp. 318–336.

448 *The Excellence of the Arabs*, ed. J.E. Montgomery and P. Webb, translated by S. Bowen Savant and P. Webb, New York: New York University Press, 2017, p. xviii. See also G. Lecomte, in *Encyclopaedia of Islam, Second Edition*, s.v. Ibn Ḳutayba; Franz Rosenthal, in *Encyclopaedia Iranica*, s.v. Ebn Qotayba, Abū Moḥammad ʿAbd-Allāh; Ahmad Ashraf in *Encyclopaedia Iranica*, s.v. Iranian Identity, iii. Medieval Islamic Period.

449 This popular account is told by several historians in different forms. Especially in modern times it is used to rouse Persian nationalistic sentiments against the Arabs. See Ṭabarī, *The History of Tabari*, Vol. XI (The Challenge to the Empires A.D. 633–635/A.H. 12–13), trans. Khalid Yahya Blankinship, Albany, NY: State University of New York Press, 1993, p. 24. Zarrinkub rela-

ingrained in Iranian minds from an early age. Such historical allusions are deployed to amplify the differences in time of war:

ز خون ما و شما آسیا بگردانند
قسم به خون که اگر روزگار
سنان ببارد بر عمود قامت ما
گمان مبر به یمین و یسار برگردد

From our and your blood, they run mills;
I swear by blood, that if the world
Were to cast a spear at the lance of our stature,
beyond doubt it would not bend to left or right.[450]

In another poem, by Naṣrullāh Mardānī (1947–2003), the soldiers are compared to Ārash, a skilled archer who appears in pre-Islamic Persian legends to define the boundary of Iran against the archenemy Turan. He shoots extremely far with a special bow and an iron-tipped arrow. According to the polymath Abū Reyḥān Bīrūnī (about 973–1048), Ārash appeared naked and said, "'Behold! my body is free of any wound or sickness; but after this bowshot I will be destroyed.' At dawn he shot and was immediately torn to pieces."[451] In popular Persian it is said that he gave his soul to the arrow, shooting the arrow beyond the regions in Central Asia. Ārash has become a symbol of patriotism, who offers his life to protect Iran. In modern war poetry, the legend is employed in various ways to emphasise the soldiers' readiness to protect the country, often interwoven with a Shiite theme, as in the following piece:

جنگجویان دلاور پیشتازان دلیر
آرشان فاتح این خاك پهناور به پیش
با سلاح کاری اَللّه اکبر میروید
پیروان راستین فاتح خیبر به پیش

---

tivises the story: "[n]ear Anbar a fourth engagement occurred on the banks of the Euphrates at a village called Ullais. The Iranian commander, whose name was Jaban, was again accompanied by Christian members of the Bakr b. Wa'il tribes. Near the battleground was a channel known as the River of Blood, perhaps connected with the legend that the Arab commander, driven to wrath by the casual air of the Iranians, caused a number of captives to be put to death so that blood flowed as a river, a legend which is, incidentally, associated with several other commanders in the history of the Arab conquests." See A.H. Zarrinkub, "The Arab Conquest of Iran," pp. 10–13.

450 This is a ghazal of sixteen couplets depicting various aspect of the front. I have retrieved this ghazal from http://mostafamohadesi.blogfa.com/1390/01 (last accessed 25.03.2021).

451 As cited by A. Tafażżolī, in *Encyclopaedia Iranica*, s.v. Āraš; also see S. Gazerani, "Why Was the Story of Arash-i Kamangir Excluded from the Shahnameh?," in *Iran-Nameh*, 29, 2, 1993/2014, pp. 43–63.

Brave fighters, valiant combatants,
Victorious Ārash of this far-stretching soil, go forward
You march with the weapon of "God is Great"
True followers of the victor of Khaybar, march forward.[452]

As these two examples show, there is no specific anti-Arab sentiment in these poems.[453] The allusions to historical events and figures are intended to motivate soldiers to defend the country. Where anti-Arab feelings do appear in Persian war poetry written by committed revolutionary poets, they are mild compared to the allusions in modern Persian nationalistic poetry, in which the Arabs are dehumanised. In the war poetry, "anti-Arab" sentiments focus on Saudi Wahhabism rather than Arab ethnicity. Iran and her ancient history and culture are honoured in many poems, but the cliché predicates for Arabs, such as lizard-eaters, bare-footed and uncivilised, are rare.[454] Rather, allusions are made to the Wahhabis as destroyers of the graves of the prophet, his daughter Fāṭima and the Shiite imams, and as betraying Islam by collaborating with the US and Israel. A typical example is the following *qiṭʿa* ("fragment")[455] by Mihrdād Avistā (1930–1991) with the title "The Wahhabi Disgrace " (*nang-i Wahhābī*):

ای مژده عدالت مهدی یکی نگر

452 Khaybar refers to a fortified Jewish oasis in the Northern Hejaz which ʿAlī conquered single-handedly, according to popular Shiite narratives.

453 Anti-Arabic sentiments appear with specific references to pre-Islamic Arab rituals such as burying young baby girls alive. See Amīnpūr's quatrain, "These little girls have Paradise as their dowry / their blood adorns the architect of their graves / There are many of these girls buried alive / as this is the tradition of the age of ignorance" (*īn dukhtarakān bihishtishān kābīn ast / bar ḥijla-yi gūr khūnishān ādhīn ast / īn zinda ba gūr dukhtarān bisyārand / z-ān rūy ki rasm-i jāhiliyyat īn ast*). The quatrain depicts an Iraqi attack during which Iranian girls were raped and buried in a massive grave. I do not know for which attack this particular quatrain was composed, and whether the girls were buried alive. The editor says in a brief note that, months later, their mass graves were found. The poet connects this abhorrent deed to the pre-Islamic Arab tradition and how they treated women. See *Naqd u taḥlīl*, Vol. I, ed. M. Akbarī, p. 283.

454 Abbas Jamshidi, "Lizard as Arab food: Representation of Arabs and the Shāhnāmeh Scholarship," in *Persian Language, Literature and Culture*, pp. 318–336. Jamshidi cites a Persian poem cited by a populist poet, Ḥājj Siyyid Riżā ʿĀlī Payām, in response to the name of the Persian Gulf using classical form and vocabulary in a blatantly racist way and he is "applauded by his audience": "*Ei ānkeh dideh dūkhteh-i be khalij-e Fārs / In loqmeh bā shekambeh-ye to sāzegār nist // Zirā dar āb-e pāk u zolālash bedun-e shak / Māhist, pā berahneh Arab, susmār nist.* You, who have set your eyes on the Persian Gulf, / This mouthful won't suit your stomach; / Since, inside its pure and clear waters, no doubt, / There are fish, barefooted Arab, not lizards."

455 *Qiṭʿa* is a literary form and is often used for occasional poetry.

دجال را به قدس و حجاز آمده فرود
ننگی چنین به دامن تاریخ کس ندید
چونان که داغ صهیون بر جبهه یهود
[...]
زآل امیه این همه بیداد و کین نرفت
کاسلام را ز آل فرو مایه سعود
ننگ وهابیست به دامان روزکار
کز دامنش نیاری الا به خون زدود
[...]
من کافرم گر اوست مسلمان چنین که فهد
زاول خدای داند و پیغمبرش نبود
دل خون شد از مصایب افغان وای افسوس
زین دیو نابکار فرو مایه عنود[456]

O! Tidings of justice, Mahdī! Just look:
Antichrist has come down, in Jerusalem, and Hejaz.
There's never been such a stain on history's hem,
like the brand-mark of Zionism on the cloak of a Jew.
[...]
The Umayyads did not bring as much injustice and hatred
as the vile Family of Saud has brought on Islam.
There's a Wahhabi stain on the hem of the world;
its hem can only be cleansed with blood.
[...]
If Fahd is a Muslim, I am a heretic;
From the start, God knows that he had no Prophet.
Alack, alas! My heart bleeds from intense lamentation,
for this vile, evil-doing treacherous demon.

In the opening lines of this poem the poet hopes that the Mahdī will come and bring justice. In eschatological accounts, the arrival of the Mahdī will be preceded by signs such as the coming of the antichrist. The accounts are not clear as to where the Mahdī will reveal himself, but Jerusalem and Mecca (in the Hejaz), both sites that are holy for Muslims, are mentioned. Having opened the poem in this way, the poet lingers on the antichrist and associates him with the Saudis. The link between the antichrist and the Saudis is not explicit, but it is axiomatic for Persian readers in that period that the antichrist refers to the Saudi kingdom. The poet then compares the Saudis' clear infamy to a Jew wearing an identifying mark. The poet uses a hyperbole by stating that the damage the Saudi family has done to Islam is more than the Umayyads could wreak. This is of course an allusion to the problem of the succession of the prophet. According to the Shiites, ʿAlī was the rightful successor, but others usurped his rights, especially the first

456 *Naqd u taḥlīl*, Vol. I, ed. M. Akbarī, p. 376.

Islamic dynasty, the Umayyads. The poet thinks that the Wahhabi "stain" will be removed only by bloodshed. The royal family of Saud was founded in 1744 by Muḥammad ibn Saʿūd, who joined forces with the founder of Wahhabism, Muḥammad ibn ʿAbd al-Wahhāb, to give the Saudis great political and religious stability.[457] In the last two couplets the poet declares the Wahhabis to be unbelievers, who did not even believe in the prophet. This allusion refers to the Arabs as heirs of the ancient Arabs who did not at first believe in Muḥammad's message, forcing him to leave Mecca and creating much hardship for him. There also appears to be an allusion to the strict monotheism of the Wahhabis, which limits even the honouring of the Prophet and his family that is characteristic of both Shiism and Sufism. The final couplet closes with an emotional trigger, referring to sufferings inflicted by the Wahhabi enemy.

8.7 Conclusion

I started this chapter by listing three fields of contentions between Iran and Saudi Arabia: Persian-Arab rivalry, Wahhabi views of Shiism and *vice versa*, and the Sufi mystical interpretation of Islam. To start with the last topic, it is clear that much of Islamic mysticism, with its doctrines and ideas that flout the most holy rituals and practices of Islam to promote individual piety, is diametrically opposed to the Saudi Wahhabi ideology. The ritual *ḥajj* remains one of the pillars of Islam for all Muslims, including Iranians, yet the profound impact of mystical ideas such as the preference for the Kaʿba of the heart over the physical Kaʿba, transmitted through popular Persian poets such as Ḥāfiẓ and Rūmī, creates a new dimension to religiosity which Wahhabism considers utterly blasphemous. The mystical interpretation of the pilgrimage allowed modern Shiiite intellectuals to politicise *ḥajj*, calling the attention of all Muslims not to the rituals alone but also to political developments in their own countries. Khomeini's political take on pilgrimage is based on both individual spiritual aspirations and freeing the Muslim world from Western dominion.

While the Islamic Republic framed the war as a Muslim struggle against despotic rulers who were puppets of Western powers, Saddam framed the war in terms of the historic defeat of the sophisticated Persian army by a smaller Muslim Arab army. That defeat had become almost a cultural trauma for Persian nationalists. By giving the title of Qādisiyya to the war against Iran, Saddam want-

457 See Wayne H. Bowen, *The History of Saudi Arabia*, Westport, CT/London: Greenwood Press, 2008, pp. 69–70.

ed to present it as a war between two historic empires, the Arab Muslims and the pagan Persians. The Shiite faith in Iran was considered heretical. Iraqi war rhetoric ignored the fact that the majority of Iraq's people are Shiites. This rhetoric fanned nationalistic sentiments, evoking Arab-Persian rivalry, bringing the Arab nations together to fight the Persians. When Saddam invaded Kuwait in 1990, leading to the first Gulf war, the Qādisiyya paradigm lost its power. Since then the Saudis have claimed the cloak of Arab legitimacy and of leadership against the Iranian government. Although nationalist Arab-Persian rivalry plays a role, the Wahhabi-Shiite conflict is more important.

In Persian war poetry the emphasis is less on ethnicity and more on religious affiliations. Saddam and the Saudi royal family are condemned not so much because of their Arab descent as because of their religious ideology and collaboration with the West, which Iran, since the 1979 Revolution, has regarded as Imperialists who want to destroy Islam. In the poetry analysed in this chapter the emphasis is on politicising Shiism as a cornerstone of the Islamic Republic, and highlighting some antinomian Sufi doctrines, themes and motifs that are absolutely disparate to the Wahhabi ideology.

9 Conclusion: Making Death Meaningful

I started this book by scrutinising the role of poetry in violent political events in Iran and how the revolutionary poets and the established dissident poets depicted the socio-political crisis of the 1979 Revolution and the Iran-Iraq War (1980–1988) for different purposes. While revolutionary poets saw poetry as a means to promote revolutionary ideas and as a means for mobilisation, established poets took a more reflective approach to the upheavals, often in a frustrated fashion. This poetry offers us insights into the use of poetry in a political context in which new generations of revolutionary literati integrated a militant Islamic ideology, often profoundly mixed with mysticism. As poetry is an essential part of Iranian culture, the first generation of revolutionaries launched a drastic programme, heavily financed by the government, to create an ideologically Islamist literature, positing a schism between pre-revolutionary poetry and revolutionary poetry. Pre-revolutionary poetry was stigmatised as secular and as aiming to introduce the "immoral" and "vulgar" norms and values of the West. Theoreticians of the revolutionary poetry stipulated a number of criteria for proper poetry, which would support the Islamic Republic's ideology.

The revolutionary poetry depicts death as love-death and martyrdom as union with God, introducing new interpretations of medieval mystical concepts and doctrines with the aim of mobilising young people for the front and instilling a new Islamic ethos, carefully defined by the state. The war poetry's role as a mobilising force was to convince soldiers that death at the front was justified, not merely as an act of patriotism, but more importantly as a means of personal spiritual growth and a marker of loyalty to the state's ideology. To achieve this goal, this poetry was framed in the discourse of Shiite paradigms and mystical doctrines while concocting ever newer metaphors and imagery. The Karbalā paradigm of Ḥuseyn's martyrdom became a model for soldiers. This paradigm presented Ḥuseyn as the "prince of martyrs," an example of a perfect human being to be imitated in all respects. To die as a martyr meant to have followed Ḥuseyn's ideals. Moreover, the guilt that Shiite Iranians have felt for not being present in 680 to aid Ḥuseyn, fighting the Sunnite enemy at his side, has played an essential role. The army of the Sunnite Saddam, occupying the territory where Ḥuseyn fought against the Umayyad Yazīd, created a perfect parallel setting where they might compensate for this sense of guilt. The Karbalā paradigm effaced linear time. Poetry and songs helped revolutionary Iranians to experience Ḥuseyn's tragedy as if it were happening before their eyes, so they could easily identify with the Karbalā martyrs. The emotionally loaded poetry bridged the space of 1,400 years connecting the medieval battlefield to a modern war setting.

https://doi.org/10.1515/9783110748734-013

Another feature of this poetry was the inclusion of Sufi mysticism, which is an integral part of Persian culture. The mystic poetry of Sanāʾī, ʿAṭṭār, Saʿdī, Rūmī and Ḥāfiẓ is deeply intertwined with everyday Persian language. The role of mysticism in the war poetry was to convince soldiers that their physical fight was a spiritual quest. The ideal of a mystical love that entails the enduring of suffering enabled soldiers to bear physical and psychological hardship at the front. They were called mystic lovers on the path of annihilation, longing to attain eternal life in and with the immaterial beloved. The parallel between a peaceful mystic quest and military action could be seamlessly created, as the medieval spiritual metaphors embraced suffering and the extermination of the ego. These lovers sometimes longed to be killed at the beloved's hands (*kushta-yi maʿshūq*).[458] Just as a mystic lover in classical poetry craved for annihilation at the hand of the beloved, like a moth in the candle's flame, so Iranian soldiers longed for a love-death, to cross the fiery boundary of death to be united with an immaterial beloved. As the lover in classical poetry is commonly advised to barter worldly interests and attachments for eternal union, it was an easy step for war poets to transform such tropes into war settings. Concepts, doctrines and key figures from the rich Persian mystical tradition provided these poets with material to present their poems in a mystical garb. Interpreting death as ascent to the presence of the Divine, after the example of the prophet Muḥammad, or performing ritual ablutions in blood as a symbol of preparing for the daily prayer in which the lover loses himself to the divine presence, and referring to the mystic Ḥallāj as a prefiguration of a self-disinterested lover, are among the recurring mystical themes and motifs employed by war poets to make death meaningful and to justify violence. In this war poetry, metaphors, similes and imagery are all given a new religious and political significance, a connotative ideological load to praise revolutionary ideals.

As we have seen, this application of mysticism could not have been successful without the intellectual developments prior to the 1979 Revolution. ʿAlī Sharīʿatī and others revived an activist Shiism while cultivating the cult of martyrdom and knitting Sufism into a living Islam. This inspired a new generation of poets to compose committed poetry on topical themes, often linked with mystical tropes and motifs. The profound familiarity of Persians with classical poetry paved the way for introducing the new ideology of the Islamic government to the next generation of Iranian youths.

---

458 See chapter seven, "When They Love, They Die," in Seyed-Gohrab, *Laylī and Majnūn*, pp. 127–138.

Although this new literary revolutionary movement, commonly known as the "literature of Sacred Defence," still exists, it has lost its vigour because the key poets of this movement distanced themselves from a purely ideologically framed poetry. What has lived on is the poetry of giant figures such as Shāmlū, Nādirpūr, Farrukhzād, and Bihbahānī (to name only a few), who are still the dominant voices in Iran. It is extraordinary that a diasporic poet such as Nādirpūr, who criticised the foundations of the 1979 Revolution and the government, is one of the favourite poets in Iran, as the number of reprints of his work and university dissertations on him testify. The same applies for other pre-revolutionary poets whose writings are inspirations for new generations of poets, forming an indispensable basis for contemporary Persian poetry.

9.1 The War's Bearing on Current Politics

The 1979 Revolution and the founding of the Islamic Republic created a new system, an ideologically-orientated order incompatible with western liberal ideas and values. This has resulted in misconceptions and misunderstandings. To read and to appreciate the committed war poetry, one must realise that many of its concepts are incompatible with western liberal culture, in which religion has a limited role in politics. This poetry is rooted in mysticism and Shiite Islam, with laws based on revelations, and not on individual reason or the wisdom of human beings. In this theocratic philosophy human reasoning is limited and human beings are incomplete creatures who may achieve perfection through gnosis and martyrdom. A consequence of this is that human beings are incompetent to manage the legislative, executive and judicial powers of the state. To emphasise the need for divine intervention, it is even stated that "if human wisdom could meet all human needs and could solve all human problems, there would have been no need for Prophets and Divine revelations."[459] The theocratic system requires, therefore, the absolute authority of a jurist, the so-called *vilāyat-i faqīh*, an individual who is in contact with God, and is designated to lead God's community in all worldly affairs. Such a person acts as the supreme leader, monitoring the laws and other essential bodies such as the armed forces. In this system God is the source of laws, and the individual is following the rules of Islam to attain to good in both this world and the Hereafter. The Hereafter plays a central role as it is a fair, just and eternal world compared to the injustice and

---

459 Mohammad Reza Chitsazian and Seyed Mohammad Ali Taghavi, "An Iranian Perspective on Iran-US Relations: Idealists Versus Materialists," in *Strategic Analysis*, 43, 1, 2019, pp. 28–41.

ephemerality of this world. The soldier's desire to die is a longing to start anew in another world. This is all in sharp contrast to the Western liberal political philosophy in which law-making is based on human reason and the "authority of the state derived from citizens' will, which gets reflected in majority rule."[460] The motivations of the soldiers to offer their lives are based on faith in this theocratic system, which derives from God himself. Death as union with God completes the soldier-lover's journey to perfection. It is for this reason that death in battle is never depicted as "murder," which we see, for instance, in the poetry of World War I. A mystic lover or a martyr does not experience the pains of death or the torments of the grave, because s/he has an instant route to God.

Unlike the European war poetry, which limns the horror and revulsion of war, with images of trenches, wounded soldiers, mutilated bodies, the fear of death, deserters and so forth, the committed Persian war poetry commonly praises death as love-death, the highest ideal a human being can achieve. I have not dealt with several topics which are worth investigating, such as suicide, deserters, executions for disobedience, etc. simply because there are no literary references to them, which does not mean that they did not happen. It is certainly possible that there are poems written on these subjects but due to the regime's censorship, they are not publically available. The committed revolutionary literati were sponsored by the state and did not mention subjects that would evoke doubts and fear among people. The established poets also avoided these subjects, due to censorship. It is worth mentioning that many Iranian youths fled to the West during the 1980s, mostly to pursue their studies. Although they are not literally "deserters," their deliberate absence during the war suggests that the Iran-Iraq War must also have had its deserters.

Persian war poetry is marked by celebrating death and suffering. Often it is not death in the hope of reward in the Hereafter, as commonly presented in Western media, but death as mystical union with God. In the following excerpt the poet Siyyid Riżā Muʿayyad depicts how in the trenches someone says that at the moment of martyrdom the martyr will be rewarded by virgin girls (*ḥūrīs*) in Paradise, but a basījī responds with tears in his eyes:

که من شهید نگردم به شوق حور و قصور
مرا ز کشته شدن غیر ازین بود منظور
منم شکسته عشق و طبیب من دگری است
قسم به عشق مقدس حبیب من دگری است
مگر حسین (ع) نیاید به بازدید شهید؟
که هست دیدن او آخرین امید شهید

460 Ibid. p. 31.

خوشا حسین (ع) و چنین عاشقان دیدارش
خوشا امام و چنین امت فداکارش
چه امتی که شکسته شکست خوردن را
به زندگانی ننگین گزیده مردن را[461]

"I do not want to die as a martyr longing for *ḥūrī*s and palaces,
I have another goal for which I am ready to be killed:
I am the one broken by love, and my physician is not what you say;
I swear by the holy love that my beloved is not what you say.
Does not Ḥuseyn come to visit a martyr?
For the dying hope of a martyr is to see him."
Blessed is Ḥuseyn and these lovers longing to see him,
Blessed is Khomeini and his community who are ready for sacrifice.
What a community? It has broken breaking (i.e. defeat),
Choosing death above inglorious life.

The motif of preferring the immaterial Beloved to rewards such as paradisiacal virgins appears in Persian mystical poetry, classical and modern. One famous example is the story of the great mystic Shiblī, also attributed to the early female mystic Rābiʿa al-ʿAdaviyya (d. 801), who runs with a torch in one hand and water in the other. When people ask Shiblī what he intends to do, he says he wants to set fire to paradise and to extinguish the fire of hell, so that people do not worship God out of fear of punishment or hoping for reward. Other modern poets such as Hūshang Ibtihāj use the words *ḥūrī*s and palaces (*quṣūr*), found in the example above, to emphasise that the lover wants the Beloved and not any reward.[462]

There is also a theme of Muslim piety and being a good Muslim in Iran-Iraq poetry. As Narguess Farzad aptly puts it, this poetry "is rather celebratory in mood and rarely does it show a negative side or utter remorse or regret."[463] This poetry celebrates death because it connects death with love, which is the highest station in the mystical journey of the faithful. For mystics, the soul originates in God and is banished from the spiritual plane. They long to return to the

461 *Naqd-u taḥlīl-i shiʿr-i difāʿ-i muqaddas*, p. 32. The poem was written by Siyyid Riżā Muʿayyad, and is quoted from *Yād-nāma-yi sivvumīn kungira-yi sarāsarī-yi shiʿr-u adab*, published by Idāra-yi kull-i irshād-i islāmī, Khurāsān, Chāp-khāna-yi dānishgāh-i Mashhad, 1363/1984.
462 See the poem entitled *rowshan-i gūyā* or "The Enlightened Eloquent," starting with the following couplet: "For some time we have been far from your beautiful face / no need to explain that we are longing for your presence."

دیری ست که از روی دل آرای تو دوریم
محتاج بیان نیست که مشتاق حضوریم

463 N. Farzad, "Qeysar Amīnpūr and the Persian Poetry of Sacred Defence," p. 353.

original state of union with God. Soldiers fully applied this paradigm to justify their exertion on the battlefield and their final extinction.

As we have seen, most of this war poetry does not describe how to kill or mutilate the enemy (although such poems also exist). Rather, the poetry is personal in the sense of celebrating one's own mystical growth by dying. It is as if passing the boundary from this world to the other is in itself a reward of having achieved union with God. Many of the poems were sung and broadcast on radio and television. Religious singers (*maddāḥ*s), such as Ṣādiq Āhangarān, prepared soldiers psychologically to justify their own deaths by hypnotising his audience through rhyme, rhythms and his voice.[464] While the emphasis was on being about to die, the enemy could also be killed as they were considered unbelievers and evil.

It is not easy to inspire soldiers with a readiness to die when their basic instinct is to live. Mystical poetry, whether from classical Persian masters or new poets, created a space for abnegating self, imagining oneself as an ideal lover who is ready to disavow everything, including giving one's life for a beloved who, according to context, is pictured as God, a Shiite saint or Khomeini. Through such mysticism death is interpreted as deliverance. This firm belief in a loving embrace with the beloved led aspirant martyrs to return to battle, even when they had witnessed the slaughter of thousands of soldiers. Another motivation was that the status of hero, achieved by being killed like the Shiite soldier-saints, elevated the martyr's position due to the high status that society conferred on that person and the material gain for the families of the fallen. Personal love of God, love for the Shiite saints such as Imam Ḥuseyn, and the promise of high social status nurtured a strong sense of loyalty that overcame rational self-interest. These prevailing motivators were reinforced by patriotism, which was innately present but was suppressed to amplify the religious dimensions of the fight against unbelief.

* * *

464 In an interview with the BBC, when Āhangarān is asked whether he was aware how his songs sent young soldiers into the arm of death, he answers that "he was completely aware of all the consequences." See https://www.youtube.com/watch?v=_qmCwn3zOFM. On his role in canonizing several war poems see F. Shams, *A Revolution in Rhyme*, 183–186.

9.2 The Reception of War Literature

The reception of the war literature in present-day Iran has not been the subject of any study to my knowledge. Collections of poetry by poets such as Amīnpūr and Bihbahānī have gone through many reprints in recent years, but the popularity of the other war poets is unclear as many collections of the committed war poetry are distributed free of charge by various government organisations. This also applies to war literature in prose. A general impression, based on the publication and distribution of this poetry, is that its consumption is limited to revolutionary people, who wish to keep alive the ideals of the 1979 Revolution and especially the ideal of martyrdom. Perhaps the broader Iranian public avoids the poetry. The devastating war caused more than one million deaths and left a large number disabled. Those who have suffered the traumas of a war often do not wish to be reminded of them. Perhaps, while the effects of the war are so pervasive through the images of martyrs in street murals and in other public spaces, people do not wish to read a poetry that also celebrates death. One observation that may be evidence that the reading public avoids this poetry is that it is not easy to buy the volumes of the lesser known war poets. Although the Centre for the Study and Research on Resistance Literature, financed by the Islamic Republic, promotes the ideals of the Revolution through art and poetry, these collections are hardly available in bookshops. Yet, to my astonishment, this poetry is widely reproduced in cyber space. It appears that it is distributed largely via many personal and organisational websites publishing a wide range of the war poetry, and not so much in books and journals.

Qeyṣar Amīnpūr is without doubt the best revolutionary war poet. He produced an immense number of poems in both classical and new poetic forms. His transformation from a revolutionary committed poet to a more apolitical poet is a good yardstick of the development of Persian war poetry. Some of his poems that I have dealt with in this book are not included in his collected poetry and are hard to find elsewhere. It is as if he wanted to remove specific poems from his *oeuvre*. This may indicate a desire to distance himself from the state's ideology. He did not openly and drastically break with the state, as several dissidents such as Muḥsin Makhmalbāf did, but his silence and withdrawn life were marked signs of an apolitical transformation. In a brief but essential biography of Amīnpūr, Fatemeh Shams observes that the "transformation of his poetics may come as a sign of his ideological disillusionment at the end of his life."[465]

465 Fatemeh Shams, "From Revolution to Silence: The Political and Literary Life of Qaysar Amīnpūr," in *The Layered Heart*, p. 551.

Several pieces of Amīnpūr's poetry have such high poetic merit and flavour that they are appreciated even outside the context of war. Like Bihbahānī's poem, "Once more, I will build you, my homeland," written at the beginning of the war and taking on a new life as a nationalistic poem after the war, several of Amīnpūr's poems are still used, but in other contexts.

Literary works financed or commissioned by the government are distributed in huge editions to those interested, while independent authors are unsupported but may still be influential. Ismāʿīl Faṣīḥ is an example: his novel *Zimistān-i 1362* has had ten reprints (1985–2018) and is extremely popular, but the Ministry of Culture and Islamic Guidence banned it from 1987 to 2003 as it did not conform to the state's doctrine of martyrdom.[466] Another example is *One Woman's War: Dā (Mother) the Memoirs of Seyyedeh Zahra Ḥuseyni*, a best-seller among Iran-Iraq war memoirs.[467] It is interesting that while poetry and prose were written on the subject of the war during the 1980s, the traumas of war inhibited authors from releasing memoirs and personal reflections on the war. Sprachman discusses the unclear situation about the distribution and popularity of war literature in his Introduction to *One Woman's War*, which created a "Dā-reading fever." It was not published until September 2008. An indicator of its influence is that it is part of the office décor in an image marking the 100th day of President Hasan Rouhani's administration.[468] While such texts show how vivid the memories of the Iran-Iraq War are, they also confirm that literature is an indissoluble part of the politics of the Islamic Republic.

---

466 For a monograph on this specific novel see S. Shahnahpur, *Writing War in Contemporary Iran: The Case of Esmāʿil Fasih's Zemestān-e 62*, New York: Peter Lang Publishing, Inc, 2019; There are several valuable studies on Persian prose fiction related to the Iran-Iraq War, among which are G. Ghardashkhani-Otter, "Narrative Geometry in ʿAli Reza Gholami's *Divar* (The Wall): New Developments in Iranian War Literature," in *Iranian Studies*, 53, 5–6, 2020, pp. 873–89,; and the collection of essays and translations in *Moments of Silence: Authenticity in the Cultural Expression of the Iran-Iraq War, 1980–1988*, ed. A. Khakpour, M.M. Khorrami & S. Vatanabadi, New York: New York University Press, 2016; invaluble research is conducted on this topic by A. Moosavi, among which is his "How to write Death: Resignifying Martyrdom in Two Novels of the Iran-Iraq War," in *Alif: Journal of Comparative Poetics*, No. 35, 2015, pp. 1–23.

467 *One Woman's War, Da (Mother): The Memoirs of Seyyedeh Zahra Ḥuseyni*, translated by Paul Sprachman, Costa Mesa, CA: Mazda Publishers, 2014, pp. xii–xiii; for an analysis see L. Nanquette, "An Iranian Woman's Memoir on the Iran-Iraq War: The Production and Reception of Da," in *Iranian Studies*, 46, 6, 2013, pp. 943–957; Shams, *A Revolution in Rhyme*, p. 254; A. Abiz, *Censorship of Literature in Post-Revolutionary Iran*, p. 140.

468 *One Woman's War*, p. xiii.

Bibliography

A'lam, H., in *Encyclopaedia Iranica*, s.v. Banafša.
Abisaab, R.J., *Converting Persia: Religion and Power in the Safavid Empire*, London/New York: I.B. Tauris, 2004.
Abiz, A., *Censorship of Literature in Post-Revolutionary Iran: Politics and Culture Since 1979*, New York/London: I.B. Tauris, 2021.
Abrahamian, E., *A History of Modern Iran*, Cambridge: Cambridge University Press, 2008.
Afary, J., *Sexual Politics in Modern Iran*, Cambridge: Cambridge University Press, 2009.
Agius, D.A., "The Shuʿūbiyya Movement and its Literary Manifestation," in *The Islamic Quarterly*, issue xxiv, 1980, pp. 76–88.
Aḥmadī, A., "Khāstgāh-i adabiyyāt-i qabl va baʿd az inqilāb," in *Majmūʿa-yi maqālāt-i simīnār-i barrasī-yi adabiyyāt-i inqilāb-i islāmī*, Tehran: Samt, 1373/1994, pp. 3–9.
Ahmed, S., *Before Orthodoxy: The Satanic Verses in Early Islam*, Cambridge, MA: Harvard University Press, 2017.
Ahmed, S., in *Encyclopaedia of the Qur'ān*, s.v. Satanic verses.
Ahmed, S., *What Is Islam? The Importance of Being Islamic*, Princeton, NJ: Princeton University Press, 2016.
Akbarī, M., "Nigāhī ba shiʿr-i inqlāb-i nūr," in *Majmūʿa-yi maqālāt-i simīnār-i barrasī-yi adabiyyāt-i inqilāb-i islāmī*, Tehran: Samt, 1373/1994, pp.18–19.
Akbarī, M., *Naqd va taḥlīl-i adabiyyāt-i inqilāb-i islāmī*, Vol. I, Tehran: Sāzmān-i Madārik-i Farhangī-yi Inqilāb-i Islāmī, 1371/1993, pp. 333–335.
Alagha, J., *Hizbullah's Identity Construction*, Amsterdam: Amsterdam University Press, 2011.
Algar, H., "Imam Khomeini, 1902–1962: The Pre-Revolutionary Years," in *Islam, Politics and Social Movements*, eds., E. Burke & I.M. Lapidus, Berkeley, CA: University of California Press, 1988, pp. 263–88.
Algar, H., in *Encyclopaedia Iranica*, s.v. Āḵūndzāda.
Algar, H., in *Encyclopaedia Iranica*, s.v. *ʿAtabāt.*
Algar, H., in *Encyclopaedia Iranica*, s.v. Behešt-e Zahrāʾ.
Algar, H., in *Encyclopaedia Iranica*, s.v. Burial.
Algar, H., *Wahhabism: A Critical Essay*, New York: Oneonta, 2002.
Allen, G., *Intertextuality*, London: Routledge, 2000.
Amanat, A., "Divided Patrimony, Tree of Royal Power, and Fruit of Vengeance: Political Paradigms and Iranian Self-Image in the Story of Faridun in the Shahnama," in *Shahnama Studies I*, ed. C. Melville, Cambridge: The Centre of Middle Eastern and Islamic Studies, University of Cambridge, 2006, pp. 49–70.
Amanat, A., *Iran: A Modern History*, New Haven, CT, and London: Yale University Press, 2017.
Amīnpūr, Q., *Dastūr(-i) zabān-i ʿishq*, Tehran: Murvārīd, 1387/1999.
Amīnpūr, Q., *Guzīna-yi ashʿār*, Tehran: Murvārīd, 12th edition, 1386/2007.
Amīnpūr, Q., *Majmūʿa-yi kāmil-i ashʿār*, Tehran: Gulshan, 9th edition 1391/2012.
Amīrī, F., "Chigūnigī-yi rushd va taṭavvur-i adabiyyāt-i kūdakān baʿd az pīrūzī-yi inqilāb-i islāmī," in *Majmūʿa-yi maqālāt-i simīnār-i barrasī-yi adabiyyāt-i inqilāb-i islāmī*, Tehran: Samt, 1373/1994, pp. 23–41.
Amoretti, B.S., "The Political Realm's Literary Convention: The Example of ʿIshqi and Iqbal," *The Necklace of the Pleiades: 24 Essays on Persian Literature, Culture and Religion*, ed. F.D. Lewis and S. Sharma, Leiden: Leiden University Press, 2010, pp. 281–93.

https://doi.org/10.1515/9783110748734-014

Anṣārī, Ḥ., "Dar bāra-yi ziyārat-i ʿāshūrā," in *Barrisīhā-yi tārīkhī dar howza-yi islām va tashayyuʿ*, Tehran: Kitāb-khāna, 1390/2011, pp. 675 – 79.

Anṣārī, Ḥ., and S. Schmidtke, "Abū Saʿd al-Ḫargūšī and his Kitāb al-Lawāmiʿ A Ṣūfī Guide Book for Preachers from 4th/10th century Nīšāpūr," in *Arabica*, 58, 2011, pp. 503 – 518.

Arberry, A.J., "Khargūshī's Manual of Ṣūfism," in *Bulletin of the School of Oriental and African Studies*, 9, 2, 1938, pp. 345 – 9.

Arjomand, S.A., *After Khomeini: Iran under His Successors*, Oxford: Oxford University Press, 2009.

Arjomand, S.A., *The Shadow of God and the Hidden Imam: Religion, Political Order, and Social Change in Shi'ite Iran from the Beginning of 1890*, Chicago: University of Chicago Press, 1984.

Ashraf, A., "The Crisis of National and Ethnic Identities in Contemporary Iran," in *Iranian Studies*, Vol. 26, No. ½, 1993, pp. 159 – 164.

Ashraf, A., in *Encyclopaedia Iranica*, s.v. Iranian Identity, iii. Medieval Islamic Period.

Atrissi, T., "Arab and Iranian Images of Each Other," in *Imagining the Arab Other: How Arabs and Non-Arabs View Each Other*, ed. T. Labib, London/New York: I.B. Tauris, 2008, pp. 316 – 56.

ʿAṭṭār, Farīd al-Dīn, *Asrār-nāma*, ed. M.R. Shafīʿī-Kadkanī, Tehran: Sukhan, second print 1388/2009.

ʿAṭṭār, Farīd al-Dīn, *Farid ad-Din ʿAttār's Memorial of God's Friends: Lives and Sayings of Sufis*, translated by P. Losensky, New York: Paulist Press, 2009.

ʿAṭṭār, Farīd al-Dīn, *Manṭiq al-ṭeyr*, ed. Siyyid Ṣādiq Gowharīn, Tehran: Shirkat-i Intishārāt-i ʿIlmī va Farhangī, 1368/1989.

ʿAṭṭār, Farīd al-Dīn, *Tadhkirat al-Owliyā*, Tehran: Manūchihrī, 1991.

ʿAṭṭār, Farīd al-Dīn, *The Conference of the Birds*, Trans. by D. Davis & A. Darbandi, Penguin Classics, 1984 (reprint 2011).

Awn, P.J., *Satan's Tragedy and Redemption: Iblis in Sufi Psychology*, Leiden: Brill, 1983.

ʿAyn al-Qużāt-i Hamadānī, *Nāma-hā*, eds. ʿAlī-Naqī Munzavī and ʿAfīf ʿUṣayrān, 3 Vols., Tehran: Asāṭīr, 3d print 1377/1998.

Ayoub, M., *Redemptive Suffering in Islam: A Study of the Devotional Aspects of in Twelver Shi'ism*, The Hague: Mouton Press, 1978.

Āzād Tabrīzī, Ḥ., *Gulzār-i maʿrifat (La roseraie du savoir)*, Leiden: Brill, 1906.

Azimi, F., "Khomeini and the 'White Revolution'," in *A Critical Introduction to Khomeini*, ed. Adib-Moghaddam, Cambridge: Cambridge University Press, 2013, pp. 19 – 42.

Barāhinī, R., *Ṭalā dar mis: dar shiʿr va shāʿirī*, 3 Vols., Tehran: Nashr-i zamān, 1371/1992.

Bauer, T., *Die Kultur der Ambiguität: Eine andere Geschichte des Islam*, Berlin: Verlag der Weltreligionen, 2011.

Bayat, M., in *Encyclopaedia Iranica*, s.v. Āqā Khan Kermānī.

Bearman, P., T. Bianquis, C.E. Bosworth, E. van Donzel, and W.P. Heinrichs, eds. *The Encyclopaedia of Islam*, Second Edition, Leiden: Brill, 1960 – 2007.

Beeston, A.F.L., in: *Encyclopaedia of Islam, Second Edition*, s.v. Abraha.

Bihbahānī, Sīmīn, *Khaṭṭī zi surʿat u az ātash*, Tehran: Zavvār, 3th print 1370/1992.

Bihbahānī, Sīmīn, *Majmūʿa-yi ashʿār*, Tehran: Nigāh, 1982/2003.

Bleiker, R., *Aesthetics and World Politics*, Basingstoke: Palgrave Macmillan, 2009.

Bosworth, C.E., "Farrukhī's Elegy on Mahmud of Ghazna," in *Iran: Journal of the British Institute of Persian Studies*, 29, 1991, pp. 43 – 9.

Bowen, W.H., *The History of Saudi Arabia*, Westport/London: Greenwood Press, 2008.
Böwering, G., in *Encyclopaedia Iranica*, s.v. ʿAyn-al-Qożāt Hamadānī.
Boyce, M., in *Encyclopaedia Iranica*, s.v. Amurdād.
Brookshaw, D.P., *Hafiz and his Contemporaries: Poetry, Performance and Patronage in Fourteenth-Century Iran*, New York/London: I.B. Tauris, 2019.
Brookshaw, D.P., "Revivification of an Ossified Genre? Sīmīn Bihbahānī and the Persian Ghazal," in *Iranian Studies*, Vol. 41, No. 1, 2008, pp. 75–90.
Browne, E.G., *A Literary History of Persia*, 4 Vols., Cambridge: Cambridge University Press, 1902–24 (several reprints).
Bruijn, J.T.P. de, "Some strip of Herbage: Gardens in Persian poetry," in *The Authentic Garden. A symposium on gardens*, eds. L. Tjon Sie Fat and E. de Jong, Leiden: Clusius Foundation, 1991, pp. 123–130.
Bruijn, J.T.P. de, in *Encyclopaedia Iranica*, s.v. Beloved.
Bruijn, J.T.P. de, in *Encyclopaedia Iranica*, s.v. Candle.
Bruijn, J.T.P. de, in *Encyclopaedia Iranica*, s.v. Elegy.
Bruijn, J.T.P. de, in *Encyclopaedia Iranica*, s.v. Farroḵī Sīstānī, Abu'l-Ḥasan ʿAlī.
Bruijn, J.T.P. de, in *Encyclopaedia Iranica*, s.v. Hafez. iii. Hafez's Poetic Art.
Bruijn, J.T.P. de, *Pearls of Meanings: Studies on Persian Art, Poetry, Sufism and History of Iranian Studies in Europe by J.T.P. de Bruijn*, ed. A.A. Seyed-Gohrab, Leiden: Leiden University Press, 2020.
Bruijn, J.T.P. de, *Persian Sufi Poetry: An Introduction to the Mystical Use of Classical Persian Poems*, Richmond Virginia: Curzon, 1997.
Buhl, F., in *Encyclopaedia of Islam, Second Edition*, s.v. Minā.
Busse, H., in *The Encyclopaedia of the Quran*, s.v. Nimrod.
Calmard, J., in *Encyclopaedia Iranica*, s.v. Ḥosayn B. ʿAli. ii. In Popular Shiʿism.
Chehabi, H.E., in *Encyclopaedia Iranica*, s.v. Zur-ḵāna.
Chehabi, H.E., "Wrestling in the Shāhnāmeh and Later Persian Epics," in *The Layered Heart: Essays on Persian Poetry, A Celebration in Honor of Dick Davis*, ed. Asghar Seyed-Gohrab, Washington, D.C.: Mage, 2019, pp. 237–282.
Chelkowski, P., "All's is not Quiet on the western Front: Graphic Arts in the Iranian War effort," in *Moments of Silence: Authenticity in the Cultural Expression of the Iran-Iraq War, 1980–1988*, ed. A. Khakpour, M.M. Khorrami & Sh. Vatanabadi, New York: New York University Press, 2016, pp. 163–75.
Chelkowski, P., and H. Dabashi, *Staging a Revolution: The Art of Persuasion in the Islamic Republic of Iran*, New York, NY: New York University Press, 1999.
Chitsazian M.R., & S.M.A. Taghavi, "An Iranian Perspective on Iran-US Relations: Idealists Versus Materialists," in *Strategic Analysis*, 43, 1, 2019, pp. 28–41.
Chittick, W., "Rūmī's View of Imam Ḥusayn," in *Papers From the Imam Ḥusayn Conference* (London, 6th-9th July 1984), Norfolk: The Thetford Press Ltd., 1986, pp. 3–12.
Clinton, J.W., "Shams-i Qays on the Nature of Poetry," in *Edebiyât: the Journal of Middle Eastern Literatures*, 1, No. 2, 1989, pp. 101–127.
Clinton, J.W., *The Divan of Manūchihrī Dāmghānī*, Minneapolis: Bibliotheca Islamica, 1972.
Clohessy, C.P., *Fāṭima, Daughter of Muḥammad*, Piscataway, NJ: Gorgias Press, 2018.
Constitution of the Islamic Republic of Iran," (1989 Edition) translated by Firoozeh Papan-Matin, in *Iranian Studies*, Vol. 47, No. 1, 2014, pp. 159–200.

Dabashi, H., *Truth and Narrative: The Untimely Thoughts of ʿAyn al-Qudat al-Hamadhani*, Richmond Virginia: Curzon, 1999.
Dabiri, Gh., "Historiography and the Shoʿubiya Movement," in *Journal of Persianate Studies*, 6, 2013, pp. 216–234.
Dah shab: shabhā-yi shāʿirān va nivisandigān dar anjuman-i farhangī-yi Iran va ālmān, compiled by N. Muʾadhin, Tehran: Amīr Kabīr, 1357/1978.
Daryaee, T., "Food, Purity and Pollution: Zoroastrian Views on the Eating Habits of Others," in *Iranian Studies*, Vol. 45, No. 2, 2012, pp. 229–242.
Davis, D., "The Journey as Paradigm: Literal and Metaphoric Travel in Attar's *Mantiq al-Tayr*," in *Edebiyât: the Journal of Middle Eastern Literatures*, 4, 2, 1993, pp. 173–83.
Davis, D., *Epic and Sedition: The Case of Ferdowsi's Shāhnāmeh*, Fayetteville Arkansas: University of Arkansas Press, 1992 (reprinted Washington, DC: Mage Publishers, 2006).
Davis, D., *Faces of Love: Hafez and the Poets of Shiraz*, Washington D.C.: Mage Publishers, 2012.
Davis, D., *Ferdowsi: The Legend of Seyavash*, New York: Penguin Classics, 1992.
Davis, D., *Shahnameh: The Persian Book of Kings*, New York: Penguin Classics, 2006.
Davis, J.M., *Martyrs: Innocence, Vengeance, and Despair in the Middle East*, New York: Palgrave Macmillan, 2003.
Dībāchaʾī bar zīyārat: pāsukh ba shubahāt-i vahhābiyyat az dīdgāh-i dānishmandān-i shiʿa va ahl-i sunnat, Qumm, Payām-i Imām Hādī, 1394/2015, written by a research group called Payām-i Imām Hādī.
Dorraj, M., "Symbolic and Utilitarian Political Value of a Tradition: Martyrdom in the Iranian Political Culture," in *The Review of Politics*, 59, 3, 1997, pp. 489–521.
Duchesne-Guillemin, J., in *Encyclopaedia Iranica*, s.v. Ahriman.
Editors of EIr in *Encyclopaedia Iranica*, s.v. Children vii. Children's Literature.
Ekhtiari Amiri, R., K. Hasnita Binti Ku Samsu and H. Gholipour Fereidouni, "The Hajj and Iran's Foreign Policy towards Saudi Arabia," in *Journal of Asian and African Studies*, Vol. 46, No. 6, 2011, pp. 678–90.
Emami, K., "Water's Footsteps: A Poem," in *Iranian Studies*, Vol. 15, No. 1/4, 1982, pp. 97–116.
Elias, J.J., "Ultimate Sacrifice: Women and Motherhood in Iranian Visual Culture," in *The 'Other' Martyrs: Women and the Poetics of Sexuality, Sacrifice and Death in World Literatures*, ed. Alireza Korangy & Leyla Rouhi, Wiesbaden: Harrassowitz Verlag, 2019, pp. 39–54.
Enderwitz, S., in *Encyclopaedia of Islam, Second Edition*, s.v. al-Shuʿūbiyya.
Ernst, C.W., "On Losing One's Head: Hallājian Motifs and Authorial Identity in Poems Ascribed to ʿAttār," in *'Attār and the Persian Sufi Tradition, the Art of Spiritual Flight*, eds. L. Lewisohn & Ch. Shackle, London/New York: I.B. Tauris, 2006, pp. 330–343.
Ernst, C.W., "The Symbolism of Birds and Flight in the writings of Rūzbihān Baqlī," in *The Heritage of Sufism*, ed., L. Lewisohn, Vol. 2, Oxford: Oneworld, 1999 (repr 2003), pp. 353–66.
Essays on Nima Yushij: Animating Modernism in Persian Poetry, eds., A. Karimi-Hakkak and K. Talattof, Leiden: Brill, 2004.
Fahd, T., in *Encyclopaedia of Islam, Second Edition*, s.v. al-Lāt.

Farāhānī, Mīrzā Muḥammad Ḥusayn, *A Shiite Pilgrimage to Mecca 1885–1886: The Safarnāmeh of Mirzā Moḥammad Ḥosayn Farāhāni*, edited, translated, and annotated by Hafez Farmayan and Elton L. Daniel, London: Saqi Books, 1990.

Farhang-i dīvān-i ash'ār-i imām Khomeini, Tehran: Institute for the Compilation and Publication of Imam Khomeini's Works, 1372/1993.

Farhat-Holzman, L., "The Shahnameh of Ferdowsi: An Icon to National Identity," in *Comparative Civilization Review*, 2001, pp. 104–141.

Farhosh-van Loon, D., *Of Love and Longing: A Study of Ayatollah Khomeini's Mystical Poetry and its Reception in Iran and Abroad*, Leiden: unpublished PhD-Dissertation, 2016.

Farzad, N., "Qayṣar Amīnpūr and the Persian Poetry of Sacred Defence," in *British Journal of Middle Eastern Studies*. 34, 3, 2007, pp. 351–74.

Farzan, M., "Contemporary Poetry in Iran," in *Persian Literature*, ed. E. Yarshater, New York: State University of New York Press (Bibliotheca Persica), 1988, pp. 336–66.

Firdowsī, Abū 'l-Qāsim, *Shāh-nāma*, 8 Vols., ed. J. Khaleqi-Motlaq, Costa Mesa, CA / New York: Mazda Publishers, 1369/1990. (Tehran: Markaz-i Dāyirat 'l-Ma'ārif-i Buzurg-i Islāmī, 1387/2008; *The Shahnameh: The Book of Kings*. Edited by D. Khaleghi-Motlagh: vol. 1: New York: Bibliotheca Persica, 1988; vol. 5: Costa Mesa, CA: Mazda Publishers, and New York: Bibliotheca Persica, 1997; vol. 8: New York: Persian Heritage Foundation, 2008.

Fleet, K., G. Krämer, D. Matringe, J. Nawas and E. Rowson, *Encyclopaedia of Islam, Third Edition*, Leiden: Brill, 2012-present.

Fry, R.N., *The Golden Age of Persia*, London: Phoenix, 1975, reprinted 2003.

Gardet L., and J.-C. Vadet, in *Encyclopaedia of Islam, Second Edition*, s.v. Ḳalb.

Gardet, L., in *Encyclopaedia of Islam, Second Edition*, s.v. Allāh.

Gasiorowski, M.J., in *Encyclopaedia Iranica*, s.v. Coup d'Etat of 1332 š./1953.

Gazerani, S., "Why Was the Story of Arash-i Kamangir Excluded from the Shahnameh?," in *Iran-Nameh*, 1393/2014, 29, No. 2, pp. 43–63.

Gazerani, S., "Zahhak's Story and History," in *The Layered Heart: Essays on Persian Poetry, A Celebration in Honor of Dick Davis*, ed. Asghar Seyed-Gohrab, Washington D.C.: Mage Publishers, 2019, pp. 199–235.

Gershon Lewental, D., in *Encyclopædia Iranica*, s.v. Qādesiya, Battle of.

Ghaeni, Z., "The History of Children's Literature (1900–1940)," in *Literature of the Early Twentieth Century: From the Constitutional Period to Reza Shah*, ed. A.A. Seyed-Gohrab, London/New York: I.B. Tauris, 2015, pp. 448–469.

Ghanoonparvar, M.R., *Prophets of Doom: Literature as a Socio-Political Phenomenon in Modern Iran*, Lanham / New York: University Press of America, 1984.

Ghazalī, Aḥmad b. Muḥammad, *Sawāniḥ. Aḥmad Ghazzālī's Aphorismen über die Liebe*, Herausgegeben von Hellmut Ritter, Leipzig: Bibliotheca Islamica 15, 1942.

Gibb, E.J.W., *A History of Ottoman Poetry*, 6 Vols., London: Luzac, 1990.

Gibb, H.A.R., "The Social Significance of the Shu'ubiya," in *Studies on the Civilization of Islam*, eds. S.J. Shaw and W.R. Polk, Boston MA: Beacon Press, 1962, pp. 62–73.

Gieling, S., *Religion and War in Revolutionary Iran*, London/New York: I.B. Tauris, 1999.

Gieling, S., in *Encyclopaedia Iranica*, s.v. Iraq. vii. Iran-Iraq War.

Goldziher, I., "Die Šu'ūbijja unter den Muhammedanen in Spanien," in *Zeitschrift der Deutschen Morgenländischen Gesellschaft*, liii, 1899, pp. 601–20.

Gölz, O., "Dah Šab: Zehn Literaturabende in Teheran 1977: Der Kampf um das Monopol literarischer Legitimität," in *Die Welt des Islams*, 55, Nr. 1, 2015, pp. 83–111.

Gruber, C., "The Writing is on the Wall: Mural Arts in Post-Revolutionary Iran," in *Persica: Annual of the Dutch-Iranian Society*, 22, 2008, pp. 15–46.
Gruber, C., "The Martyrs' Museum in Tehran: Visualizing Memory in Post-Revolutionary Iran," in *Visual Anthropology*, 25, 1–2, 2012, pp. 68–97.
Haeri, S., "Temporary Marriage and the State in Iran: An Islamic Discourse on Female Sexuality," in *Social Research*, 59, No.1, 1992, pp. 201–23.
Haeri, S. *Law of Desire: Temporary Marrigaes in Shiʿi Iran*, Syracuse, NY: Syracuse University Press, 1989.
Ḥāfiẓ, Muḥammad Shams al-Dīn, *Dīvān*, ed. P. Nātil Khānlarī, Tehran: Khvārazmī, 1362/1983.
Ḥāfiẓ, Muḥammad Shams al-Dīn, *The Collected Lyrics of Háfiz of Shíráz*, Translated by Peter Avery, Cambridge: Archetype, 2007.
Ḥakīmī, I., "Barrisī-yi adabiyyāt-i inqilāb az buʿd-i ʿirfānī," in *Majmūʿa-yi maqālāt-i simīnār-i barrasī-yi adabiyyāt-i inqilāb-i islāmī*, Tehran: Samt, 1373/1994, pp. 149–66.
Hanaway, W.L., "The Cross and the Clock," in *Iranian Studies*, Vol. 30, No. 3/4, 1997, pp. 301–303.
Hawting, G.R., in *Encyclopaedia of Islam, Second Edition*, s.v. Yazīd (I) b. Muʿāwiya.
Heinrichs, W.P., "Observations on an Arabic Literary Debate," in *Dispute Poems and Dialogues in the Ancient and Mediaeval Near East: Forms and Types of Literary Debates in Semitic and Related Literatures*, ed. G.J. Reinink and Herman L.J. Vanstiphout, Leuven: Peeters, 1991, pp. 179–198.
Heinrichs, W.P., in *Encyclopaedia of Islam, Second Edition*, s.v. Ta<u>kh</u>yīl.
Hooglund, E., *Twenty Years of Islamic Revolution: Political and Social Transition in Iran Since 1979*, Syracuse, NY: Syracuse University Press, 2002.
Hovannisian, R.B., & G. Sabagh, ed., *The Persian Presence in the Islamic World*, Cambridge: Cambridge University Press, 1998.
Hunarjū, Ḥ., *Barf-i gul-i yās: majmūʿa-yi shiʿr-i kūdakān*, Tehran: Shāhid, 1376/1997.
Hunsberger, A.C., *Nasir Khusraw: the Ruby of Badakhshan, a Portrait of the Persian Poet, Traveller and Philosopher*, London/New York: I.B. Tauris, 2003.
Ḥuseynī ʿĀmilī, Siyyid Muḥsin Amīn, *Kashf al-irtīyāb*, (Persian Trans. by ʿAlī Akbar Tihrānī, Tehran: Bītā, 1357/1978).
Ḥuseynī, S.Ḥ., *Guzīda-yi shiʿr-i jang va difāʿ-i muqaddas*, Tehran: Sūra-yi Mihr, 1381/2002.
Ḥuseynī, S.Ḥ., *Ham-ṣidā bā ḥalq-i Ismāʿīl*, Tehran: Sūra-yi Mihr, 1387/2008.
Ibn Qutayba, *The Excellence of the Arabs*, ed. J.E. Montgomery and P. Webb, Translated by S. Bowen Savant and P. Webb, New York: New York University Press, 2017.
ʿIshqī, Muḥammad Rizā Mīrzāda, *Kulliyyāt-i Muṣavvar-i ʿIshqī*, ed. ʿAlī Akbar Mushīr Salīmī, New York, Piedmont: Jahan Book, 1985.
Jacobi, R., in *Encyclopaedia of Islam, Second Edition*, s.v. ʿU<u>dh</u>rī.
Jamālī, Ḥāmed ibn Fażl-Allāh, *The Mirror of Meanings*, trans. By A.A. Seyed-Gohrab, Costa Mesa, CA: Mazda Publishers, 2002.
Jamshidi, A., "Lizard as Arab Food: Representation of Arabs and the Shāhnāmeh scholarship," in *Persian Language, Literature and Culture: New Leaves, Fresh Looks*, ed. K. Talattof, London / New York: Routledge, 2015, pp. 318–36.
Jazayeri, M.A., "Recent Persian Literature: Observations on Themes and Tendencies," in *Critical perspectives on Modern Persian Literature*, ed. T.M. Ricks, Washington: Three Continents Press, 1984, pp 70–87.

Kahdūʾī, M.K. "Barrisī-yi adabiyyāt-i takhdīrī, bī-hadaf va mutiʿahhid dar dowrān-i muʿāṣir va taḥavvul-i ānhā dar dowra-yi inqilāb-i islāmī," in *Majmūʿa-yi maqālāt-i simīnār-i barrasī-yi adabiyyāt-i inqilāb-i islāmī*, Tehran: Samt, 1373/1994, pp. 479–493.
Kamrava, M., "Khomeini and the West," in *A Critical Introduction to Khomeini*, ed. A. Adib-Moghaddam, Cambridge: Cambridge University Press, 2014, pp. 161–62.
Karamustafa, A.T., *Sufism, the Formative Period*, Edinburgh: Edinburgh University Press, 2007.
Karimi, P., "Imagining Warfare, Imaging welfare: Tehran's Post Iran-Iraq War Murals and their Legacy," in *Persica: Annual of the Dutch-Iranian Society*, 22, 2008, pp. 47–63.
Karimi, P. and C. Gruber, "Introduction: The Politics and Poetics of the Child Image in Muslim Contexts," in *Comparative Studies of South Asia, Africa and the Middle East*, Volume 32, Number 2, 2012, pp. 273–293.
Karimi-Hakkak, A., "Revolutionary Posturing: Iranian Writers and the Iranian Revolution of 1979," in *International Journal of Middle East Studies*, 23, 4, 1991, pp. 507–531.
Karimi-Hakkak, A., "Introduction: Iran's Literature 1977–1997," in *Iranian Studies*, Vol. 30, No. 3/4, 1997, pp. 193–213.
Karimi-Hakkak, A., *A Fire of Lilies: Perspectives on Literature and Politics in Modern Iran*, Leiden: Leiden University Press, 2019.
Karimi-Hakkak, A., *Recasting Persian Poetry: Scenarios of Poetic Modernity in Iran*, Salt Lake City: University of Utah Press, 1995.
Kāshānī, ʿIzz al-Dīn Maḥmūd, "Kunūz al-asrār va-rumūz al-aḥrār," in *Shurūḥ-i savāniḥ*, ed. A. Mujāhid, Tehran: Surūsh, 1372/1993.
Kāshānī, S., "Adabiyyāt-i inqilābī va mubāriza bā istikbār," in *Majmūʿa-yi maqālāt-i simīnār-i barrasī-yi adabiyyāt-i inqilāb-i islāmī*, Tehran: Samt, 1373/1994, pp. 401–10.
Katouzian, H., "The Campaign against the Anglo-Iranian Agreement of 1919," in *British Journal of Middle Eastern Studies*, 25, No. 1, 1998, pp. 5–46.
Katouzian, H., *Musaddiq and the Struggle for Power in Iran*, London: I.B. Tauris, 1990.
Kermani, N., in *The Encyclopaedia of the Qur'ān*, s.v. Intellect.
Keshavarzian, A., "How Islamic Was the Revolution?" in *Middle East Report*, No. 250, The Islamic Revolution at 30, Spring, 2009.
Khaleghi-Motlagh, Dj., in *Encyclopaedia Iranica*, s.v. Aždahā. ii. In Persian Literature.
Khāqānī-yi Shirvānī, Afżal al-Dīn Bādil Ibrāhīm ibn ʿAlī, *Dīvān*, ed. ʿAlī ʿAbd ʿl-Raṣūlī, Tehran: Marvī, 2537/1979.
Khomeini, Ruḥullāh Musavī, *Dīvān*, Tehran: Muʾassisa-yi Tanẓīm-u Nashr-i Āthār-i Imām Khomeini, 16th edition, 1377/1998.
Khomeini, Ruḥullāh Musavī, *Islam and Revolution*, Trans. H. Algar, London: New York, 2010 (earlier edition 2002, Kegan Paul International)
Khorrami, M.M., "Narratives of Silence; Persian Fiction of the 1980–1988 Iran-Iraq War," in *Moments of Silence: Authenticity in the Cultural Expression of the Iran-Iraq War, 1980–1988*, ed. A. Khakpour, M.M. Khorrami & Sh. Vatanabadi, New York: New York University Press, 2016, pp. 217–35.
Khorrami, M.M., *Literary Subterfuge and Contemporary Persian Fiction: Who write Iran?*, London / New York: Routledge, 2015.
Khosronejad, P., "Introduction: Unburied Memories," in *Unburied Memories, Visual Anthropology*, 25, 1–2, 2012, pp. 1–21.
Khushnām, M., "Nigāhī gudharā bar shiʿr-i Nādir Nādirpūr," in *Irān-Nāma*, 1378/1999, issues 68–9, pp. 839–48.

Kian, A., "Gendered Khomeini," *A Critical Introduction to Khomeini*, ed. Adib-Moghaddam, Cambridge: Cambridge University Press, 2013, pp. 170–92.
Knysh, A., "'*Irfān* Revisited: Khomeini and the Legacy of Islamic Mystical Philosophy," *Middle East Journal*, 46, 4, 1992, pp. 631–53.
Korangy, A., "A Literary and Historical Background of Martyrdom in Iran," in *Comparative Studies of South Asia, Africa and the Middle East*, 29, No. 3, 2009, pp. 528–543.
Kramer, M., *Arab Awakening and Islamic Revival: The Politics of Ideas in the Middle East*, New Brunswick / London: Transaction Publishers, 1996.
Landau, J., "Naṣīr al-Dīn Ṭūsī and Poetic Imagination in the Arabic and Persian Philosophical Tradition," in *Metaphor and Imagery in Persian Poetry*, ed. A.A. Seyed-Gohrab, Leiden / Boston: Brill, 2012, pp. 15–65.
Lange, Ch., *Justice, Punishment, and the Medieval Muslim Imagination*, Cambridge: Cambridge University Press, 2008.
Lecomte, G., in *Encyclopaedia of Islam, Second Edition*, s.v. Ibn Ḳutayba.
Levi Della Vida, G., in *Encyclopaedia of Islam, Second Edition*, s.v. Salmān al-Fārisī.
Lewental, D.G. "'Saddam's Qadisiyyah': Religion and History in the Service of State Ideology in Ba'thi Iraq," in *Middle Eastern Studies*, 2014, Vol. 50, Issue 6, pp. 891–910.
Lewis, F.D., "Review of Joya Blondel Saad's The Image of Arabs in Modern Persian Literature," *Iranian Studies*, issue 32, No. 1, (1999), pp. 163–167.
Lewis, F.D. *Rumi. Past and Present, East and West: The Life, Teachings and Poetry of Jalâl al-Din Rūmī*. Oxford: Oneword Publications, 2000.
Lewisohn, L., "Prolegomenon to the Study of Ḥāfiẓ: 2- The Mystical Milieu: Ḥāfiẓ's Erotic Spirituality," in *Hafiz and the Religion of Love in Classical Persian Poetry*, London: New York: I.B. Tauris, 2010, pp. 31–6.
Maghen, Z., in *Encyclopaedia of Islam, Third Edition*, s.v. Ablution.
Marashi, A., *Nationalizing Iran: Culture, Power, and the State, 1870–1940*, Seattle, W.A.: University of Washington Press, 2008.
Marashi, A., "The Nation's Poet: Ferdowsi and the Iranian National Imagination," in *Iran in the 20th Century Historiography and Political Culture*, ed. T. Atabaki, London: I.B. Tauris, 2009, pp. 93–111.
Martin, V., *Creating an Islamic State: Khomeini and the Making of a New Iran*, London / New York: I.B. Tauris, second print 2003.
Marzolph, U., "The Martyr's Way to Paradise: Shiite Mural Art in the Urban Context," in *Ethnologia Europaea*, 33, 2, 2003, pp. 87–98.
Matini, J., "Nādir Nādirpūr Shā'ir-i chīra-dast (1308–1378)," in *Irān-shināsī*, 1379/ 2000, 46, pp. 402–03.
McAuliffe, Jane Dammen, ed., *The Encyclopaedia of the Qur'ān*, Leiden: Brill, 6 Vols. 2001–2006.
Mehran, G., in *Encyclopaedia Iranica*, s.v. Education. xxiv. Education in Postrevolutionary Persia, 1979–95.
Meisami, Julie Scott, "Allegorical Gardens in the Persian Poetic Tradition: Nezami, Rūmī, Hafez," in *International Journal of Middle East Studies*, Vol. 17, No. 2, May, 1985, pp. 229–260.
Meisami, Julie Scott, *Medieval Persian Court Poetry*, Princeton: Princeton University Press, 1987.
Melchert, Ch., "Khargūshī, *Tahdhīb al-asrār*," in *Bulletin of the School of Oriental and African Studies*, 73, 2010, pp. 29–44.

Melville, C.P., in *Encyclopaedia of Islam, Second Edition*, s.v. Sarbadārids.
Milani, F., "Simin Behbahani: Iran's National Poet," in *Iranian Studies*, Vol. 41, No. 1 (2008), pp. 3–17.
Mīrshakkāk, Y-ʿA, *Sitīz bā khīshtan: Majmūʿa-yi maqālāt*, Tehran: Barg, 1369/1990.
Mohaddessin, M., *Islamic Fundamentalism: The New Global Threat*, Washington D.C.: Seven Locks Press, 1993.
Momen, M., *An Introduction to Shi'i Islam: The History and Doctrines of Twelver Shi'ism*, New Haven, CT, and London: Yale University Press, 1985.
Montgomery Watt, W., in *Encyclopaedia of Islam, Second Edition*, s.v. Abū Djahl.
Montgomery Watt, W., in *Encyclopaedia of Islam, Second Edition*, s.v. Āmina.
Montgomery Watt, W., in *Encyclopaedia of Islam, Second Edition*, s.v. Abū Lahab.
Moosavi, A., "How to write Death: Resignifying Martyrdom in Two Novels of the Iran-Iraq War," in *Alif: Journal of Comparative Poetics*, No. 35, 2015, pp. 1–23.
Moosavi, A. "Stepping Back from the Front: A Glance at Home Front Narratives of the Iran-Iraq War in Persian and Arabic Fiction," in *Moments of Silence: Authenticity in the Cultural Expression of the Iran-Iraq War, 1980–1988*, ed. A. Khakpour, M.M. Khorrami & Sh. Vatanabadi, New York: New York University Press, 2016, p. 120–37.
Mottahedeh, R., "The Shuʿubiyah Controversy and the Social History of Early Islamic Iran," in *International Journal of Middle Eastern Studies*, 7, 1976, pp. 161–82.
Muʾayyad, Siyyid Riżā, *Yād-nāma-yi sivvumīn kungira-yi sarāsarī-yi shiʿr-u adab*, Khurāsān: Idāra-yi kull-i irshād-i islāmī, Chāp-khāna-yi dānishgāh-i Mashhad, 1363/1984.
Mudarrisī, F., "Rāzhā-yi Āyatollāh," in *Shahrvand*, 1386/2007, Ābān, No. 23.
Mumtaḥin, Ḥuseyn-ʿAlī, *Nihzat-i shuʿubiyya: junbish-i milli-yi irāniyān dar barābar-i khalāfat-i umavī va ʿAbbāsī*, Tehran: Kitābhā-yi Jībī, 1354/1975, second print 1370/1991.
Mūsavī Khuʾīnīhā, Muḥammad, "Ḥajj az dīdgāh-i imām," in *Pāsdār-i islām*, 5, 55 issue, 1365/1986, pp. 32–35.
Mūsavī Khuʾīnīhā, Muḥammad, "Hamrāh bā imām ba sū-yi ḥajj: pāygāh-i inqilāb-i jahānī-yi islām," in *Pāsdār-i islām*, 5, 67 issue, 1366/1987, pp. 27–42.
Mushīrī, F., *Guzīna-yi ashʿār*, Tehran: Murvārīd, 1371/1992.
Naderpour, N., "Une contradiction: L'âme iranienne et l'esprit islamique," in *Die Welt des Islams*, Vol. 23/24, 1984, pp. 129–135.
Nādirpūr, N., *'Een schipper van was, kleiner dan God': Gedichten van Nader Naderpur*, translated by J.T.P. de Bruijn and A. Seyed-Gohrab, Leidschendam: Quist, 2006.
Nādirpūr, N., "Huviyyat-i millī va zabān-i mushtarak," in *Kitāb-i Nīmā*, no. 3, 1990, pp. 19–37.
Nādirpūr, N., "Irānīyān yikka-savārān-i du-gānigī (andīshihāʾī dar bāra-yi milliyyat va farhang-i īrānī va peyvandishān bā zabān-i pārsī," in *Irān-nāma*, 1373/1994, issue 47, pp. 439–72.
Nādirpūr, N., *Majmūʿa-yi ashʿār*, California, Los Angeles: Kitāb Corp, 2002.
Nādirpūr, N., *False Dawn: Persian Poems*, Introduction and Translations by M.C. Hillmann, afterword by Leonardo P. Alishan, Literature East & West, Austin, Texas: 1986.
Naficy, H., *A Social History of Iranian Cinema, The Islamicate Period 1978–1984*, Vol. 3, Durham / London: Duke University Press, 2012.
Najmabadi, A., "The Erotic Vatan [Homeland] as Beloved and Mother: To Love, to Possess, and To Protect," in *Comparative Studies in Society and History*, Vol. 39, No. 3, 1997, pp. 442–467.

Nanquette, L., "An Iranian Woman's Memoir on the Iran-Iraq War: The Production and Reception of Da," in *Iranian Studies*, 46, no. 6 (2013): 943–957.
Naqd-u taḥlīl-i shiʿr-i difāʿ-i muqaddas, Vol. I, ed. M. Akbarī, Tehran: Sāzmān-i madārik-i farhangī-yi inqilāb-i islāmī, 1377/1998.
Nematollahi Mahani, M., *'Do Not Say They Are Dead': The Political Use of Mystical and Religious Concepts in the Poetry of the Iran-Iraq War*, Unpublished PhD Dissertation, Leiden University, 2014.
Niʿmatullāhī Sālihī Najafābādī, *Shahīd-i Jāvīd*, Tehran: Fardā, 1382/2003.
Niẓāmī ʿArūżī, *Chahār maqāla*, ed. Muḥammad ibn ʿAbd al-Vahhāb Qazvīnī, Berlin; Iranschahr, 1927. (*Revised Translation of the Chahar Maqala*, Edward G. Browne, London: Luzac, 1921)
Niẓāmī Ganjavī, *Layli and Majnun*, transl. by Dick Davis, Washington DC.: Mage Publishers, 2020.
Niẓāmī Ganjavī, *Laylī u Majnūn*, ed. V. Dastgirdī, Tehran: Armaghān, 1313/1934, second edition, ʿIlmī, 1363/1984.
Norris, H.T., "Shuʿūbiyya in Arabic Literature," in *Cambridge History of Arabic Literature: Abbasid Belles-Letters*, eds., J. Ashtiany et al, Cambridge: Cambridge University Press, 1990, pp. 31–47.
Omidsalar, M., in *Encyclopaedia Iranica*, s.v. Kāva.
Omidsalar, M., *Iran's Epic and America's Empire*, Santa Monica, California: Afshar Publishing, 2012.
One Women's War, Da (Mother): The Memoirs of Seyyedeh Zahra Ḥuseyni, translated by Paul Sprachman, Costa Mesa, CA: Mazda Publishers, 2014.
Oostrom, F., van, *Het woord van eer: literatuur aan het Hollandse hof omstreeks 1400*, Amsterdam: Ooievaar, 1996.
Pannewick, D. ed., *Martyrdom in Literature: Visions of Death and Meaningful Suffering in Europe and the Middle East from Antiquity to Modernity*, Wiesbaden: Reichert Verlag, 2004.
Papan-Matin, F., *Beyond Death: The Mystical Teaching of ʿAyn al-Qudāt al-Hamadāni*, Leiden: Brill, 2010.
Pourshariati, P., "The *Akhbār al-Tiwāl* of Abū Ḥanīfa Dīnawarī: A *Shuʿūbī* Treatise on Late Antique Iran," in *Sources for the History of Sasanian and post-Sasanian Iran*, ed., R. Gyselen, (collection *Res Orientales* 19), Bures-sur-Yvette: Groupe pour l'Étude de la Civilisation du Moyen-Orient, 2010, pp. 201–289.
Pūrjavadī, N., "Manbaʿī kuhan dar bāb-i malāmatiyyān-i Neyshābūr," in *Maʿārif*, 15, No. 1–2, 1377/1998, pp. 3–50.
Rādfar, Abū 'l-Qāsim, "Digargūnīhā va vīzhigīhā-yi adabiyyāt-i inqilāb-i islāmī dar yik nigāh," in *Majmūʿa-yi maqālāt-i simīnār-i barrasī-yi adabiyyāt-i inqilāb-i islāmī*, Tehran: Samt, 1373/1994, pp. 183–192.
Rahnema, A., *An Islamic Utopian: A Political Biography of Ali Shari'ati*, London: I.B. Tauris, 1998.
Rakel, E.P., "Iranian Foreign Policy Since the Iranian Islamic Revolution: 1979–2006," in *The Greater Middle East in Global Politics*, ed. M.P. Amineh, Leiden: Brill, 2007, pp.147–77.
Rakel, E.P., *The Iranian Political Elite, State and Society Relations, and Foreign Relations Since the Islamic Revolution*, PhD Dissertation, University of Amsterdam, 2008.

Raven, W., in *Encyclopaedia of the Qur'ān*, ed. Jane Dammen McAuliffe, Brill, Leiden–Boston–Koln, Vol. I, 2001, s.v. Martyrdom, pp. 281–86.

Rāzī, Najm al-Dīn, *Mirṣād al-ʿibād*, ed. M.A. Riyāḥī, Tehran: ʿIlmī va Farhangī, 1371/1992.

Reckendorf, H., in *Encyclopaedia of Islam, Second Edition*, s.v. ʿAmmār ibn Yāsir.

Reinert, B., "Ḫumainī im Spiegel seiner Gedichte," in *Islamische Grenzen und Grenzübergänge*, Vol. 4, Bern: Peter Lang AG, 2007, pp. 191–293.

Renard, J., "Images of Abraham in the Writings of Jalāl ad-Dīn Rūmī," in *Journal of the American Oriental Society*, Vol. 106, No. 4, 1986, pp. 633–40.

Rezvani, S., in, *Encyclopædia Iranica*, s.v. Bihbahani, Simin ii. Poetry.

Richter-Bernburg, L., "Linguistic Shuʿūbīya and Early Neo-Persian Prose," in *Journal of the American Oriental Society*, 94, 1, 1974, pp. 55–64.

Ridgeon, L., "Hidden Khomeini: Mysticism and Poetry," in *A Critical Introduction to Khomeini*, ed. A. Adib-Moghaddam, Cambridge: Cambridge University Press, 2014, pp. 193–210.

Ridgeon, L., "The Zūrkhāna between Tradition and Change," in *Iran: Journal of the British Institute of Persian Studies*, Vol. 45, 2007, pp. 243–265.

Ritter, H., *Das Meer der Seele: Mensch, Welt und Gott in den Geschichten des Fariduddin ʿAṭṭār*, Leiden: E.J. Brill, 1955 (*The Ocean of the Soul: Man, the World and God in the Stones of Farīd al-Dīn ʿAṭṭār*, Translated by John O'Kane with Editorial Assistance of Bernd Radtke, Leiden / Boston: Brill, 2003).

Robson, J., in *Encyclopaedia of Islam, Second Edition*, s.v. Abū Dharr Ghifārī.

Rosenthal, F., in *Encyclopaedia Iranica*, s.v. Ebn Qotayba, Abū Moḥammad ʿAbd-Allāh.

Rūmī, Jalāl al-Dīn, *Dīvān-i Shams-i Tabrīzī*, ed. B.Z. Furūzānfar, Tehran: Amīr Kabīr, 1378/1999, 10 Vols.

Rūmī, Jalāl al-Dīn, *Mathnavī-yi maʿnavī*, 6 Vols. ed. Muḥammad Istiʿlāmī, Tehran: Zavvār, 1372/1993.

Rūmī, Jalāl al-Dīn, *The Mathnawí of Jalálu'ddín Rúmí*, edited and translated by R.A. Nicholson, 8 Vols., Cambridge: University of Cambridge, 1925–1940.

Rūmī, Jalāl al-Dīn, *The Masnavi of Jalāloddin Rumi Book 2 The Ending of the Self, A New English Translation with Explanatory Notes Alan Williams With the Persian Text Edited by Mohammad Esteʿlami*, London / New York: I.B. Tauris, 2020.

Rustow, D.A., "The Political Impact Of The West," in *The Cambridge History of Islam*, eds. P.M. Holt, A.K.S. Lambton, B. Lewis, Cambridge: Cambridge University Press, 1977, pp. 673–697.

Saad, J.B., *The Image of Arabs in Modern Persian Literature*, Lanham, New York and London: University Press of America, 1996.

Saʿdī, Muṣliḥ al-Dīn, *Būstān*, ed. G.H. Yūsufī, Tehran: Khᵛārazmī, 1375/1996.

Sanāʾī, Abū 'l-Majd Majdūd ibn Ādam, *Ḥadīqat al-ḥaqīqa va sharīʿat al-ṭariqa*, ed. Maryam Ḥuseynī, Tehran: Markaz-i Nashr- Dānishgāhī, 1382/2004.

Sanāʾī, Abū 'l-Majd Majdūd ibn Ādam, *Ḥadīqat al-ḥaqīqa*, ed. Mudarris-i Rażavī, Tehran: Intishārāt-i dānishgāh-i Tehran, 1368/1989.

Ṣanʿatī, Muḥammad Ḥuseyn, *Āshnā'ī bā adabiyyāt-i difāʿ-i muqaddas*, Tehran: bunyād-i ḥifẓ-i āthār va nashr-i arzishhā-yi difāʿ-i muqaddas, 1389/2010.

Savant, S.B., "Shu'ubis" in *The Princeton Encyclopedia of Islamic Political Thought*, ed. Gerhard Böwering, Princeton: Princeton University Press, 2013.

Schimmel, A., *A Two-Colored Brocade: The Imagery of Persian Poetry*. Chapel Hill & London: University of North Carolina Press, 1992.

Schimmel, A., *Deciphering the Signs of God: A Phenomenological Approach to Islam*, New York: State University of New York 1994.

Schimmel, A., "Reason and Mystical Experience in Sufism," in *Intellectual Traditions in Islam*, ed. F. Daftary, London / New York: I.B. Tauris, 2000, reprinted 2001, pp. 130–45.

Schimmel, A., *Mystical Dimensions of Islam*, Chapel Hill: The University of North Carolina Press, 1975.

Scott, Aghaie Kamran. "Fatemeh, Zeynab, and Emerging Discourses on Gender," in *The Martyrs of Karbala: Shi'i Symbols and Rituals in Modern Iran,* Washington, Seattle: University of Washington Press, 2004, pp. 113–130.

Sells, M., in *Huffington Post* entitled "Wahhabist Ideology: What It Is And Why It's A Problem" (published 12/20/2016) (last accessed 16.11.2018)

Seyed-Gohrab, A.A., "'Martyrs of Love': Genesis, Development and Twentieth Century Political Application of a Sufi Concept," in *Martyrdom: Canonization, Contestation and Afterlives*, ed. I. Saloul & J.W. van Henten, Amsterdam: Amsterdam University Press, 2020, pp. 129–51.

Seyed-Gohrab, A.A., "'The Traveller' and the Sun's Companionship: Universal Mysticism in Sohrâb Sepehri," in *Writings and Writing: From Another World and Another Era*, ed. R.M. Kerr & T. Milo, Cambridge: Archetype, 2010, pp. 393–447.

Seyed-Gohrab, A.A., "Khomeini the Poet Mystic," in *Die Welt des Islams: International Journal for the Study of Modern Islam*, 51, 2011, pp. 438–458.

Seyed-Gohrab, A.A., "Life, Cult and Impact of Khāja ʿAbdullāh Anṣārī of Hirāt." in *Āshnāyān-i rah-i ʿishq: majmūʿa maqālātī dar muʿarrifī-yi shānzda ʿarif-i buzurg*, ed. M.R. Isfandyār, Tehran: Iran University Press, 2005, pp. 135–66.

Seyed-Gohrab, A.A., "Martyrdom as Piety, Mysticism and National Icon in Iran," in *Der Islam: Zeitschrift für Geschichte und Kultur des islamischen Orients*. 87, 1–2, 2012, pp. 248–73.

Seyed-Gohrab, A.A., "Of Poetry and Politics: Poetry as Awakening," in *Literature of the Early Twentieth Century: From the Constitutional Period to Reza Shah*, ed. A.A. Seyed-Gohrab, London: I.B. Tauris, 2015, pp. 103–10.

Seyed-Gohrab, A.A., "Poetry as Awakening: Singing Modernity," in *Literature of the Early Twentieth Century: From the Constitutional Period to Reza Shah*, ed. A.A. Seyed-Gohrab, London / New York: I.B. Tauris, 2015, pp. 30–132.

Seyed-Gohrab, A.A., "Satan as the Lover of God in Islamic Mystical Writings," in *The Beloved in Middle East Literature: The Culture of Love and Languishing*, edited by Alireza Korangy, Hanadi Al-Samman, Michael Beard, London / New York: I.B. Tauris, 2017, pp. 85–101.

Seyed-Gohrab, A.A., "The Erotic Spirit: Love, Man and Satan in Hafez's Poetry," in *Hafiz and The School of Love in Classical Persian Poetry*, ed. L. Lewisohn, London: I.B. Tauris, 2010, pp. 107–21.

Seyed-Gohrab, A.A., "The Rhetoric of Persian Verbal Contests: Innovation and Creativity in Debates between the Persians and the Arabs," in *Disputation Literature in the Near East and Beyond*, ed. Enrique Jiménez and Catherine Mittermayer, Berlin: De Gruyter, 2020, pp. 261–82.

Seyed-Gohrab, A.A., "The Rose and the Wine: Dispute as a Literary Device in Classical Persian Literature," in *Iranian Studies*, 2013, Vol. 47, No. 1, pp. 69–85.

Seyed-Gohrab, A.A., "The Tuin Qom," in *ZemZem: Tijdschrift over het Midden-Oosten, Noord-Afrika en Islam*, Issue 15, No. 1, 2019, pp. 34–7.

Seyed-Gohrab, A.A., "Waxing Eloquent: The Masterful Variations on Candle Metaphors in the Poetry of Hafiz and his Predecessors," in *Metaphor and Imagery in Persian Poetry*, Leiden / Boston: E.J. Brill, 2012, pp. 81–123

Seyed-Gohrab, A.A., *Courtly Riddles: Enigmatic Embellishments in Early Persian Poetry*, Leiden: Leiden University Press, 2010.

Seyed-Gohrab, A.A., in *Encyclopædia Iranica*, s.v. Leyli o Majnun.

Seyed-Gohrab, A.A., *Laylī and Majnūn: Love, Madness and Mystic Longing in Niẓāmī's Epic Romance*, Leiden: Brill, 2003.

Seyed-Gohrab, A.A., "Rūmī's Antinomian Poetic Philosophy," in *Mawlana Rumi Review*, Issue IX, No. 1–2, 2018, pp. 159–99.

Seyed-Gohtrab, A.A., "The Flourishing of Persian Quatrains," in *A History of Persian Literature: Persian Lyric Poetry in the Classical Era 800–1500: Ghazals. Panegyrics and Quatrains*, Vol. II, ed. E. Yarshater, London: I.B. Tauris, 2019, pp. 488–568.

Shafī'ī-Kadkanī, M.R., *Dar hargiz-u hamīshigī-yi insān: az mīrāth-i 'irfānī-yi Khāja 'Abdullāh Anṣārī*, Tehran: Sukhan, 1994/2015.

Shafī'ī-Kadkanī, M.R., *Chirāgh-u āyina: dar justijū-yi taḥavvul-i shi'r-i mu'āṣir-i Iran*, Tehran: Sukhan, 4th print 1392/2013.

Shahbazi, Sh.A., in *Encyclopaedia Iranica*, s.v. Flags. i. of Persia.

Shahnahpur, S., *Writing War in Contemporary Iran: The Case of Esmā'il Fasih's Zemestān-e 62*, New York: Peter Lang Publishing, 2019.

Shaki, M., "An Introduction to Modern Persian Literature," in *Critical perspectives on Modern Persian Literature*, ed. T.M. Ricks, Washington: Three Continents Press, 1984, pp. 26–41.

Shakibi, Z., *Pahlavi Iran and the Politics of Occidentalism: The Shah and the Rastakhiz Party*, London: I.B. Tauris, 2020.

Shamīsā, S., *Shāhid-bāzī dar adabiyyāt-i Fārsī*, Tehran: Firdows, 1381/2002.

Shams al-Dīn Muḥammad ibn Qays al-Rāzī, *al-Mu'jam fī ma'āyir ash'ār al-'ajam*, re-edited by S. Shamīsā (this edition is based on the original critical edition by Qazvīnī [London, 1909] and red-edited by Mudarris Rażavī, [Tehran, 1959]), Tehran: Rāmīn, 1388/ 2009.

Shams, F., "Dialogues with the Dead: Necropoetics of Zahra's Paradise," in Iranian Studies, Vol. 53, Nos. 5–6, 2019, pp. 893–909.

Shams, F., "From Revolution to Silence: The Political and Literary Life of Qaysar Amīnpūr," in *The Layered Heart: Essays on Persian Poetry, A Celebration in Honor of Dick Davis*, ed. Asghar Seyed-Gohrab, Washington D.C.: Mage Publishers, 2019, pp. 551–88.

Shams, F., "Ideology of Warfare and the Islamic Republic's Poetry of War," in *International Journal of Persian Literature*, Vol. 1, 2016, pp. 5–58.

Shams, F., *A Revolution in Rhyme: Poetic Co-option under the Islamic Republic*, Oxford: Oxford University Press, 2021.

Sharī'atī, 'Alī, *Shahādat*, Tehran: Sāzmān-i Intishārāt-i Ḥuseyniyya Irshād, 1350/1971.

Sharma, S., *Persian Poetry at the Indian Frontier: Mas'ūd Sa'd Salmān of Lahore*, Delhi: Permanent Black, 2000.

Siegel, E., "The Politics of Shahid-e Jawid," in *The Twelver Shia in Modern Times: Religious Culture & Political History*, ed. Rainer Brunner and Werner Ende, Leiden: Brill, 2001, pp. 150–77.

Soroudi, S., in *Encyclopaedia Iranica*, s.v. Constitutional Revolution, vii. the Constitutional Movement in Literature.

Sprachman, P., "The Poetics of *Hijāb* in the Satire of Iraj Mirzā," *Iran and Iranian Studies: Essays in Honor of Iraj Afshar*, ed. K. Eslami, Princeton, NJ: Zagros, 1998, pp. 341–57.

Steingass, F., *Persian-English Dictionary*, London: Routledge, 1892, fifth print 1963.

Ṭabarī, Muḥammad ibn Jarīr, *The History of Tabari*, Vol. XI (The Challenge to the Empires A.D. 633–635/A.H. 12–13), trans. Khalid Yahya Blankinship, Albany: State University of New York Press, 1993.

Tafażżolī, A., in *Encyclopaedia Iranica*, s.v. Āraš.

Taheri Shemirani, S., "The War of the Cities," in *The Iran-Iraq War: The Politics of Aggression*, ed., F. Rajaee, Gainesville, Florida: University of Florida Press, 1993, pp. 31–40.

Talattof, K., "'I Will Rebuild You, Oh My Homeland': Simin Behbahani's Work and Sociopolitical Discourse," in *Iranian Studies*, 41, 1, 2008, pp. 19–36.

Talattof, K., "What Kind of Wine Did Rudaki Desire? Samanids' Search for Cultural and National Identity," in *The Layered Heart: Essays on Persian Poetry, A Celebration in Honor of Dick Davis*, ed. A.A. Seyed-Gohrab, Washington DC: Mage Publishers, 2019, pp. 127–171.

Talattof, K., "Sexuality and Cultural Change: The Presentation of Sex and Gender in Pre- and Post-revolutionary Iranian Cinema," in *Conflict and Development in Iranian Film*, Leiden: Leiden University Press, 2010, pp. 31–48.

Talattof, K., *Modernity, Sexuality, and Ideology in Iran the Life and Legacy of a Popular Female Artist*, Syracuse, N.Y.: Syracuse University Press, 2011.

Talattof, K., *The Politics of Writing in Iran: A History of Modern Persian Literature*, Syracuse, NY: Syracuse University Press, 2000.

Taqavī, M., "Jahat-gīrī-yi adabiyyāt-i muʿāṣir va taḥavvul-i ān pas az inqilāb," in *Majmūʿa-yi maqālāt-i simīnār-i barrasī-yi adabiyyāt-i inqilāb-i islāmī*, Tehran: Samt, 1373/1994, pp. 103–113.

Tavakoli-Targhi, M., "From Patriotism to Matriotism: A Tropological Study of Iranian Nationalism, 1870–1909," in *International Journal of Middle East Studies*, Vol. 34, No. 2, 2002, pp. 217–238.

Ṭūsī, Naṣīr al-Dīn, *Shiʿr va shāʿirī dar āthār-i khāja Naṣīr al-Dīn Ṭūsī*, ed. Muʿaẓẓama Iqbālī (Aʿẓam), Tehran: Sāzmān-i Chāp va Intishārāt-i Vizārat-i Farhang va Irshād-i Islāmī, 1992.

Utas, B., "The Munājāt or Ilāhī-nāmah of ʿAbdu'llāh Anṣārī," in *Manuscripts of the Middle East*, 3, 1988, pp. 83–7.

Vaḥīdī, S., *Dīvān*, Tehran: Vizārat-i Farhang va Irshād-i islāmī, 1389/2010.

Vaḥshī Bāfqī, *Nāẓir and Manẓūr*, in *Dīvān*, ed. P. Bābā'ī, Tehran: Nigāh, 1373/1994.

Venzlaff, H., "Mohr-e Namāz: Das schiitische Gebetssiegel," in *Die Welt des Islams*, Vol. 35, Issue 2, 1995, pp. 250–275.

Waardenburg, J., in *Encyclopaedia of the Qur'ān*, s.v. Death and the dead.

Waugh, E.H., in *Encyclopaedia of the Qur'ān*, s.v. Blood and Blood Clot.

Webb, P., *Imagining the Arabs: Arab Identity and the Rise of Islam*, Edinburgh: Edinburgh University Press, 2016.

Webb, P., "Fragmentation and Integration: A Response to the Contributions by Hugh Kennedy and Walter Pohl," in *Empires and Communities in the Post-Roman and Islamic World c.*

400–1000 CE, eds Walter Pohl and Rutger Kramer, Oxford University Press, 2021, pp. 76–88.
Wensinck, A.J., and J. Jomier, in *Encyclopaedia of Islam, Second Edition*, s.v. Kaʿba.
Yarshater, E., "A Star Ceases to Shine," in *Persica: Annual of the Dutch-Iranian Society*, Vol. 17, 2001, pp. 137–53.
Yarshater, E., "The Theme of Wine and Wine-drinking and the concept of the Beloved in Early Persian Poetry," in *Studia Islamica*, Vol. 13, 1960, pp. 43–53.
Yarshater, E., *Encyclopaedia Iranica*, Encyclopaedia Iranica Foundation, 1987-, http://www.iranicaonline.org/.
Yavari, H., *Encyclopaedia Iranica*, s.v. Fiction. ii(d). The Post-Revolutionary Short Story.
Yavari, H., in *Encyclopaedia Iranica*, s.v. Nader Naderpour.
Yazaki, A., *Islamic Mysticism and Abu Talib al-Makki: The Role of the Heart*, London: Routledge, 2013.
Yūsufī, Gh.Ḥ., "Dar jangal-i shab," in *Chishma-yi rowshan: dīdār bā shāʿirān*, 4th ed., Tehran: ʿIlmī, 1371/1992, pp. 766–71.
Zarrīnkūb, A.ʿḤ., "The Arab Conquest of Iran," in *The Cambridge History of Iran*, Cambridge: Cambridge University Press, 1975, Vol. IV, pp. 1–56.
Zarrīnkūb, ʿA-Ḥ., *Tārīkh-i Īrān baʿd az islām*, Tehran: Amīr Kabīr, 1368/1989.
Zia-Ebrahimi, R., "Self-Orientalization and Dislocation: The Uses and Abuses of the "Aryan" Discourse in Iran," in *Iranian Studies*, Vol. 44, No. 4, 2011, pp. 445–472.
Ziai, H., "Ḥāfeẓ, Lisān al-Ghayb of Persian Poetic Wisdom," in *Gott ist schön und Er liebt die Schönheit* (*God Is Beautiful and He Loves Beauty*), A. Giese, and C.J. Bürgel, Bern: Peter Lang, 1994, pp. 449–469.
Zipoli, R., "Poetic Imagery," in *History of Persian Literature: General Introduction to Persian Literature*, ed. J.T.P. de Bruijn, London: I.B. Tauris, 2009, pp. 172–232.
Zipoli, R., "Semiotics and the Tradition of the Image," in *Persica: Annual of the Dutch-Iranian Society*, 20, pp. 155–72.
Zulkifli, *The Struggle of the Shiis in Indonesia*, Canberra: Australian National University Press, 2013.

Index

Ābādān 84
Abbasid dynasty (750 – 1258) 237 – 38
ʿAbd al-Wahhāb, Muḥammad ibn (1703 – 1791) 235
Ablutions 112 – 13, 123, 258; performing ~ in the heart's blood 112, 258
Abraha 100, 233 – 34,
Abraham 32, 41, 115, 117 – 18; ~ in fire 115; ~'s offering his son 183
Abrahamian, Ervand 163
Abū Bakr, the first Caliph (573 – 634) 29
Abū Jahl (d. 624) 206, 208, 210
Abū Lahab 173, 177
Abū Dharr 150 – 51
acacia 123
Academic Board of the University of Tehran 11
Academy of Persian Language and Literature 72
Academy of Islamic Isean and Arts 71
Adam 32, 37 – 8, 122, 128
aesthetic xviii, xx, 2, 15, 34, 46, 89 – 90, 98, 159; ~ engagement 2
aesthetised politics xviii
affliction 37, 39 – 40, 176
Afrāsiyāb xvii, 213
Āhangarān, Ṣādiq 262
Aḥmadī, Aḥmad 16 – 7, 19 – 21
Ahriman 176, 178 – 79, 202, 208, 218
Ahūrā Mazdā 218
Aida 12, 15
Akbarī, Manūchihr 11, 13 – 6, 85
Akhavān Thālith, Mihdī (1929 – 1990) 24
Ākhūndzāda, Fatḥ-ʿAlī (1812 – 1878) 214, 228
alcohol xviii, 10
Algar, Hamed 224, 238
Āl-i Aḥmad's (1923 – 1969) *Gharbzadagī* ("Westoxification") 30 – 1, 33
ʿAlī Ibn Abī Ṭālib (c. 600 – 661) 29, 33, 45, 250; the usurpation of ~'s position 29, 237
āl-i Saʿūd, "family of Saud" 230
alms-giving 240
altruism xvii, 41, 43, 48, 134
ambiguity 3, 5 – 7, 28, 130
American Embassy xiv, 222
Āmina, the name of the prophet Muḥammad's mother 142 – 43
Amīr Naṣr II ibn Aḥmad (re. 914 – 43) 4
ʿAmūzāda-Khalīlī, Firaydūn 71
analogy 3, 183
anemone 14, 65 – 8, 93
angels 67, 134, 136, 144 – 46, 155
annihilation (*fanā*) xviii, 40, 101, 115, 128 – 29, 258
Anṣārī, ʿAbdullāh (1006 – 1089) 127
anti-Arabic 214
anti-Arab 216, 234, 250 – 51, 253
anti-imperialism 8
anti-Islamic 214, 216
antinomian 7, 21, 47, 241, 243 – 44, 256
antinomian mystics, see qalandar
antithesis 6, 8, 152, 190,195
anti-western sentiment 30 – 1, 48
Anvarī, Ḥasan 133
ʿaql ("intellect") 6, 109, 116, 118
ʿAql-i surkh ("The Crimson Reason") 118
Arabic literature 27
Arabism 237 – 38, 246
Arab-Persian rivalry 256
Ārash, a mythic archer 252 – 53
archery 44
Arghūn, Fakhr ʿUẓmā 157
ʿĀrif from Qazvīn (1882 – 1934) 57, 179; ~'s "From the Blood of the Homeland's Youth ...," 57
Āryā-Mihr, see Muḥammad Riżā Shah 214
Aryan heritage 9
Aryan race 214; ~ theory 24, 228
Aryanism 214
Asadī from Ṭūs (ca. 1000 – 1072) 249
ascension xviii, 15, 40, 103 – 05, 118
ascetic 59, 112, 126, 128, 201, 241
asceticism 244
ashes 53 – 4, 65, 79, 83, 189

https://doi.org/10.1515/9783110748734-015

Ashraf, Ahmad 214
ʿĀshūrā 28, 31, 38, 233; ~ paradigm as a prefiguration of contemporary socio-political events 31–38
astronomer 5
ʿatabāt-i ʿalīyāt ("the lofty or sacred thresholds") 33
ʿAṭṭār, Farīd al-Dīn (c. 1145–1221) 37–8, 40, 52, 76, 102, 105, 112, 129, 242, 245, 258
Avistā, Mihrdād (1930–1991) 253; ~'s "Wahhabi Disgrace" (*nang-i Wahhābī*) 253
ʿAyn al-Qużāt Hamadānī (1098–1131) 120–22

Bachelard, Gaston (1884–1962) 1
Bahār, Muḥammad Taqī (1886–1951) 179
Balkans 27
ballad 57
Bāqirī, Sāʾid (b. 1339/1960) 39–41, 54, 69
Bashshār ibn Burd (714–784) 248
Basīj ("mobilisation") xx, 87, 134–36, 145, 147–48, 260; Khomeini's phrase "mobilisation is the school of love" (*basīj madrasa-yi ʿishq ast*) 148
Baʿth party 237
baths 240
bats 78, 82
battle 28–9, 43, 53, 89, 225, 246, 251, 260; ~ Against Arrogance 21; the ~ of Badr 29; "~ of Blood River" 251; ~ of Qādisiyya 246, 255–56
Battlefield 42, 48, 50, 101, 111, 116–17, 185, 257, 262
bazaar of heart sellers (*bāzār-i dil-furūshān*) 109
Bed for Three (1972) 18
beloved xvii, xviii, xix, 14–5, 21, 27, 33–4, 37–40, 47, 53, 68, 73–4, 76, 86, 101–04, 106, 108–09, 112, 115–16, 124, 126–30, 157, 169, 171, 179, 197–201, 204, 217, 220–21, 241, 244, 245, 258, 261–62; immaterial ~ xix, 27, 38, 74, 103, 129, 258, 261
Bengal 27
Beygī Ḥabīb-Ābādī, Parvīz 50, 52, 54, 69
Beyt al-ḥarām ("the Sanctified House") 222
Beyt al-Muqaddas 182
Bīdakī, Zahrā 66–7
Bihbahān 99, 103
Bihbahānī, Sīmīn (1927–2014) xx, 45, 157–186, 259, 264
birthday 49
Bīrūnī, Abū Reyḥān (about 973–1048) 252
Black Friday (17 Shahrivar / 8 September 1978) xiv, xx, 162–63, 166
Black Shroud 180–81
blasphemous 51, 103, 122, 192, 255
blasphemy 9, 115, 192
Bleiker, Roland 2
blossom 20, 98, 152–53, 157, 171
bombardment 22, 81–4, 92–3, 129, 147, 154, 180
bombs xv, 63, 81
Böwering, G. 122
bread 88, 107, 249, 251
bride 27–8, 129
Bu'l-Ḥasanī, Ibrāhīm 63
Bukhara 4
bull 162; mythical ~ 162
bullet xix, 12, 20, 78, 81, 137–38, 160–62, 164–68, 207, 209–10
Būrāq 104
burning 113, 128, 161–62, 175, 179, 207, 211
Burūjirdī, Siyyid Ḥuseyn, Ayatollah (1875–1961) 30
butterfly 145–46, 152–53, 155
Buzurg ʿAlavī (1904–1997) 16

cabarets 18
cadaver 129
cage 57, 59, 73, 112, 126
Cain and Abel 42, 44, 168–69
camel 250
candle xvii, 53, 61, 68–9, 105, 127–28, 172, 207, 210, 258
candle and the moth 53, 61, 127–28
celebrations of 2,500 years of Iranian monarchy 223

cemetery of Baqīʿ 235; ~ of Bihisht-i Zahrā 58
censorship 10, 13, 18, 22, 24, 260
chafiyye 134–35, 140–41, 149
Chahār-maqāla ("Four Discourses," 1155–1157) 4–5
chemical attack 93; ~ bombardment 92–3; ~ rain 91–2; ~ weapons 48, 85, 90, 92
children's literature 131–33
Christian 18, 200, 234; ~ girl 113
Christianity 243
church 234, 242–43
CIA 10
classical Persian poetry 26, 74, 81, 109, 125–26, 130, 162, 171, 180, 210, 241
cliché images 53, 57, 67, 162
colour xx, 7, 28, 43, 50, 57–9, 63, 99, 103, 111, 125, 134, 138, 145, 149, 155, 184, 194, 209, 217, 230, 233, 237
comb 53–4
committed revolutionary poets ix, xix, 11, 253
community (*umma*) 238
condolences xix, 44, 56, 59
congratulations 44, 55, 64
constitution 8, 227
Constitutional Revolution (1906–1911) 3, 9, 16, 36, 57, 179, 190
correspondence (*Mukātabāt*) 122
corruption 16, 48, 219
coup d'état 1953 10, 212
crimson 42, 87, 118, 120, 125, 150, 171
crone 129
Ctesiphon 180–81
cup-bearer 116, 241, 244–45
cypress 57, 123, 171–72

dance 18, 73, 84, 114, 117, 171; "a ~ without feet and head," (*raqṣ-i bī pā-u sar*) 117
dancers 18, 84
Dānishvar, Sīmīn (1921–2012) 178, 181
Day of Judgement 180
day of unity (*rūz-i vaḥdat*) 227
debate poetry 120, 220, 244, 248–51; ~ between a Persian Muslim and an Arab Muslim 249
democracy 3, 9, 36, 57, 213
demonstrations xiii, 14, 30, 161, 163, 221–22, 227
deserters 260
devil 212–13
diaspora xxi, 159, 187, 189, 192, 197
die before you die 108
divinity 109
Dizfūl 71, 78, 85
dog-tags 63, 64
doll 80, 83–4, 137–38, 145, 154, 184
door 17, 35, 50, 56, 59, 73, 127, 138–39, 239–40
dustman 79, 83

earthquake 187
ecstatic state 117, 126, 200
education 8–9, 45, 71, 101, 131–33, 188
elegy 53–4, 67, 154
elephant 100, 234
emigration 159
enemy xvii, 20–2, 29, 32–3, 39, 41, 48, 54, 74, 76, 78–9, 81, 85, 95, 100–02, 104, 118, 129, 133, 152, 166, 168–69, 173, 175–76, 178–79, 182, 184–85, 213, 217, 237, 240, 246–47, 251–52, 255, 257, 262
England 209, 224
Eqbali, Dariush 177
eroticism 15, 18
eschatological 122, 254
European 8–9, 163, 188, 190, 214, 260
evil 6, 79, 168–70, 185, 202, 204, 212–13, 217–19, 228, 230, 254, 262
exaggeration 27
excommunication (*takfīr*) 202
exile ix, xiii, xiv, xvii, xxi, 11, 30, 52, 111, 125, 187, 189, 211, 216–19, 223

Fahd 228, 233–34, 254; ~ compared to the second Umayyad Caliph Yazīd ibn al-Muʿāviyya (r. 680–683) 234
Fahmīda, Muḥammad Ḥuseyn 12, 152–53, 182

Family Protection Law (1967) 30
Farrukhī of Sīstān (d. about 1038) 190
Farrukhī-yi Yazdī (1889–1939) 179
Farrukhzād, Furūgh (1934–1967) 13, 17, 259
Fars 45
Farzad, Narguess 72, 77, 90, 261
Faṣīḥ, Ismā'īl (1935–2009) ix, 264; ~'s *Zimistān-i 1362* ix, 264
Fasting 42–3, 126, 240
Fāṭima al-Ma'ṣūma, the sister of the eighth Shiite imam 215
Fāṭimat al-Zahrā (604–632), daughter of the Prophet 31–2, 45, 58, 236, 253
fatwa 30, 80
feigned ignorance (*tajāhul al-'ārif*) 49, 55
Fireydūn 13, 203, 205–06, 208, 211
fighter 32, 173, 207–08, 253
Film-Farsi 18
Firdowsī, Abū 'l-Qāsim (940–1019 or 1025) xxi, 2, 9, 42, 63, 82, 162, 176, 188, 190, 194, 196–97, 202, 204, 213, 250–51; *Rustam and Suhrāb* 162; ~'s "seven feats" 42; ~'s *Shāh-nāma* millennium celebration 9
fire xiii, xiv, xvii, 12, 28, 39, 41–2, 53, 61, 65, 68, 73, 84, 87, 93, 99, 105, 107, 115, 117–18, 127–29, 160–61, 175–76, 179, 189, 207–08, 213, 216, 233, 247, 261
fish 142–43, 161–62, 175
flight 12, 40, 59, 75–6, 88, 128, 138, 141, 153, 155, 175, 206, 208
flora and fauna metaphors 57, 162
Foucault, Michel (1926–1984) 163
Four Elements 127
freedom of expression 10, 13, 18, 158
Frits van Oostrom 2
Fry, Richard N. (1920–2014) 248

Gabriel, archangel 105
gallows 50, 52, 103
Garmārūdī, 'Alī Musavī 18
Gaumātā 212
gender 17, 47, 158–59, 180; ~ and female sexuality 17
Ghadīr Khumm 29
ghazal 14, 19, 20–1, 34, 36, 38–9, 45–6, 51, 53–6, 64–5, 67, 72–3, 99, 102–03, 105, 108, 114, 158, 160, 179, 185, 200, 218, 236, 241, 243–44, 251
Ghazālī, Aḥmad (c. 1061–1126) 104, 106, 116, 122, 129–30, 169, 169–70, 239
Ghazālī, Muḥammad (1058–1111) 122
Gnosis 12, 14, 240, 239, 259
gnostic knowledge (*ma'rifa*) 110
Gnosticism 12
Goethe Institute in Tehran 13, 18
grain 126
grape 125, 188
Greater Occultation 156
Greek 1, 3, 36
green xiii, 32, 42, 50, 62–3, 67, 116, 135–38, 143–44, 149, 152–53, 155, 164–65, 171–72, 175, 195, 207, 215–16
Gruber, Christiane 152
guilt 48–9, 147, 257
Gulshan-i rāz ("The Rose-Garden of Mystery") 118
guns 46, 81, 207, 209
Gurgānī, Fakhr al-Dīn Asad (d. about 1039) 82

Ḥāfiẓ, Muḥammad Shams al-Dīn (1315–1390) 40, 102, 157–58, 177, 188, 198, 200–04, 213, 218, 238, 243–45, 255, 258
hagiography 52
haiku 25
hair 53–4, 194, 199, 201–02, 206–11, 243, 245; curly ~ 244; facial ~ 243
ḥajj xxi, 150–51, 182, 220–24, 226–27, 237–39, 243, 255; ~ as a setting for unmasking the imperialist policies of the West 226; ~ as worshipping an idol 221; ~ as worshipping the Owner of the House 221; ~ deaths of 402 pilgrims 227; ~ protests during 220; ~ ritual pilgrimage 220; ~ rituals 220–21, 239
Ḥakīmī. Ismā'īl 14
Halabja 90

Ḥallāj, Ḥuseyn Manṣūr (executed 922) 26, 50–1, 103, 115–16, 169, 258; ~'s saying "I am the Truth" 51, 103, 115
Hanaway, William L. (1929–2018) 217
hanging judge, see Khalkhālī
harp 50, 51
Ḥasan b. ʿAlī b. Abī Ṭālib (625–670) 29
Hāshimī Rafsanjānī, ʿAlī-Akbar (1934–2017) 17, 228
hashish 12
hat (*kulāh*) 165
hatred 48, 110, 147, 161,164, 167–68, 254
Heinrichs, Wolfhart (1941–2014) 3
hell 26, 112, 173, 175, 207–08, 210–11, 228, 262
Herat 4
Hereafter 104, 156, 259–60
heroism xx, 12, 115, 147
Hijaz 223, 244
Ḥijāzī, Fakhr al-Dīn 99, 105
homeland xx, 20, 24, 57, 87, 108, 111, 125, 147–48, 173, 175, 177–86, 189, 191, 193, 195, 197, 216, 264
hoopoe 37
horse 20, 50–1, 137, 250
horsemanship 44
houris (*ḥūrīs*) 26 (see also paradisiacal virgins)
Hoveyda, Amir-Abbas (1919–1979) 166
Hoveyze 64
Hunarjū, Ḥamīd 133–34; ~'s *Barf-i gul-i yās: majmūʿa-yi shiʿr-i kūdakān* ("Snow of Jasmine Petals: Collection of Poetry for Children" 133
Ḥuseyn b. ʿAlī b. Abī Ṭālib, (d. 680) xx, 26, 28–34, 38, 41, 43–4, 48, 50–1, 74, 115–16, 148, 230, 234, 257, 261–62; ~ as a model for Iranian soldiers 28, 257; ~ as the "King of martyrs" 28; ~'s horse Zu'l-Jināh 51
Ḥuseynī, Siyyid Ḥasan (1956–2005) 69, 74, 77, 103–04, 113, 117–19, 121–23
Ḥuseyniyya Irshād 31
hyperbole 5, 40–1, 44, 254
hypocrisy 7 n.18, 221, 231, 233, 239, 243–44

Ibn ʿArabī, Muḥyī al-Dīn (1165–1240) 245
Ibn Quteyba (828–889) 251; ~'s *Excellence of the Arabs* 251
Ibn Saʿūd, ʿAbd al-ʿAzīz 235
Ibn Saʿūd, Muḥammad 255
Ibtihāj, Hūshang 261
idol (*ṭāghūt*) 12; ~ worshippers 41
Iḥyāʾ ʿulūm al-dīn ("The Revivification of the Religious Sciences") 122
Ikhvāniyya ("Epistle") 118
imagery 7, 21–22, 26, 34, 40, 44, 51, 54, 56–7, 59, 61–3, 65–6, 68, 74, 84, 89, 93, 102, 109, 112, 117; bacchic ~ 40; bird ~ 126; dancing ~ 117; floral ~ 56, 63, 65–6, 93, 135, 164, 171; maritime ~ 61, 66; nature ~ 44, 142, 195; tactile ~ 68; wine ~ 21
Imam Ḥuseyn, see Ḥuseyn b. ʿAlī b. Abī Ṭālib
immorality 15–6, 257
immortality 33, 161 n. 256
imperialist 9, 48, 224, 226–27, 256
imperialism xiv, 8, 223–24
imprisonment 18, 30, 218
independence xiii, 8, 21
indigo 58
Indo-European languages 214
inequality 21, 24
innocence xvii, 28, 93
intercession 236
intertextuality 92, 101
Iranian civilisation 1, 36
Iranian intellectuals xviii, xxi, 11, 13–4, 22, 214, 228
Iraqi bombers 82; ~ border 85; ~ mirages 82; ~ missiles 99, 180; ~ soldiers 33, 209, 246–47; ~ tank 182
Islamic community 29, 191, 230, 237
Israel 30, 209, 225–27, 253
Iṭṭilāʿāt newspaper 99

jāhiliyya, "the age of ignorance" 237, 253 n.453
Jamālī, Muḥammad Khalīl 231
Jamālzāda, Muḥammad-ʿAlī (1892–1997) 16
jasmine 133–34, 154–55

Jesus 180–81, 195, 242–43; ~ reviving the dead 180–81
journey 7 n.18, 8, 12, 37, 40, 61, 68, 76, 103, 105, 111, 114–15, 117–18, 125–26, 149–50, 225, 239, 249, 260–61
Judaic 1
judas tree 171–72
Jurjānī, ʿAbd al-Qāhir, al- (d. 1078 or 1081) 3

Kaʿba xxi, 7 n.18, 32, 51, 123, 192, 221, 230, 234, 239, 241–45, 249–50, 255–56; ~ in Chains (*Kaʿba dar zanjīr*) 32, 243; ~ of clay (*Kaʿba-yi gil*) 234, 241; ~ of the Goal (*Kaʿba-yi maqṣūd*) 241; ~ of Love (*Kaʿba-yi ʿishq*) 241; ~ of the heart (*Kaʿba-yi dil*) 239, 241–42, 255
Kahdūʾī, Muḥammad Kāẓim 16
Karamustafa, Ahmet T. 240
Karbalā xviii, 28–31, 33, 39, 41–4, 48, 50–1, 116, 229, 233–34, 257; ~ paradigm 31, 43–4, 51; the clay of ~ (*turbat*) 33
Karimi, Pamela 152
Karimi-Hakkak, Ahmad 13
Karrāmiyya 241
Kārūn 43, 177
Kāshānī, ʿIzz al-Dīn Maḥmūd (d. about 1335) 128
Kāshānī, Sipīda (1936–1992) 19–21, 23–4
Key Kāvūs 213
Keyhān, newspaper 167
Khālid ibn Valīd 251
khalīl, see Abraham
Khalīlī, ʿAbbās 157
Khalkhālī, Ṣādiq (1927–2003) 166–67
Khamenei, ʿAlī 13 n.33, 24, 50, 192
khamriyya, (*khamriyyāt*, "wine-poetry") 21, 244
Khargūshī, Abū Saʿd, al- (d. about 1016) 240; ~'s *Tahdhīb al-asrār* ("Refining the Secrets") 240
Khatami, Mohammad (presidency 1997–2005) 191
Khātib, Muḥibb al-Dīn, al- (1886–1969) 223
Khaybar 253
Khayyām, ʿUmar (d. either 1123 or 1132) 188
Khomeini, Ruḥullā Mūsavī, Ayatollah xiii–xiv, xviii–xix, xxi, 11, 14, 16, 21, 24, 30, 38, 41, 44, 74, 84, 108, 115, 132, 134, 148, 152, 182, 187, 191–92, 195–96, 201–04, 208, 211–12, 217, 222–26, 235–38, 241, 243–47, 255, 261–62; ~ as a spiritual leader 14; ~'s rank elevated to *Ayatollah al-ʿUẓmā* 30; ~'s identification with the qalandars 241, 243–44; ~'s image in the moon 191, 201, 203–04, 208; ~'s mystical exegesis of the Quran 14; ~'s poetry 244–45
Khotan 57
Khuʾī, Ismāʿīl 187
Khuʾīnīhā, Muḥammad Mūsavī 222–23
Khūnīn-shahr, see Khurram-shahr
Khurram-shahr 182–83
Khursandī, Hādī 187
Khusrow Parvīz II 181
Khuzistan 71
Kirmānī, Mīrzā Āqā Khān (1854–1896) 214
Kramer, Martin 220
Kristeva, Julia 92
Kūcha ("Alley") by Firaydūn Mushīrī 15
kufr ("unbelief") 6, 7 n.18, 63 n.118, 221
Kuwait 247, 256; ~i ships 227

lamentation 44, 150, 254
land reforms 30
law 6, 8, 28, 239, 241, 259–60; codified ~ 8; tribal, religious and ethical ~ 28
Laylī 27–8, 106; as a figuration of God 27
Laylī and Majnūn 27, 59, 102
legends xxi, 2, 183, 196, 217, 252
legendary 211, 219, 245, 251
lightening 46, 104
lips 42, 61, 67, 73, 87, 89, 98, 107, 128, 141, 143, 146, 164–66, 204
literary manuals 3

literature of the Islamic Revolution" (*adabiyyāt-i inqilāb-i islāmī*) 11, 13
lizard 250, 253
love xvii–xxii, 5–7, 12, 14–6, 18, 20, 23–4, 27–8, 33–5, 37–41, 47–50, 54, 58, 61, 63, 65, 69, 72–3, 87, 93–4, 98, 134, 144, 146–48, 150, 153, 157, 159, 167–69, 171, 176, 179, 181–82, 198–201, 218, 230, 233, 239, 241–43, 245, 250, 257–58, 260–62; ~ as an attractive force 124; ~ as a bird 126–27; ~ as gravity 124; ~'s ladder 115; ~ magnetism 124; ~ poetry xviii, xix, 33–4, 58, 108; ~-death xxii, 38, 101–03, 105, 108; ~-madness 40; ~-making scenes 17; ~ and reason 39, 101, 105–08; book of ~ 100–01, 103, 105, 127; dagger of ~ 127; door of ~ 127; Freudian ~ 16; grammar of ~94, 130; homo-erotic ~ 243, 18 n.49; house of ~ 127; mystical philosophy of ~ 121, 130, 245; pen of ~ 101; physiognomy of ~ 117, 128; profane ~ 15; school of ~ 99, 101–04, 129, 148; seven valleys of ~ 37, 39, 40, 76; steed of ~ 104; teacher of ~ 101

madness 39–40, 106
mafqūd al-athar ("lost trace of") 140
magic 34 n83; black ~ 204; satanic ~ 204
Mahdī, Twelfth Shiite Imam 45, 115, 156, 201 n.324, 254
Mahyār Deylamī, Abū 'l-Ḥasan (d. about 1037) 248
Majnūn 27–8, 106; as a selfless lover 27
Makhmalbāf, Muḥsin 24, 263
Makkī, Abū Ṭālib, al- (d. 996) 109, 240; ~'s *Qūt al-qulūb* ("The Sustenance of Hearts") 109, 240
malāmatiyya 241
male gaze 18
Malikī, Buyūk 71
Manṭiq al-ṭeyr ("The Conference of Birds") 7 n.18, 37, 76, 112
Mardānī, Naṣrullāh (1947–2003) 41, 252
marg-i surkh ("the red death," i.e., martyrdom) 31
maʿrifa, God's intimate knowledge 109, 239
marriage 17, 29, 240
marriage contract 17; temporary ~ 17
Marxist ideology 9
mass graves 64–5, 253 n453
maẓlūm ("oppressed") 156
Mecca xxi, 7 n.18, 29, 32–3, 123, 127, 182, 192, 208, 221–23, 225, 229–30, 234, 238–39, 245, 250, 254–55
Medina xxi, 29, 32, 221–22, 235, 238, 250
Mehran, Golnar 132
memories 4, 54, 69, 76, 141–42, 141–42, 146–47, 149, 154, 173, 176, 194, 210, 264
merciful (*luṭf*) 169
metaphor xvii, 3, 6, 22, 26, 34, 36, 38, 40, 43, 45–8, 50, 54–7, 59, 61, 66, 68–9, 74–6, 84–5, 92, 101, 103–05, 108–09, 116–18, 122, 127–29, 134, 139, 141, 148, 155, 157, 160–62, 180, 184–85, 189–90, 192, 195, 201, 204, 216, 241, 257, 258; ~ becoming reality 26
metaphysical 6
Milani, Farzaneh 158
Mīlānī, Muḥammad Hādī, Ayatollah (1895–1976) 30
mill 251–52
Minā 182–83
minefields 12
Ministry of Culture and Islamic Guidance 132–33, 264
Miqdād 150, 152
miʿrāj (ascent to heaven) 40, 50, 100, 103, 258
mirror for princes 5
Mirṣād al-ʿibād ("The Path of God's Bondsmen") 11
Mīrzāda ʿIshqī, Muḥammad Riżā (1893–1923) 180; ~'s opera 180
Missile xv, xix, 40–1, 44, 46, 78, 81, 92, 100, 102, 137–38, 144–46, 178, 180
Miʿyār al-ashʿār ("the Standard of Poetry") 4

mobilising (people) xix, xxii, 33, 86, 89, 135–36, 257
modernism 16
Mongols 43, 52
mortars 46, 137–38
Moses 73
mother 27, 45–7, 79–84, 89, 94–5, 97–8, 101, 134, 138–39, 142–43, 145–46, 156–57, 172–73, 176–77, 188, 194–95, 207, 210–11, 264
Mount Qāf 37
Mount Sinai 73
mourning 48–51, 55–6, 58–9, 61–2, 67, 207–08, 210
Mu'ayyad, Siyyid Rižā 260
Muḥammad Rižā Shah 10, 24, 159, 204–05, 214; ~ compared to Caliph Yazīd 30; ~'s westernisation programme 18, 31; compared to Żahhāk 204
Muḥammad, the prophet of Islam (d. 632) xviii, 28–9, 32, 40, 40, 45, 63, 73, 103–05, 118, 142, 173, 192, 202, 230–31, 234–35, 237–38, 241, 245, 250, 253–55, 258–59
Muḥarram 28–9, 48
Mujāhidī, Muḥammad-'Alī (pen-name Parvāna) 64
Mu'jam fī ma'āyir ash'ār al-'ajam, al- (1232–33) 4
Mullā Ṣadrā, Ṣadr al-Dīn Muḥammad (d. about 1635) 245
murshid 242
Muṣaddiq, Muḥammad (1882–1967) 10, 188
Mūsavī Khu'īnīhā, Muḥammad, see Khu'īnīhā
Mushīrī, Fireydūn (1926–2000) 13, 15; ~'s *Yāghī* or "Rebel" 16
Muṣībat-nāma ("Book of Affliction") 37
music 2, 4, 19, 54, 84, 113, 176, 188–89, 218; ~al instrument 117; ~al performance 54
mucisian 84, 188, 197, 200, 245
musk 44
Mustamlī of Bukhara 239
mustaż'afān ("oppressed") 132
Mutivassilīyān, Aḥmad 140
myths xxi, 2, 196, 217, 228
mythical xxi, 44, 162, 200, 204, 217–18

Nādirpūr, Nādir ix, xx, xxi, 187–219, 228, 259
nafs, "lower self" 240
Nahj al-balāgha 14, 236 n415
Najaf 30, 223–24
Najafābādī, Ni'matullāhī Sālihī 30
Nāṣir-i Khosrow (d. about 1071) 218
nationalism 8, 16, 214, 226, 237; ~ opposed to Islam 16; ethnic ~ 237
nationalistic sentiments 9, 31, 73, 96, 177, 214, 220, 251 n.449, 253, 256
new poetry (*shi'r-i now*) 77, 157, 189, 190
newspapers xiv, 3, 8, 93, 166, 184
night journey, see ascension
nightingale 57, 216
Nimrod 32, 115, 117–18
Niẓāmī 'Arūżī 4
Niẓāmī Ganjavī (c. 1141–1209) 27–8, 59, 63, 82, 102, 124
Nobel Prize for Literature 159, 189
Nowrūz 21
Nūrī, Abū 'l-Ḥuseyn, al- (d.c. 907–908) 239; ~'s *Maqāmāt al-qulūb* ("Stations of the Heart") 239

ocean 12, 20–1, 39, 61, 120–21, 150, 152, 239
offspring 37
One Woman's War: Dā (Mother) x, 264
operation Beyt al-Muqaddas 182
operation, Va-'l-Fajr 113
operations Ḥajj Imrān, Fāv and Fakka 150
opium 12
oppression 13, 20–2, 161, 168, 170, 193, 225, 230, 236
orthodoxy 51, 192, 202, 241
Ottoman Empire 246
Owen, Wilfred (1893–1918) 147; ~'s *Dulce et Decorum est* 147

Pahlavi dynasty (1925–1979) xiii, xiv, 9, 13, 18, 30–2, 41, 163, 166, 170, 195–96, 214, 222, 224
Palestinians 18, 134, 225

pan-Islamism 8
paradise 26, 38, 58, 101, 134–36, 150–51, 156, 169, 207–08, 210–11, 218, 260–61
paradisiacal virgins 261
paradox 6, 7 n. 18, 8, 20, 48, 53, 82, 130, 166, 179–80
parallelism 54, 62, 190
pāsdārān see Revolutionary Gaurds
patriotism 9, 20, 44, 147, 153, 173, 177, 181, 191, 252, 257, 262
peace xix, 82, 94–8, 117, 137, 145, 154, 158, 177, 209–10, 258
pearl 61, 116, 150–51
pen-name (*takhalluṣ*) 38, 64, 118
philosophy 1, 3, 8, 36, 121–22, 130, 166, 189, 245, 259–60
physician 5, 203, 261
piercings 243
piety xv, xxi–xxii, 6, 7 n.18, 30, 112, 142, 156, 230, 239, 240–45, 249, 255, 261–62; paradoxical ~ 6
pilgrimage xxi, 33, 120, 192, 220, 222–26, 228–30, 233–34, 237, 239–41, 245, 249, 255
poetic argumentation 4–6
poetic manual 5
poetry eliciting mercy 5
poetry topical 3, 8, 160, 258
polytheism 225, 230, 233, 242–43
poppy 65, 93
popular culture 27, 250
possessed 12, 117
prayer tablet (*muhr*) 12, 33, 34 n. 83
pretext 61, 209
propaganda xiv, 34, 44, 49, 56, 64, 69, 76, 197, 218, 226
prophecy 1
prophethood 122
prostitution 17, 159
prostitute-poet 12
purity 19, 28, 112, 156, 168, 219, 240

Qādisīyya (battle of, AD 636) 246, 255–56
Qajar court 8
qalandar 241–44; ~iyya 241; ~*iyyāt* ("poems with antinomian themes") 244
qaṣīda 4, 182
Qeys al-Rāzī, Shams al-Dīn Muḥammad ibn 4
qiṭʿa ("fragment," occasional poetry) 253
quatrain (*rubāʿī*) 47, 72–3, 83, 103–04, 110–13, 116, 124–25, 127, 129, 140, 190, 253 n. 453
quietist xviii, 28, 30
Quran xiii, xx, 7 n. 18, 14, 21–2, 24, 37, 73, 104, 109, 113, 115, 117–18, 121, 128, 130–31, 136–37, 141, 155–56, 161, 169–71, 173, 180, 182, 191, 201–02, 208, 211, 221, 234–35, 237, 239, 241, 245, 248, 250; Sūra (2:154; 3:169) 155; (2:259) 180; (3:157–8) 156; (3:163) 115; (5:54) 130; (7:172) 37; (11:7) 161; (14: 24) 239; (21:67–9) 117; (28:38) 118; (37:102) 182; (40:60) 36; (47:4–6 and 9:111) 156; (48:1) 171; (49:13) 248 n. 440; (57:25) 170; (89:27–28) 104; (102:5–7 and 56:95) 128; (105:1–5) 234; (111:3) 173
Qūt al-qulūb ("The Sustenance of Hearts") see Makkī, Abū Ṭālib

Rābiʿa al-ʿAdaviyya (d. 801) 261
Rāzī, Najm al-Dīn (1177–1256) 111
refugees 52, 159
religiosity xxi, 6, 7 n. 18, 113, 235, 239, 243, 245, 255
religious singers (*maddāḥ*s) 262
resistance xviii, 12–3, 20–1, 84, 183–84, 263
Revolutionary Guards (*pāsdārān*) 43, 116, 207, 209
rhyme 36, 54, 56, 62, 77, 88–9, 110, 121, 140, 157, 166, 173, 179, 190, 262
*rind*s ("libertines") 243
Ritter, Hellmut (1892–1971) 101, 108–09, 129–30
river 19–20, 42–3, 97, 149, 177, 239, 251, 252 n. 450

Riżā Shah (1878–1944) 10; ~'s sympathies for the Germans 10
Riżā, ʿAlī ibn Mūsa, al- (d. 818), the eighth Shiite imam 215
rooster 35–6
roses 20, 57, 97–9, 121, 134, 138, 150–51, 154–55, 165, 172, 194, 207, 209–10, 216; wild ~ 65–6
Rouhani, Hasan (Pr. 2013–2021) 264
Rūdakī, Abū ʿAbdullāh Jaʿfar ibn Muḥammad (c. 860–940) 4, 190
Rūmī, Jalāl al-Dīn (1207–1273) 73, 92, 102, 115, 118, 122, 124, 234 n 408, 238–39, 255, 258; ~'s pen-name "Silent" 118; ~'s *Mathnavī* 92
Russia 8
Rustam 42, 162, 185 n. 299
Rustam Farrukhzādān 251

Sabzivār 43, 52
sacrifice xx, 6, 20, 26, 29, 42–3, 47, 51, 74, 76, 80, 84, 74, 76, 80, 84, 101, 108, 117, 129, 133, 152–53, 171, 180, 182–84, 210–11, 230, 261
Saʿd b. Vaqqās 251
Saʿd Salmān, Masʿūd (d. about 1131) 218
Saddam Hussein (1937–2006) xiv, xxi, 12, 34, 41, 43, 48, 85, 90, 93, 118, 145, 173, 220–22, 227, 230, 237–38, 246–47; ~'s invasion of Kuwait 247, 256
Saʿdī, Musharrif al-Dīn Muṣliḥ b. ʿAbd-Allāh (c. 1210–1292) 1, 51, 102, 157, 177, 188, 221 n. 366, 258
Ṣādiq Hidāyat (1903–1951) 16
Safavid dynasty (1501–1722) 29
Ṣaffārzāda, Ṭāhira (1936–2008) 18
sainthood 122
Salmān 53 n. 106, 150–51
salvation 21, 125 n. 214
samāʿ ("mystic audition") 100, 117, 122
Sanāʾī, Majdūd b. Ādam Ghaznavī (d. 1131) 7 n. 18, 104, 106, 108, 126–27, 242, 245, 258
Ṣanʿān, Shaykh 7 n. 18, 112–13
sanctification 11, 24 n. 65, 192
Sarbidārān 42–3
Sardasht 90
Sarhangī, Māshāllāh 113
Sasanian Empire (A.D. 226–652) 180–81, 251
Satan 12, 169, 197–204, 218–19, 230–31, 233, 242–43, 247
satanic verses 208
satire 25, 200
Saudi Arabia xxi, 220–256
scales of justice (*mīzān-i ʿadl*) 156, 168, 170
Schimmel, Annemarie (1922–2003) 115
Schoolbooks 41, 44
Scott Meisami, Julie 124
sea 40, 61, 116, 130, 139, 150; ~ as a lover 61
secretaries (*dabīrs*) 5, 248
secular xvii, xviii, xxi, 6, 10, 14–5, 18–9, 21, 24, 108, 132, 218, 257
secularism 8, 10, 16–7, 132
Sells, Michael 235
senses 4, 43, 46, 120, 166, 200
sewing machine 79, 83, 94
sex 15, 18; ~ual desire as *fiṭrat*, ("inborn nature") 17; ~ual freedom 17; ~ual morals 10; ~ual transgression xvii, xviii
sexuality 17–8, 24
Shabistarī, Maḥmūd (c. 1250–1320) 118
Shafīʿī Kadkanī, Muḥammad Riḍā 71
shahādat 31, 36
Shahīd-i jāvīd ("The Eternal Martyr," 1968) 30
Shāh-nāma, see Firdowsī
shame 42, 44, 117, 148, 177, 207, 213, 231; ~ful 29, 44, 147, 194–95
Shāmlū, Aḥmad (1925–2000) 13, 15, 22–3, 204, 211 n. 341, 259; ~'s *Aida in the Mirror* 15; ~'s *ʿishq-i ʿumūmī* 23
Shams, Fatemeh 263
Sharīʿatī, ʿAlī (1933–1977) xviii, 31–3, 258; ~'s definition of martyrdom 31–3
Sharīʿat-Madārī, Muḥammad Kāẓim, Ayatollah (1906–1986) 30
Shaṭṭ al-ʿArab, see *Kārūn*
Shiblī 116, 261

shi'r-i now, see "New Poetry"
shroud 28, 53–4, 65, 67, 148, 180–81, 209
shu'ūbiyya ("confessors of equality") 238 n. 419, 247, 248 n. 440, 251
silver 71
Sīmurgh 37
singer xx, 49, 54, 57, 159, 177, 262
Sipihrī, Suhrāb (1928–1980) 122; ~'s *The Sound of Water's Footsteps* (1964) 122
Siyāvash xvii, 213
sleep of negligence (*khᵛāb-i ghaflat*) 36
smell 43, 67, 94, 135, 138–39, 141, 144–45, 151, 178
snow 133–34, 154–55
soil 20, 34 n. 83, 173, 253
soldier xvii, xix, xx, 14, 26–8, 33, 38, 40–1, 44, 46–52, 56, 61, 63, 65–9, 73–7, 87, 93, 96, 98, 101–02, 104, 106, 108–09, 115, 118, 124–26, 128–30, 134, 136, 140, 148, 152–53, 162, 173, 179, 183–85, 209–10, 246–47, 252–53, 258, 260, 262
soul king 37
source of imitation (*marja'-i taqlīd*) 226
Soviet Union 223–24, 236
spiritual journey 12
star 42, 78–9, 82, 136, 157, 164, 177
steed (of longing) 4, 43, 104–05, 126
suffering xviii, xix, 22, 28, 32, 59, 85, 112, 137, 147, 154, 156, 194, 233, 258
Sufi xxi, 2, 221, 238, 242, 245, 255, 258; ~ brotherhood 221, 245; ~ doctrine 256; ~ monastery 117; ~ saint 245; ~ shrines 236
Sufism xix, xxii, 129, 221, 258
Suhrāb 162, 185 n. 299
Suhravardī, Shihāb al-Dīn (d. 1191) 118, 124
suicide 16, 260
Sulṭānpūr, Sa'īd (1940–1981) 14
Sunnite 29, 33, 41, 43, 48, 192, 220–21, 224, 234, 237, 241, 257
syllogism 3
Syria 48, 237

taboo 17
Tabūk 29
Ṭahmāsbī, Qādir (b. 1952) 251
tajallī, "manifestation" 20
Tajikistan 9
takhyīl, "make-believe" 3–4
Talattof, Kamran 18–9, 158, 177–78
tank 12, 137–38, 152, 178, 182
Taqavī, Muḥammad 16
tarṣī' or "setting in jewels" 165
Tataristan 44
tavern 53, 241, 244–45
tears 23, 42, 44, 46, 51, 54–6, 61, 64, 70, 134–35, 140–41, 143, 150–53, 158, 163–64, 166, 176, 178, 180, 194–95, 207, 250, 260
Tehran University 71–2
temperaments (*ṭabā'*) 6
Ten Nights (*dah shab*) 13, 16 n. 42, 18
theologian xiii, 122, 169, 238, 242
throne 4, 39–41, 104, 160–61, 205, 208, 212, 239
tongue 68–9, 78–9, 82, 87–9, 158, 164, 176, 182
touch 28, 43, 68, 126, 141, 245
towḥīd ("unicity of God") 21, 239
traditional schools (*maktabs*) 131
traditionalism 8
trauma xix, xx, xxii, 25, 84, 86, 123, 141, 162, 164, 166, 256, 263–64
Tudeh party 188
tulip 36, 42, 44, 50, 56–8, 65–6, 78, 81, 87, 93, 100, 103, 111, 115, 118, 145–46, 151, 207, 209–10, 233; the black colour of the ~'s heart 57–8, 209; ~ as a symbol for martyrs 93, 209–10
Turan xvii, 213, 252
Ṭūsī, Naṣīr al-Dīn (1201–1274) 4
tyranny xiii, 20–1, 31, 33, 197, 202, 204, 211

'Udhrite love (*al-ḥubb al-'udhrī*) 102
'ulamā' 9, 30, 121, 241
Umayyad army 28, 48
Umayyad Caliph, Yazīd I (ca. 647–683) 28, 234, 258

Umayyad dynasty (661–750) 28–9, 43, 102, 234, 237–38, 254–55, 258
ʿUthmān (the caliph, 644–656) 250

Vaḥīdī, Sīmīndukht 45–7
vengeance 5, 48, 170, 194, 234 n. 408
Vilāyat-i faqīh ("guardianship of the jurist") 187, 259
violence xv, xviii, 1–25, 199, 201, 210, 224, 258; justification of ~ xviii, 1–25
violet 56, 58–9, 145; ~ as a symbol of mourning 58
virgin girls in Paradise, see houris

Wahhabis xxi, 223, 228, 230, 235–38, 253–56
Wahhabism xxi, 222, 230, 235, 253; ~ versus Shiism 230, 235, 255, 256
watermill 251 (also see mill)
weeping 44, 49, 55–6, 146, 150–51, 161
westernisation 18, 31
Westoxification (*gharbzadagī*) 10, 30, 132
Westwood Village Memorial Park and Mortuary 189
Wheel 51, 57–8, 100–01, 233, 250
whirling dervishes 117
White Revolution 30, 223
wine xviii, xxi, 7 n. 18, 15, 21, 39–40, 47, 53, 57, 66, 113, 116, 125, 157, 159, 197, 199–201, 218, 229, 244–45; bubbling of ~ 116; ~-cup 116, 220, 244; ~-houses 12, 54, 241, 244; ~ of *lā* or "No" 115; ~-vat 116
women's rights 9, 158
women's suffrage 30
wrath 5, 12, 39, 41, 169, 252 n. 450
Writers' Association of Iran (1968) 13–4, 189

Yarshater, Ehsan (1920–2018) 1, 190
Yazīd ibn Muʿāvīyah (647–683) 28–30, 233–34, 257
yellow 62–3, 91–2, 94, 125
Yūshīj, Nīmā (1897–1960) 16, 158, 190
Yūsufpūr, Muḥammad Kāẓim 228

Żahhāk 202–217
Zeyn al-ʿĀbidīn Marāghaʾī (1840–1910) 16
Zhāla Square 162–63
Ziai, Hossein (1944–2011) 1
Zipoli, Riccardo 59
Zoroastrian xvii, 202, 216
Zoroastrianism 243
Zu'l-Jināh, see Ḥuseyn b. ʿAlī b. Abī Ṭālib
zuhdiyyāt ("poems of abstinence") 244

www.ingramcontent.com/pod-product-compliance
Lightning Source LLC
Chambersburg PA
CBHW031422150426
43191CB00006B/356
* 9 7 8 3 1 1 1 2 7 7 1 4 1 *